Working Well, Living Well

Discover the Career within You

FIFTH EDITION

Clarke G. Carney
Kenyon College

Cinda Field Wells

Brooks/Cole Publishing Company

I(T)P® *An International Thomson Publishing Company*

Pacific Grove • Albany • Belmont • Bonn • Boston • Cincinnati • Detroit • Johannesburg
London • Madrid • Melbourne • Mexico City • New York • Paris • Singapore
Tokyo • Toronto • Washington

Sponsoring Editor: *Eileen Murphy*
Editorial Assistant: *Julie Martinez*
Marketing Team: *Steve Catalano, Jean Thompson,*
   and Aaron Eden
Production Service: *Greg Hubit Bookworks*
Production Editor: *Janet Hill*
Manuscript Editor: *Molly Roth*

Cover Design: *Laurie Albrecht*
Interior Design: *John Edeen*
Permissions: *The Permissions Group*
Illustrations: *Lotus Art*
Typesetting: *ColorType, Inc.*
Printing and Binding: *WebCom*

For more information, contact:

BROOKS/COLE PUBLISHING COMPANY
511 Forest Lodge Road
Pacific Grove, CA 93950
USA

International Thomson Publishing Europe
Berkshire House 168-173
High Holborn
London WC1V 7AA
England

Thomas Nelson Australia
102 Dodds Street
South Melbourne, 3205
Victoria, Australia

Nelson Canada
1120 Birchmount Road
Scarborough, Ontario
Canada M1K 5G4

International Thomson Editores
Seneca 53
Col. Polanco
11560 México, D. F., México

International Thomson Publishing GmbH
Königswinterer Strasse 418
53227 Bonn
Germany

International Thomson Publishing Asia
60 Albert Street
#15-01 Albert Complex
Singapore 189969

International Thomson Publishing Japan
Hirakawacho Kyowa Building, 3F
2-2-1 Hirakawacho
Chiyoda-ku, Tokyo 102
Japan

Printed in Canada

10   9   8   7   6   5   4   3   2   1

Library of Congress Cataloging-in-Publication Data

Carney, Clarke G.
   Working well, living well : discover the career within you /
Clarke G. Carney, Cinda Field Wells. — 5th ed.
      p.   cm.
   Rev. ed. of: Discover the career within you. 4th ed.   1995.
   Includes bibliographical references and index.
   ISBN 0-534-35767-9
   1. Vocational guidance.   2. Job hunting.   I. Wells, Cinda Field.
II. Carney, Clarke G.   Discover the career within you.   III. Title.
HF5381.C3153   1999
331.7′02—DC21   98-26828

CONTENTS

CHAPTER *8*

INSIDE / OUTSIDE   152

CHAPTER *9*

FINDING A JOB IS A JOB!   179

CHAPTER **10**

WORK ADJUSTMENT AND CAREER EXPANSION   *227*

APPENDIX **A**

SELF-ASSESSMENT INVENTORY   *259*

APPENDIX B

APPENDIX C

PREFACE

When you stop and think back on your life—no matter how long it has been—you can probably think of times when you have felt surprised or betrayed because things did not turn out the way that you expected. We can all remember moments when we heard ourselves or others say, "It isn't fair!" or "I didn't know! Why didn't someone tell me?" Even after we should be old enough to know better, a part of us still hopes that things will turn out the way they do in movies and fairy tales: The hero rides off into the sunset, the frog turns into a prince—the good (and the bad) get what they deserve. We make choices and go about our daily business believing (or hoping) that if we do what is right and work hard we'll live happily ever after. Career choice, a major factor shaping our lives, is one of the decisions most subject to this myth. Many of us are encouraged to believe that if we choose well, our occupation will provide fulfillment and security for life. Some of us have parents who did that. But the economy, the workplace, and the entire way that society views careers have all recently changed drastically. Along with rapidly developing technology have come the periodic creation and disappearance of groups of jobs and entire industries. The fallout from these sudden changes and resulting fluctuations in the world economy have made the restructuring of business and changes in job descriptions a regular part of what we must now contend with during our careers. On a personal level, increasing affluence and education have brought greater mobility and higher expectations. In summary, we now have both the need and the opportunity to use change to improve the quality of our careers, to try new things, and to look for jobs that are meaningful as well as financially rewarding.

A readiness for flexibility, growth, and change thus must be part of how we define a career. Because we are both producers and products of change, it must lie at the heart of our dreams and decisions about every major factor in our lives, especially one as central to our identities as our career. As we grow and learn about ourselves and the world, our goals, interests, and needs will change. We must arrange our work or educational settings to make them flexible enough to accommodate new visions. We must be aware that we are constantly meeting and adapting to changing demands from all areas of our environment; in this way, we can have as much control over these changes as possible and be prepared to meet them positively. Sometimes we will be sad about what we must leave behind or scared because a change is not under our control. In spite of these feelings, we can usually go forward anticipating new opportunities and can discover ways to benefit from and enjoy the changes.

Focus on Text

Social scientists have observed that the people who thrive in the midst of change are those who can anticipate it, have the skills to deal with it, and, ideally, can take advantage of it. *Working Well/Living Well* will help you acquire the skills and attitudes to plan for and effectively manage the changes you will experience during your career. We believe that people who are effective in organizing and carrying out their career goals possess these important skills:

1. They can look at their lives and themselves and see "the big picture" by understanding their development and the roles they will play in life, as well as how these can change over time. Such people know what needs they must fill and what their priorities are.

2. They know how to use several decision-making strategies and know when different situations require different approaches. They also know how to find and explore options, assess what is best for them, and determine what is most realistic.

3. Such people know how to explore and learn about themselves. Aware of their values, interests and abilities, goals, hopes, and dreams, they understand their beliefs and feelings and know how to figure these things out if they are confused.

4. They have learned how to learn and how to work for what they want. With a sense of their own identity and of what beliefs, activities, and people matter to them, they balance the different areas of life that keep them happy and healthy.

5. They understand how the world of work is organized and how to obtain information about it. Further, they can look at this information realistically and assess it in light of their preferences, abilities, goals, and desired lifestyle.

6. Aware of what is happening in society and in the world of work, such people can integrate this external information with their own needs and goals as well as with the feelings and preferences of the important people in their lives. They can make a choice that seems right for them, one that is realistic and satisfying and fits well with other aspects of their lives and future goals.

7. Such people are willing and able to take the initiative to approach others about training, internships, or interviews that will lead to job experience and to securing employment. They have the necessary social and communication skills to meet new people and situations with confidence.

8. They have the ability to follow through after being hired: form good working relationships and get along with co-workers, translate their education into a practical setting, and continue learning. They have good written and oral communication skills as well as the confidence and patience to negotiate new challenges gracefully and continue to learn on the job.

This text presents these skills and their components in an easy-to-follow sequence in which one skill builds on another. You will learn and practice skills through exercises, practical activities, diagrams, and examples of real situations.

Organization of the Text

Working Well/Living Well: Discovering the Career Within You starts with an overview of how we shape our lives and how work meets our needs and fits into the overall patterns of our lives. We identify important questions to consider and skills that need to be developed for effective career and life planning. Next, we present a process for identifying needs or problems and making decisions about them. The focus then shifts to self-awareness—understanding the lifelong process of developing our identities and goals and how our careers or vocational identities develop and change with our lives. Exercises, examples, and inventories are provided to help you clarify how your personal qualities—preferences, beliefs, values, interests, and abilities—affect you in the world of work.

Following an overview of the structure and functions of occupations in the world of work today, we present techniques for gathering information about occupations and for assessing this information in light of individual needs and lifestyle preferences. In the next step of the career-planning process, personal and occupational exploration come together as information about self and career is integrated. The integration process involves fitting the realities of possible career options with your own goals and hopes as well as confronting any differences with significant people in your life. Once you have chosen a career goal, you will learn ways to carry out effective strategies for locating and securing employment. The book concludes with an in-depth discussion of several important adjustment issues, such as the hidden social requirements of the workplace, problems you might encounter and how to deal with them, and how to continue your self-development through work.

In this way, the text completes a circle that starts with self-awareness and growth and ends with self-enrichment and new opportunities for growth. Our goal is to stimulate exploration and understanding that will lead to a career that fits well with your sense of self and of how you want to live and will provide practical skills for building your career and a life you can enjoy in a changing world.

New to This Edition

As the new title of this book suggests, we have always believed that the process of career development is interwoven with the development of our personal identities and our lives. We endeavor to present the process of career choice in its context—the unfolding of our larger selves that occurs as we engage in our educational and occupational pursuits during the course of our lives. *In Working Well/Living Well: Discovering the Career Within You,* we have expanded this view, focusing on how people can integrate career choices and pursuits with a healthy lifestyle. To this end, we have added a wellness concept developed by William Hettler, M.D., the head of the National Wellness Institute at the University of Wisconsin at Steven's Point. According to Hettler, the occupational part of our lives is linked with five other important areas: social, emotional, spiritual, intellectual, and physical. As we explore career development, we examine how these aspects of life affect and are affected by occupational choices. Our objective is to help you recognize that you have the freedom and the responsibility to make career choices consistent with your inner vision of yourself and your capacities. We hope that learning the career-planning skills identified in this book will empower you and provide a process that you can use to pursue a satisfying career and to make lifestyle choices that will enhance it.

You will also find that each chapter of this edition includes new and expanded information about personal development and factors that influence it, about understanding yourself and your needs, and about our changing society and the world of work. In particular, Dale Prediger, Ph.D., at American College Testing Program has graciously provided us with information and paradigms that he and his colleagues have developed to describe the world of work. He differentiates clusters of occupations in a clear and useful way in easy-to-understand language. Some students who have taken the ACT prior to college entrance may already have a profile that will help them to identify where they fit on the world-of-work map. We have also added new material from the U.S. Department of Labor. This includes the newest occupational projections and a listing of 500 possible occupations, as well as a new way of breaking down occupations into 11 separate categories based on levels of training and skills required. This edition pays special attention to the current realities of the job market and the economy. This includes increased information about the job-search process, new resumé examples, and suggestions for how to cope with leaving a job, shifting job descriptions, and the threat of downsizing. Also included are new activities to help you understand and use this information. Finally, an instructor's manual is available for *Working Well/Living Well*. The manual includes learning objectives, suggested instructional activities, suggested homework assignments, and supplemental instructional resources.

We believe the changes in this edition help us better demonstrate how career planning and life planning can be done together and can enhance each other. We hope the changes provide a more complete picture of the skills needed for career success and satisfaction and of how you can apply these skills throughout life. We welcome your comments on how effective we have been in strengthening the text in these ways. If you have specific suggestions for change, including new ideas and classroom activities, please contact Clarke G. Carney in care of the Health and Counseling Center, Kenyon College, Gambier, OH 43022.

Acknowledgments

This book is the product of many people. Whenever possible, we have identified and acknowledged the creators and publishers of material in the book. We appreciate their willingness to allow us to adapt their material to our framework. In particular, William Hettler, of the National Wellness Institute at the University of Wisconsin at Steven's Point, and Dale Prediger, of the American College Testing Program, have been especially gracious in their willingness to share their resources with us and our student audience, as has the staff of the U.S. Department of Labor. Similar thanks are due to Ginny Hiller, Robert Milt, and Virginia Romfh, who shared their resumés with us and our readers.

Our highest praise also goes to Beth Hillier, the secretary in the Health and Counseling Center at Kenyon College, who typed the manuscript, often under intense pressures to meet deadlines.

Thanks to Tracy Schermer, the director of the Health and Counseling Center at Kenyon College, and the mental health professionals on the staff—Camille Collett, Tim Durham, and Beth Mansfield—who gave needed encouragement and understanding as the pressure to complete our work grew greater over time.

Special thanks also to Vicki and Leland, our spouses, and the Carney kids, Ian and Kaitlin, who have now survived our struggles and delights in preparing this book.

We would like to thank the following reviewers for reading the manuscript and making helpful comments and suggestions on this edition: Susan Ekberg, Webster University; Marie Nowakowski, Hagerstown Junior College; and Vaughn Worthen, Brigham Young University.

We also feel very fortunate to have had Greg Hubit and Molly Roth guiding our work through the final stages of editing and proofreading.

Finally, we also want to share our appreciation for the support and helpful guidance that has been given us by the staff of Brooks/Cole during our 20 years of collaboration.

CHAPTER 1

BEING WELL, DOING WELL

Calvin and Hobbs, © 1993 Watterson. Dist. by Universal Press Syndicate. Reprinted with permission. All rights reserved.

There is no heavier burden than a great potential.

—Charlie Brown, cartoon character

The classroom fills slowly. Students come in one at a time, sometimes in twos, only occasionally in larger groups. Those who aren't sorting through books and papers or looking out the window at the sunny afternoon sky chat about their hometowns, how they spent their vacations, people they know in common, or courses they're taking. They don't talk about their majors or their plans for after graduation. Instead, they concentrate on topics that don't remind them that they haven't yet made up their minds about what to major in or what they want to do with their lives.

Dee sits with Pam and Pat, high-school acquaintances of hers. Dee entered college intending to become an engineer. She heard about promising employment prospects in that field and has always liked math and science. But she likes to work with people and wonders whether an engineering career will fill that need. Pam likes to work with people too, but she has difficulty with the science courses in her nursing program. Her adviser has suggested that she choose another major, but Pam has always wanted to be a nurse like her mom. Pat wants to be an art major but knows that her choice will disappoint her father, who wants her to become a partner in his firm. It's difficult to argue with him when he points out how hard it is to make it as an artist, predicting that she'll wind up waiting tables for the rest of her life.

Kaitlin enters the room and finds a seat away from the others. Because she's the oldest member of the class, she feels isolated. She thinks other students wouldn't understand what it's like to be a recently divorced mother of three starting college after being out of school for 15 years. Kaitlin isn't sure how she'll manage a full load of classes while raising her children, but she believes it may be her best shot at finding a fulfilling career. She has done volunteer work, but feels she's starting at the bottom because it wasn't paid employment. She needs and wants to do something in addition to being a homemaker, but she isn't sure what, and she doesn't know whether she can work full-time at first.

Vijay, an international student, and Akiko, who know each other from other classes, take seats together. Vijay has been taking courses for several years but doesn't seem to be heading anywhere. His parents have begun pressuring him to do something, and he feels guilty about spending their money being a professional student. His adviser wants Vijay to declare a major because he's accumulated too many hours as an undecided student. Vijay has considered several career fields but can't decide what appeals to him. He spends a good part of his leisure time in sports activities. Akiko's story is different. She is financing her education through loans and part-time work. She realizes that she may have to take a job that isn't exactly what she wants at first. She can't afford to continue in school or she'll fall too deeply into debt. Knowing she can get more education later after she saves some money, she's thinking of getting a 2-year degree and then some work experience.

Stacey enters the classroom and slowly moves forward, looking for a vacant seat. She ends up sitting next to Tracy, who notices that she carries a white cane, and so she offers to help. They start talking and discover that they have career confusion in common. With several interests, Stacy finds it hard to choose just one. She fears some employers will see her impaired vision as a problem, even if she can do the job. Her adviser has urged her to consider rehabilitation counseling, where she can help people like herself. Tracy, who has learning disabilities, wants to help others with similar problems. She knows, however, that earning a college degree will be hard work for her because she still reads slowly and has difficulty memorizing.

Other students enter the room. Mary Pat, who has many talents and interests, finds it difficult to focus on a specific major. Ian had hoped to use college as a springboard to a career as a basketball player but was forced to give up his dream because of a serious knee injury. Now he's not sure what he wants to do. Camille, the last to enter the room, is anxious to make the right career choice but can't find a career that suits her. She hopes her counselor will give her a test that will tell her what to pursue.

As he walks from his office to the classroom, Dr. Morrow, the director of the campus counseling service, reflects on the past few days. It has been hectic preparing for this class and being involved in important administrative activities at the same time. He has also been assisting a group of teachers who want to find alternative careers. And he began this day by helping Tracy explore career possibilities and learning resources relevant to her particular strengths. Despite being busy, Dr. Morrow is looking forward to teaching this class and dislikes the idea that he should be starting to think about retirement.

Which of the students described here do you identify with most, in terms of career uncertainty? In what ways do you resemble that person? In what ways do you differ? If you could advise that person about what to do, what would you say? Do you have any advice for the other students in the class?

Like the students in this imaginary class, career undecidedness has many faces, and it will affect most students at some point in their lives. In fact, studies show that changing one's mind about a college major or occupational goal is quite natural for college students.

Some 30 to 40 percent of an entering college class will not complete their studies with their classmates. Some of them will find that college is not to their liking and then seek other forms of training or go directly to work. Others may drop out for a while to earn money to support their studies, to support their families during a difficult time, or to raise children.

Depending on the college, some 30 to 75 percent of a graduating class will change their majors two or more times (Lewallen, 1993). Many of those students may have been certain about their majors when they enrolled in classes but later found that they couldn't handle class requirements or that their major was not compatible with their interests. Others have difficulty making a choice because their college offers too many majors (some institutions offer more than 100!) or because they experience a conflict with their family over their career goals. Still others may have difficulty finding a major that satisfies all their diverse talents and interests. Even after the choice of a major is made, further exploration into the realities of the work environment and the job description (through research or experience) may reveal to some students that a particular choice is not a good fit because of personality, lifestyle, or values and priorities.

The 5-year bachelor's degree is becoming increasingly common. Some college administrators estimate that as few as 20 percent of students finish within the traditional 4 years. The need for additional time to complete a degree has arisen from rapid changes in the economy and technology, as well as the complexity, specialization, and growing number of career options in the 1990s. These and other changes will continue to affect students after they graduate. For example, the U.S. Department of Labor predicts that 25 percent of college graduates who enter the labor force between 1997 and 2005 will be either unemployed or in jobs that do not require a college degree.

The Labor Department also predicts that, because of a slowed economy, college-level jobs will grow more slowly over the next decade. Many 20-somethings now stay in or return to their parents' home during or after college for a time while trying to find a job (or a job in their field), save money, or decide what to do next. Not everyone needs this additional time or help from parents, but for those who do, it is reassuring to know that this isn't a "failure" or abnormal. Further, after the job search is over, 48 percent of college graduates will find employment in the fields that do not directly relate to their college majors (Grites, 1981).

At one time, labor analysts predicted that the average 20-year-old worker in the United States would change jobs six or seven times during his or her career. Now, they expect people who enter the labor force to change their professions— not simply their jobs—three to four times during their lives (Naisbitt and Aburdene, 1991). Given the importance of work in our lives and the rapid changes in the job market, it is not surprising that many students are uncertain about their majors or career choices, but they can face any anxiety, guilt or embarrassment knowing that these feelings are common and understandable.

A Few Questions . . .

Do you plan to spend more than the "usual" amount of time finishing your degree? Why? If you were unable to get the job you most want after graduation, what would your "back-up" plan be? Would you consider returning to live with your family temporarily? Would you take a job in a field related to your first choice? Or one in the same organization that would allow you to work your way into your desired position? Can you visualize yourself taking a job unrelated to your major and liking it enough to abandon your plans and strike out in a new direction?

Even though most students change majors at least once during their college years and change jobs or professions after they graduate, many students still believe that there is one right job for them. For this reason, choosing a career may seem a scary and irreversible undertaking. Students may be afraid of losing time and money or may feel that changing their minds is a sign of immaturity. Robert Frost expressed some of these feelings in describing his decision to become a poet:

The Road Not Taken

Two roads diverged in a yellow wood,
And sorry I could not travel both
And be one traveler, long I stood
And looked down one as far as I could
To where it bent in the undergrowth;

Then took the other, as just as fair,
And having perhaps the better claim,
Because it was grassy and wanted wear;
Though as for that the passing there
Had worn them really about the same,

And both that morning equally lay
In leaves no step had trodden black.
Oh, I kept the first for another day!
Yet knowing how way leads on to way,
I doubted if I should ever come back.

I shall be telling this with a sigh
Somewhere ages and ages hence:
Two roads diverged in a wood, and I—
I took the one less traveled by,
And that has made all the difference.[1]

Like Robert Frost, some people will follow only one path. Most of us, though, will follow several related or unrelated paths during the course of our careers. Often, like Frost, we will be traveling a road we have chosen and come to an unexpected fork, where we stand feeling indecisive and unable to get a clear idea of which direction will fit us better. We worry about regrets we may have later. Our best option is to get as much data as possible and choose the fork that seems to feel right and to lead toward our goals, and then to explore and reevaluate as we go. For some, this will lead to another fork, and another, until they end up somewhere fulfilling but totally unforeseen. After they learn more about what they want and what lies ahead, others decide to double back to the first fork and pursue "the road not taken." This may mean a major change in lifestyle or training, or simply in perspective.

During your lifetime, you will have many opportunities for exploration and change as you choose a major, take your first job after graduation, consider op-

---

[1]In E. C. Lathem (Ed.), *The Poetry of Robert Frost,* copyright © 1916, 1969 Henry Holt and Company, Inc. Copyright © 1944 Robert Frost. Reprinted with permission of the publisher.

portunities for advancement, change employers, and prepare for retirement. Over time, these choices will form a pattern that reflects your career, affects other important areas of your daily life, and eventually defines you as a unique person. Although this pattern may become clear to you only later in life, as you look back on choices you have made and paths you have taken, right now you can learn and do many things that will help define that pattern and take you in the direction you want to go.

WORK AND LIFE: A HOLISTIC VIEW

How Careers Affect and Reflect Our Lives

From popular advertising, most of us are acquainted with the term *lifestyle*. We frequently hear, for example, about the California lifestyle, the singles lifestyle, the executive lifestyle, and the lifestyle of the retiree. Those lifestyles that differ greatly from our own may greatly appeal to us. The snowbound person may envy the life of someone in warmer climates. A bored worker stuck in a routine job or a homemaker with small children may fantasize about being a jet-hopping consultant or a powerful executive who solves the challenging problems. Our daily lives reflect our attempts to reconcile our fantasies and aspirations with the reality of what we can do and the opportunities we really have.

The career decisions we make will shape our lives in several important ways. Work produces resources that meet our physical and other needs. It fills our time and sets a structure that provides continuity, helping us feel anchored and secure. It challenges our abilities and forces us to grow; it meets our intellectual needs and motivates continued learning. By providing us the opportunity to socialize and meet new people, work helps us form friendships and professional relationships. It also enables us to discover and afford leisure activities and companions who share them. Our accomplishments create self-respect, confidence, and emotional fulfillment, while our sense of purpose helps give us spiritual satisfaction. Work may also dictate to some extent where we live geographically. This is an important consideration if you believe that meeting your other needs hinges on a specific climate or the availability of such things as isolation and quiet, urban activities, the ocean, or the mountains. Your career choices will greatly affect all areas of your life and the lives of significant others, as their choices will affect you. Clearly, you will benefit from exploring and understanding how your work can fulfill your personal needs and fit into the total pattern of your life.

Our actions reflect how we see ourselves. If you had your way, what would you do on a daily basis in your studies or work to reflect your ideal image of yourself? Would you prefer to work with people, data, things, or ideas? Just with your brain or with your hands and body as well? Indoors or outdoors? Early or late? In a "team" or alone? For yourself or for a large organization? What are the most important things you want to do during your life? What interests you? Excites you? In which activities do you excel? Do your skills match what you like to do and what matters most to you? Your answers to these questions will reflect who you

Figure 1-1 The wellness wheel (*Note:* Adapted from figures from the National Wellness Institute at the University of Wisconsin at Stevens Point, William Hettler, Director.)

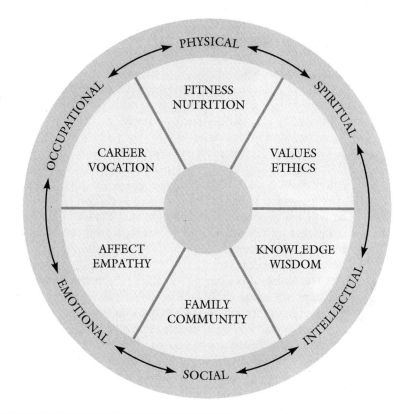

The Wellness Wheel

How would you describe your preferred way of living? To help you, we have developed the "wellness wheel," which has six dimensions (see Figure 1-1) and has been adapted from William Hettler's work at the National Wellness Institute. The occupational dimension, of course, is the main focus of this book. We shall examine job and career plans and concerns in the larger context of the lifespan. This dimension stresses one's interests and abilities, education and training, and the goal of establishing financial responsibility and independence. However, it also involves finding ways to integrate career choices with the other aspects of the wellness wheel: social and intellectual stimulation, achievement and recognition, meaning and structure for our lives, contributions to the society we live in, and enjoyment and emotional fulfillment for ourselves.

The intellectual side of life encompasses the ability to engage in activities that stimulate and challenge us, expand our knowledge, and foster learning. We all need to train ourselves in a process we can use for a lifetime of learning, since

are as a person and suggest ways you can express yourself through your career and in other areas of your life as well.

life's changes and maturation will require continued growth and adaptation. If our intellect is a dominant part of us, we will probably seek such stimulation not only through life's challenges and changes, but also through games and puzzles, reading, and hobbies.

The physical dimension of the wellness wheel involves maintaining fitness through proper nutrition, exercise, necessary medical care, and the avoidance of self-destructive behaviors such as smoking, drug abuse, and reckless driving. Many new and intriguing ideas have been added to our options for physical care in the 1990s. Treatments from many and diverse cultures are becoming increasingly popular: Eastern disciplines such as yoga, tai chi, and varied forms of meditation; massage, raki and other types of energy work; and holistic treatments such as acupuncture, hypnosis, imagery, and herbs and vitamins. Medical professionals have begun to accept these techniques as valuable by themselves or as adjuncts to traditional treatments. Current research clearly shows that the emotional, spiritual, and social aspects of people's lives profoundly affect the immune system, healing, and health.

The social side of our personalities reflects the extent to which we value relationships, the company of others, and the feeling of contributing and belonging to our community and society. As individuals, we place varying degrees of importance on interactions with friends and co-workers, on dates, and on social leisure activities. Our awareness of and comfort with our interdependence with others will affect how each of us chooses to express the social side of ourselves.

The emotional area of the wellness wheel represents our awareness, acceptance, and understanding of our own feelings. This self-knowledge strongly affects our ability to meet our needs in acceptable ways and to manage behaviors generated by these feelings. Emotional self-awareness helps determine our outlook on life, our self-esteem, and our self-expression. It also forms the basis for our ability to empathize with other people's feelings and viewpoints. All of this creates the foundation for important emotional capabilities: to be intimate, to be assertive, to achieve, and to be happy with our lives. Emotional awareness is also a necessary component of intuition, or "gut feelings." Knowing how you feel about something when making a decision will give you a great deal of crucial information about what is right for you.

The spiritual aspect of human identity may be the heart of the wellness wheel. Some of us choose to express this in a religious context, while others do not. But for all of us, spirituality involves a continuing search for the meaning and purpose of existence. We all have questions at some time about our place in the universe, our reason for being here, and whether we are part of something larger. This also includes our thoughts about "inner space"—what is inside us. Often, people search for this internally through meditation, psychotherapy, religion, and philosophy; many express it by reaching out in some way to give of themselves.

In summary, we can view the six sides of the wellness wheel as a kind of ecosystem in which we give and receive energy in our relationships, activities, and choices. During a typical day, we engage in some activities or behaviors that deplete our energies and other actions that restore us and provide us with a sense of well-being. Often, the same activity depletes us in some ways and "feeds" us in others. For example, your values might lead you to enter a field such as medicine, which would challenge you intellectually, physically, and emotionally while fulfilling your need to have a career with a sense of spiritual and social purpose.

Applying the Wellness Wheel

Stop for a minute and think about your present lifestyle. How do you think the six dimensions of the wellness wheel apply to your life? Is one (or more) especially important to you? Why? Are there sides you know little about or haven't really thought about? Do you think you might be missing something? If you already know that certain areas are important to you, how do you think they will affect your career choice?

To learn more about yourself, try the following exercise. During a typical week, how many hours would you say you spend on each of the six dimensions of the wellness wheel?

Activity	Sun.	Mon.	Tues.	Wed.	Thurs.	Fri.	Sat.
Emotional							
Social							
Intellectual							
Occupational							
Physical							
Spiritual							

When you look at your estimates, you'll probably see imbalances. Some may be due to the varied levels of awareness, others to genuine differences in behavior or opportunity. Which (if any) areas are you satisfied with? Are there areas that you would like to improve or change? If so, how would you change your behaviors to increase your sense of well-being? When could you start to make these changes?

The occupational and intellectual areas make the most obvious demands in the college years, since they focus on learning and vocational training. Keep in mind that although these things are important, you need not sacrifice a healthy and balanced life to them. If you feel overloaded or pressured in these areas, as most students do, start looking for ways in which you could be more efficient or "work smarter" to free time (even small amounts) for other priorities.

If you aren't happy with your sense of physical health or level of physical activity, you may find yourself increasingly tense, uncomfortable, and low in energy and resilience, all of which can undermine your effectiveness in other areas of your life. What might you do to improve in this area? Would you stop smoking? Drive more carefully? Alter your diet? Change your sleep habits? Spend more time in quiet relaxation? Learn stress-management skills or techniques? Have a physical exam?

Social connections and activities, both for fun and to establish relationships, are important both emotionally and developmentally at this stage in life. For this reason, students usually notice if their social needs are not being met, but sometimes they feel guilty about setting aside time for socializing or are unsure how to start. If you feel dissatisfied about this area of your life, what steps can you take? Do you need to reserve time for friends and learn to use other blocks of time more wisely? Would it help to find extracurricular activities or clubs where you could have fun and meet people? Or to seek some counseling to boost your interpersonal skills and confidence? On the other hand, if your calendar is overflowing with social activities at the expense of study, rest, exercise, or down time, you may need to examine your priorities and start saying no in order to avoid burnout. As Abraham Lincoln said, "Do not worry; eat three square meals a day; say your prayers; be courteous to your creditors; keep your digestion good; exercise; go slow and easy. Maybe there are other things your special case requires to make you happy, but my friend, these I reckon will give you a good life."

In the remaining two dimensions of the wellness wheel—emotional and spiritual—deficits and lack of balance are more subtle and sometimes difficult to see. Maybe your survey sheet shows gaps in these areas because you're not even sure how to recognize them or how they fit into your life. Our emotional growth and balance often remains outside of our awareness unless something external forces a reaction—breaking up a relationship, flunking a test, a money or job crisis. Sometimes an overload of unacknowledged emotion forces its way to the surface in the form of a "crash"—feelings of stress or depression so intense that we find it difficult to concentrate or to summon the motivation or energy to go on. Many students can avoid paying attention to physical and emotional strain until exams are over, but once the pressure is off, they get sick. If you recognize any of these behaviors, ask yourself if you know how to recognize and accept your feelings. If you have trouble identifying your feelings, you have important work to do in this area, because feelings will provide much important information about what's right for you in your career as well as other areas of life. What if you do know how you feel but not what to do about it or how to express yourself? Can you see opportunities to make a decision or to do something about a problem instead of burying it? Would working out or talking with a friend help release the tension? What do you need to do to express your opinions, values, and priorities? Besides conserving your health and energy, self-awareness helps you develop many other skills you'll need in jobs and relationships.

People's spiritual needs are personal and internal, deeply rooted in their histories, values, and beliefs. When people feel a sense of emptiness or a lack of motivation and direction, the problem is often spiritual. If you feel confused about the meaning of your life or wonder what you're getting up for in the morning, ask yourself about your goal or purpose. What are your thoughts about your place in the universe? Is there a larger meaning in the career or lifestyle you're planning? Do these plans allow you to express "the real you?" How might you learn more about yourself and your relationship to the universe? What about meditation? Religion? Philosophy? Is there a way to expand your focus beyond the immediate and see a "bigger picture?"

If you've gotten any ideas about changes you could make to your personal wellness wheel or about things you need to be more aware of, write them down. Notice any things that "hit home." Anything you can do to form healthy habits and learn balance will pay dividends both now and for the rest of your life. You may also find it valuable to keep the wellness wheel in mind as you explore career possibilities and employment opportunities in the future. The wheel can help you to evaluate each potential job or change that you pursue in terms of how well it matches your preferred lifestyle in each dimension. You may also use the wheel to evaluate how responsive a company or specific job will be to your needs. A growing number of employers offer "perks" to help their staff maintain good physical and emotional health and a balanced lifestyle: fitness facilities, healthy cafeteria meals, personal-growth seminars, team-building exercises, continuing education, flexible work schedules, telecommuting, and family-focused corporate attitudes.

Just as other priorities do, the balance within the wellness wheel shifts during our lives. Different areas of our lives have different levels of importance at each age and stage: social skills in adolescence, career questions in college, emotional and family decisions when we marry, and spiritual issues as our world view enlarges. With change or crisis, we may choose to set aside certain needs in order to make room for those that seem more urgent. Although new ideas about adult stages of development and the opinions of those close to us matter a great deal, the best barometer is what feels balanced to us.

Web Sites for Personal Health and Development

Frequently Asked Questions	http://www.dentistinfo.com./topics/faq.html
Mayo Clinic	http://www.mayo.ivi.com
Rodale Press (A rich resource of printed information)	http://www.Rodalepress.com
Wellness Web	http://www.wellweb.com
World Health Network	http://www.worldhealth.net./

THREE REASONS WE WORK

The career paths we follow greatly affect our views of ourselves and others. As the writer Eugene Delacroix once said, through work "we seek not only to produce but to give value to time." The everyday process of getting acquainted also reflects the special value we give to our work in our society. When people first meet, their conversations often begin with references to work: "What's your job or major?" "What do you plan to do when you graduate?" When asked, "Who are you?" most people respond, "A teacher," "A student," or "A homemaker," rather than "An extrovert" or "A U.S. citizen."

We Work to Fulfill Life Needs

If asked why they work, most people would probably say, "To earn a living, of course." In other words, to support their basic needs and other aspects of their lifestyles. People for whom work is not an absolute economic necessity might say that they enjoy their work, that it gives them a sense of identity or status, that it fills their time, or that they want to contribute something. Social scientists have examined people's motives. Do they *really* work for other reasons besides money and what it can buy—a new car, a bigger house, dinner out, vacations?

The psychologist Abraham Maslow (1954) developed a way of viewing people's life needs that has now become a classic in the field of human behavior. Maslow suggested that we work to satisfy five important life needs, which are arranged like the rungs of a ladder. Once the first need at the base of the ladder is met, the need at the next rung increases in importance and presses for satisfaction. First, and most basically, we work to survive—to earn money to purchase necessities, such as food and shelter. Second, we earn an income to live in a safe and secure setting. Third, we work to belong. To put it simply, we need to share our talents, interests, and career aspirations with others and need to know others care about them. The fourth reason for working, according to Maslow, is that success at work enhances our self-esteem. Through work, we achieve a sense of mastery, value, respect, and prestige. The fifth and last need—self-actualization—is the most complex. It involves expressing our creativity, using our potential, experiencing a sense of purpose in life, and feeling that we're part of something greater than ourselves. As we approach the year 2000, we see increasing evidence that the old motivations—money, security, and status—no longer carry the same meaning for many of today's workers. Many workers today seem to feel they have a right to a secure living and that the most important rewards of their jobs are found higher up on Maslow's "ladder"—things like self-esteem, independence, recognition, self-fulfillment, and a sense of purpose. Workers whose jobs do not fill these needs often look to leisure and hobbies for their main source of satisfaction and identity. How we meet our needs through work has a lot to do with our values, priorities, and views of how and why we live.

We Work to Fill Important Roles

In addition to playing the important role of *worker,* we assume many other social and emotional roles in order to satisfy our own needs and contribute to society and the groups within it that nurture us. We can review these roles in chronological order, adding the developmental tasks identified by Erik Erikson (1968), well-known developmental theorist.

Our first role is that of *child,* which can also include grandchild, niece or nephew, godchild, and so forth. As children, we learn from family members how to give and receive affection, how to express ourselves and get our needs met, how to take care of ourselves, and how to be part of an intimate social network. According to Erikson, the preschool years center on three developmental tasks. First, we must develop trust in both ourselves and the world outside. Second, we develop autonomy—the ability to say no and be separate while cooperating and accepting help. Third, we learn to take initiative and not to feel guilty about our needs.

Next come our elementary-school years, when we learn how to have and to be a *friend,* as well as how to take direction and finish a task—our first experience with work. With grade school comes another important role—*student* or *learner*—that will serve us in different forms throughout our lives. Even *play* at this age, which we remember as being carefree, is often a rehearsal for work. We play house, teacher, doctor; we play "dress-up," either in our parents' clothes or in costumes that represent jobs such as fire chief or airline pilot. Erikson refers to this in his fourth stage as "industry"—being productive, doing, or achieving. As we move toward the end of grade school, we become more aware of our obligations to the world around us. We learn about being a contributing *family member,* and we learn about citizenship through school organizations, community service, and religious or other groups. By this time we begin to realize that all basic roles, such as friend, student, and *member of society,* keep getting more complex, demanding refinement of our skills as we get older. Being a *worker* has expanded to the point where we may now be paid for such jobs as babysitting or delivering newspapers.

Then we hit puberty—or it hits us! According to Erikson, in these years our task is to begin the development of our individual identity, which is really a process rather than a goal and will take the remainder of our lives. We start to define ourselves through our choices of everything from clothing and music to what friends and what career we find appealing. At this age, play often involves trying out new behaviors and experiences and usually includes peers. We try on new roles such as *boyfriend* or *girlfriend, part-time worker, helper* and *confidant* to friends, and *leader* in school or other groups. Though we move into the role of young adult when we want to and can, we often regress back into "childhood" behavior if we are highly emotional or confused.

As our teen years end, we move into *adulthood*. For some, this involves immediate full-time work or some kind of training or apprenticeship. Others participate in further education, often with full or partial financial assistance from parents, spouses, or agencies. Work may mean an unrelated job to pay tuition or rent, or it may be some type of internship or job connected with educational goals that allows students to try on future career roles "for size." Erikson claims that at this stage our task is to develop intimacy through learning to commit and to face the fear of loss and hurt that goes with loving people in a changing world. As young adults, we need to develop an emotional support system that will function as our family did when we were small. This can include a spouse or partner, friends, co-workers, and mentors or advisors. Sometime in this stage, we begin to realize that play is not a luxury but a necessary stress reliever—time to "re-create" ourselves. We also notice that after fitting our work and/or school, friends and family, and time for our own development into the day, there is often no free time. Leisure for play, self-enrichment, or exercise becomes another priority we need to set aside time for. As we grow into new stages of our lives, we continue to add new roles. In our personal lives, these may include *spouse, parent,* or *community member.* In our work lives, new roles could evolve from new responsibilities (such as *supervisor, manager,* or *entrepreneur*) or from a change of specialty or career.

At some point in our adult lives (depending on how old we feel), we start thinking of ourselves as *middle-aged* and begin to set goals and priorities for the second half of our lives. Erikson calls this the age of "generativity," a term he defines as sharing with and guiding the next generation. This will probably mean a *mentoring* role at work, which may have already started and should be enjoyable. In our personal lives, the new roles of this age may be more stressful; they often involve reversing lifelong roles, as in caring for aging parents. We must also learn how to have an adult-to-adult relationship with children who are now grown, and we may have another new role: *grandparent!* Finally, we reach *retirement.* Although it now comes later for many of us than it did for our parents, we also live longer and in better health, so we have a large chunk of free time before us. For people who have defined themselves and their value primarily by their vocational identity, this can be frightening and depressing. Erikson suggests that to enjoy this last segment of our lives, we must develop "ego integrity," or the ability to integrate the various sides of our identity and to see ourselves as part of the larger culture and history. It seems clear that people who have made time for and developed all sides of themselves are better prepared to enjoy this stage, because they have hobbies, interests, friends, ways of spending leisure time, and the ability to feel that their contribution can be important even without a paycheck. People who have viewed work as only one part of their lives can see retirement as a new beginning and a chance to bring other parts of their identities to the forefront. This may mean more time for the role of *golfer, painter, traveler,* or *friend,* a move to a warmer climate and the role of "*sunbird,*" an unpaid career as a *volunteer,* or even the birth of a new business—and the discovery of parts of ourselves yet unknown.

We Work to Complete Life Tasks

Another way of looking at how our career plans fit into our lives is to think about how the college years involve the learning of important developmental tasks. Researchers who study the idea of life tasks or stages suggest that the accomplishment of a particular task leads to feelings of happiness, confidence, and self-esteem; approval from others; and the ability to succeed at other important tasks. Convictions about the importance of specific life tasks and the speed with which they are accomplished arise from the individual's physical and emotional maturation, intelligence, social skills and expectations, level of self-awareness, and personal aspirations and values. One vital thing to know about developmental stages and life tasks is that they are never really "done." Although we're told we must develop *competence* in what we undertake, *resilience* in facing difficulty, *cop-*

Figure 1-2 The four developmental tasks of college students (Carney, 1975)

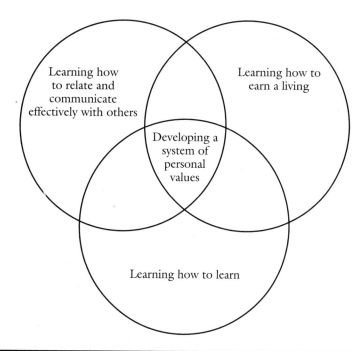

Learning how to relate and communicate effectively with others

Learning how to earn a living

Developing a system of personal values

Learning how to learn

ing skills to manage stress, *intimacy skills* for relationships, as well as qualities like *trust, autonomy, initiative* and a sense of *identity* (to name a few), these are merely goals meant to keep us heading in the right direction. We can't realistically expect ever to be "finished" or "all grown up" with respect to these qualities. Rather, when we feel stuck or encounter problems through our lifetimes, we can refer to these concepts to help us discover what area might need additional attention or adjustment.

Based on our experience in counseling college and university students over the past two decades, and on the work of theorists such as Arthur Chickering and Linda Reisser (1993), who have applied the concept of developmental tasks to college-student development, we have come to believe that students who enter college directly after high school are confronted with four developmental tasks during their college years, as Figure 1-2 shows. Like all the developmental tasks shown in this figure, learning how to learn starts at home, with the adoption of family attitudes toward school, reading, and other learning activities such as vocabulary and language use; educational toys; problem solving; use of creativity and imagination; and even elementary computer use. Difficulties in mastering the task of learning become evident during the college years among students who can not cope with academic requirements, cannot understand complex ideas or clearly present their thoughts in writing, are not motivated to study, are not well organized, and have poor study habits. The need to master the task of learning how to learn extends beyond college into the workplace, where we are expected to motivate ourselves, to keep learning from others, to manage stress, and to complete work assignments on time without prompting. In addition, the need for the ability to learn extends throughout our lives into all areas that matter to us. Changes, mistakes, and problems bring challenges and require us continually to adapt, break old habits, and develop new ones. As we learn about ourselves, we move into new jobs, relationships, social arenas, hobbies and sports, and levels of awareness about our inner selves. An 80-year-old who has never mastered a process for continued learning has not lived one lifetime of 80 years but rather one year 80 times.

The task of learning how to relate effectively with others strongly affects the other two spheres of our lives, linking them in several ways. Learning how to relate involves learning how to recognize, manage, and express our feelings while being empathic and accepting, direct and open, and (whenever possible) fair and reasonable with others. Obviously, our ability to connect effectively with others has been important since our earliest friendships and family ties, but this skill takes on new significance and complexity as we grow to adulthood and establish families of our own and a support network of friends. Connections with people help us meet needs on all fronts. We get physical affection, intellectual stimulation, social and recreational opportunities, and emotional and spiritual satisfaction. At work, we need the ability to form good relationships with friends, mentors, and bosses, as well as to work comfortably with other co-workers whose tastes, beliefs, attitudes, and lifestyles differ from ours. Our occupational endeavors—starting with education, interning, and interviewing and continuing through adjustment to the world of work and career advancement—center on skills in relating to and communicating with others.

The task of learning how to earn a living involves developing specific work skills based on our preferences, interests, abilities, and values. It also involves understanding ourselves and our feelings and priorities in regard to who we are and how we want to live, so that our career choices will continue to be compatible with our self-image and our chosen lifestyle.

At the center of these three developmental tasks—learning, relating, and working—we find the development of our personal values. Our values represent the things we cherish most in life. They shape our attitudes and actions regarding how and what we choose to learn, the type and quality of our relationships, and the direction we give to our career pursuits. Our values give purpose and coherence to our lives and guide us as we strive to satisfy our life needs, fulfill our social roles, and create a satisfying lifestyle. Knowing and living by our values leads us to a better understanding of who we are (Erikson's task of developing an identity) and what principles will guide our choices and behavior. According to Stephen Covey (1989), these values and principles provide the starting point and most lasting foundation for long-term success. In Chapters 3 and 4, we will describe in greater detail the forces that shape our life roles, stages, and tasks. The next two sections summarize the important questions about ourselves and the skills we need for effective career planning that the rest of the book will explore.

CAREER-PLANNING QUESTIONS

In her book on career planning, Celia Denues (1972) points out: "To know where you want to go, you must know where you are and who you are." The best place to start the career-planning process is with yourself—specifically with your wants and preferences. Let's begin with questions about *you*. You'll need to answer five questions about yourself as you chart your current and future career path, but you don't have to be concerned with answering them yet. Here, we're simply going to identify them and emphasize their importance in order to give you guidelines for understanding the process of career and life planning.

1. Who are you?
2. How do you want to live?
3. Where do you want to live?
4. What will you do for a living?
5. Whom will you spend your time with?

In addition to answering these basic questions, we need to learn many less concrete things about ourselves if we are to fit our vocational identity into a lifestyle that fulfills our larger dreams and goals. And we need to be prepared to keep on learning, since the answers may change as we do. For example:

1. What type of environment are you most comfortable in?
2. Do you like things casual and flexible or structured?
3. Do you prefer time alone, with other people, or some of each?
4. Will your chosen work be physical, mental, or both?
5. Which is more important to you: intellectual or emotional stimulation?
6. What do you think of as the most important purposes of work?
7. What is the most important need work will satisfy for you?
8. How will you spend your time outside of work?
9. What forms of recreation are most enjoyable to you? What others interest you?
10. How do you use free time? Do you plan it out? Do you need "couch potato" time?
11. Is an active social life a priority to you? What about family life? Children?
12. How do you want to be seen or see yourself as a person?

To explore these questions, we need to look at all sides of our lives—ways of filling those needs essential to our development, self-esteem, and energy in all areas of life, including work.

By the time you have finished this book, you'll have the skills and knowledge to answer most of these questions in detail. In addition to knowing who you are and where you are in the career-planning process, you'll also know where you want to go. Now let's turn to the skills you'll need to build your career effectively, now and in the future.

SIX SKILLS FOR EFFECTIVE CAREER AND LIFE PLANNING

How can we plan for the future and still remain open to change as our needs and goals, and those of society, evolve over time? The answer to this question is to develop now the skills that will prepare you for a lifetime of career decision making. Doing so will allow you to anticipate and manage your career effectively in a changing world.

Whether you are making a choice today or preparing to make future choices, you'll need to master six essential career-planning skills. This book is organized around these skills. The first skill you'll need is *effective decision making*. Our decisions form a bridge between our wants and needs and the world around us. We shape our lives through our decisions. Every day, each of us makes a great many of them. Some require little thought and planning; others require a great deal. Whether your decisions are large or small, if you have not developed the skills for effective decision making, you may find yourself feeling powerless and directionless. Chapter 2 will help you focus on and refine your career decision-making skills.

Effective career decision making begins and ends with ourselves, with the way we shape our world to accommodate our unique capabilities, interests, and values. The second essential skill—*self-assessment*—involves the ability to pull together the bits and pieces of information you have about yourself to create a picture of who you are occupationally, and in a larger context, how other aspects of your life goals, preferences, and sense of identity fit with your career choices. Because you're likely to change as you gain life experience, the image you have of yourself is more like a frame in a motion picture than a snapshot. Consequently, you need to plan for self-review throughout your career.

If you learn how to obtain and apply information about yourself and to understand how your goals, dreams, and needs are likely to change over the course of your life, you can manage your career more effectively. Chapters 3, 4, and 8 explore in depth how personal and environmental influences can shape the course of your career.

The third essential skill is that of *gathering and assessing career information*. We are all probably familiar with some occupations, but only a few of us have a real sense of how seemingly unrelated occupations fit together to form unified industries and economic networks. Like pieces of a puzzle, each occupation shares characteristics with the pieces around it. As you acquire knowledge of the puzzle as a whole, you'll begin to see how you can use your particular interests and talents in various settings. Skills for gathering accurate occupational information will enable you to identify several career areas that suit your work and lifestyle preferences. Chapters 6 and 7 provide an overview of the world of work.

In Chapter 8, you'll learn the fourth essential skill—fitting together occupational information and your knowledge of yourself with external influences and people important to you, in a process of *developing personally satisfying career options.*

When you've completed your studies or other forms of training, you'll probably begin the process of securing employment. The fifth essential career planning skill is *effectively communicating your skills, interests, and aspirations to an employer.* Although you may not go right out and look for work after reading this book, we encourage you to learn and practice the skills necessary to conduct an effective job campaign. To do so, you must learn to identify job leads and present yourself effectively to an employer through telephone contacts, correspondence, and interviews. Whatever your level of work experience, Chapter 7 will greatly help you in conducting your first job campaign or later in your career as you face changes in the workplace, redefine your personal goals, and develop new skills to remain a viable candidate for new jobs.

Our society exerts tremendous pressure on people to be flexible and to adapt to a variety of interpersonal situations. Donald Super (1980) has observed that at different times during our working lives we will be called on to fill many roles, including learner, friend, co-worker, team member, mentor or teacher, boss or manager, and family and community member. Each role requires that we be sensitive to our needs and those of others, that we recognize differences and commonalities with others and be able to communicate effectively with them, and that we take direction, act independently, or work interdependently as the need arises. Many people who find these requirements difficult lose jobs or fail to get them because they can't get along with other people. So the sixth career-planning skill is that of *work adjustment and career expansion.* Chapter 10 is devoted to this subject and shows how you can promote the development of your career by managing the stress of the job, negotiating the culture of the work setting with integrity and professionalism, and taking advantage of new learning opportunities. Although you may believe that the content of Chapter 10 isn't relevant to you now because you're a student, we encourage you to read it and think about how the concepts presented there can be applied to any clubs or social organizations you belong to; your part-time or summer jobs; the faculty, staff, and students at your college; and even your family. Learning and using these concepts now will help you be better prepared to negotiate the culture of the organization that employs you when you graduate and enter the "real world."

These six skills—decision making, self-assessment, occupational exploration, integration of information and development of options, job campaigning, and work adjustment and career expansion—form the core of this book. They build and spiral back on one another with each career decision you make. Essential to a self-directed lifestyle, these skills can be learned and refined with practice and used throughout your career as you make new choices and enter new situations. People who achieve these skills can meet a changing world with hope, optimism, and confidence in their own personal resources.

Some Questions to Consider

1. Here is a list of feelings that might apply to the career search. Circle the ones you feel or have felt.

ambivalent	disorganized	intimidated	frustrated	responsible	determined
angry	anxious	burdened	confused	capable	eager
different	pressured	threatened	impatient	excited	exhilarated
helpless	isolated	panicked	competitive	happy	strong
worried	stressed	insecure	prepared	centered	calm

    a. Which negative feeling is strongest? How might it affect your career search? How do you deal with it?

    b. Which positive feeling is strongest? How is it affecting your attitude and behavior?

    c. What feelings would you like to have? How might you cultivate them?

2. Find a family member or friend who has been working for a while and is willing to talk with you about his or her career. Ask that person the following questions:

    a. What influenced your decision to choose your field of work?

    b. Why do you work?

    c. What is most satisfying about your job? What do you like to do when you aren't at work?

In addition, try to find out which needs are being met through family and friendships. What are the most important roles that the person is playing in his or her life? What challenges or developmental tasks is the person working on? Ask the same questions of yourself and identify how you resemble or differ from the person you've interviewed.

3. Review this list of life roles:

child	player	leader/manager	friend
young adult	worker	entrepreneur	boyfriend/girlfriend
middle-ager	paid worker	mentor	spouse/partner
retiree	co-worker	family member	helper/confidant
student/learner	supervisor/boss	community member	volunteer

    a. Which life roles have you already played? Which were your favorites? Why? Which were difficult? Why? Some are easy to spot—you know you've been a child, a student, and so forth. Before you dismiss some of the other roles, try to expand your view of how they might express themselves. For example, did you ever head a committee (boss or leader), knock on doors and offer to shovel snow or mow lawns (entrepreneur), or help teach a younger sibling or classmate (mentor)? What do the elements of your most and least favorite roles tell you about what you might want to do for a living? Review your memories of the various roles you played and what that was like. Did you do them voluntarily or did someone pressure you? Did you get along with "co-workers" or were you impatient? Bossy? Were you more comfortable leading or following instructions? What did you learn about yourself?

b. Which life roles are you playing now? List them in order of their importance to you—most important to least. Starting with the least important, pretend you have the opportunity to give it up. Would you exchange it for another role? If so, why? If not, why not? What role would you replace it with? Repeat this sequence for each of your current roles. Then examine the patterns and ask yourself—what stands out? What have you learned? How would you change your life right now if you could? If you choose to stay in an imperfect situation, what are your reasons? Goals? Is it worth the effort?

c. What roles do you hope or expect to be filling in 5 years? In 10 years? By then, will you be able to institute the changes you want? How do you think your career will affect which roles you'll keep and which ones you'll be adding?

4. What does the term *career* mean to you personally? How does your definition differ from the way the word is used in this chapter?

5. In your own words, describe the six important skills for career planning. Which skill(s) have you already developed? Which do you want to develop or refine by using this book?

6. What do you want from college? From this book? From your career?

7. Write down an important change you've made in your life and describe how that change occurred by answering the following questions:

a. What changed?

b. How did the change occur? Did you make it by choice? Did a specific event create the need to change?

c. How did you cope with or manage the change?

d. Who supported you in making the change? If anybody got in the way, how did you work with or around that person?

e. As you look at it now, what would you do differently?

f. How is this particular change affecting your life now?

Beetle Bailey, ©1994. Reprinted with special permission of King Features Syndicate.

REFERENCES AND RESOURCES

Carney, C. (1975). Psychological dimensions of career development: An overview and application. Paper presented at a training conference for the Ohio Department of Education, Columbus.

Chickering, A., & Reisser, L. (1993). *Education and identity.* (2nd ed.) San Francisco: Jossey-Bass.

Covey, S. R. (1989). *The 7 Habits of Highly Effective People.* New York: Simon & Schuster.

Denues, C. (1972). *Career perspective: Your choice of work.* Worthington, OH: Charles D. Jones.

Erikson, E. H. (1968). *Identity: Youth and Crisis.* New York: Norton.

Foote, B. F. (1980). Determined—and undetermined—major students: How different are they? *Journal of College Student Personnel, 21,* 29–34.

Goodson, W. D. (1981). Do career development needs exist for all students entering college or just the undecided major students? *Journal of College Student Personnel, 22,* 413–417.

Grites, T. J. (1981). Being "undecided" may be the best decision they could make. *School Counselor, 29,* 41–46.

Havinghurst, R. J. (1972). *Developmental tasks and education.* (3rd ed.) New York: David McKay.

Healy, C. C. (1991). Exploring a path linking anxiety, career maturity, grade point average and life satisfaction in a community college population. *Journal of College Student Development, 32,* 207–211.

Kojaku, L. K. (1972). *Major field transfer: The self-matching of university undergraduates to student characteristics.* Los Angeles: University of California Press (ERIC Document No. ED 062 933).

Lewallen, W. (1993). The impact of being "undecided" on college persistence. *Journal of College Student Development, 34,* 103–112.

Maslow, A. (1954). *Motivation and personality.* New York: Harper & Row.

Naisbitt, J., & Aburdene, P. (1991). *Megatrends 2000.* New York: Morrow.

Noel, L. (1985). Increasing student retention: New challenges and potential. In L. Noel, R. Levitz, D. Saluri et al. (Eds.), *Increasing student retention: Effective programs and practices for reducing the dropout rate* (pp. 1–27). San Francisco: Jossey-Bass.

Slaney, R. B. (1980). Expressed vocational choice and vocational indecision. *Journal of Counseling Psychology, 27,* 122–129.

Steele, G. E., Kennedy, G. J., & Gordon, V. N. (1993). The retention of major changers: A longitudinal study. *Journal of College Student Development, 34,* 58–62.

Super, D. E. (1980). Life-span, life-space approach to career development. *Journal of Vocational Behavior, 16,* 282–298.

Tinto, V. (1985). Dropping out and other forms of withdrawal from college. In L. Noel, R. Levitz, D. Saluri et al. (Eds.), *Increasing student retention: Effective programs and practices for reducing the dropout rate* (pp. 28–43). San Francisco: Jossey-Bass.

Titley, R. W., Titley, B., & Wolfe, W. M. (1976). The major changers: Continuity of discontinuity in the career decision process. *Journal of Vocational Behavior, 8,* 105–111.

York-Anderson, D., & Bowman, S. L. (1991). Assessing the college knowledge of first and second generation college students. *Journal of College Student Development, 34,* 103–112.

CHAPTER *2*

CHOICES IN ACTION

Funky Winkerbean, ©1992. Reprinted with special permission of North America Syndicate.

Planning is bringing the future into the present so that you can do something about it now.

—Alan Lakein, time-management specialist

Emilio tips his head back, closes his eyes, and sighs. Lines of print dance inside his eyelids. Only a few more weeks of writing and tests and he will have his M.B.A. Even this close to his goal, he still wonders what he wants to be when he grows up. He has worked so hard to find a comfortable fit with a career choice, and sometimes that scares him. If this choice is really right, why hasn't it come more easily? His friend Alison, who has always loved all things medical, is now a med tech. His neighbor Jon, who is a natural at math, fell easily into computer studies and a job with a local business. But Emilio has had to struggle and search for a career path, and he still sometimes wonders whether the one he has chosen will really work for him.

Emilio remembers his discomfort when high-school friends started choosing careers. Emilio tried to examine his interests and abilities. Then he tried to match his vocational self to the working world. The B.S. in computer science and the M.B.A. in marketing seemed likely to open many doors while combining his technical and detail aptitudes with his interest in people and psychology. With that training, he could work for many different types of businesses.

Emilio takes a drink of his Coke and turns back to his book with a sigh. His biggest fear about business or corporate work is about the demands—a lot of time, possible relocation. Growing up in a big, active Latino home, he looks forward to a family with several children and the time to be involved in their lives. Emilio worries about whether he can make these conflicting needs work together, but he figures this problem "goes with the territory." He plans to find a job where he feels comfortable and put his energy into blending his lifestyle and career effectively. He knows he can keep reevaluating his choices, with the help of his fiance. Later, if things aren't working as they hope, he can adjust his goals and make different choices.

Our self-concepts—the images that come to mind when we ask ourselves "Who am I?"—provide continuity as we grow and change. Our self-image and sense of identity appear most in the decisions we make and the actions we take and reflect the wisdom gained from our past experiences, our priorities and values, and our opinions of ourselves. Further, any marked change in our lives challenges our self-concepts and causes feelings of uncertainty. Graduating from college, changing majors, taking a new job, getting married, moving, being promoted, or going on vacation are all common changes that most of us experience during our lives. Each change requires us to make decisions that reflect our self-concepts.

Even though we may not be aware of it, our decisions are based on the beliefs, attitudes, and values that are woven into the fabric of our self-concepts. These beliefs, attitudes, and values are shaped by messages we receive from and behaviors we observe in our family and culture. Our *beliefs* represent our personal views about how the world operates and what reality is and should be. Our *attitudes,* on the other hand, predispose us to like some situations or people and not like others. Because we cannot have direct experience in every area, many of our attitudes and beliefs are based on information we get from others (even though it may be distorted or inaccurate). Our *values* tell us what we should or should not do. What we define as right or proper is a reflection of our values. Our values are also shaped by the society in which we live and by parents, teachers, and friends.

All these influences—our society, culture, family, friends—affect our decisions indirectly through our beliefs, attitudes, and values. To be sure that our decisions reflect what we want for ourselves rather than what we've been told by others, we must learn to look at our feelings and experiences objectively. We must separate our reality from the biases and distortions we absorbed while growing up, as well as from our fears about making mistakes and about our own adequacy. In Chapter 8, we shall discuss strategies for doing this.

Because of the changing nature of society and of ourselves, each of us must frequently try to balance what we have now against what we think will exist in the future. We're torn between the security that comes with keeping things as they are and the insecurity involved in deciding to reshape our lives. In making decisions, each of us must be willing to say, "This is what I value," by freely choosing to give up some options and by assuming responsibility for the consequences of our choices. We're free to choose and to take responsibility for our choices only when we have two or more options based on our independent assessment and are capable of acting on them. Lacking choices and the ability to act, we cannot make real decisions.

Many of our choices will not be permanent. Living involves growth and change, and the future holds twists and turns we cannot predict. Even though the decisions we make as we adjust to such changes may be looked at separately, each is actually a link in a long chain of choices. Every decision builds on our previous decisions and in turn stimulates and influences future decisions.

In looking at an individual decision, we need to distinguish between the *decision process* and the *decision outcome*. The decision-making process is irreversible in the sense that we cannot reverse time. It propels us forward through a series of decisions. We often can change the outcomes of our decisions—the actions we take and their consequences—by making new decisions as alternatives become available.

Both the information we use as well as the way we make our decisions affect the quality of those decisions. If we lack the proper information, we can run into blind alleys. If we fail to consider carefully all available information, we limit the number of alternatives to consider or make a premature choice. In addition, the information we use may be distorted because it's outdated or misrepresented by its source. For example, if we examine the information, beliefs, attitudes and values we have internalized from our families, we may find that some of them are right for our parents or other family members but not for us. We ourselves can even unwittingly distort information when we view it through our personal be-liefs, attitudes, and values. All it takes to illustrate how frequently this occurs is a discussion with friends about the meaning or value of a book, movie, or event; just about everything can be interpreted in different ways by different people.

New information may also change our decisions. Suppose you're planning to spend your summer working at a camp, but your academic adviser says you must take classes during the summer to graduate on schedule. Instead of facing the single decision of how to obtain a camp job, you now need to decide between camp and graduation.

Finally, our attitudes and effectiveness in decision making are affected by how confident we are of our own skills and our ability to succeed. For all these reasons, we need to learn, understand, and practice a decision-making process, which we can use repeatedly to guide us in exploring new information, feelings, and varied experiences. This can give us confidence by showing us we have the structure and tools to succeed.

DECISION STRATEGIES

The situations that require us to make decisions will vary greatly throughout our lives. The pressure to change or to decide may come from ourselves or from the environment—or often from both. How realistic or efficient we are at making a decision often depends on how well we know ourselves and our environment.

Figure 2-1 demonstrates graphically how information affects our decisions over our lifetimes. As infants, we had no real control over what happened—all we could do was vocalize our discomfort while our parents tried to guess its source. As chil-dren, we learned more about ourselves and the world and began to use new strate-gies for decision making. If we didn't really know what we wanted to do but knew about our environment, we probably tended to make *dependent decisions*. ("I'll get

Figure 2-1
Learning decision strategies

		Self	
		Not known	Known
Environment	Not known	Confusion and/or paralysis	Intuitive decisions
	Known	Dependent decisions	Informed decisions

spanked if I don't do what Mommy says. I'd better do it her way.") If we knew what we wanted to do but were less certain about the conditions in the environment, we probably made *intuitive decisions.* ("I don't want spinach. I want ice cream.") As we grew older, we retained the ability to make these two types of decisions by adding another strategy—the *planful decision,* which takes into account our knowledge both of ourselves and of the environment. When we use this strategy, we weigh the internal and external demands of the situation and the pros and cons (or costs and benefits) of the various alternatives. If there's time, we may gather and consider additional information about alternatives, look at possible consequences for ourselves and our environment, and consider our intuition and feelings.

We shall now discuss three strategies for the decision process, each with its own advantages and disadvantages, and present hints about how each one might be used and how you can combine them. Note that we don't address confusion and paralysis; this is the state of not being able to decide.

Dependent Decision Strategy

The *dependent decision strategy* may appear to be the easiest—we've certainly had the most time to practice it! All we need to do is defer the choice to others: let someone else decide. In a situation where the outcome matters little to us, this approach can save time and energy. If you're like most people, you make many of your dependent decisions in the spirit of compromise, as in a group decision. Some situations may call for a more informed dependent choice. If your doctor recommends surgery, for example, you may wish to get a second opinion or have the reasons carefully explained. Knowing that you don't have enough medical knowledge to make the final decision, you must depend partly on your doctor's judgment.

A dependent decision can be self-defeating and produce unhappy results if it stems from fear of making a choice on your own or is made to avoid the work of exploring options. Deferring an important choice out of fear or indecision does not help us to avoid the problem. It means only that the decision will be out of our control and will eventually be made by others or by circumstances. The results will affect our lives just as if we had made the choice. Even if we have transferred the decision making elsewhere, we will still have to cope with the results.

"Let us not look back in anger or forward in fear, but around in awareness."
—*James Thurber*

Intuitive Decision Strategy

Decision makers who use the *intuitive decision strategy* rely on gut-level reactions. They check out their internal signals to find out whether something feels right. Because one can make intuitive decisions spontaneously and below one's level of awareness, they take little time, data gathering, or conscious planning. They are useful in situations where time is at a premium, such as emergencies or unforeseen opportunities. Intuition often helps us in interpersonal, social, and emotional situations, where factual data may be unavailable, inaccurate, or misleading. When

---

Dependent Decision Worksheet

One decision I made with the help or advice of others was _____

My reason for choosing a dependent decision was _____

It did/didn't work out well because _____

I'm glad/sorry I asked for help because _____

If I could do it over, I would _____

What I learned about dependent decisions is _____

What I learned about myself is _____

Intuitive Decision Worksheet

One decision I made intuitively was _____

My reason for choosing an intuitive decision was _____

It did/didn't work out well because _____

I'm glad/sorry I based the decision on my intuition because _____

If I could do it over, I would _____

What I learned about intuitive decisions is _____

What I learned about myself is _____

---

used appropriately, intuition can help us retain both authority and responsibility in making a difficult decision.

But an intuitive decision can have uncomfortable results if it is used as a substitute for or to avoid gathering needed information. In emotional or very important situations, intuitive hunches are sometimes hard to distinguish from wishful thinking or personal bias. If the information and time to review a decision are available, it is usually wise to take advantage of them. After exploring, however, intuition or feelings may still play an important part in the final decision. Intuition enjoys a better reputation now than in the past, since we realize that hunches may really be perceptions based on information that is taken in over time but not consciously remembered. In emotional and spiritual terms, we also realize that at some point any major decision involves a leap of faith based on our belief in ourselves and in the resources that we have. Nevertheless, it is probably wiser not to decide something on the basis of intuition alone if other information is available.

Informed Decision Worksheet

One decision I made by gathering information and data was _____

My reason for choosing an informed decision was _____

It did/didn't work out well because _____

I'm glad/sorry I gathered data and information because _____

If I could do it over, I would _____

What I learned about informed decisions is _____

What I learned about myself is _____

Informed Decision Strategy

The *informed decision strategy* involves exploring our needs and feelings along with information and feedback from the environment then rationally weighing the various alternatives, costs, and benefits. Though slower than others, this approach allows maximum time for data gathering, exploring, and experimenting. Attention can be paid to details, and questions can be raised and answered. These questions will help us anticipate possible problems and implement the decision more smoothly and efficiently.

Because the informed approach to decisions can consume a great deal of time and energy, it's not always appropriate. Many decisions aren't important enough to be worth this amount of effort, and sometimes needed information isn't available. Another problem is that in any situation the data are never all in, and waiting for everything we need to know can be a way of avoiding a decision. Finally, anyone who takes this decision style literally runs the risk of making a totally rational or totally independent decision, which may not reflect reality, since our feelings and the opinions of significant others are important.

This approach is most effective when combined with other strategies to include consideration of personal concerns and gut feelings about the choices (intuitive) and the opinions of experts and loved ones (dependent). We may also want to include personal and idiosyncratic decision strategies that have worked for us in the past, including everything from the serious—prayer and meditation, list making—to carrying lucky charms, casting spells, and other superstitious behaviors. Ideally, a balanced decision includes elements of all three decision styles. First, we consider information available from internal and external sources, weigh the validity of that information, and formulate possible steps or plans. Next, we check this against feedback and advice that we consider valid. We might invest time in further exploration if necessary. Finally, we refer to our own priorities and comfort level with any decision. Ideally, we "sleep on it," taking time to review how we would feel about or respond to possible outcomes and consequences. Our most productive decisions take into account information from all these resources.

STAGES OF AN INFORMED CAREER DECISION

One may describe an informed career decision process in several ways. The decision stages that we have found most useful are summarized in Figure 2-2.

Awareness

The awareness stage is usually heralded by a feeling of increasing discomfort in some area of our lives—an awareness of pressure for change. Often we can't make a change immediately, because the early stages of awareness may arrive before we can identify the problem or even be sure what area of our lives the problem involves. Still, unless we're willing to let the circumstances control us, we feel the need to *do* something. The natural first step, then, is to locate the origin of the problem and clearly define it before beginning the search for a solution. If unsure where the problem lies, we need to take a moment to look over our lives. Using a framework such as the wellness wheel or a set of goals or principles by which we guide our lives, we can look at areas that are important to us and evaluate our inner experience. We can also ask trusted friends and advisors to give us constructive feedback about what they see and feel. Understanding the problem requires referring to our own beliefs, attitudes, and values as well as those of our society. As we begin to realize where the discomfort comes from, we can localize our search and "close in" on a clear definition of the problem. However, sometimes we're so anxious to learn about alternatives that we fail to spend enough time sorting out the elements that make up the problem. Time devoted to defining the problem is well spent, particularly for those who feel confused by a multitude of options that they can't organize or compare in any meaningful way.

Once we have determined what change is needed, or if we can already see one coming (such as a career choice), we tend to have mixed feelings. A new venture is often a positive one, bringing excitement and anticipation. However, most changes also introduce risk, potential mistakes, or the fear of a wrong choice. Our anxiety can affect our decision process negatively by either slowing it down or

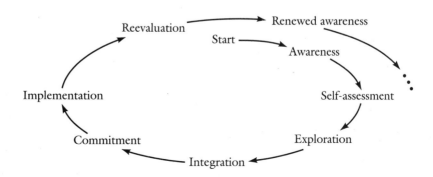

Figure 2-2 The decision cycle

speeding it up. The latter can occur if we grow so uncomfortable that we want to act before being ready, just to "get it over with." More often, however, fear and doubt lead to delay, and we procrastinate or ignore the problem for fear of making a bad choice. If the changes that awareness demands frighten us, we sometimes postpone making the decision until it's almost upon us. This delay may contribute to the fear or even panic that sometimes accompanies awareness. We can often alleviate confusion and anxiety by pinpointing specific fears, irrational expectations, or skill and information deficits that contribute to the problem.

Examining what's blocking a decision can provide clues about where to look for help and what to do first. Awareness of an unresolved problem can be confusing and distressing, but it is important not to block the feelings out, since they are the source of much information about our own needs and preferences. They signal in a positive way when we're on the right track. Being headed toward the "right" goal for us doesn't always feel wonderful, though, because it can imply hard work and uncertainty. But we may notice that our "gut feelings" are good (although confused), and we often notice the absence of that feeling that says, "This isn't for you." Sometimes we have a feeling that tells us we're ready to decide, but an important element of readiness is still work: learning, examining, and refining ourselves, our environment, and our decision-making strategies. As mentioned in Chapter 1, decision making is the first of six skills crucial to planning our careers.

Self-Assessment

As in defining the problem, the best source of information for identifying desirable alternatives is ourselves. At this stage, we begin to use the second of the six career-planning skills—self-assessment.

We need to focus on two kinds of information within ourselves. One is information about our self-concept, specifically answers to "Who am I?" and "How do I want to live?" We need to clarify our beliefs, attitudes, and values so we can check the strategies, goals, and outcomes we generate to see if they fit comfortably with our self-concepts. We need to determine what we want and what we're willing to sacrifice to get it. Self-assessment includes not just career but all six dimensions of the wellness wheel, since juggling all our different needs involves sacrifices and compromises. On examination, we may discover that past decisions have been largely dependent or intuitive or that we have put other people's wants and needs ahead of our own. If so, we need to work to get better acquainted with our inner selves—there may be a lot there that we're not aware of because we haven't used it consciously.

The second type of internal information we need to focus on is more specifically career related. Most of us since early childhood have held our own ideas and fantasies, as well as messages received from others, about what we want to do when we grow up. Research indicates that this is (believe it or not) an excellent predictor of what career we choose. What were some of the things you played at being or wondered about as a child? What appealed to you about those childhood dreams, and what common thread might they have? What did you dress up as on Halloween? Did you notice people who wore uniforms to work? Did you notice adults working? What kinds of jobs attracted your attention? Why? In any case, it's important to review these ideas to learn whether they fit us, whether they're still appealing, and whether they're really ours rather than someone else's. Even if none of them fits us today, they still serve as a valuable source of information about ourselves. The more knowledge you have about your inner self as you work on the career decision process, the easier it will be to determine whether the options that you uncover will fit with your self-concept and your lifestyle goals.

Exploration

The purpose of exploration is to make sure we have enough data and information as well as alternative ways of achieving our desired goals and outcomes. This third career planning skill involves learning strategies for gathering career information. Such strategies can include reading biographies or other books about people who work in professions that interest you, talking with people about their jobs, spending a day "shadowing" someone in his or her job, attending local job fairs, and gaining experience through part-time jobs, internships, or volunteering. What is your preferred mode of research? Which of the following appeals to you: thinking and analyzing information, reading, exploring your feelings, talking with others, action and experimentation, interviewing people with experience, or surfing the web? Chapters 6 and 7 will examine in depth the world of work and strategies for information seeking.

As you explore, you'll start to notice and pull together ideas that point to various options. Spend some time on each alternative, trying to think through possible outcomes and how they might feel or fit. As you discover appealing alternatives, you can weigh the probability and cost of possible positive and negative outcomes. For example, you might say, "If I complete pre-med and can't get into medical school, or major in political science and change my mind about law school, what other options will I have? Can I live with them?" After you've collected several realistic alternatives, you can approach deciding among these courses of action in two ways. First, you can eliminate the least acceptable alternatives and examine what's left. Second, you can start with the attractive ones and weigh each to identify the most practical and attainable one.

The process of exploring can be uncomfortable. It often creates confusion, conflict, and anxiety. The sheer amount of information available in many career areas increases the complexity of decision making and presents new considerations or options that cause us to feel like we have to start over. Awareness of requirements and commitments involved in many choices can awaken fears of risk and failure. Such awareness can also bring the unwelcome realization that favored dreams and solutions may be blocked or perhaps too difficult to be worthwhile. Although we can imagine ourselves as corporation presidents, we may discover that we do not have the personal resources to strive to the corporate world's top levels.

People who have very many—or very few—areas of interest often discover several alternatives that appear to be equally attractive, but they have difficulty prioritizing them. Greater in-depth exploration or volunteer or trial work experience may help differentiate interests, test abilities, and increase confidence. Reviewing one's personal beliefs and goals may also help.

Integration

Before we can make a commitment to go forward in any specific direction, we must assess how the career ideas or options we found in our information search fit what we know about ourselves and our lives. In weighing the likelihood of turning our hopes into realities, we must review what we learned about our self-concepts and lifestyle preferences and examine the influence of important external factors as well. These include commitments to significant others (spouses or serious relationships, family members, employers), financial resources, and constraints of time and location.

The process of integration, which leads to readiness for commitment, is not smooth sailing for many of us. Many people encounter some conflicts when they attempt to fit their desires and options with these other realities. Some conflicts are with loved ones whose opinion we value—for example, parents who feel we are taking the wrong path, or a spouse who may experience hardship because of our career choice. We may also find ourselves in conflict with reality. For example, a career requiring years of graduate training will take time, money, and probably outstanding grades just to be admitted. A choice that has few or specific locations may necessitate a move that was not in our plans. Other conflicts will be internal—such as difficulties in deciding how best to spend limited time or money, discomfort because what we want is not what we believe we *should* want, or the inability to see clearly or choose wisely among options because of guilt, fear, or dependence on others. Further, we may find ourselves reevaluating some of our own beliefs and attitudes as we explore career possibilities and the world outside our family structure. In Chapter 8, we shall fully examine the varied aspects, problems, and possible resolutions of this process of integration.

Commitment

As we examine ourselves, our lives, and the world of work, we reach a point where we feel ready to move ahead with an alternative or at least to experiment. Reaching this point doesn't mean we're ready to make a final decision or that we have no fears. It simply means that we've learned enough about ourselves, our options, and what kind of lives we envision that we're willing to accept the unavoidable risks and go forward on the basis of our hopes and preparations. Often, we're not sure we're ready, but we do know that we're tired of being undecided, that we have done the best informed decision making that we can, and that the only way to find out whether our tentative choice will work is to try it!

For some of us, this is a difficult point in the process. Although we may be unsure, we must choose one alternative to pursue, while keeping others in reserve. Choosing one solution means eliminating others—at least temporarily, but sometimes permanently. Eliminating options before we're through with them is difficult. We fear we'll be wrong, and we hate to close off other pathways. Unfortunately, we can pursue no single course of action to its most successful conclusion if we're emotionally divided or spending energy trying to keep other choices alive. The only way to discover whether something will really work for us is to commit our focus, energy, and resources to it wholeheartedly. Although some choices may involve irreversible expenditures of time and personal resources, almost any decision can be reevaluated, altered, or abandoned at a later stage if we have the courage to look at it and our feelings honestly. Research on adult development indicates that the outcomes of a commitment made and pursued to the best of our abilities are generally very positive in terms of growth and learning. Research shows that even if people change or abandon their commitments, these people will be more successful with later endeavors—apparently because they have had practice in deciding, communicating, and following through.

Implementation

Once we've made a commitment, we implement the decision by initiating new courses of action or behaviors. We may gather information and start acquiring new skills or equipment. We may begin formal procedures for entering a training program or begin a job campaign. We may be able to change an old situation or create a new one using skills and opportunities that are already available. In all these situations, we will need the fourth career-planning skill: the ability to find available jobs and to market ourselves. As we implement our decisions, we need to be aware of feedback about the choice we've made. Does it fit our values? Have we done enough exploring? Have any of the circumstances changed?

If self-assessment, exploration, and integration have been complete, any difficulties encountered in implementing a goal will not come as a complete surprise. (However, things do happen that we cannot foresee or control, such as financial reversals, illness, or sudden changes in the environment.) Of course, hurdles and setbacks on the road to any goal—especially a long-term goal—may appear bigger or more discouraging in reality than they did in imagination, but discouragement can often be remedied with a little rest or moral support. If the path to implementation seems full of unpleasant surprises, however, the exploration may have been incomplete or the goals unrealistic.

Implementation of a chosen goal may still be blocked or delayed. An undergraduate aiming for graduate school may find that his or her grades are not high enough or that needed funds will not be available. A person whose decision seems permanently blocked may spend some time coping with the disappointment before returning to the beginning of the decision cycle to search for attractive alternatives. In some cases, implementation of choices is simply delayed and can be successfully completed only at a later time. People in such situations must wait, investigate other alternatives, or alter dreams to fit their present circumstances.

Reevaluation

After we implement a decision, we put new behaviors into practice, thereby altering our life patterns. This stage of career development starts with the final career-planning skill identified—work adjustment. Adjusting to a new work situation involves learning how to do tasks and how to take and give direction while working cooperatively with other people. Keeping in tune with the job means finding out how to get new information and learning new skills as needed.

After satisfying the requirements of a new environment or role, we can begin to examine more closely whether it's fulfilling our expectations. If the change has not had the anticipated or desired results, we may want to evaluate goals and alternatives. For example:

1. Feelings, rewards, and goals may no longer seem appropriate or satisfying. They have changed or need to be changed.
2. Anticipated courses of action may no longer be practical, or perhaps things are going so well that they're not necessary.
3. Preferred alternatives that were previously unattainable may now be within reach.

We need to examine new information and experiences regularly to see whether they have brought about a change in our perspectives or possibilities.

Even if the initial choice has good results, circumstances may change or the situation may become monotonous if new challenges do not arise after a while. If unforeseen changes occur or hoped-for changes fail to occur, awareness of the need to reevaluate leads us back to the beginning of the decision cycle, to go through each stage again. Even if we feel we know our present situation well, taking shortcuts in the decision process may keep us from uncovering information essential to our next step. We may fail to reevaluate decisions, thinking that we have a right answer that will work indefinitely. As noted later, fear of change can keep us from recognizing the need to reevaluate, even if we are in a position that is beyond our abilities.

The most important thing to remember about decision making and about what to look for in reviewing decisions is the inescapable nature of change. Everything changes. Our own beliefs, attitudes, and values will change. Our environment is changing with ever-increasing rapidity. In 25 or even 5 years, many of our goals and skills will be obsolete. Even when we do control the externals, growth goes on within us long after we think we are grown-up. We can never be sure that a decision will be the right one beyond the moment we make it. Our decisions and our world must grow and change with us.

"I can give you a six-word formula for success: 'Think things through—then follow through.'"

—*Eddie Rickenbacker*

Marvin, ©1994. Reprinted with special permission of North America Syndicate.

DECISION STYLE WORKSHEET

In this supplementary exercise, each of the following boxes focuses on one of the three decision-making approaches just discussed. List three situations in each box that might prompt you to use the form of decision making represented in that box. Think of decisions you have made or discussed, or decisions in such areas as family, friends, activities, classes, or jobs.

After you complete each box, review your answers. Do the situations in each box share anything in common? If they do, what is it?

How do the decisions you listed in each box differ from the decisions noted in each of the other boxes?

Three decisions that I might let others make for me:

1. _____
2. _____
3. _____

Three decisions that I might make intuitively:

1. _____
2. _____
3. _____

Three decisions that I would want to be well informed about:

1. _____
2. _____
3. _____

WHERE AM I IN THE CAREER DECISION-MAKING PROCESS?

Each of the following boxes contains a stage in the process of making an informed career decision. The goal or desired outcome of each stage is described and an example is provided. Review each of the stages and identify what stage in your own career decision making you are now in. Then write what you have to do to move to the next stage. When you complete this exercise for your own plans, you may wish to use the vignettes in the following section to sharpen your decision-making skills. Each vignette presents a person who is attempting to make a career decision. Try to formulate an informed decision-making approach for that individual.

1. *Awareness*

GOAL To define clearly the decision you need to make

EXAMPLE I need to decide on the academic major at the end of this term.

A decision I need to make soon:

_____

_____

_____

_____

The feelings or issues surrounding this decision:

_____

_____

_____

_____

I can start to clarify or resolve these feelings and issues by doing the following:

_____

_____

_____

_____

Possible obstacles I see:

_____

_____

_____

I can start to remove or overcome these obstacles by doing the following:

_____

_____

_____

2. Self-Assessment

GOAL To decide how important the decision is to you, what you want to accomplish by it, and what effort or sacrifice you're willing to make to achieve it

EXAMPLE My decision about an academic major is very important to me. I want to go to law school, and I need to major in the area that will most help me get into law school. I need to make this decision by the end of this term so I can graduate on schedule.

On a scale of 1 to 10 (with 10 being the most important), how important is this decision to me?

_____

What I want to accomplish:

_____

_____

How does this fit with my goals for other parts of my life? With my career dreams?

_____

_____

What can I do now to facilitate this decision?

_____

_____

Do I feel equipped to do this? Why or why not?

_____

_____

Are there things I need to clarify about myself and my feelings?

_____

_____

How much effort or sacrifice will this action take?

_____

_____

When do I expect to complete this action?

_____

_____

3. *Exploration*

GOAL To identify and explore at least two possible courses of action

EXAMPLE I'll explore political science and psychology, since both are applicable to law. I'll take 3 weeks to explore both fields by reading about them in the *Occupational Outlook Handbook* and professional literature, talking to people in both fields, and talking to academic advisers in each area. Before I do, I'll make a checks-and-balances sheet about each field. This will allow me to compare them with each other in terms of things that I like and don't like about each.

Two areas that I want to explore:

A. _____

_____

B. _____

_____

The ways that I will explore them:

A. _____

_____

B. _____

_____

C. _____

_____

D. _____

_____

Doubts I have about these choices:

_____

_____

_____

_____

I will complete my exploration by _____
                                           (date)

Other areas I might explore later:

A. _____

_____

B. _____

_____

4. *Integration*

GOALS

- To develop a prioritized list of career options that reflect your preferences, interests, values, and abilities and that are realistic for you to pursue
- To consider the feelings of significant others without being totally dependent on their wishes and needs
- To examine and change any beliefs you may have—about your social role or about occupations— that may unnecessarily restrict your career options

EXAMPLE I'll review my information about psychology and political science and decide what about those courses of study appeals to me and what bothers me. I'll talk over my feelings with my family and a few friends and listen to their feedback. Then I'll go over everything carefully and try to weed out myths and prejudices so that my choice will be realistic and personally satisfying.

In order of priority, the most personally fulfilling and feasible career options for me to pursue:

A. _____

B. _____

C. _____

D. _____

How do I feel about each of the options I've listed?

A. _____

_____

B. _____

_____

C. _____

_____

D. _____

_____

(continued)

4. *Integration* (continued)

What areas of disagreement or misunderstanding might I encounter when I discuss these options with others?

A. _____

_____

B. _____

_____

C. _____

_____

How might I or my family have a limited view of my choices or my actions because of prejudices or stereotypes?

A. _____

_____

B. _____

_____

C. _____

_____

On what concerns of mine do I want feedback from others?

A. _____

_____

B. _____

_____

C. _____

_____

I'll talk with the people I've listed by _____
                                                    (date)

5. *Commitment*

GOAL To choose one alternative and inform others about your choice

EXAMPLE I've decided on political science. I'll tell my academic adviser about my decision. I'll inform my family as well, since they're interested in what I do. I'll let them know about my decision in 4 weeks.

I've decided to do the following:

_____

_____

_____

_____

To pursue this choice I'll do this:

_____

_____

_____

_____

My fears or feelings about moving ahead:

_____

_____

_____

_____

The people I want to inform about my decision:

A. _____

_____

B. _____

_____

C. _____

_____

I'll inform all of them by _____

(date)

6. *Implementation*

GOAL To act on your decision

EXAMPLE After I ask my adviser which political science courses I should take, I'll sign up for them at preregistration for next term.

The actions I need to take to implement my decision:

A. _____

_____

B. _____

_____

C. _____

_____

D. _____

_____

E. _____

_____

Problems that might delay me or cause discomfort:

A. _____

_____

B. _____

_____

C. _____

_____

My timeline for each of these actions:

A. _____

B. _____

C. _____

D. _____

E. _____

7. Reevaluation

GOAL After you've lived with your choice for a reasonable length of time, to review it and if necessary identify new choices to be made

EXAMPLE At the end of the next term, I'll spend some time reviewing how I feel about political science. If I'm comfortable with it as a choice, I'll identify what makes me uncomfortable and look at other possible majors that may be more consistent with what I like to do.

I'll reevaluate my decision by _____
                                                                (date)

When I do this, I'll make my judgment using the following criteria:

A. _____

_____

_____

_____

B. _____

_____

_____

_____

C. _____

_____

_____

_____

I'll reexamine the following areas of concern:

A. _____

B. _____

C. _____

Vignettes[1]

1. Jim left a sales job to return to school; his dream is eventually to go to medical school. Jim's counselor says that he is not sure that Jim will be able to get into medical school. His past grades have been good but not spectacular. The way Jim sees it, he can take two more years of pre-med training and risk wasting that time, or he can decide right now to be practical and switch to a related major, such as something in the field of biology or an allied medical profession.

2. Jesse likes people and has always been good at understanding their personalities and problems. He feels he'd be successful in a business setting, such as sales or public relations. He also likes the idea of helping people and has been interested in counseling the disabled, which he did one summer as a volunteer. He found this work especially satisfying because he himself uses a wheelchair. However, at this point he's leaning toward business. He thinks the business world would probably be faster-paced and more exciting, and he is sure it will be more financially rewarding, than counseling. He wants to be able to support a nice lifestyle and a family. Although he has been successful so far, he still wonders how well the business community will accept someone who uses a wheelchair.

3. LaShanda is 31 and quit work when she and her husband had their first baby. Their children are 12 and 7 now, and LaShanda wants to take some training courses so she can get a job working with computers to add to the family income. Tonight, though, she's asking herself whether it will be worth it. She feels snowed under by household chores, and one of the kids is sick. Her husband isn't crazy about the idea of her working, and she's beginning to wonder if he's right.

4. Peggy is in business school. Her father has a large accounting firm and has always planned on Peggy's becoming his partner after college, since she is the best mathematician in the family. Peggy likes accounting, but since starting college she has been longing to explore some of the other careers she has heard about, especially teaching. Her friends envy her because she has a secure, high-paying job waiting for her in accounting. They tell her she'd be crazy to change to education. Her father would be terribly disappointed, and she'd be out there competing for a limited number of jobs.

REFERENCES AND RESOURCES

Dinklage, A. B. (1966). *Adolescent choice and decision-making: A review of models and issues in relation to some developmental tasks of adolescence.* Cambridge, MA: Harvard University Press (ERIC Document No. ED 010 371).

GeLatt, H. B., Varenhorst, B., Carey, R., & Miller, G. P. (1973). *Decisions and outcomes.*

---

[1]Adapted from an exercise created by Cinda Field Wells, Ph.D., Dale Alexander, A.C.S.W., and Pat Jonas, M.D., The Ohio State University, March 1980.

New York: College Entrance Examination Board.

Gordon, V. N. (1984). *The career undecided college student*. Springfield, IL: Thomas.

Harren, V. A. (1979). A model of career decision-making for college students. *Journal of Vocational Behavior, 14,* 119–133.

O'Neil, G., & O'Neil, N. (1974). *Shifting gears: Finding security in a changing world.* New York: M. Evans.

Tiedeman, D. V., & O'Hara, R. P. (1963). *Career development: Choice and adjustment.* New York: College Entrance Examination Board.

CHAPTER *3*

THE EMERGING SELF:
BIRTH TO ADOLESCENCE

"Are you the opposite sex or is it ME?"

Dennis the Menace® used by permission of Hank Ketcham and
Copyright © 1993 by North America Syndicate.

Sow an act and reap a habit;
Sow a habit and reap a character;
Sow a character and reap a destiny.

—*Boardman*

Here's how one writer for the *Chicago Tribune* describes the miraculous pace of her daughters' young lives.

I ended my daughters' kindergarten careers as I began them—with a lump in my throat and a glance over my shoulder at the approaching tidal wave of time.

The felt-tip markers came home in the backpack, the picnic was held and then it was over.

I have sent my last child to classroom with wood blocks and a pet turtle. My youngest is ready for first grade. I am not.

How did it happen? Their little-girl years once stretched before me so far that I couldn't see the end. Surely I always would hold their little hands crossing the street. Surely their hands always would be little.

I surely was wrong.

Their baby days have faded so much that I don't even remember the milestones that once loomed so large. When did they first roll over, talk, get a tooth? If it weren't that they roll, talk and have teeth now, I wouldn't be sure they had done it at all.

Like my parents looking at decades-old pictures of my older sister and me, I can no longer even tell my children's baby pictures apart. They were only babies for a moment.

It was a moment I thought would last forever, followed by early childhood years that seemed similarly enduring. Their youth defined them: My children were little girls, not girls who were temporarily little.

With the end of kindergarten, they are both officially big girls. And I am the baby.

I'm a fool for ever wishing, even as briefly and rarely as I did, that my children would grow up a little bit faster so they could amuse themselves/feed themselves/walk by themselves, and I could finally get a break.

What was I thinking? Didn't I see that I would take a deep breath, and six years would be gone? Didn't I realize that my whole life was the break, and the time when my children would need so much of my time was the momentary, marvelous interruption?

Veteran parents told me as much, with a quiet ruefulness that I did not understand when I was chasing toddlers around a party and wishing I had more time to talk to grown-ups.

I have plenty of time to talk to grown-ups now. I understand now.

Here's to the future. But the last day of the last child's kindergarten calls forth the past.

It was the best ride ever. I wish I could go around with my daughters one more time. (Brotman, 1997, p. 10H)

The call for growth and change in our lives—some call it an identity crisis—can be as quiet as a whisper or as loud as a thunderclap. Like the Chinese symbol for crisis, change presents us with both danger and opportunity. The danger is that we won't hear the call or will ignore it, and things will become worse, with new chances being lost. The opportunity comes when we recognize and listen to the call, modify old choices we once saw as permanent, learn new skills and face new challenges. In short, we can make our lives richer and more satisfying.

At some point in their lives, people of all ages and backgrounds struggle with the question, "Who am I?" As they experience change, they discover that they no longer feel comfortable with themselves or their situations and that something must go—or that they must grow. Old decisions and commitments once seen as permanent may need to be reviewed. When new situations occur in which old behaviors and solutions don't work anymore, people need to create new behaviors and solutions.

Choices having to do with a career are among the most far-reaching decisions of a person's life. They also represent the greatest challenges and cause the strongest feelings of "no turning back." Self-expression through work fills not only a large part of each day but also many of our personal and larger needs as well. Consequently, any career changes can impact someone vocationally as well as personally, socially, physically, intellectually, and emotionally. For people who see their work as a "calling," the choice of a career direction may have spiritual elements as well.

This chapter and the next will help you better understand the internal and external forces that shape a person's career and lifestyle. Together, these two chapters will provide you with a kind of map to help you become more aware of who you are, how you got to be where you are, and where you might go from here.

CHILDHOOD IDENTITY: *YOU ARE A PERSON WHO . . .*

The processes that shape a person's self-concept—including their vocational self-concept—begin at birth, although no one knows for certain exactly how they work. Current research has repeatedly confirmed that infants and children become aware of and understand their environment and people's responses to them much sooner and more clearly than we have previously realized. Further, recent research suggests that a person's inborn temperament is evident in infancy. The early months and years of life are therefore more significant than we once thought.

The critical influences on a person's development are largely social and cultural. Because people learn their beliefs and values at an early age and in subtle ways, they may not be aware that they have them or how they acquired them.

Thus, by age 18, many expectations and stereotypes, especially those associated with gender, race, and occupation, are firmly established in a person's mind (Fitzgerald, Fassinger, & Betz, 1995; Gottfriedson, 1981). Interestingly, men appear to be more limited by gender stereotyping than are women in one respect. Specifically, research studies have consistently revealed that girls are much more likely to prefer and choose stereotypically male careers than men are to prefer stereotypically female careers (Hannah & Kahn, 1989). Further, the range of occupational possibilities that a person will consider varies as a function of his or her beliefs about the types of work that men and women should pursue based on their gender. In contrast to individuals who limit their options this way, people with an androgynous attitude tend to consider an occupation regardless of its gender associations or social prestige (Leung & Harmon, 1990).

In school, students learn that study is the order of the day, with recess as a treat to be earned through successful work. The work ethic thus becomes an early influence in life. And an important prejudice gets passed on—the idea that real work is associated with being away from home and with external reinforcements such as grades or money.

During childhood and into early adolescence, fantasy role tryouts play an important part in vocational development. Vocational role models may be found in teachers, relatives, and other socially significant people. Models may also come from storybooks and TV. Especially significant is the role that fathers play in encouraging a child to do well in school. A recent survey conducted by the U.S. Department of Education illuminates this point very well. Over four months, January through April, the department interviewed almost 17,000 kindergarteners through twelfth graders, and their parents and guardians. The results yielded a simple but significant point: Kids do better when their fathers get involved in their child's education by participating in parent–teacher conferences, PTA, and other school-related activities. This was especially true in two-parent households.

In single-parent households, children living with their mothers tended to perform better than children living with their fathers. As one might expect, children of the least involved parents did not do as well academically or socially as their peers did (Columbus Ohio Dispatch, 1997).

Tommy, reprinted by permission of United Feature Syndicate, Inc.

Robert Fulghum, a Unitarian minister and author, has suggested that, in elementary school, children receive other important values and bits of wisdom that will serve as guides in adulthood:

> All I really need to know about how to live and what to do and how to be I learned in kindergarten. Wisdom was not at the top of the graduate school mountain, but there is the sandpile at Sunday School. These things I learned:
>
> Share everything.
>
> Play Fair.
>
> Don't hit people.
>
> Put things back where you found them.
>
> Clean up your own mess.
>
> Don't take things that aren't yours.
>
> Say you're sorry when you hurt somebody.
>
> Wash your hands before you eat.
>
> Flush.
>
> Warm cookies and cold milk are good for you.
>
> Live a balanced life—learn some and think some and draw and paint and sing and dance and play and work every day some.
>
> Take a nap every afternoon.
>
> When you go out into the world, watch out for traffic, hold hands, and stick together.
>
> Be aware of wonder. Remember the little seed in the Styrofoam cup: The roots go down and the plant goes up and nobody really knows how or why, but we are all like that.
>
> Goldfish and hamsters and white mice and even the little seed in the Styrofoam cup—they all die. So do we.
>
> And then remember the Dick-and-Jane books and the first word you learned—the biggest word of all—LOOK.
>
> Everything you need to know is in there somewhere. The Golden Rule and love and basic sanitation. Ecology and politics and equality and sane living.
>
> Take any one of those items and extrapolate it into sophisticated adult terms and apply it to your family life or your work or your government or your world and it holds true and clear and firm. Think what a better world it would be if we all—the whole world—had cookies and milk about three o'clock every afternoon and then lay down with our blankies for a nap. Or if all governments had as a basic policy to always put things back where they found them and to clean up their own mess.
>
> And it is still true, no matter how old you are—when you go out into the world, it is best to hold hands and stick together. (1988, pp. 4–6)

ADOLESCENCE: WHO AM I?

In adolescence, young people are expected to start looking ahead and thinking about how they live and achieve financial independence after high school or college. Such decisions are sometimes predetermined by family influence ("You can work at Uncle John's office when you graduate and climb your way up the ladder with his help"), by a person's special talent, or by trial and error. For some indi-

Zits, ©1997. Reprinted with special permission of King Features Syndicate.

viduals, adolescence heralds a struggle to be free from family directives and to "do their own thing," which often means doing what their peers are doing or something that the family doesn't agree with. Although many people tend to focus on the negative aspects of peer influence on adolescents, "peer pressure" usually helps individuals make wise, socially acceptable choices.

Even as their horizons expand, many students feel pressured to declare a career direction or at least an educational objective. Thus, dreams about the future give way to further exploration and action in the form of part-time and summer jobs, which serve to introduce students to the responsibilities of the work world and help them explore vocational options rather than make a premature commitment to a specific occupation.

Romantic relationships in adolescence serve a similar purpose, introducing young adults to the responsibilities and beliefs that undergird a lasting intimate relationship. Thus, through work and other forms of self-discovery, the process of socialization advances, and a person's vocational and personal identity become more clearly defined.

Gender Issues

Confusion in the gender-role socialization process may have painful consequences for young men and women. Unlike some societies that expect men to set limits on sexual involvement, U.S. society has traditionally placed this responsibility on its women. Consequently, many American male adolescents struggling to define themselves socially and sexually may feel that they must push the limits of sexual involvement with women to prove their masculinity or to meet various physical and emotional needs. In their way of thinking, *no* means *maybe,* or even *yes* if they push. Surveys of college men and women support this point in disturbing ways. More than 4 percent of college men surveyed by one investigator admitted to the use of violence to obtain sex, while an additional 27 percent had used lesser degrees of physical and emotional force when a woman was unwilling to have sex with them. More than half of college women surveyed reported experiences of sexual aggression in the form of verbal threats, physical coercion, or violence at some time from someone they knew. Although they did not use the term *rape,* one in eight students reported an experience of assault that met the legal definition of rape. Further, women ages 16 to 24—the age span of most college students—are at greatest risk for rape. Seventy-five percent of first-year college women said they had experienced an act of sexual aggression, most often during their senior year of high school or first year of college.

Many people carry some stereotypical beliefs and attitudes into adulthood without understanding how these may limit and disrupt their personal relationships and career pursuits. As a result, they may have blind spots or prejudices that make them see their abilities and vocational opportunities—or those of others—restricted by gender, race, or age. Sometimes, because of such childhood learning, they may believe they can't do or aren't interested in activities that they've never tried. And men who cling to the image of men as strong willed and sexually privileged may carry this attitude into the work setting, where it may come out as sexual harassment. Times continue to change, however. Federal and state laws provide protection from harassment in the workplace. Colleges are doing a better job at preventing acquaintance rape and handling such cases in a judicious and fair manner. Many communities and schools offer support groups and resources to encourage personal and work-role experimentation.

In our society, work continues on gender equity in attitudes and opportunities. Many more women are now in the work force, with many now working in formerly male-dominated fields. Women receive fairer wages and have better legal protection from discrimination and sexual harassment. Nonetheless, their salaries continue to be lower than those of men.

Modern Risks

David Hamberg and Ruby Takinashi (1989) have observed that U.S. society changed dramatically when the economy lost its agricultural basis. Adolescents who grew up in farming communities usually had a stable base of support in their families and family friends, a base that offered them cultural guidance, support for coping with the stresses of life, and vocational wisdom. With industrialization, our society became more mobile, and extended families now have fewer adults for teens to turn to for support, comfort, and advice.

Adolescents grow at a faster rate physically than they do socially, emotionally, and vocationally. Thus, where earlier generations of teens learned about adult roles gradually through instruction and observation prior to puberty, today's adolescents reach puberty before being socialized into adult ways of thinking and acting. Because they have easier access to alcohol, drugs, cars, and weapons, today's adolescents are at greater risk for accidents, suicide, unplanned pregnancies, sexually transmitted diseases, lethal conflict, substance abuse, and just plain poor judgment (Hamberg & Takinashi, 1989).

Although social scientists have described adolescence as a period of "storm and stress" (Hall, 1904), the fact remains that four out of five adolescents will not have significant emotional and behavioral problems that will place them at risk socially or vocationally. Thus, most adolescents in U.S. society are confident, hopeful, and well-adjusted individuals with a high potential for personal and career success (Weiner, 1992).

THE COLLEGE YEARS: I AM A PERSON WHO...

In young adulthood, the pressure is on to make decisions and carry them out. The playful question, "What are you going to be when you grow up?" is no longer amusing—it demands an answer. Young adults are expected to make choices for themselves even though they may not feel ready. Young adults cope with this threatening freedom in many ways. Some are challenged and excited, some try to avoid their freedom, and some keep their options open while making tentative commitments.

Separation from the family physically and emotionally is the primary goal of college-age individuals. They strive for a balance between autonomy and dependence on others as they work toward achieving interdependence. College often entails living away from home and enjoying the pleasure of self-direction, but these freedoms may conflict with continued dependence on family money. Thus, college students often spend more energy in gaining control over their lives by learning to make important personal decisions. The emotional isolation and responsibility that come with young adulthood can be lonely and confusing. The family may no longer meet a person's emotional needs, yet he or she may lack the skills and courage to start building a new emotional support system. An individual may fill this gap with school friends and roommates, fraternities and clubs, a romantic commitment or marriage, or an organization such as a religious group.

People this age need to consider their lifestyle, personal relationships, emotional needs, and religious and political affiliations. Young adults form new ideas about where they might want to work and with what kind of hours and co-workers. Such decisions about lifestyle can be joyous and exciting, but when one makes commitments out of fear of freedom, one often merely hands responsibility for important life decisions to someone else.

It is especially important for young adults to strive to sort our their own feelings and dreams free of social and familial pressures. Rebelling against a career option even though it might be the right one, or conforming to someone else's choice because it's safe or comfortable, is often all too easy, and a knee-jerk reaction. People tend to gravitate toward careers for which they match the stereotype—for example, men have tended to go into business or science, women into teaching or nursing. Young adults especially need opportunities to explore their motives and enthusiasms to see whether they are shying away from an unexpected career choice because of outside pressures. For some people, occupational or life decisions may come easily; others may remain confused or choose goals hastily to escape uncertainty. It takes courage to choose to remain confused. However, if undecided people keep their minds open to new information about the world and themselves, they will eventually begin to identify leisure and vocational activities that represent a comfortable combination of what they want and what they perceive as possible and acceptable. The building blocks people use as they deal with the tasks of adulthood can be shaped and fit together to form their preferred lifestyle, which may involve all or some of the elements of the wellness wheel: being healthy physically, spiritually, emotionally, socially, intellectually, and, of course, vocationally. The balance of all the pieces will never be perfect and each will require periodic adjustment as new opportunities arise.

Table 3-1 describes the parts of our vocational self, when we most likely acquire them, and how they influence our career. As you can see, the hallmark of childhood is acceptance of what others believe and the surrounding world. Children often use fantasy to project their ideal vocational self-image and express an emerging awareness of how best to balance time and energies. Adolescence involves questioning, exploring, and sometimes challenging old standards in order to realistically assess ourselves. With experience, preferences about work give way to a more realistic assessment of interests and skills. In young adulthood, the urge to become our own person—to become autonomous—leads to the clarification of personal values and wants and how we can use work to achieve our personal goals.

Table 3-1   Factors Affecting Vocational Self-Concepts

What	Influence in your career
	Childhood
Your *energy level* is the amount of physical and mental energy you have. It influences the amount of energy you wish to invest in each of your daily pursuits, including your work and leisure activities.	Your energy level is affected by heredity, diet, patterns of activity and rest, age, and health. Since your energy level influences the amount and intensity of your activities, it will shape the level and types of responsibilities you pursue at work, the amount of stress you can handle, and the amount of physical and mental exertion you can invest in work and leisure tasks (your lifestyle).
Your *attitudes and beliefs* are your subjective views of the world around you—the way you expect things to be and believe they should be, the way you perceive and form opinions about things.	Your attitudes and beliefs can have a positive or negative effect on the way you view yourself and your work. Decisions based on unrealistic, incomplete, or outdated career-planning myths and beliefs may cause you to restrict your options or undertake too much and can result in disappointment with your career.
Your *aspirations* are the things you fantasize or dream about doing soon or "someday."	During childhood most of us saw work in idealized ways. We dreamed of being somebody special and often played at being people of high status or prominence, largely because of their uniforms, their work, their ability to influence others, or the excitement of their jobs. Whether you fulfill your childhood dreams depends largely on your talents, the opportunities to develop them, and the time and energy you invest in developing them. The chapters that follow show how the balance between your dreams and what you can actually achieve may affect how you see yourself as an adult and the levels and kinds of work at which you can be most successful.

Table 3-1 Factors Affecting Vocational Self-Concepts *(continued)*

What	Influence in your career
	Childhood (continued)
Your *preferences* are what you would like to do if reality permits them.	As we gain in life experiences and are exposed to more information about the world of work, fantasies give way to preferences, and mental self-portraits become clearer. We can identify occupations that appeal to us, but we can also recognize that we may not have the skills to be successful at all of them. Understanding what your most preferred occupations have in common can help you identify the skill and interest areas you would like to develop and related majors and occupations to explore.
	Adolescence
Your *interests* are more realistic than your preferences. They reflect the experiences or ideas you have had about work-related activities that you like or dislike.	Because our interests reflect the direct experiences we've had with different occupationally related activities, they tend to become more stable as we get older. Occupational interest surveys can be used to compare your interests with those of people who are successful and satisfied in a variety of occupations. Such comparisons can help you identify occupational areas that employ people who have interests similar to yours. Surveys can also give you an idea of how you would have to reshape your interests in order to enter and enjoy occupations that employ people whose interests are not like yours.
Your *skills* or abilities are the things you can do. They help you define the level on which you could operate within various areas of interest.	Our skills reflect the experiences we've had with work-related activities, especially those that require particular ways of thinking, moving, or relating to others to achieve a goal or to produce a product. Like interests, your skills can be measured and compared with the skill requirements of different professions and academic areas. Your *functional skills* can be transferred to and implemented in many different interest areas. Your *adaptive skills* reflect your ability to get along smoothly with others in the work setting and to manage various stressors on the job. Your *technical skills* reflect your ability to perform the tasks associated with a specific occupation or profession. It is important to identify your skills in each of these three areas and to separate them in your mind from interests.
	Adulthood
Your *values* are what you are for or against and what matters to you in which order. They determine what you want from your life.	Because our values reflect the things that we cherish or prize, they help us judge the appropriateness of specific work activities for us and the importance we place on work relative to our other needs and to the other elements of our preferred lifestyle.

What Do I Want to Do?

As we begin to know and understand ourselves, we need a way to organize our self-knowledge and to determine how our personal characteristics fit into the requirements of differing educational and work settings. The exploration of how people go about making career decisions has a long history, and research on the topic continues today. In fact, we can trace this history back into the late 1800s, when the mental-testing movement began. This form of study continues to be important in "matching people to jobs."

The major thrust of the budding vocational guidance movement occurred in 1909, when Frank Parsons, a service-oriented youth counselor, published a book titled *Choosing a Vocation,* which presented his view that a person's adjustment to the world of work is a function of the compatibility between the individual's capacities and characteristics (e.g., interest, skills, and values) and the demands of the occupation (Crites, 1969). Researchers in the U.S. Department of Labor and psychologists such as John Holland and Dale Prediger have continued this legacy. As the following pages describe, other research on occupational choice examines how one may cluster different occupations by their common characteristics.

The Three Spheres of Work Activity

From its ongoing studies of individual traits and the requirements of different occupations (job factors), the Department of Labor has identified three spheres of activity—data, people and things—that appear to capture the common characteristic of workers in differing occupations. The three spheres are shown in Figure 3-1. The spheres in this figure overlap because individuals are frequently interested or engaged in work activities that involve more than one sphere. Because we have the basic endowment and opportunities to develop a variety of abilities, we may have skills in all three areas but tend to be oriented toward work activities in only one or two. Avocational activities may balance these areas or provide outlets for interests and skills not tapped in the work setting.

Figure 3-1
Spheres of work
activity

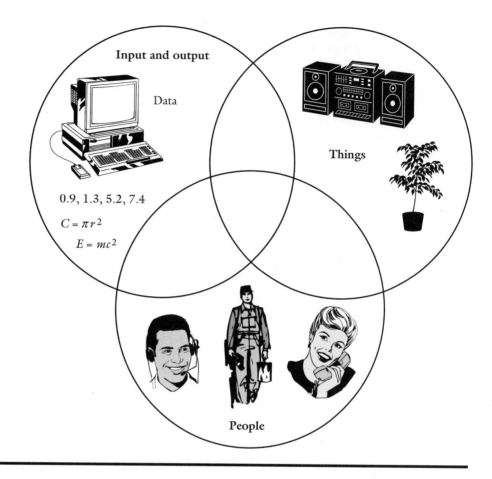

Input and output

Data

Things

0.9, 1.3, 5.2, 7.4

$C = \pi r^2$

$E = mc^2$

People

Generally speaking, an individual oriented toward and skilled at working with people enjoys involvement with others and prefers interpersonal situations that allow opportunities to lead, persuade, teach, or counsel. The individual with interests and competencies more strongly focused on the data dimensions tends to enjoy working with numbers and abstract concepts expressed through words and symbols. As the name implies, an individual oriented toward things likes working with machinery, tools, and instruments and enjoys solving problems concerning physical objects.

Table 3-2 summarizes the *functional skills* associated with the data/people/things dimensions of work. Note that the skills in each area are arranged in a hierarchy: Those at the top of the list are the most complex and require the most education and training. You may have noticed that the skills in Table 3-2 can be transferred from one occupation to another. For example, *instructing* (listed under

Table 3-2   Hierarchy of Functional Skills Associated with Working with Data, People, and Things

Data	People	Things
Synthesizing	Mentoring	Setting up
Coordinating	Negotiating	Precision working
Analyzing	Instructing	Operating/controlling
Compiling	Supervising	Driving/controlling
Computing	Diverting	Manipulating
Copying	Persuading	Tending
Comparing	Speaking/signaling	Feeding/offbearing
	Serving	Handling
	Taking instructions/helping	

people) applies to a variety of jobs, including teaching in the classroom, training others on a specific task in an industry, or child raising. Knowing which skills you can bring from one situation to another may help you in selecting a new area of study, looking for a job at graduation, or changing jobs, which has become a common occurrence in today's rapidly changing workplace.

Other skill areas identified by the Department of Labor are adaptive skills and technical skills. *Adaptive skills* are primarily related to specific work settings and to the people in those settings. The ability to manage a complex and demanding work routine is an example of an adaptive skill, as are such personal qualities as courteousness, dependability, cooperativeness, initiative, creativity, leadership, tolerance, and persistence. *Technical skills* are essential to perform specialized tasks, such as the skills a pharmacist uses to fill a prescription. Because technical skills are so narrowly focused, they are more easily transferred to identical jobs than from one occupation to another.

World of Work

The psychologist Dale Prediger (1976) and his colleagues at ACT (American College Testing Program) have separated the "data" dimensions in Figure 3-1 into two categories: data and ideas. These four dimensions—data/ideas/people/things—form the basis of the ACT career-planning program used by many high schools to guide graduating seniors and by colleges to place students in different academic majors. Table 3-3 describes the four dimensions.

Prediger also suggests these four categories be further divided into six job clusters and families linked to the data/ideas and people/things dimensions described in Table 3-3. These clusters and families—business contact, business operations, technical, science, arts, and social services—are displayed in Figure 3-2. Examples of related occupations in each job cluster are displayed in Figure 3-3, which indicates how we can use the ACT job families to classify different occupa-

Table 3-3 Basic Work Tasks

Data/Ideas Dimension	*People/Things Dimension*
Data (facts, records, files, numbers; systematic procedures for facilitating goods/services consumption by people). "Data activities" involve *impersonal processes* such as recording, verifying, transmitting, and organizing facts or data representing goods and services. Purchasing agents, accountants, and secretaries work mainly with data.	**People** (no alternative terms). "People activities" involve *interpersonal processes* such as helping, informing, serving, persuading, entertaining, motivating, and directing—in general, producing a change in human behavior. Teachers, salespeople, and nurses work mainly with people.
Ideas (abstractions, theories, knowledge, insights, new ways of expressing something—for example, with words, equations, or music). "Ideas activities" involve *intrapersonal processes* such as creating, discovering, interpreting, and synthesizing abstractions or implementing applications of abstractions. Scientists, musicians, and philosophers work mainly with ideas.	**Things** (machines, mechanisms, materials, tools, physical and biological processes). "Things activities" involve *nonpersonal processes* such as producing, transporting, servicing, and repairing. Bricklayers, farmers, and engineers work mainly with things.

Source: ACT, 1997, p. 2

tions based on their commonalities. For example, the business contact job cluster contains two general business-related clusters: "Marketing and Sales" and "Management and Planning," which provide a common organization of many occupations and jobs based on their overlapping characteristics.

Holland's Personality Types

John Holland (1973), a psychologist, developed a different classification system based on the Department of Labor's worker trait groups. He suggested six ways to classify occupations and worker personality types. These types are presented in Figure 3-4, along with the activities associated with each type. According to Holland, a person's work personality type is clearly established by early adulthood and remains stable. Changes in a person's choice of job over time may reflect choices more congruent with a person's work personality, forced changes such as loss of employment, or an inability to make wise career decisions, but they do not reflect changes in the person's work personality as a result of aging.

Types on adjacent corners of the hexagon are said to be consistent. That is, the closer two types are on the hexagon, the more psychologically similar they are. Thus, a person with "realistic" characteristics will most likely exhibit a personality pattern that shares "conventional" and "investigative" interests, skills, and values. Similarly, an individual with a "social" orientation may have some "artistic" and "enterprising" qualities (see Chapter 6). Sometimes types compete within one person, in which case the individual may find it hard to determine a preferred occupational direction, especially if his or her preferences relate to several types with equal intensity or the competing types are opposite points of the hexagon.

Figure 3-2 The world of work map (ACT, 1993, p. 1)

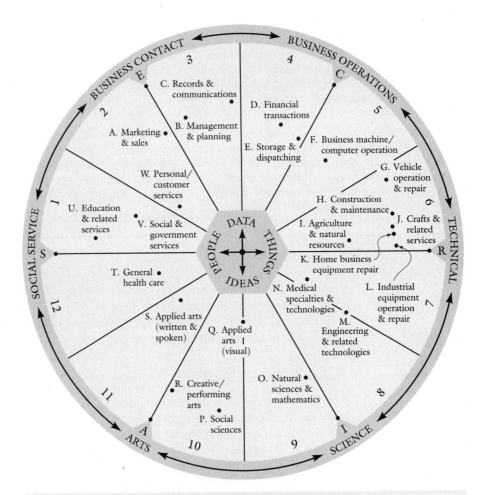

About the Map

- The world of work map arranges job families (groups of similar jobs) into 12 regions. Together, the job families cover all U.S. jobs. Although the locations of the jobs in each family differ, most are located near the point shown.

- A job family's location is based on its primary work tasks—working with DATA, IDEAS, PEOPLE, and THINGS.

- The edge of the map presents six general areas of the work world. The letters RIASEC refer to occupational and personality typologies created by John Holland.

BUSINESS CONTACT JOB CLUSTER

A. MARKETING AND SALES JOB FAMILY

Sales workers in stores; route drivers (milk, etc.); buyers; travel agents; sales workers who visit customers (real estate and insurance agents; stock brokers; farm products; office and medical supplies sales workers)

B. MANAGEMENT AND PLANNING JOB FAMILY

Store, motel, restaurant, and agribusiness managers; office supervisors; purchasing agents; managers in large businesses; recreation/parks managers; medical records administrators; urban planners

BUSINESS OPERATIONS JOB CLUSTER

C. RECORDS AND COMMUNICATIONS JOB FAMILY

Office, library, hotel, and postal clerks; receptionists; computer tape librarians; office, medical, and legal secretaries; court reporters; medical record technicians

D. FINANCIAL TRANSACTIONS JOB FAMILY

Bookkeepers; accountants; grocery check-out clerks; bank tellers; ticket agents; insurance underwriters; financial analysts

E. STORAGE AND DISPATCHING JOB FAMILY

Shipping and receiving clerks; mail carriers; truck, cab, and airline dispatchers; cargo agents; air traffic controllers

F. BUSINESS MACHINE/COMPUTER OPERATION JOB FAMILY

Computer console, printer, etc., operators; office machine operators; typists; word-processing equipment operators; statistical clerks

TECHNICAL JOB CLUSTER

G. VEHICLE OPERATION AND REPAIR JOB FAMILY

Bus, truck, and cab drivers; auto, bus, and airplane mechanics; forklift operators; merchant marine officers; airplane pilots

H. CONSTRUCTION AND MAINTENANCE JOB FAMILY

Carpenters; electricians; painters; custodians (janitors); bricklayers; sheet metal workers; bulldozer and crane operators; building inspectors

I. AGRICULTURE AND NATURAL RESOURCES JOB FAMILY

Farmers; foresters; ranchers; landscape gardeners; tree surgeons; plant nursery workers; pet shop attendants

J. CRAFTS AND RELATED SERVICES JOB FAMILY

Cooks; meatcutters; bakers; shoe repairers; piano/organ tuners; tailors; jewelers

K. HOME/BUSINESS EQUIPMENT REPAIR JOB FAMILY

Repairers of TV sets, appliances, typewriters, telephones, heating systems, photocopiers, etc.

L. INDUSTRIAL EQUIPMENT OPERATION AND REPAIR JOB FAMILY

Machinists; printers; sewing machine operators; welders; industrial machinery repairers; production painters; laborers and machine operators in factories, mines, etc.; firefighters

SCIENCE JOB CLUSTER

M. ENGINEERING AND OTHER APPLIED TECHNOLOGIES JOB FAMILY

Engineers and engineering technicians in various fields; biological and chemical lab technicians; computer programmers; computer service technicians; drafters; surveyors; technical illustrators; food technologists

N. MEDICAL SPECIALTIES AND TECHNOLOGIES JOB FAMILY

Dental hygienists; EEG and EKG technicians; opticians; prosthetics technicians; X-ray technologists; medical technologists; dentists; optometrists; pharmacists; veterinarians

O. NATURAL SCIENCES AND MATHEMATICS JOB FAMILY

Agronomists; biologists; chemists; ecologists; geographers; geologists; horticulturists; mathematicians; physicists

P. SOCIAL SCIENCES JOB FAMILY

Marketing research analysts; anthropologists; economists; political scientists; psychologists; sociologists

ARTS JOB CLUSTER

Q. APPLIED ARTS (VISUAL) JOB FAMILY

Floral designers; merchandise displayers; commercial artists; fashion designers; photographers; interior designers; architects; landscape architects

R. CREATIVE/PERFORMING ARTS JOB FAMILY

Entertainers (comedians, etc.); actors/actresses; dancers; musicians, singers; writers; art, music, etc.; teachers

S. APPLIED ARTS (WRITTEN AND SPOKEN) JOB FAMILY

Advertising copywriters; disk jockeys; legal assistants; advertising account executives; interpreters; reporters; public relations workers; lawyers; librarians; technical writers

SOCIAL SERVICE JOB CLUSTER

T. GENERAL HEALTH CARE JOB FAMILY

Orderlies; dental assistants; licensed practical nurses; physical therapy assistants; registered nurses; dietitians; occupational therapists; physicians; speech pathologists

U. EDUCATION AND RELATED SERVICES JOB FAMILY

Teacher aides; preschool teachers; athletic coaches; college teachers; guidance/career/etc., counselors; elementary and secondary school teachers; special education teachers

V. SOCIAL AND GOVERNMENT SERVICES JOB FAMILY

Security guards; recreation leaders; police officers; health/safety/food/etc., inspectors; child welfare workers; home economists; rehabilitation counselors; social workers

W. PERSONAL/CUSTOMER SERVICES JOB FAMILY

Grocery baggers; bellhops; flight attendants (stewards, stewardesses); waitresses and waiters; cosmetologists (beauticians); barbers; butlers and maids

Figure 3-3 Job cluster and job family list (ACT, 1993, pp. 3–4)

Figure 3-4
Holland's work and
worker personality
types (Adapted
from Holland,
1973, pp. 12–13
and updated from
Campbell, 1974,
pp. 126–137)

Realistic

Likes and is able to perform activities
requiring mechanical ability or physical
strength or coordination in working with
objects, machines, tools, athletic equipment,
plants, or animals.

Some common traits: Hardheaded, mechanical,
quiet, reserved, unassuming, highly trained,
low in self-understanding

Conventional

Likes and is able to perform activities requiring attention to
detail, accuracy, and clerical skills to record, file, and
organize numerical and verbal data according to specified
instructions or procedures.

Some common traits: Content, conforming, not original,
conscientious, neat, practical, methodical

Likes and is able to perform activities
requiring persuasive, managerial, supervisory,
and leadership skills to obtain an institutional,
political/social, or economic gain.

Some common traits: Ambitious, power or
status seeking, confident, popular, sociable,
shrewd, dominant

Enterprising

MAKING PRODUCTIVE USE OF YOUR LEISURE TIME

One way to explore careers, often overlooked by college students, is using leisure
activities as vehicles for promoting occupational awareness and developing or enhancing their skills. Paul Bloland (1984) has suggested that students can use their
leisure time on campus to promote their career goals in at least eight ways. He
proposes the following:

1. Use your leisure time to observe people at work in order to explore potential occupations.
2. Develop new vocational competencies by participating in extracurricular
   activities such as serving as a stage hand for plays and recitals on campus.
3. Extend and refine your job-related skills by participating in campus activities. For example, if you're an accounting major, you might donate your
   time to serve as the budget officer for a campus organization.
4. Serve as an apprentice to a campus official to learn more about that person's job.

Likes and is able to perform activities requiring intellectual or analytical skills to observe, assess, evaluate, and theorize in order to solve problems.

Some common traits: Scientific, intellectual, curious, scholarly, mechanical, has broad interests, logical

Investigative

Likes and is able to perform activities requiring artistic, creative, expressive, and intuitive skills to convey esthetics, thoughts, and feelings in words, movements, sound, color, or form.

Some common traits: Imaginative, nonconforming, original, sensitive, expressive, introspective, complicated

Artistic

Likes and is able to perform activities requiring work with people to inform, enlighten, help, train, develop, or heal them.

Some common traits: Friendly, understanding, helpful, sociable, enthusiastic, competent, trusting

Social

5. Use the same skills in work and leisure settings. For example, if you're a senior majoring in education, you might serve as a teacher's assistant in an elementary school or child-care center, or coach a kid's sports team.
6. Use your off-campus involvements to practice and refine your interpersonal skills by working with a variety of people. For example, you could donate your time to a homeless shelter or teach English to immigrants.
7. Use your leisure time to escape from academic pressures or job-related stress by helping out at a nursing home.
8. Use leisure time to supplement your studies and achieve balance in one or several facets of the wellness wheel. For example, you could meditate to reduce stress and restore clarity of thinking.

Given the highly competitive, rapidly changing, and global nature of the world of work today, you will also need to add the following activity to Bloland's list of learning experiences:

9. Use your leisure time to refine and expand your communication skills by keeping current in your computer knowledge, participating on a debate

Factors Affecting Vocational Self-Concept

Try to trace the development of aspects of your vocational identity from childhood to the present. Talk with classmates or friends to stimulate memories. If you can't remember, ask a family member, or someone who knew you when, for some hints.

	Prior to grade school	*Grade school*	*High school*	*College*
A. Dreams or fantasies	1.			
	2.			
What were (are) these based on?	1.			
	2.			
How realistic were (are) they?	1.			
	2.			
B. What were (are) you interested in?	1.			
	2.			
C. What skills were (are) you especially proud of?	1.			
	2.			
How do these reflect your or your family's values?	1.			
	2.			

Look back over these experiences and memories that have helped shape you and compare them. How do they fit into the four spheres of data/ideas and people/things? How do they fit with the ACT world of work map? What threads can you see in your development that link your childhood with your present vocational self? What significant or noticeable changes have occurred between then and now? What is the most important dream you have for your vocational future right now?

team, writing for the student newspaper on your campus, learning a foreign language, or enhancing your public speaking skills by joining Toastmasters International.

These uses of your leisure time can benefit you and promote your growth in various ways. Many of the previous examples could take you into new areas and experiences that not only will expand and clarify your vocational identity but also can meet needs other than those on the wellness wheel. For example, coaching would be primarily physical or accounting intellectual, but all such endeavors would likely meet some social and emotional or spiritual needs.

"The strongest principle of growth lies in human choice"

—*George Eliot.*

The next three sections present exercises to help you apply this chapter to your own life. We hope they will clarify your career goals and orientations.

PREDICTING YOUR OCCUPATIONAL ORIENTATION

Carefully read the descriptions that follow. Then rank the six orientations, writing "1" next to the one most like you, "2" beside the type next most like you, and so on, until you have a number beside each of the six types.

Ranking   **Occupational Orientation**

_____ **Technical**   I am interested in and skilled at activities requiring mechanical ability, physical strength, or coordination in working with objects, machines, tools, athletic equipment, plants, or animals.

_____ **Science**   I am interested in and skilled at activities requiring intellectual or analytical skills to observe, assess, evaluate, and theorize in order to solve problems.

_____ **Arts**   I am interested in and skilled at activities requiring artistic, creative, expressive, and intuitive skills to convey esthetics, thoughts, and feelings in words, movement, sound, color, and form.

_____ **Social Service**   I am interested in and skilled at activities requiring work with people to instruct, educate, train, or counsel them or to treat their ailments.

_____ **Business Contact**   I am interested in and skilled at activities requiring persuasive, managerial, supervisory, and leadership skill to obtain an instructional, political/social, or economic gain.

_____ **Business Operations**   I am interested in and skilled at activities requiring attention to detail, accuracy, and clerical skills to record, file, and organize numerical and verbal data according to specified instructions or procedures.

In ranking the types of activity just listed, you have, in a way, predicted the outcome of any interest or abilities inventory you might take that uses the ACT Job

Families and Job Clusters or Holland's personality types as its format. One inventory that uses the ACT approach is provided in your workbook. To get a sense of how well your predictions about yourself compare with your inventoried preferences, interests, and abilities, complete the inventory there or contact the counseling service on your campus to take other interest and ability tests to survey your work personality. Another way to get feedback about your work orientation, is to give the descriptions just provided to a close friend or family member and ask that person to rank the types according to how he or she sees you. You can then compare your self-assessment with those of others to determine whether others see you as you see (or would like to see) yourself. Similarly, you can make lists of activities that you enjoy and do well and look for commonalities among them that you can translate into work activities. You can also use self-scored inventories that tap your interests, values, and abilities.

REFERENCES AND RESOURCES

American College Testing Program. (1993). *A guide to the world of work*. Iowa City, IA: Author.

American College Testing Program. (1997). *ACT assessment user's handbook*. Iowa City, IA: Author.

Bloland, P. (1984). Leisure and career development: For college students. *Journal of Career Development, 11*(2), 119–128.

Brotman, B. (1997, June 29). With the blink of an eye, time flies and they're no longer little. *Columbus Dispatch* (OH), p. 10H.

Campbell, D. (1974). *If you don't know where you're going, you'll probably end up somewhere else*. Niles, IL: Argus Communications.

Columbus Dispatch (OH). (1997, Oct. 3), p. 3a.

Crites, J. O. (1969). *Vocational Psychology*. New York: McGraw-Hill.

Eccles, C. M., Wingfield, A., Buchanan, C. M., Reuman, D., Flanigan, C., & Maclvern, D. Development during adolescence: The impact of stage-environment fit on young adolescent experiences in schools and families. *American Psychologist, 48*, 90–99.

Fitzgerald, L., Fassinger, R., & Betz, N. E. (1995). Theoretical advances in the study of women's career development. In W. B. Walsh & S. H. Osipow (Eds.), *Handbook of vocational psychology: Theory, research and practice*. 2nd ed. Mahwah, N.J.: Erlbaum.

Fulghum, R. (1988). *All I Really Needed to Know I Learned in Kindergarten*. New York: Random House.

Gottfriedson, L. S. (1981). Circumspection and compromise: A developmental theory of occupational aspirations. *Journal of Counseling Psychology, 28*, 545–579.

Hall, G. S. (1904). *Adolescence*. Vol. 2. Englewood Cliffs, NJ: Prentice-Hall.

Hamberg, D. D., & Takinashi, R. (1989). Preparing for life: The critical transition of adolescence. *American Psychologist, 44*, 825–827.

Hannah, J. S., & Kahn, S. E. (1989). The relationship of socioeconomic status and gender to the occupational choices of grade 11 students. *Journal of Vocational Behavior, 34*, 161–178.

Holland, J. L. (1973). *Making vocational choices: A theory of careers.* Englewood Cliffs, NJ: Prentice-Hall.

Koss, M. P., Gidyez, V. S., & Wisniewski, N. (1987). The scope of rape: Incidence and prevalence of sexual aggression and victimization in a national sample of higher education students. *Journal of Consulting and Clinical Psychology, 55,* 162–170.

Leung, S. A., & Harmon, L. W. (1990). Individual and sex differences in the zone of acceptable alternatives. *Journal of Counseling Psychology, 37,* 153–159.

Parsons, F. (1909). *Choosing a vocation.* Boston: Houghton-Mifflin.

Prediger, D. J. (1976). A world of work map for career exploration. *Vocational Guidance Quarterly, 24,* 198–208.

Weiner, I. B. (1992). *Psychological disturbance in adolescence.* New York: Wiley.

CHAPTER 4

THE EMERGING SELF: BEYOND ADOLESCENCE

The Middletons. © Tribune Media Services, Inc. All Rights Reserved. Reprinted with permission.

Be not afraid of growing slowly,
Be afraid only of standing still.

—*Chinese proverb*

A s autumn returns, it brings with it the memory of an October evening 2 years ago when I stood in the front pew of a church and watched my daughter Paget walking toward me, her bridal gown shimmering with beads and pearls. After stopping to give me a rose and a hug, she proceeded the last few steps to the altar. On her right stood my beloved husband, who escorted her down the aisle at her request. On her left stood her father, whom she had asked to give her away.

During these quiet moments before the start of the ceremony, I asked myself, "How did so many years fly by?" In many ways, I still feel the same inside as when I was 21 and starting down the aisle on my father's arm. If I'd even imagined a day when I might be the mother of the bride, I'm sure I thought I'd be the same person I was then. Crowding in on me was an awareness of all the unexpected changes in my life and of how so many things were not as I thought they would be. I was so sure when Paget's father and I were college sweethearts that we should marry. By the time I had doubts, the voice of intuition was weak compared with the security of the plans and commitments we had made over 4 years. When we started trying to have a baby, I felt more doubts. Growing up, I'd fantasized about a glamorous career, not motherhood. I wasn't sure I felt ready to be a parent. By contrast, I had no doubts about the career I chose in college. I forged ahead with great success and enjoyed teaching immensely.

Sometime in my early 30s, I noticed that all my decisions seemed to have stood on their heads. My first marriage was indeed crumbling. The career chosen without misgivings had lost its vitality, while the daughter who scared me and made me feel incompetent was—and is—my best work. I left the marriage and my job, went back to school, and started over—terrified and excited. Now, after many unforeseen detours, decisions, and mistakes, I listened in joy and peace as Paget and Chris shared their wedding vows. I looked back on a second marriage and a second career which have continued to challenge and fulfill me for the last 18 years. I had a whole life and an identity that I hadn't planned for when I had stood in her place, contemplating a future I felt was largely decided. Now I have a daughter and a new "son" who, at 26 and 30, are still exploring and remaking decisions about their careers and trying to be both realistic and optimistic. They seem to be much more comfortable seeing their lives and vocational identities as a "work in progress" than my generation ever was.

Until recent research on adult development, we in this culture believed that at a certain point (age 18, or maybe 21) we become grown up, mature, officially "adult." Children were expected to go through stages. Adults, however, were expected to sort out their values, choose a vocation and a lifestyle, and become independent. We believed that people who made the "right" choices would be safe and secure. However, we now realize how difficult it is to define adulthood or pinpoint exactly when it starts. Certainly it isn't a static condition at which we arrive and stay, but a process marked by constant growth and change as we gather information, accumulate experience, and encounter crises and opportunities, all of which lead us to reevaluate our goals and direction.

So much for the myth of instant adulthood, of a moment when we become finished products, stable and permanently decided about our lives—adults who weren't supposed to get confused, change their minds (careers, marriages), reevaluate their goals, or start over. Fortunately, research is teaching us that adulthood is more complex than it has appeared. We continue to grow, change, and learn about ourselves. In the endeavors that affect various aspects of our lives, such as marriage, we continue to work at knowing ourselves better and making our first decision one that will last. However, this does not seem to be the case with career choice. Today, people often change jobs multiple times, and often entire career directions as well, with positive results for both the individual and the business and professional world. However, we mustn't make such decisions in adulthood in the same cavalier and impulsive way we often did as children. We have a responsibility to use our increased capacity to foresee consequences, to plan ahead, and to consider the people in our lives who may be involved in the outcome. But we also need to develop our own identity and allow room to make mistakes and change our minds. It's crucial to realize how valuable and necessary exploration and trial and error are, even though they may prove embarrassing or slow us down. Without them, we risk buying into what others tell us we should do instead of finding our own path. If we follow someone else's formula for success or happiness in an effort to gain approval or security, we'll most often find as we age that we feel betrayed, disappointed, empty, or bitter. Security grows boring, we're baffled by our own need for continued growth and change, and we miss out on the anticipation, excitement, fulfillment, pride, and confidence that come with defining and following our own dreams. An old cliché says that we can have "too much of a good thing," and security is no exception. As Germaine Greer put it, "Security is when everything is settled, when nothing can happen to you. Security is a denial of life."

ADULT LIFE STAGES: AN OVERVIEW

Researchers on adult development now know that children are not the only ones who grow, change, make mistakes, and have an evolving identity. More and more evidence points to a consistent series of adult stages and transitions through which we change and grow as long as we live. As scary as this prospect may seem, it does take the pressure off. We no longer have to have it all together or make all our decisions by a certain age. We no longer have to pretend to others, ourselves, our parents, or our children that we're faultless. We can take our confusions and problems out from under wraps.

Maturity is not an outcome but a growth process. However, we may find it difficult to win permission from ourselves and society to grow, experiment, and change. Roger Gould and fellow researchers in adult development attribute this difficulty to the magical expectations of adulthood and adults that we learn as children. Gould (1978) warns of minimal growth and maximal misery unless we accept that continuing growth is a part of adult life and stop expecting ourselves to be perfect and have all the answers.

Growth circles back on itself. Change serves as both the impetus for growth and its product. Change is where career decisions—like all major decisions—begin and end. Both exciting and frightening, change is unavoidable. It's often paired with crisis; this pairing in part has to do with timing. Sometimes change comes when we're not ready for it: graduation from school, a personal loss, or a job that's phased out. Or we may be ready for a change that does not come—a promotion, a raise, or some new friends. Even when a change is well timed, it involves an act of faith, a letting-go of the familiar to embrace the unknown. Part of coping with change is learning to believe in growth, to put aside fear and frustration long enough to realize that change is a catalyst for transition. Everything around us is growing. If we try to stand still, we won't avoid change; we'll simply be giving up our option to choose and to help direct the change. A crisis is often the chance for a ride to the next stage of our development—not a free ride, but often a real bargain in terms of experience.

Adult life stages appear to be ordered. Each one must be worked with and to some extent completed before the next one can be genuinely undertaken. People sometimes feel a great pressure to jump ahead. Time and competition are important to Americans. Sometimes we're so anxious to go forward that stopping to sort out and tie up loose ends seems like wasted time, but there are no shortcuts. Stephen Covey, the author of *The Seven Habits of Highly Effective People* (1989), talks about the impossibility of avoiding these natural processes, using a metaphor familiar to all students—cramming for exams. He says, "Did you ever consider how ridiculous it would be to try to cram on a farm—to forget to plant in the spring, play all summer and then cram in the fall to bring in the harvest? The farm is a natural system. The price must be paid and the process followed. You always reap what you sow; there is no shortcut" (p. 22). Like infants, we must crawl before we can walk. People who try to circumvent growth phases by leaping forward to keep up with the expectations of a parent, employer, or spouse are setting the stage for serious trouble for themselves and for their relationships.

Each person's existence is guided by internal beliefs and external demands. It's much easier to see and understand the external elements. Our social, familial, and job roles involve many factors that we perceive as controlling us: I should do this, I have to do that, I can't do something else. We may be tempted to define our lives in terms of external success and the opinions of others, and to blame failures and distress on spouses, jobs, or social conditions. We may try to decide the appropriateness of our attitudes and the values according to external events and expectations, but as with development, this is not a workable long-term strategy.

The first place we need to look to find our own direction—not the last, as we sometimes think—is inside ourselves. Which of these choices is right for me? How do I feel about each of them? Although crises and growth experiences may be altered by and attuned to our environment, they frequently begin and end inside us. Covey says that this is the real message of his book. He advocates "a principle-centered, character-based, 'inside-out' approach to personal and interpersonal effectiveness" (p. 42). *Inside-out* here refers to the fact that effectiveness, success, and fulfillment start with our own investment in and responsibility for our growth, principles, integrity, priorities, and decisions. Covey believes that this process leads to "an upward spiral of growth" and indicates that "in all my experience, I have never seen lasting solutions to problems, lasting happiness and success, that came from the outside in" (p. 43).

The basis of what is inside is what Covey calls the "Character Ethic"—a self and a life built around basic, natural principles we integrate into our lives. These include values and beliefs such as integrity and honesty, quality and excellence, human dignity, fairness and justice, and growth. He refers to approaching success through such avenues as public relations, influence techniques, and "positive thinking" as the "Personality Ethic." He states that these strategies can be useful in some short-term situations but not as a foundation for long-term plans or relationships. Interestingly, although Covey's views sound psychological and sometimes spiritual, much of the experience that led him to these conclusions was gained and fine-tuned in work settings, where he has long been sought after as a consultant by many high-profile employers and Fortune 500 companies.

Although Covey's concepts sound clear and even simple, living them is neither. It requires thought, self-awareness, and understanding, and the courage to express ourselves and stick to our principles—even when no one's looking. Seeing the process of our growth and the changes in our lives in the context of adult developmental stages is further complicated by differences in subgroups and their roles and goals. We have just begun to understand these differences. Most early studies were conducted with white males, so this research may have limited application to women and minorities. Increasingly, new research implies that, although the ultimate goals of human development may be the same for all human beings, the paths by which women and members of minority groups arrive at these goals differ from those of white men. Some of these differences will be pointed out in this chapter. Keep in mind that many basic similarities remain.

Each life stage has its own implications for all the decisions we make—for our work, our personal development, and our lifestyles. In general, discoveries about adult development have triggered the realization that a career choice is in fact usually a series of choices. As the environment changes, our internal landscape does as well. As we gain new life experiences, our values, interests, feelings, and capacities may shift. To be fulfilling, a career choice may need to be reevaluated too.

EARLY ADULTHOOD (AGES 20 TO 30)

In our early 20s (or sooner), we face a conflict between the desire for stability and the desire to explore. At this age, we are expected to start making commitments to a life system of our own and to detach ourselves from our parents. Many post-adolescents feel this push to commitment when they still have too many loose ends in their lives. Young adults respond to this confusion in many ways. Some continue to explore different sets of values and attitudes by experimenting with various kinds of living arrangements and temporary jobs. But many appear to turn their backs on unexplored horizons and begin working to establish themselves. Some may have sorted out what they want and feel ready to settle down. For others, a career choice or marriage may seem to be the right path to adulthood and security. Misfortune may be the result when people believe that making a decision simply in order to decide will guarantee happiness.

Social Change

Society has traditionally given us the message that we should start a family and establish a career direction in our 20s. In the last two decades, however, national surveys have shown that social change is accelerating. New and varied lifestyle choices are emerging, fueled by the perspectives of new generations and by burgeoning options for women in particular. Changes in women's choices in turn reshape the attitudes of both genders about work, marriage, and children, as the following points examine.

1. Women have been entering the labor force and college in increasingly greater members. Some people predict that by the year 2005, women will make up nearly half of the labor force. More than half of all full-time first-year college students are women. This increasing ability of women to value personal development represents a gradual but significant change that has created problems as well as opportunities. Women's gender-role confusion and ambivalence regarding autonomy were first spotlighted by Horner's research on the "fear of success" (Horner, 1972). Briefly, Horner found that women fear that achievement or autonomy will mean the loss of femininity, relationships, or social acceptance. Although women are trying many new things and shifting priorities, they're having difficulty reconciling these changes with the traditional roles of wife, mother, and homemaker they still fill.

2. Despite the difficulties that change presents for everyone, our attitudes about marriage and work are changing. According to census figures, the median age at first marriage has gone up for both genders, as increasing numbers of men and women postpone marriage for college and career. (*The 1997 Information Please Almanac,* 1997). Decades ago, people married in their late teens or early 20s. By 1992, the average age had risen to 26.5 for men and 24.4 for women. In a Virginia Slims survey, published in *USA Today* (October 21, 1985), 72 percent of the women said that marriage is not a prerequisite for happiness, and only 48 percent ranked a loving husband as more important than self-fulfillment (compared with 64 percent a decade ago). Given a choice between homemaking and working outside the home, 51 percent of the women said they would choose the job (up from 35 percent a decade earlier), and 85 percent of working women said they received "great" or "moderate" satisfaction from their work.

3. As a result, the number of dual-career couples (and families) in the labor force keeps increasing. The 1985 Virginia Slims survey reported that 63 percent

of women wanted to combine career and marriage and/or family. According to the early 1992 census, in 60 percent of all married couples in the United States, both spouses were employed outside of the home, compared with 45 percent in 1976.

4. Our attitudes toward work and childbearing have also changed. The number of working mothers has increased dramatically over the past four decades. As a result, many couples have postponed having children until their 30s so that the woman can get a head start on her career. According to 1992 census figures, 81 percent of dual-career couples with children were age 30 and older, compared with 50 percent of those without children. Further, many couples no longer see having children as vital to a happy marriage. Data from the 1985 Virginia Slims survey reveal that 80 percent of the women and 76 percent of the men did not feel that they needed children to have a happy marriage—another view thought to be unhealthy or selfish in the past.

5. Changes in the role of husband and father have come with the evolution of dual-career families. As more men marry women with ongoing careers and with women's incomes more crucial to the couple's lifestyle, men take on more of the responsibility for home and children. In the traditional roles of past generations, men rarely cooked, and their time watching the kids was often seen as "baby-sitting" instead of parenting. Now, we have many kinds of role changes, including families where the wife's income supports the family and the husband cares for the children, as well as families where one or both spouses work at home (self-employed or "telecommuting") and care for families simultaneously. The Family and Medical Leave Act of 1993 mandates that all businesses over a certain size must allow up to 12 weeks of leave time for any employee after the birth or adoption of a baby, or for the illness of a spouse, child, parent, or oneself. This allows paternity leave, for example, without discrimination by employers. Such steps serve to humanize the workplace and acknowledge the need for the balance represented by all sides of the wellness wheel, such as emotional, spiritual, social, and physical (see Chapter 1).

6. Other changes in society and in family structure stem from new attitudes, efforts to fight discrimination, and the increased financial independence of women. Some women now choose to have a child without marrying, and single people of both genders adopt children. With the increasing divorce rate, and more fathers obtaining custody of their children, single parenthood, stepparenting, and blended families are becoming common. With joint custody, children often commute between two residences. Partners of the same gender are now celebrating "unions," buying homes, and raising children. Single mothers will join households to share parenting duties and expenses. Many of those who find that the traditional family structures no longer serve them must struggle to get their varied needs met and find new ways to maintain balance in their lives.

7. Work has a positive effect on a woman's self-esteem and family life. A national survey of adults conducted by the Target Group Index (published in *Working Women* in March 1979) found that women who work described themselves in more positive terms than did nonworking women. Women employed outside the

home tended to rate themselves higher than homemakers did in terms of their self-assurance, intellect, humor, and ability to get along with and support others. A survey of the goals of readers of *Working Women* found that being financially well off, having a good family life, and having a job or career were all endorsed by 50 percent of the female readers. In 1989, the psychologist Lois W. Hoffman published a survey in *American Psychologist* that summarized the results of several studies comparing working mothers and homemakers. She concluded that, compared with nonemployed mothers, working mothers had fewer psychosomatic and stress-related ailments and experienced less depression. She also observed that children, especially daughters, of working mothers had fewer stereotyped attitudes about gender roles and that husbands of working mothers were more involved in family life if they also worked. Finally, Hoffman reported that the quality of interactions between working mothers and their daughters is more positive, whereas relationships with male children change little when the mother works. It does appear, based on anecdotal evidence, that men who had working mothers are more comfortable with working wives and often assume their wives will work. This can create marital problems if the wife wishes to be a full-time mother. The reverse may occur if a man with a mother who was at home has a wife who expects support for her career.

8. Finally, it appears that numerous homemakers and workers of both genders are returning to school or to work after their 20s to launch new careers. Half of all college students are older than 25, and one in every four is older than 35 (Clinton, 1987). Women now have more "permission" and opportunities to start or change careers during or after starting a family. Men also are increasingly able to add to or retool their training. Because they are no longer the sole wage earners in the family, they can afford a temporary loss of income that would have been impossible a few decades ago. Interestingly, older returning students, especially women, tend to be more liberal than their younger classmates in attitudes toward women's roles (Etaugh & Spiller, 1989).

In effect, as social change occurs, many people are changing their attitudes and lifestyles. Some are forced to change because of loss of a job or spouse. Others

Sally Forth, ©1993. Reprinted with special permission of King Features Syndicate.

are choosing change in order to take advantage of new opportunities. Thus, a commitment during the 20s that later turns out to be uncomfortable need not become a devastating mistake. In fact, research seems to indicate that those who make some kind of a wholehearted commitment at this stage—even if they eventually outgrow it—are better equipped for much of the growth that occurs later in life.

One implication of these changes and options is that growth and development tasks become more complex. For men in their 20s, priorities must be realigned to include attention to home, family and parenting, or career—and a wife's job—unlike in the past, when almost all of a man's energy during those early years went into career building. Women in their 20s have, in addition, new priorities and some difficult choices. Women who want both a career and a family must develop themselves simultaneously as nurturers and achievers, because statistics suggest that, despite slowly changing attitudes, most nurturing and homemaking tasks still fall to women. If women choose to postpone or give up one of these options, they must deal with risk and loss. Whether they do family and career serially or simultaneously, women involved in both must learn to deal with frequent guilt about shortchanging one area or the other. Even with a career, women in their 20s continue to think about and work on developmental tasks concerning relationships and commitment to others—emphasizing the emotional, social, and spiritual areas of their lives. Men usually focus first on occupational development. Intellectual, physical, and social activities may play a role, either as part of the job or as recreation, while emotional and relationship issues may be postponed until career or lifestyle priorities are in place.

Mentors

In addition to the varied relationships that satisfy different sides of us, there is one type of relationship specific to work and career that we begin learning about in early adulthood, usually in our first "real" job. This is a relationship with a mentor—a person far enough along in his or her own emotional and career development to guide and help younger workers. The mentor has more experience than do younger colleagues and is usually at a higher occupational level. He or she can provide an informal source of information, influence, and support, helping the protégé learn shortcuts, informal (often unspoken) rules, and processes in a particular business environment or career area. Most inexperienced workers find a mentor tremendously helpful in developing not only their skills and career direction but their professional identity as well.

Though sometimes helpful or appropriate for the mentor to be the same gender as the "mentee," many career women have male mentors because bosses and executives in many organizations still tend to be men. As more women reach higher levels, younger workers of both genders will have more opportunities to have women as mentors. Mentor relationships can be particularly significant for women, who may have a greater need for sponsorship and "clues" if entering a career or organization built around a male network. This works well as long as both parties take care to make it clear through their behavior that it is strictly a business relationship. Developing a mentor relationship is an important work skill in itself, since most people will acquire new mentors as they change jobs or advance in their careers. Many will also keep former mentors as colleagues, business contacts, or friends.

REEXAMINATION (AGES 30 TO 40)

No matter how settled the 20s may seem, the pathway into the 30s often involves a reappearance of some of the confusion and self-doubt that we put aside or thought we had solved in adolescence. In this stage, conflict may arise between obligations and unfulfilled personal desires. We begin to understand that we've accepted some ideas about what we should do from our families and society, and we ask "Why *should* I?" We begin to realize that the rewards we expected for doing what we were told may not materialize. We may think about rearranging our priorities to reflect our revised hopes and dreams.

Around this age, many of us also begin to feel pressed for time. Feelings of lost opportunity, combined with the prospect of middle age and old age ahead, create a feeling of urgency. We feel that if we miss the opportunity to do what we really want to do now, it may be too late. This feeling often impels people at this stage to reexamine and reevaluate personal values and attitudes, as well as their career progress and goals. In doing so, we may find that some of our beliefs and goals no longer fit.

People in their 20s usually focus much of their energy on learning to meet their basic needs and establishing a career and/or marriage and family. So, for many the 30s becomes a time to notice and evaluate what may be missing in other areas of their lives. This can mean another review of the wellness wheel. Is the hard-working sales executive missing out on hobbies or recreation? Is the parent at home with two small children getting enough intellectual stimulation? Is the computer programmer tense from lack of exercise? Is the lawyer working a six-day week now ready to marry or start a family? For people who feel successful and comfortable about their choices, concerns about career, money, and security may start to take a back seat to some of these other needs.

Maslow's Hierarchy of Needs

One of the most respected theories of human motivation and behavior is the model developed by Abraham Maslow. It states that human needs are arranged in a hierarchy. The most basic are physiological: hunger and thirst. Once assured of physical sustenance, we work toward the second level: safety from harm as well as comfort and security about both present and future. When we feel secure about our physical needs, we move to level three: "belongingness" and love. This is achieved through relationships, group memberships, and working with others toward a mutual purpose. These things give us a sense of validation and identity. They also contribute to meeting the need composing Maslow's fourth stage: esteem. Through work and other commitments of our choosing, we strive for a sense of competence, worth, and recognition. The need at the final and highest level of the hierarchy is the most complex: self-actualization, or the use of our abilities and values in ways that create a sense of personal meaning and integrity.

Maslow's research indicates that we're likely to meet needs at the upper levels of the hierarchy only after we've successfully coped with our most basic needs. He also suggests that if we wonder where we currently stand in the hierarchy, we can look at our feelings. When our physiological and safety needs are threatened, we experience anger. When the higher needs go unmet, we're more likely to feel anxiety. Learning how to meet these needs on our own is a pressing task during adolescence and early adulthood. Deciding how to do this involves understanding our individual dreams, interests, abilities, resources, and values.

Maslow's hierarchy gives us a way of looking at how work relates to meeting the needs expressed by different sides of the wellness wheel. Crucial for physical and emotional survival, nourishment and safety are the most obvious things that we provide for ourselves through work. On the third level, belonging and love, we satisfy social, emotional, and spiritual needs through the collegiality of work and the contributions it makes to individuals and society. This is the foundation for self-esteem, which grows when we challenge ourselves and develop competence, confidence, pride, and recognition. We do this in many ways through our occupations and/or avocations, which can involve gaining expertise in any area—intellectual, physical, social, emotional, spiritual—or in several. The peak use of our potential, self-actualization, brings intellectual, emotional, and spiritual satisfaction—the sense of making a commitment and seeing it through with our best effort. This kind of internal reward can come from within our occupation or from some other kind of work that "pays" in an intangible way (such as volunteerism, community service, or parenting).

Job and Career Changes

One result of the U.S. worker's increased affluence, mobility, and questing after self-fulfillment is a new attitude toward job change. Many of our parents or grandparents were loyal employees of one firm for 30 or 40 years and retired with a ceremony and a gold watch. Today the average worker changes jobs several times during his or her career and may retrain at some point to enter a partly or an entirely different area. External influences we face include competition for jobs, changing social attitudes and legislation, and a growing number of overcrowded or obsolete jobs. Over our working lives, many kinds of changes can occur. In addition to a job shift—being fired, laid off, quitting, taking a new job, or even starting a whole new career—changes are common within one company or enterprise, or even within a job. These changes include promotion; demotion; shifts in job duties; a leave of absence; a transfer to a new location; a change of income; additional school or on-the-job retraining; the loss of employees, bosses, or colleagues; or even something as subtle as a change in feelings about one's job.

Although we often can't foresee these changes when training ourselves for a first career, we can deal with them constructively and turn them to our advantage if we are observant and informed. We must continue to learn, stay flexible, and keep our options open. Whether we view these changes as good or bad, they will require adjustments and decisions on our part and will affect our present and future feelings and behaviors as well as those of others. Single workers may find that such changes affect friends, roommates, dates, or parents. Career-related events in the lives of married workers will affect their spouses (and any other family members). Dual-career marriages present special problems, such as finding a location where both spouses may pursue their career interests. The feelings and the household routines of husbands and children can present problems for a woman who wants to begin working or continue to advance in her career while continuing to have a family.

Any change in family routines and expectations demands intellectual and emotional growth of everyone. Each has to learn new roles and tolerate inconveniences. A parent who takes a job in a new city requires everyone in the family to make sacrifices both social and emotional, and sometimes intellectual and occupational as well if family members must change schools or jobs. If someone wants to invest time or money in school or job training, doing so may mean asking others to cut back on their standard of living or to assume new responsibilities. Handling such changes also requires continual evaluation of our lives on all sides of the wellness wheel so that we can assess how change will affect the things that matter to us and, in turn, what role the things we value play in shaping our decisions.

Women in their 30s today are being affected by inflation, divorce or widowhood, social attitudes, and the realization that the job of motherhood fills only 10 to 20 of their 40 (or more) working years. Women in their 30s who have chosen the more traditional career paths or who have had their children while young may have developed themselves in the context of commitment to others. According to Maggie Scarf (1980), these women reach a point at which they prepare to let go of these roles in order to develop a more independent identity. Other women, whose principal investment during the 20s was in a full-time or nontraditional career, may feel a need to develop their nurturing side as they enter their 30s and may thus turn to marriage or childbearing. Women are gradually taking on more "masculine" roles—and not just in the workplace. They're doing household repairs, learning to fix their own cars, and making financial and business decisions for themselves and for the family that were traditionally made by men when they provided the sole income for the family.

Men also face some confusing—although not so well-publicized—new options. Job changes and even second careers are much more acceptable now than in the past, and a man who has a working wife may have more freedom to make changes than he anticipated. Of course, these new options and pressures provide sources of imbalance and conflict in marriage, parenthood, and other relationships, as well as within the self. As a result, many men are shifting toward more active involvement in running the household and in parenting. More men function as single parents, and married men sometimes take on the role of homemaker as a full-time job while their wives work outside the home. These changes in roles within the family are sometimes based on preference or personality, and other times on the job market or economic necessity. In all cases, the challenge of these new roles and perspectives requires flexibility and continued learning. By their 30s, many people have learned to carry within them their own personalized

Hagar the Horrible, ©1987. Reprinted with special permission of King Features Syndicate.

version of the wellness wheel. This allows them to weigh how potential changes may affect the balance they need in their lives and enhance or block their progress in important areas.

Any job or career change, whether a small step up in responsibility or a cross-country move, a hoped-for promotion or an unchosen event, will likely shift the internal and external balances we have established in our lives, as well as those of the people around us. For example, a difference in career responsibilities can mean more time spent at work and a temporary neglect of activities that satisfy other sides of the self, such as leisure and fun, sleep, or exercise. It could mean a change in how we meet social needs, if we are expected to entertain clients, or increased intellectual effort, if we must learn new skills or information. Any change in the occupational side of our lives will "unbalance" other areas as well, stimulating a reevaluation of our needs and how we can meet them. The best thing we can do for ourselves throughout our working lives is to try to be prepared emotionally, financially, and vocationally to make change work for us when it comes our way.

MIDLIFE SHIFT (AGES 40 TO 50)

The big "4-0" is a birthday celebrated by many with great fanfare and teasing. However, as people live longer and in better health, the attitude about "middle age" is shifting in a very positive way. Plates and napkins that used to say "Over the hill" now say "When you're over the hill, you pick up speed."

This change has occurred in part because people now often change jobs or start a second or third career after age 40 or even after retirement. In fact, people sometimes take advantage of "early retirement" to use a pension as a springboard to a new career. Aging brings with it the awareness of limitations of time and opportunity. We see that some of our dreams have not been realized, or that this may be our last chance at them, or that we have dreams we didn't even know we had. People unhappy with their personal or vocational lives may reexamine their values and goals or the balance of various elements in their lives. People who have tried to do what they were "supposed to" and don't feel satisfied may decide to try something else. People who don't see a happy ending to their present job may opt to take more risks. We leave jobs to start over, go back to school, become self-employed, or do something we've always wanted to do. Women whose changing attitudes and experiences have caused them to outgrow old roles may start a new phase of their lives. Homemakers may opt for school or work, and women who have devoted themselves to a career may marry and have children—something women in their 40s are doing with increasing frequency.

For more and more people, pursuing a series of different vocations is beginning to make sense, because we grow and change and because our productive and energetic years are being prolonged. It doesn't make sense to stagnate in one job all your life or be dead-ended in one at age 40—especially because in the current economy the promised security is often not forthcoming anyway. Companies are bought and merged; jobs or whole departments are phased out by changes in policy or management; highly paid executives are let go to save money on salaries or to avoid paying retirement benefits.

More people are taking risks; retraining in their 30s, 40s, or 50s; changing jobs if the old one is a compromise; and starting new businesses at 50 or second careers after retirement. When life expectancies were shorter, facing disappointments and unfinished dreams at 40 might have been an invitation to depression. Now, it can be the beginning of a new reality, based on the opportunity to be the new you. People who value highly something about their present job (for example, security, salary, or location) may not want to leave it. Instead, they may shift their search for personal fulfillment or recognition to hobbies, community involvement, or family activities. Or, sometimes, if they have met their vocational goals they want to change or cut back on work time to focus energy on some other area of life that has taken on greater importance. They may find new challenge and fulfillment in new roles or opportunities. Again, reevaluation of jobs, roles, or values by one or both partners in a relationship may create a need for change in the balance of the family.

Gender Differences

Men's and women's experiences during this reevaluation period may differ significantly. Men may change careers or adjust to loss or disappointment, but more often they will consolidate career decisions and actions already taken—pushing for a promotion or cutting back on work time to enjoy more leisure. On the other hand, women who have had children, particularly if they did not have a full-time job outside the home, are really being forced into a retirement of sorts. As their children grow up and leave home, mothers must adjust to the loss of a major life role. At this point, women may be eager to try making their way competitively in a career (a developmental task that most men start in their 20s), or they may not want to give up the role of full-time wife and homemaker.

During this period of reevaluation and change, many men become more aware of their nurturing side. They may seek increased involvement with their spouses and growing children, or they may become mentors to younger co-workers. Women who have been primary caregivers for children or others may now discover a more aggressive side of themselves, which men may have developed earlier in their careers. These changes give rise to a disturbance in the balance and harmony of some relationships, as expressed humorously in this poem by Ric Masten:

Coming and Going

i have noticed
that men
somewhere around 40
tend to come in from the field
with a sigh
and removing their coat
in the hall
call into the kitchen
> "You were right, Grace
> It ain't out there.
> Just like you always said."
and she
with the children gone at last
breathless
puts her hat on her head
> "The hell it ain't!"
coming and going
they pass in the doorway

A husband and wife (or family) may have to work at rebalancing their needs and activities at this point. They may pursue lifestyle changes that promote growth in areas of the wellness wheel that they previously ignored in the effort to establish a foundation of physical and financial security. As Maslow points out, these needs come first, and they put on a lot of pressure in the first decades of adulthood. Only later do we feel we have more time to devote to relationships, leisure, and fun, additional education or unfinished dreams—expanding our identities to include parts of ourselves pushed aside in our earlier scramble to "grow up." The changing, reaching and risking, and letting go of old "selves" that occur at this stage can be painful but also open the door to new adventures. At 40, we still have at least 25 years left to work—and now people often work past age 65. With exercise and good health care, we can hope for even more years to enjoy life beyond work: the physical and intellectual challenges as well as opportunities for social, emotional, and spiritual sharing and contributions to our world.

REFOCUSING (AGES 50 TO 60)

To live constructively and positively from age 50 on, we must possess integrity in many senses of the word. We need the kind of integrity that stems from internal motivation, from self-determination and self-reward, because many of the life activities that generated external approval, such as work and child-rearing, are drawing to a close. And we need the kind of integrity that comes from the root of the word *integrate:* to face and accept as a part of ourselves the inevitable aging, changed dreams, and mistakes that we can't undo. For those who have dealt with these realities and determined to move on, the 50s can indeed be a time of redirection.

Even as we grow concerned about diminishing time and increasing wrinkles, thinning hair and fat grams, keeping fit and keeping our teeth, these same limitations sharpen our sense of the preciousness of the remaining years. The work that society has designated as ours is largely done. If we have been careful with our health and money, we now have the luxury of feeling unhurried and redefining our values, with other human beings often becoming more important than influence or material possessions.

Many people at this age develop new activities and goals to implement this new outlook on life. With ever-increasing affluence and spectacular strides in health care, many in this age group are joining those in their 40s in extending and changing their work lives in the years prior to retirement. They may start businesses, begin new full-time or part-time work, give time to community action, or develop leisure pursuits such as hobbies and travel. These ways of branching out are also great beginnings for a necessary learning process: that of structuring one's own time, something many people never have to do until retirement.

REDIRECTION (AGES 65 AND ON)

To those of us wrapped up in responsibilities to school, jobs, or families, the idea of waking up one morning with permission to do nothing sounds like a dream. Retirement is something most of us look forward to and dream about in our busiest years. But the approach or arrival of that moment causes anxiety or depression in many people. Work, a source of social contacts, recognition, intellectual challenge, emotional growth, and structure, has been removed from our lives. In addition to income, the paycheck provided reassurance that we were needed and appreciated. Learning to provide these feelings for ourselves means replacing work-related activities with other activities that we enjoy and that motivate us to get up in the morning. We must create opportunities that meet our needs to exercise, socialize, challenge our minds, open our hearts, and feel valuable and involved. This takes time, effort, creativity, and often help and support.

An additional problem of retirement is the psychological impact of the concept itself. There is prejudice against older people. They are often depicted as incompetent drivers or as jealously guarding their fixed incomes and shaking their gray heads at the younger generation. We don't venerate or use their wisdom and experiences as many other cultures do. We isolate the elderly, in part because they remind us that old age and death wait for each of us. Consequently, our attitudes cannot help but convey the idea that retirement is not a time to look forward to. Many older people do have real reasons to worry about dependence, ill health, financial problems, and loneliness. But for as many others, nothing but that fear itself is standing in the way of another 15 or 20 years of active enjoyment of life

Back to the Future: A Questionnaire

I'm studying career decision making and how careers are affected by the different needs we have and the roles we play at different stages in our adult lives. Your answers will help me develop a better understanding of the stages ahead and how they may affect my life and career choices. Thank you for your time.

The stages of adult development are Early Adulthood (20–30), Reexamination (30–40), Midlife Shift (40–50), Refocusing (50–60), and Redirection (65 and up).

1. What stage are you in now? _____

2. What is the meaning of work in your life at this time?

_____

_____

_____

3. Was its meaning different in past stages of your life? When and how?

_____

_____

_____

4. How do you think it might be different in the future?

_____

_____

_____

This figure is called the wellness wheel.
It represents different areas of our lives.

5. Which areas do you find most meaningful now? Do you know why?

_____

_____

_____

(continued)

Back to the Future: A Questionnaire *(continued)*

6. Has the importance of the different areas shifted throughout your life? How?

_____

_____

_____

Following is a list of life roles. Underline those you have filled and briefly describe your experiences in the areas your interviewer is most interested in. Rank the underlined roles in order of importance.

child	player	leader/manager	friend
young adult	worker	entrepreneur	boyfriend/girlfriend
middle-ager	paid worker	mentor	spouse/partner
retiree	co-worker	family member	helper/confidant
student/learner	supervisor/boss	community member	volunteer

7. What roles do you expect to play in the future?

_____

_____

_____

8. Have you played any important roles which are not listed?

_____

_____

_____

Choose one activity or relationship that has been important over time and has changed with you.

9. How has it changed at different stages in your life?

_____

_____

_____

10. How has it affected your different roles?

_____

_____

_____

11. How have your different roles affected the activity or relationship?

_____

_____

_____

and continued growth. They can feel satisfied with the contributions they have made and can continue to share their wisdom, memories, perspectives, and knowledge in leisure activities or part-time jobs, in volunteer capacities, or with younger friends and relatives. Many communities now have senior centers, "golden age" craft centers, where items produced can be sold, or organizations that make retired professionals available to advise or mentor younger workers.

The work of growth is seldom easy and is never completed. The realization that maturity is a process that will never be finished can seem tiring, but it can also give us hope. It gives us permission to be unfinished, to make mistakes, to ask for help. We can continually re-create ourselves and our lives. We can change our minds, alter our lifestyles, experiment with new ideas, acquire new skills, accept new challenges, and start over. New learning and new beginnings are always available. We can now be comfortable with the knowledge that we will never be finished growing.

> [Don't wait] for the day when "you can relax" or when "your problems will be over." The struggles of life never end. Most good things in life are fleeting and transitory. Enjoy them. Don't waste your time looking forward to the "happy ending" to all your troubles.
>
> —Robert L. Woolfold and
> Frank C. Richardson

BACK TO THE FUTURE: *A QUESTIONNAIRE*

Interview someone a generation older than you are—a parent, a grandparent, or other relative. If relatives are not available, choose an acquaintance you admire or like at your school or job or in your community, or even the parent of a friend. Give or mail them the questionnaire that follows. Be sure to have them contact you if they need help. You could also give the interview in person.

REFERENCES AND RESOURCES

Clinton, B. (1987). Undergraduate education in an increasingly complex world. *National Forum, 67,* 43–44.

Covey, S. R. (1989). *The seven habits of highly effective people.* New York: Simon & Schuster.

Etaugh, C., & Spiller, B. (1989). Attitudes toward women: Comparisons of traditional aged and older college students. *Journal of College Student Development, 30,* 41–43.

Gould, R. L. (1978). *Transformations: Growth and change in adult life.* New York: Simon & Schuster.

Hoffman, L. W. (1989). Effects of maternal employment in the two-part family. *American Psychologist, 44,* 283–292.

Horner, M. S. (1972). Toward an understanding of achievement-related conflicts in women. *Journal of Social Issues, 28,* 157–176.

The 1997 information please almanac. (1997). Boston: Houghton Mifflin.

Scarf, M. (1980). *Unfinished business: Pressure points in the lives of women.* New York: Doubleday.

CHAPTER **5**

A WORLD OF CHANGE

ZIGGY, © 1992 Ziggy and Friends, Inc. Dist. by Universal Press Syndicate. Reprinted with permission. All rights reserved.

A SHORT HISTORY OF MEDICINE:

"Doctor, I have an ear ache."

2000 B.C.—"Here, eat this root."

1000 B.C.—"That root is heathen, say this prayer."

1850 A.D.—"That prayer is superstition, drink this potion."

1940 A.D.—"That potion is snake oil, swallow this pill."

1985 A.D.—"That pill is ineffective, take this antibiotic."

2000 A.D.—"That antibiotic is artificial. Here, eat this root!"

—Source Unknown

Mary sits alone in her darkened room looking out her window at the moonlight on the fresh snow. A slight wind blows the snow toward the streetlight, creating a sparkling dance among the snowflakes. The city is quiet. Only a few people can be seen hurrying home from work or out toward the city's nightlife.

Like most students on campus, Mary's roommate has gone home for midterm break. But Mary can't afford to go home. She needs the time to catch up on her studies and doesn't think it would be wise to spend 2 days on a bus for a short visit with her family. She also worries about her finances, because she's barely surviving on summer earnings and study grants.

In the middle of her random thoughts, Mary is struck with the contrasts and changes in her life. A Native American raised on a small remote reservation, she finds it unreal to be a first-year student at a prestigious private university in a major eastern city. She recalls conversations with friends at home who don't understand her academic goals and her decision to experience city life, if only for a brief period as a student. She also recalls the distress that her adjustment to the social aspects of college life has caused her. She deeply values her cultural heritage but often feels alone because she's the only Native American on campus. She also feels her privacy invaded by other students' curiosity—questions about her home life and innermost thoughts as well as their occasional stares. She also dislikes the competition among her roommates regarding grades and career aspirations. Her culture has always greatly emphasized interdependence among tribal members, living in harmony with nature, and a deep reverence for the spirit world, which provides wisdom and guidance for those who listen to the voices of nature and understand the interconnectedness of all life. Being identified by her heritage is both special and lonely for Mary; it makes her stand out yet feel isolated in many ways.

Mary's thoughts drift back to the last gathering of her family 2 months ago at the bus stop near her home. She remembers the sense of pride and apprehension they shared as they sent their only child off to college. Although they openly assured themselves that she would come home when she completed her studies, they shared an unspoken understanding that the promise would be hard to keep, because jobs are scarce at home, with most members of the tribe subsidizing their earnings by farming, fishing, and hunting. Someone with a liberal arts degree and no technical skills might have little to do in such a place. She promises herself that she'll write home tomorrow to ease some of her uncertainty and loneliness.

Although born in the United States, Mary shares her dilemma with many students whose families have recently immigrated from Africa, Asia, the Middle East, and South America. They stand at a cultural crossroads that reaches far back to history yet presently affects all of us in our work and personal lives.

TECHNOLOGY SHAPES OUR FUTURE

A major force in the evolution of human cultures, technological advances have made possible new and broader visions of ourselves and the world around us. They have provided us with an ever expanding means of acquiring food and comfort, of moving about, and of communicating.

The Industrial Revolution

Only 250 years ago, with the harnessing of water power and mechanization, the industrial revolution began to change Western society dramatically. Great numbers of new and attractive jobs were created in urban centers, requiring individual initiative but at the same time disconnecting many workers from their families and the land. The unprecedented rate of technological change that accompanied this revolution brought unforeseen options and often confusing consequences. Time came to be measured by the clock rather than the changing of the seasons or social events. As new emphasis was placed on mobility and personal gain, families that lived in the same community for many generations began to split apart. Old values were soon called into question.

As technology continued to conquer environmental limitations, it also challenged and altered the existing social organization in complex and far-reaching ways. Prior to the industrial revolution, each generation passed trade skills to the next. Thus, family surnames such as Miller, Carpenter, and Farmer had their origins in the context of work. When the work setting moved from the home and the farm to the factory and office building, greater numbers of people than ever before could enter occupations either new or previously closed to them.

While advances in technology have altered the workplace, they've also significantly affected Americans in many other ways. For example, when Willis Carrier patented the air conditioning system in the early 1900s, he could not have envisioned that his idea would significantly alter U.S. social patterns. Prior to Carrier's invention, most Americans attempted to cool themselves on hot summer nights by sitting on their front porch talking and playing games or visiting with neighbors. The advent of air conditioning soon changed that pattern. Families who could afford the new technology began to spend their summer nights in their homes, while others headed out to local air-conditioned movie houses or restaurants. Thus, a new and more private social existence began to replace the community connectedness that had existed for many generations. This pattern of privacy became further established with the advent of television. Further, air conditioning spurred a continuing migration of Americans to the sun-belt states in the South and Southwest, previously avoided because of their high temperatures (Fussell, 1997).

Computers

Like air conditioning, the personal computer is now significantly affecting our social interactions. In days gone by, the primary form of communication in U.S. society was face-to-face conversations with family, friends, and co-workers. Research findings suggest that this pattern of interaction has begun to change. A recent national study conducted by the Scripps Howard News Service (1997) and Ohio University has revealed that despite having telephones, e-mail, and the Internet, Americans average 13 significant discussions daily. However, fewer than 6 of those discussions occur outside of the work setting. In fact, full-time workers who were surveyed reported that two-thirds of all their conversations take place at work. Findings such as these have led social scientists such as Robert Putnam of Harvard University to conclude that "social connections are moving to the workplace and out of the neighborhood." Rollin Hawley, the director of the Achron Institute of Leadership Development, has interpreted survey results somewhat differently. He suggests that "people talk to many more people today than they did 20 or 30 years ago. But we have less time for the highest form of friendship. We spend so much time working, watching television, and driving vehicles to get to and from work" (Scripps Howard News Service, 1997).

Thus, it seems that although technology has helped us in many ways by allowing us to communicate with co-workers in the office or on another continent, it has deprived us of the intimacy of physical and visual contact. Seeing each other in person allows nonverbal communication, such as hugs, eye contact, facial expressions, gestures, tone of voice, laughter, and a sense of connectedness that comes with someone's physical presence.

Technology and Meaningfulness

As technology extended the realm of the practical, it expanded our vision of what's possible. The science fiction writer has become the prophet of our time. Journeys into space or beneath the sea are no longer far-fetched exercises in imagination. In the past three decades, people have walked on the moon and lived for extended periods in space. And, we can now clone animals and determine a person's health risk through genetic testing. Oceanographers have descended to previously unexpected depths and discovered new life forms.

As technology pulls us into the future, it forces us to reconsider the meaning and purpose we give to our lives. New technological advances confront us with ethical dilemmas that require us to stretch our traditional notions of right and wrong. Now, as never before, we must grapple with the sometimes painful and complex issues determining who shall live, how, and for how long. These are the questions of life purpose as well as personal survival. The history of our culture is thus a story of values in transition, reflecting an endless dance of belief and technology.

> To keep our faces toward change and behave like free spirits in the presence of fate is strength undefeatable.
>
> —*Helen Keller*

Thirteen Changes Affecting Our Life and Work

Change is becoming increasingly rapid as computer technologies and advances in medicine (see Figure 5-1) transform our lives. And, while earlier generations of Americans expected that their job would last a lifetime, today's generations are aware that change is not only possible, it is often unavoidable. We've presented thirteen of the most significant changes, as follows.

1. We are no longer a farm-based society. According to the U.S. Bureau of the Census, 70.5 percent of the U.S. labor force was employed in farming occupations in 1830. In 1990, 98.4 percent of the labor force was employed in non-farming occupations. (*Information Please Almanac*, 1997, p. 156)

2. Our population is getting older. U.S. census data (1994 *Information Please Almanac*) indicates that at the beginning of the 20th century, only 4 percent of Americans were over 65 years of age; by 1990, that figure had risen to 12.4 percent. According to U.S. Department of Labor statistics, the group that includes people 85 and older is growing three times faster than any other segment of the population. In 1990, the median age of U.S. citizens was 36.3 years; it is expected to reach 40.6 years by 2005. Figure 5-2 shows how the age distribution of workers in the labor force, 1975–2005, reflects the aging spiral of the larger society. Figure 5-2 also demonstrates that the fastest-growing segment of the labor force during the years ahead will be those who are age 25 and older. The increasing median age of people in the United States will affect the labor force in at least three ways. First, career opportunities in the medical and social service fields will increase as a result of the rising health-care needs of our older population. Second, a shortage of skilled workers will develop during the latter part of this century because fewer well-trained young people will be entering the labor force. Third, the labor force will become more diverse as more immigrants and women who pursue work to provide additional family income enter jobs that younger workers would normally take. And, later on as now, a growing number of retired workers will replace the declining number of teenagers available to fill lower-level positions in the service industries.

3. The U.S. population is on the move. Census data cited in the 1992 *Information Please Almanac* (p. 771) show that in recent years the northeastern and

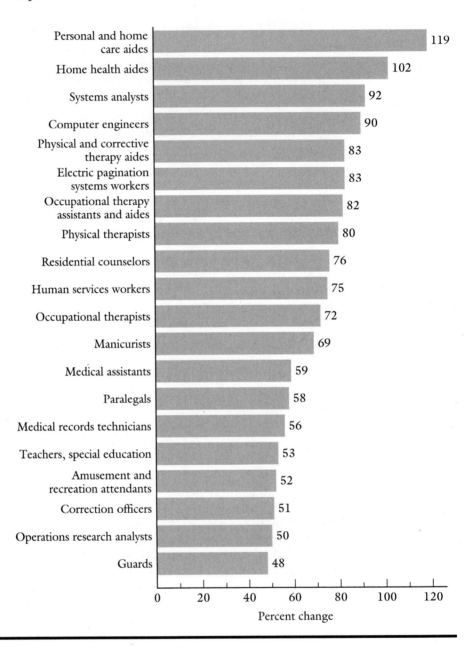

Figure 5-1 Fastest growing occupations, 1994–2005 (U.S. Department of Labor, 1995, p. 15)

Personal and home care aides — 119
Home health aides — 102
Systems analysts — 92
Computer engineers — 90
Physical and corrective therapy aides — 83
Electric pagination systems workers — 83
Occupational therapy assistants and aides — 82
Physical therapists — 80
Residential counselors — 76
Human services workers — 75
Occupational therapists — 72
Manicurists — 69
Medical assistants — 59
Paralegals — 58
Medical records technicians — 56
Teachers, special education — 53
Amusement and recreation attendants — 52
Correction officers — 51
Operations research analysts — 50
Guards — 48

Percent change

midwestern sections of the United States have seen a significant loss of population, while the western and southern parts have shown substantial increases in population (thanks to air conditioning!). Metropolitan areas have continued to grow, while central cities and rural areas have declined.

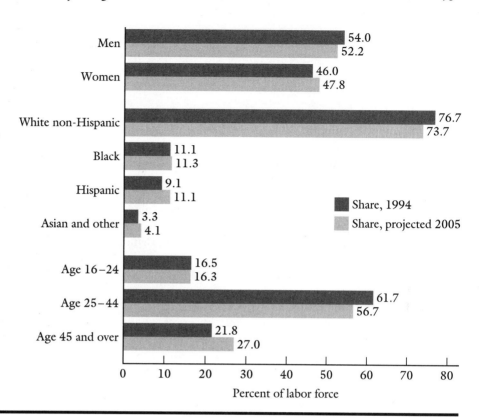

Figure 5-2
Changes in the share of the labor force by gender, age, and race and Hispanic origin, 1994–projected 2005 (U.S. Department of Labor, 1995, p. 10)

Men 54.0 / 52.2
Women 46.0 / 47.8
White non-Hispanic 76.7 / 73.7
Black 11.1 / 11.3
Hispanic 9.1 / 11.1
Asian and other 3.3 / 4.1
Age 16–24 16.5 / 16.3
Age 25–44 61.7 / 56.7
Age 45 and over 21.8 / 27.0

■ Share, 1994
▨ Share, projected 2005

Percent of labor force

4. Birthrates in the United States are on the decline. Data from the National Center for Health Statistics (*Information Please Almanac*, 1997, p. 962) show that in 1910 the birthrate was 30 per 1000 people. In 1950, the figure was 24; by 1991, the rate had dropped to 14.8. If these trends continue, we'll reach zero population growth by the year 2050 (p. 783).

5. U.S. society is becoming more ethnically varied. Current birthrates suggest that in the future, members of ethnic minority groups will be entering the U.S. labor force in greater numbers than they are now; U.S. birthrates, though, do not show a similar increase. This change, coupled with higher numbers of women entering the labor force, will probably create a large number of female and minority workers who will enter at lower-level positions and eventually compete with white men for upper-level positions in the workplace. (See Figure 5-2).

6. The labor force has become more gender balanced. Increasing numbers of women are postponing marriage and childbearing for college and career. (see Figure 5-2). Because of economic necessity and the desire of many women to combine family and career, more dual-career couples are in the work force, and increasing numbers of homemakers are returning to college to advance their careers.

In 1975 women represented 40% of the labor force; it is expected that by 2005 their numbers will increase to 48%.

—*Information Please Almanac*, 1997, p. 426

As a consequence of this change women are assuming greater influence in corporate settings. Now, they have reached a critical mass of 30 to 50 percent in many parts of the business world. Their numbers continue to increase in other professional areas such as administration and management, medicine, and law. However, their salaries continue to be about 20 percent lower than those of men in the same occupations.

The gains women currently experience in the workforce appear to reflect their recent acquisition of needed technical skills and their ability to work effectively with people in an open and democratic manner. Leaders in the corporate world recognize the need for a new style of leadership to respond effectively to better-educated employees and a rapidly changing and highly competitive international marketplace. They now realize that the best way to lead well-educated and self-motivated workers is not by directing and ordering but by encouraging employees' creative insights in carrying out projects and in guiding corporate policy. Given the general orientation toward teaching and service that has been passed down to women over many generations as family caretakers, women are perhaps more effective than men in adapting to these changes. Nonetheless, some women and minority group members working in less socially aware settings still face an artificial glass ceiling that limits their upward social mobility.

7. **Downsizing is occurring with greater frequency in corporate settings.** Recently, major changes in corporate structures have affected the U.S. workplace. Because of both the need to reduce costs in a highly competitive marketplace and advances in technology, large corporations and governmental agencies have been "downsizing" or cutting back on their staff in large numbers, especially in areas such as manufacturing, farming, mining, and clerical work. Like ripples from a pebble thrown into a pond, downsizing affects society in a variety

Sally Forth, © 1992. Reprinted with special permission of King Features Syndicate.

of ways. For one, professional outplacement firms have been doing a very active business. For two, in the future, smaller companies will provide the most jobs. Still another consequence is that some corporations now hire a series of temporary or part-time employees for the same position in order to make sure a position is needed and to search for the most suitable person to fill it. Unfortunately, some workers may find themselves becoming permanently locked into a role as a temporary employee, which may mean they never receive benefits such as sick leave, retirement, or health insurance. Downsizing has also led employees to leave their jobs to create their own small home businesses to subcontract their services to larger organizations, including their former employers.

Today, however, it also appears that the use of downsizing as a way of reducing costs may be slowing down in some areas of corporate America. A recent survey by the American Management Association found that more than half of the participating firms had taken back in-house at least one previously outsourced activity. Further, only 25 percent of the respondents reported that downsizing actually reduced their costs. Despite such tidbits of "good news," employers continue to outsource functions in nine areas, with finance, accounting, information systems, and marketing being the primary areas for cutbacks (Kleman, 1997).

8. We're more conscious of the need to protect our environment. This statement from an article in *Science* magazine presents several observations about humanity's impact on the environment:

> Human alteration of earth is substantial and growing. Between one-third and one-half of the land surface has been transformed by human action; the carbon dioxide concentration in the atmosphere has increased by nearly 30 percent since the beginning of the Industrial Revolution; more atmospheric nitrogen is fixed by humanity than by all natural terrestrial sources combined; more than half of all accessible surface fresh water is put to use by humanity; and about one-quarter of the bird species on earth have been driven to extinction. By these and other standards, it is clear that we live on a human-dominated planet. (Vitousek et al., 1997, p. 494).

Because social scientists and environmentalists have made us aware of humanity's threat to the environment, we have become more attentive to the need to live in harmony with nature and the importance of taking a global social view, in which cooperation and interdependence prevail over individualism, competition, and abuse of natural resources.

9. The knowledge explosion continues. More than 2 decades ago, British authors B. Hopson and P. Hough (1973) noted that at the rate knowledge is accumulating, by the time children born in 1973 completed their education, the amount of knowledge in the world would be 4 times greater than in 1973. By the time those individuals turn 50, in the year 2023, the amount of knowledge will be 32 times greater—and 97 percent of the knowledge in the world will have been acquired within their lifetimes.

10. A free trade movement is afoot throughout the world. According to John Naisbitt and Patricia Aburdene, authors of *Megatrends 2000* (1991), trade barriers separating North and South American, European, and Pacific Rim countries are falling as economic considerations transcend political ideologies. As

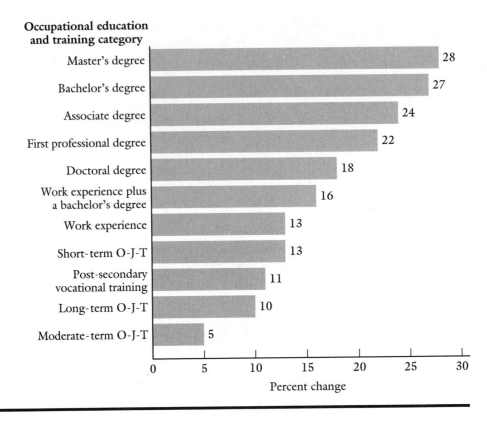

Figure 5-3
Percent change in
occupational em-
ployment by edu-
cation and train-
ing category,
1994–2005 (U.S.
Department of
Labor, 195, p. 7)

described by Naisbitt and Aburdene, "economic forces of the world are surging across national borders resulting in more democracy, more freedom, more trade, more opportunity, and greater prosperity" (p. 20). Consequently, a growing number of nations have been entering into joint ventures with U.S. companies overseas or establishing plants in the United States. This change will place many U.S. workers in the position of working in more international settings under supervision of foreign managers and will require that they become more sensitive to intercultural differences and more fluent in foreign languages.

11. **We are becoming a high-tech and service-oriented society.** Futurists such as John Naisbitt and Patricia Aburdene (1991) and Walter Kiechel III ("How we will work in the year 2000," *Fortune*, May 17, 1993, pp. 41–52), have observed that we are rapidly moving away from a manufacturing and industrial base toward a service-oriented economy involving high technology, rapid communication of information, rapid advancement in biotechnology for use in agriculture and medicine, increased utilization of health care services, and a rising volume of wholesale and retail sales. The U.S. Department of Labor's projections of the most declining and fastest growing occupations, shown in Figures 5-1 through 5-4, mirror these observations about the changing nature of the workplace in our society.

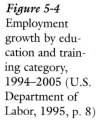

Figure 5-4
Employment growth by education and training category, 1994–2005 (U.S. Department of Labor, 1995, p. 8)

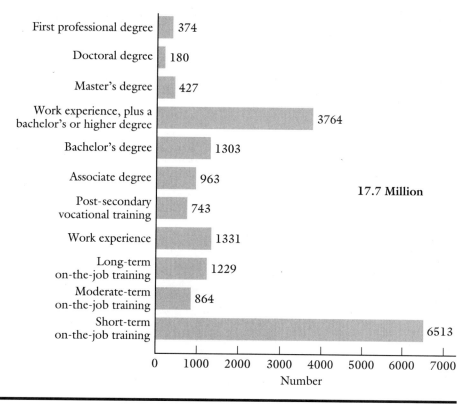

12. Lifelong learning through continuing education has become a necessity. To cope with change, people of diverse ages and backgrounds are going back to the classroom. Some, largely women, are new to the workforce; some are changing jobs; some are upwardly mobile within a field or are required to accumulate additional classes to keep their jobs or maintain professional credentials. As such, the educational level of the population continues to spiral upward. (See Figure 5-3). The Bureau of Labor Statistics projects that 75 percent of graduates who enter the labor force between now and 2005 can expect to find college-level jobs. The remaining college graduate entrants will end up in jobs that traditionally don't require a college degree (U.S. Department of Labor, 1996b, p. 4).

As shown in Figure 5-4, the greatest number of jobs available in the near future will require short-term training experience. However, the salaries for individuals who work these jobs will be considerably lower than the salaries of their more educated counterparts.

13. Over the next decade, job opportunities will be shaped by two factors: job growth and replacement needs. The fastest-growing occupations do not necessarily offer more jobs than slower-growing occupations do. Opportunities in large corporations tend to stem from staff retirements, promotions,

Figure 5-5 Total
job openings due
to growth and re-
placement needs,
1994–2005 (U.S.
Department of
Labor, 1996a)

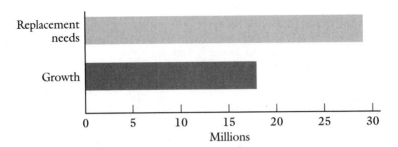

Figure 5-6
Projected job open-
ings due to growth
and replacement
needs by major oc-
cupational group,
1994–2005 (U.S.
Department of
Labor, 1996a)

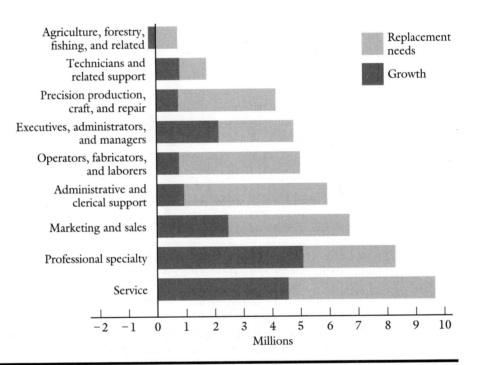

employees seeking new educational and training experiences, career changes, and individuals leaving the workplace to assume homemaking responsibilities.

Replacement needs, which are greatest in low-status and low-paying occupations, tend to be filled by young and part-time workers who have minimal training. The U.S. Department of Labor projects that replacement jobs, of which 29.4 million will open from 1994 to 2000, will provide 12 million more jobs than those arising from employment growth (see Figures 5-5 and 5-6).

Hagar the Horrible, © 1997. Reprinted with special permission of King Features Syndicate.

14. A new paradigm for work is emerging in U.S. society. Organizational development and career planning specialists have noted that the "top-down" administrative structure of organizations that emerged during the industrial revolution is becoming obsolete. In the past, most workers spent their workdays performing repetitive tasks. Although promotions provided relief for some employees, most of them remained trapped in unchallenging routines and had little, if any, input into decisions that affected their jobs.

In recent years, employers have begun to acknowledge that workers perform best when they join together in work teams in which all members have a say in their production efforts. As a consequence of this shift in attitude, a growing number of companies have reorganized themselves to create small flexible teams that they can reconfigure in response to changing market demands. The president of Action Career Management, R. Scott Glendhill (1997), projects that the most successful businesses will have fewer top-level executives and fewer support staff. Those who work in the mid level of the organization will possess specialized knowledge coupled with an ability to perform their own support functions such as using computers to compile and analyze data, monitor the economy, prepare written and oral reports, and interact with the global business community, sometimes in foreign languages.

In addition to making these changes, some wellness-oriented corporations have decided to address the lifestyle needs of their employees by allowing them to work at home, creating flexible hours for workers, providing child- and elder-care services for employee families, offering job-sharing possibilities, and providing healthy cafeteria options.

Glendhill also notes a new attitude emerging among workers. This new view reflects a belief that professionals can no longer rely on their employers to define their destinies. Instead, they view themselves as "free agents" and believe they can shape their careers by acquiring and marketing an array of transferable skills needed to achieve success in changing work environments. Simply put, the next generation of professionals will be guided by the principle "Have skills, will travel."

NEWS RELEASE ACTIVITY

This activity is meant to help you pull together the information presented in this chapter, in a way that's meaningful to you. Your task is to create a news release for public presentation that discusses the state of the American workforce both right now and in the year 2005.

Which of the facts in this chapter do you consider to be the most relevant for college students as they contemplate entering the workforce after they graduate? How can they best prepare for life after college?

REFERENCES AND RESOURCES

Fussell, J. A. (1997, Aug. 14). Well, are you comfy? Bless the man who made our summer bearable. *Columbus Dispatch* (OH), p. 3g.

Glendhill, R. S. (1997). The changing paradigm in career development. *Counseling Today, 40*(3), 54.

Hopson, B., & Hough, P. (1973). *Exercises in personal and career development.* New York; APS Publications.

Information please almanac. (1992), 45th ed. Boston: Houghton Mifflin.

Information please almanac. (1994), 47th ed. Boston: Houghton Mifflin.

Information please almanac. (1997), 50th ed. Boston: Houghton Mifflin.

Kleman, C. (1997). Many firms say they haven't saved money by outsourcing. *Columbus Dispatch* (OH), Employment guide, p. 255.

Naisbitt, J., & Aburdene, P. (1991). *Megatrends 2000.* New York: Avon.

Scripps Howard News Service. (1997, Aug. 14). Chit chat moves out of the neighborhood into the workplace. *Columbus Dispatch* (OH), Section A, p. 1.

U.S. Department of Labor. (1991, May). *Occupational projections and training data.* Washington, DC: U.S. Government Printing Office.

U.S. Department of Labor. (1995, Dec.). *Employment Outlook: 1994–2005. Job quality and other aspects of projected employment growth.* Bulletin 2472. Washington, DC: U.S. Government Printing Office.

U.S. Department of Labor. (1996a). *Occupational outlook handbook.* Lincolnwood, IL: VGM Horizons.

U.S. Department of Labor. (1996b). *Occupational Outlook Quarterly, 40*(2), 4.

Vitousek, P. M., Mooney, H. A., Lubchenco, J., & Meillo, J. M. (1997, July 25). Human dominations of earth's ecosystems. *Science, 277,* 494–499.

CHAPTER 6

PATHS IN THE WORKPLACE

Calvin & Hobbes, © 1992 Watterson. Dist. by Universal Press Syndicate. Reprinted with permission. All rights reserved.

The future is not some place we are going to, but one we are creating. The paths are not to be found, but made, and the activity of making them changes both the maker and the destination.

—*John Schaar*

Randall looks up at the morning sun and the colorful display of autumn leaves in the park. He sits back, closes his eyes, and takes in the warmth of the sun.

For the first time in many years, Randall feels truly alone. When he and Kathie became engaged during their last year of college, they agreed that whoever had the lowest income would work at home and take on the child-care responsibilities for the family. The decision about who would take that role was made for them when Randall created a small mail-order sporting goods business he ran at home via telenetwork.

Now, 18 years later, with his daughter in college in another state, Randall sits alone, wondering if his business skills are current enough for him to enter the corporate world successfully. After giving further thought to his situation, he concludes that not having a specific job objective right now may be a good thing. He wants to work for a large firm in the near future, but needs some time to explore new career options for himself. He decides to take some refresher classes at the nearby junior college and explore other options at the placement office on campus. He knows he can count on Kathie's support and chuckles when he thinks of being a college student at the same time as his daughter.

Knowing how the world of work is organized will help you identify new possibilities and make choices that match your interests and abilities with your level of aspiration. As we shall see, the overall structure of the world of work remains essentially the same, despite shifts in the economy and new technologies. Remember this as you read newspaper articles about how the world of work is dramatically changing. For example, widespread use of the computer and fax machine has created profound changes in the work setting. And it has certainly affected our home lives as well. Yet like the telephone, radio, and TV before it, the computer is essentially a resource for sharing information quickly across great distances. Like any new technology, potential downsides accompany this important resource. For example, computerization may create an atmosphere in which quick responses are expected or favored over reflective thinking. Further, worker roles may become more regimented and impersonal, thus creating a hunger for human contact among workers (Naisbitt & Aburdene, 1991). Can you think of other ways that new technologies affect your life both positively and negatively?

QUESTIONS TO KEEP IN MIND

As you explore potential career paths, keep the following questions in mind:

Who Am I?

Our actions reflect how we see ourselves. If you had your way, what kinds of things would you do on a daily basis in your studies or work to reflect your ideal image of yourself? Do you like working most with things, ideas, data, or people? What do you believe are the most important things you can do during your life, at work, with others, or through leisure pursuits? In which activities do you excel? Are your skills matched with what you like to do and with what matters most to you? Your answers to these questions will reflect who you are as a person and suggest ways you can best express yourself through your career pursuits.

Where Do I Want to Live?

How you live is influenced by where you live. Because some occupations are concentrated in specific geographical areas of the nation, your preferences may limit the occupations you consider. Other factors to consider include the type of climate you prefer, the size of community you'd like to live in, and the cultural and recreational features of that community.

What Will I Do for a Living?

Once you've pulled together some of your lifestyle preferences, you can begin to identify the more specific rewards and demands that will help make a college major or a career suit your goals. A description of the duties and rewards of any major or career you consider would be helpful; such a description should include entry requirements, time commitments, the amount of flexibility the major or career affords, and the level of responsibility it requires. On the rewards side, you need to know what the major or career provides in terms of potential job security, opportunities for entry and advancement, and physical surroundings.

Finally, you'll need to know the types of educational and training experience required in order to enter and advance successfully in an occupation. You'll need to consider carefully your skills, resources, and opportunities, as well as how willing you are to invest your time, energy, and money in meeting these requirements.

Who Will I Spend My Time With?

Since few of us work alone, the people you'll be associating with will be an important ingredient in your daily life as a student or worker. As you explore a major or a career, ask yourself: What are the people who choose this field like? Do I share many interests and values with them? If I do not, how will I deal with the differences? How will my choice of this field affect the people I'm close to now? Will they support my choice, or will they challenge it? If they disagree with my decision, how will I deal with them?

CHOOSING A CAREER PATH

What Types of Work Do I Wish to Pursue?

Thinking about work orientations can help us understand why people gravitate toward particular educational and vocational activities. As discussed in Chapter 3, various environmental, social, and hereditary factors have shaped each individual's work orientation. Similarly, work environments are shaped by the history of the organization, its corporate values, the styles of its key administrators, its resources, and external economic and social demands.

People create their work environments and organize them around more than just common tasks. A work setting is a social fabric woven around common tastes, problems, interests, goals, needs, and ideals. The underlying element in any work setting is the orientation of the individuals attracted to that environment. For example, people who work in the business and sales departments of an organization usually need strong persuasive, managerial, and leadership skills, which they may use to help their company achieve economic, corporate, or social gains. Working in support of the organizational leader may be the business operations staff— accountants, computer specialists, and secretaries—who record, organize, and transmit needed information to their supervisors. Individuals with this type of orientation tend to have more in common than they do with the people in other occupational clusters, such as those with art and science leanings.

When used flexibly, the job cluster–job family scheme can be a helpful tool for describing individuals and organizations. Although a particular occupation or profession may be characterized as most appealing to people with a particular work orientation, actual individuals are less easily stereotyped. Thus, for example, professional accountants working under the same job title in the same firm may differ greatly, depending upon their specialized interest and abilities.

What Levels of Work Am I Most Suited For?

More than four decades ago, 1658 public school students in the city of Cincinnati were asked to state their choice of occupation. Here are the results, summarized by Rebecca Van Namm Dale (1948, p. 419):

> What would Cincinnati be like if these students became the sole inhabitants of the city in the jobs of their choices ten years from now? . . . Health services would be very high, with every eighteen people supporting one doctor. . . . It may be, however, that they would be needed in a city that had no garbage disposal workers, no laundry workers, and no water supply, since no one chose to do that kind of work. . . . The two bus drivers . . . will find that their customers get tired of waiting

and use the services of the sixty-seven airline pilots. It may be difficult getting to Crosley Field to see the forty baseball players.

Have things changed since Dale's survey? Let's find out by having you take a quiz based on a national survey conducted by James Patterson and Peter Kim in 1991. In their book, *The Day Americans Told the Truth,* the authors asked Americans across the country to share their attitudes about a variety of topics, including the occupations they most admire and the sleaziest ways to make a living in the United States. Let's see how your beliefs about the "best" and the "worst" occupations compare with the views of other people in the United States.

In the following columns, write in the titles of the five occupations you most admire and the five you least admire:

Five Occupations I Most Admire	*Five Occupations I Least Admire*
1.	1.
2.	2.
3.	3.
4.	4.
5.	5.

On what basis did you select the "most admired" and the "least admired" occupations? What do your "best" occupations have in common? What do the "worst" occupations share? What adjectives would you use to describe people who work in the "best" and "worst" occupations? Now, turn to Table 6-3 at the end of this chapter. How do your views compare with those of folks from around the country? How great a role do you think stereotypes play in the public view of occupations? In your own views?

Dilbert reprinted by permission of United Feature Syndicate, Inc.

Although many students believe that one should strive for the highest rung on the occupational ladder, our society needs people working in diverse fields and at all levels of the work hierarchy. The U.S. Department of Labor has identified eleven general levels of work available to you. People who work at the highest levels have more responsibility for making decisions and supervising others than do people at the lowest levels. Starting at the highest rung on the ladder, the eleven levels are as follows (U.S. Department of Labor, 1996c):

11. *Occupations that require a first professional degree.* The first professional degree is the minimum preparation required for entry into several professions, including law, medicine, dentistry, and the clergy. Completion of this academic program usually requires at least 2 years of full-time academic study beyond a bachelor's degree. There is no ambiguity about the training requirements for these occupations.

10. *Occupations that generally require a doctoral degree.* The doctoral degree can also be easily related to specific occupations. It usually requires at least 3 years of full-time academic work beyond the bachelor's degree. Completion of this program is required for entry into 6 occupations in academia and the physical, biological, and social sciences.

9. *Occupations that generally require a master's degree.* Completion of a master's degree program usually requires 1 or 2 years of full-time study beyond the bachelor's degree. The master's degree is the usual training requirement for . . . occupations such as management analyst, urban planner, and librarian.

8. *Occupations that generally require work experience in an occupation requiring a bachelor's or higher degree.* Most occupations in this category are managerial occupations that require experience in a related nonmanagerial occupation. Jobs in these occupations generally are filled with experienced staff who are promoted into a managerial position, such as engineers who advance to engineering manager. It is very difficult to become a judge without first working as a lawyer, or to become a personnel, training, or labor relations manager without first gaining experience as a specialist in one of these fields.

7. *Occupations that generally require a bachelor's degree.* This is a degree program requiring at least 4 but not more than 5 years of full-time academic work after high school. The bachelor's degree is considered the minimum training requirement for most professional occupations, such as mechanical engineer, pharmacist, recreational therapist, and landscape architect.

6. *Occupations that generally require an associate's degree.* Completion of this degree program usually requires at least 2 years of full-time academic work after high school. Most occupations in this training category are health related, such as registered nurse, respiratory therapist, and radiologic technologist. Also included are science and mathematics technicians and paralegals.

5. *Occupations that generally require completion of vocational training provided in postsecondary vocational schools.* Workers generally qualify for jobs by completing vocational training programs or by taking job-related college courses that do not result in a degree. Some programs take less than a year to complete and lead to a certificate or diploma. Others last longer than a year but less than 4

years. Occupations in this category include some that only require completion of the training program, such as travel agent, and those in which people who complete the program must pass a licensing exam before they can go to work, such as barber and cosmetologist.

4. *Occupations that generally require skills developed through work experience in a related occupation.* (Some) jobs require skills and experience gained in another occupation. This category includes occupations in which skills may be developed from hobbies or other activities besides current or past employment or from service in the Armed Forces. . . . Among them are cost estimators, who generally need prior work experience in one of the construction trades; police detectives, who are selected based on their experience as police patrol officers; and lawn service managers, who may be hired based on their experience as groundskeepers.

3. *Long-term on-the-job training.* This category includes occupations that generally require more than 12 months of on-the-job training or combined work experience and formal classroom instruction before workers develop the skills needed for average job performance. This category includes occupations such as electrician, bricklayer, and machinist that generally require formal or informal apprenticeships lasting up to 4 years. Also included in this type of training are intensive occupation-specific employer-sponsored programs that workers must successfully complete before they can begin work. These include the fire and police academies and schools for air traffic controllers and flight attendants. In other occupations—insurance sales and securities sales, for example—trainees take formal courses, often provided at the job site, to prepare for the required licensing exams. Individuals undergoing training are generally considered to be employed in the occupation. This group of occupations also includes musicians, athletes, actors, and other entertainers, occupations that require natural ability that must be developed over several years. Eighty-nine occupations employing 13.7 million workers rely on this type of training.

2. *Moderate length on-the-job training.* Workers [in this group] can achieve average job performance after 1 to 12 months of combined on-the-job experience and informal training, which can include observing experienced workers. Individuals undergoing training are generally considered to be employed in the occupation. This type of training is found among occupations such as dental assistants, drywall installers and finishers, operating engineers, and machine operators. This training relies on trainees watching experienced workers and asking questions. Trainees are given progressively more difficult assignments as they demonstrate their mastery of lower level skills.

1. *Short-term on-the-job training.* [This is the] largest training category. Included are occupations like cashier, bank teller, messenger, highway maintenance worker, and veterinary assistant. In these occupations, workers generally can achieve average job performance in just a few days or weeks by working with and observing experienced employees and by asking questions.

You can find examples of how the fastest-growing occupations fit into these levels of training and experience in Table 6-1. Circle the levels and occupations that interest you. After you've circled the occupations, try to figure out what they have in common.

Table 6-1   Jobs Growing the Fastest and Having the Largest Numerical Increase in Employment, 1994–2005, by Level of Education and Training

Fastest-growing occupations	*Occupations having the largest numerical increase in employment*
First-professional degree	
Chiropractors	Lawyers
Lawyers	Physicians
Physicians	Clergy
Clergy	Chiropractors
Podiatrists	Dentists
Doctoral degree	
Medical scientists	College and university faculty
Biological scientists	Biological scientists
College and university faculty	Medical scientists
Mathematicians and all other mathematical scientists	Mathematicians and all other mathematical scientists
Master's degree	
Operations research analysts	Management analysts
Speech-language pathologists and audiologists	Counselors
Management analysts	Speech-language pathologists and audiologists
Counselors	Psychologists
Urban and regional planners	Operations research analysts
Work experience plus bachelor's degree	
Engineering, mathematics, and natural science managers	General managers and top executives
Marketing, advertising, and public relations managers	Financial managers
Artists and commercial artists	Marketing, advertising, and public relations managers
Financial managers	Engineering, mathematics, and natural science managers
Education administrators	Education administrators
Bachelor's degree	
Systems analysts	Systems analysts
Computer engineers	Teachers, secondary school
Occupational therapists	Teachers, elementary school
Physical therapists	Teachers, special education
Special education teachers	Social workers
Associate degree	
Paralegals	Registered nurses
Medical records technicians	Paralegals
Dental hygienists	Radiologic technologists and technicians
Respiratory therapists	Dental hygienists
Radiologic technologists and technicians	Medical records technicians
Postsecondary vocational training	
Manicurists	Secretaries, except legal and medical
Surgical technologists	Licensed practical nurses

Table 6-1 Jobs Growing the Fastest and Having the Largest Numerical Increase in Employment, 1994–2005, by Level of Education and Training *(continued)*

Postsecondary vocational training (continued)

Data processing equipment repairers

Dancers and choreographers

Emergency medical technicians

Hairdressers, hairstylists, and cosmetologists

Legal secretaries

Medical secretaries

Work experience

Nursery and greenhouse managers

Lawn service managers

Food service and lodging managers

Clerical supervisors and managers

Teachers and instructors, vocational and nonvocational training

Marketing and sales worker supervisors

Clerical supervisors and managers

Food service and lodging managers

Instructors, adult education

Teachers and instructors, vocational education and training

Long-term training and experience (more than 12 months of on-the-job training)

Electronic pagination systems workers

Correction officers

Securities and financial services sales workers

Patternmakers and layout workers, fabric and apparel

Producers, directors, actors, and entertainers

Maintenance repairers, general utility

Correction officers

Automotive mechanics

Cooks, restaurant

Police patrol officers

Moderate-length training and experience (1 to 12 months of combined on-the-job experience and informal training)

Physical and corrective therapy assistants and aides

Occupational therapy assistants and aides

Human services workers

Medical assistants

Detectives, except public

Human services workers

Medical assistants

Instructors and coaches, sports and physical training

Dental assistants

Painters and paper hangers, construction and maintenance

Short-term training and experience (up to 1 month of on-the-job experience)

Personal and home care aides

Home health aides

Amusement and recreation attendants

Guards

Adjustment clerks

Cashiers

Janitors and cleaners, including maids and housekeepers

Salespersons, retail

Waiters and waitresses

Home health aides

Source: U.S. Department of Labor, 1996a, p. 7.

See Table 6-2 near the end of this chapter for a more complete listing of the categorization of occupations by job family.

The medical professions offer an example of how a common set of "scientific" skills may be defined differently, depending on whether you attend a 2- or 4-year program to enter a different level of work within the same professional area. Many people are interested in medicine, but they differ in their interests, abilities, person-ality, level of aspiration, finances, and the amount of authority and responsibility they want to assume at work. Those who aspire to and have the capacity for high levels of achievement might attend a professional college and wind up as surgeons, dentists, medical researchers, or head nurses. Other students might attend 2-year programs to be trained as medical technologists, physicians' assistants, paramedics, or practical nurses. Those who do not choose training beyond high school might find on-the-job training opportunities and become aides or orderlies.

Starting at a lower level doesn't mean you have to stay there. For example, a person trained in a medically related specialty at the 2-year level may decide to ad-vance by seeking a 4-year college degree in a related area and perhaps later a grad-uate or professional medical specialty degree. A photographer who has an arts orientation may move up the ladder from a 2-year technical training course to a higher professional level by pursuing an advanced degree. A shop supervisor with a business-contact orientation may take night courses and eventually take a man-agerial position that becomes vacant when the manager moves up to company president.

You can use the same basic skills across a variety of occupations and settings. This fact is good to keep in mind when you're job hunting after graduation. For example, teachers who face a tight job market or who are considering entering a new field may use their teaching skills in business as salespersons, staff develop-ment specialists, public relations specialists, and managerial trainees.

Once you have an idea of the fields or types of work that appeal to you, you need to explore your values, abilities, and desires further and decide at what level in your present or new field you want to start and what level you might ultimately want to reach. You should also think about how the same set of skills can be transferred to different work settings.

Be a pianist, not a piano.

—*A. R. Orange*

What Types of Enterprises Appeal to Me?

Gerald Cosgrave (1973) has identified 11 broad occupational clusters, each com-posing a certain type of enterprise. Although you may prefer certain enterprises because of their purposes, surroundings, or personnel, remember that you can perform the same types and levels of work across a variety of enterprises. Clerical, teaching, and numerical skills serve in many occupational settings, not just the most obvious ones. Keeping this idea in mind will help you to see a broader range of opportunities in today's job market.

As you read the descriptions of the types of enterprises, which follow, try to identify several areas that appeal to you and what you like about them. Imagine how you could use your skills and interests in each area.

Agriculture   Agriculture, which includes fishing and forestry, comprises many occupations we would call "technical." Unskilled work in this area might involve physical labor or maintenance on a farm, at a park, or at a resort. Other jobs in agriculture require more education, such as breeding dairy cattle, managing a fish hatchery, or reforesting a lumber site. Professional-level jobs could range from heading an oceanography expedition to managing or teaching in the parks and recreation program of a large city or running a landscaping or agricultural business.

Mining   Mining industries need unskilled labor, trained workers such as mine inspectors, and even more highly educated workers, such as geologists, mining engineers, and researchers who deal with the extractions and use of minerals.

Construction   The construction industry requires unskilled laborers as well as numerous skilled tradespeople—carpenters, electricians, masons, welders, and other technical types. Higher-level professionals whose work is related to construction include architects and engineers, who may have a scientific or business operations as well as a technical orientation.

Manufacturing   Manufacturing is a vast network of industries that includes jobs in almost every area of interest. Common jobs are assembly line worker and supervisor. Some workers might be managers or technicians who design and run equipment and plants. The upper levels in these enterprises can include product testers, researchers, or engineers. Although many of these jobs are technical or scientific, technical people are also needed in personnel and public relations, and those with business-contact talents may find outlets in sales and advertising.

Utilities   Utilities require a large number of employees for function and upkeep. Lower levels in this area require technical and business-operations interests. Workers at these levels include repair persons, switchboard operators, and clerks. Other jobs may include managing staff at lower levels or may be more business-contact oriented, such as sales managers and public relations specialists. People with the highest level of education in these industries might be engineers, who solve problems and develop new products, or top-level managers with financial specialties.

Transportation   The transportation industry tends to be technical and oriented toward business operations. It offers many semiskilled jobs, such as jobs in loading and delivery and the occupations of dispatcher, trucker, and flight attendant. The next level includes fleet managers, vehicle repairpersons, and highway inspectors, among others. Airline pilots, urban planners, and highway designers require the highest levels of training in this field.

Communication   Communication fields expand to include almost all fields. Although this area has fewer semiskilled jobs than many fields do, it does have some, such as apprentice technician who assists in setting up audio and video equipment for radio or camera operators broadcasting from a site some distance away from the home station. Many entry-level jobs require an intermediate level of skill or education, such as the jobs of newspaper reporter, copy editor, TV camera operator, or photographer. Professional-level jobs may require substantial experience or skill: news managers for TV stations, newspaper editors, publicity or

Beetle Bailey, © 1997. Reprinted with special permission of King Features Syndicate.

public relations and advertising executives, or more glamorous jobs such as those of TV commentators, foreign correspondents, or novelists.

Trade   Trade and related enterprises offer many opportunities for a relatively untrained worker to make a start. Some are technical, such as loading trucks or stocking retail stores. Others require business-operations interests such as inventory ordering or cashiering. Still others require business-contact persons such as salespeople or product demonstrators. Jobs with more training or experience include those of buyer, department manager, or regional sales representative. Advertising employs people with art interests for copyrighting, photography, or layout and design. The highest-level jobs often involve business-contact skills for managing employees or buying for whole areas or chains. Also employed at this level may be personnel or labor relations experts, industrial and consulting psychologists, educators, and public relations people. Many large companies have programs that permit an entry-level worker to work up to or train for middle- or higher-level jobs with the firm.

Finance   Finance often attracts people oriented toward business operations and contacts. One may begin in this area as a bank teller or as a clerk for an insurance or loan company. Jobs with more responsibilities include auditor and loan officer. Higher-level jobs include accountant or financial manager for a business.

Service   The service industries include jobs in which something is being done for someone. For this reason, they attract people who have service and business-contact orientations. Jobs in service areas requiring some training include those of beautician or barber, lab technician, or probation officer. Higher-level social-service professionals include doctors, nurses, psychologists, teachers, and museum curators.

Government   City, county, and federal governments hire people for varied kinds of work at all levels and in all job families. Many jobs available in private industries have counterparts in government. Admission and advancement in most government jobs are regulated by civil service tests, which one must pass to qualify for a certain job or level. Exams for beginning-level jobs test literacy and common sense as well as specific skills. Such jobs include clerk/typist or mail carrier. Middle-level jobs include office management, law enforcement, and the inspection of government-supported institutions such as schools and hospitals. High-level jobs include such varied positions as judge, environmental specialist, and economist. Many government jobs—from dog catcher to U.S. president—are not part of the civil service system and are elected or appointed. These may require credentials or assets beyond one's ability or training, such as money for campaigns, political influence, and a willingness to take risks. Of course, like any profession, civil service carries with it a particular public image:

> Three boys were heading home from school one day when one started the time-honored game of paternal one-upmanship. He said, "My dad's faster than any of yours. He can throw a 90-mph fast ball from the pitcher's mound and run and catch it just after it crosses the plate!"
>
> One of the other boys said, "Oh yeah? Well my dad can shoot an arrow from a bow and run to the target and hold it up to make sure the arrow hits the bullseye!"
>
> The last boy said, "Your dads don't even come close to being faster than mine. My dad's a civil servant, and even though he works every day until 4:00, he always gets home at 3:30!"

Your satisfaction with a job rests on the interaction of three elements we've discussed: orientation, level, and kind of job. You'll need to investigate and evaluate your orientation, skills, and work environments. Which combination of work orientations—business contact, business operations, technical, science, arts, social service—best describes you? (See Chapter 3.) Look at the eleven levels of work for each of those orientations and within your areas of interest. Pinpoint the various enterprises and areas of interests that appeal to you, and investigate the types of jobs they offer. Begin to evaluate how these match up with your aspirations and abilities. Job satisfaction is determined not by any single factor but by the relationship among what we aspire to do, what we can do, and the rewards and demands at a specific level of work.

FUNCTIONAL SKILLS SURVEY

Listed here are the functional or transferable skills identified by the U.S. Department of Labor that may be used in settings that require working with data, people, and things.[1] Place a check mark next to each skill you believe you possess. For example, under the category "Data," you'd check "Synthesizing" if you think you have that skill.

---

[1] *Source:* U.S. Department of Labor, 1977.

Data

Information, knowledge, and conceptions, related to data, people, or things, obtained by observation, investigation, interpretation, visualization, and mental creation. Data are intangible and include numbers, words, symbols, ideas, concepts, and oral verbalization.

_____ *Synthesizing:* Integrating analyses of data to discover facts and/or develop knowledge, concepts, or interpretations.

_____ *Coordinating:* Determining time, place, and sequence of operations or action to be taken on the basis of analysis of data; executing determination and/or reporting on events.

_____ *Analyzing:* Examining and evaluating data; presenting alternative actions in relation to the evaluation is frequently involved.

_____ *Compiling:* Gathering, collating, or classifying information about data, people, or things; reporting and/or carrying out a prescribed action in relation to the information is frequently involved.

_____ *Computing:* Performing arithmetic operations and reporting on and/or carrying out a prescribed action in relation to them; does not include counting.

_____ *Copying:* Transcribing, entering, or posting data.

_____ *Comparing:* Judging the readily observable functional, structural, or compositional characteristics (whether similar to or divergent from obvious standards) of data, people, or things.

☐ Total Checked

People

Human beings; also animals dealt with on an individual basis as if they were human

_____ *Mentoring:* Dealing with individuals in terms of their total personality in order to advise, counsel, and/or guide them with regard to problems that may be resolved by legal, scientific, clinical, spiritual, and/or other professional principles.

_____ *Negotiating:* Exchanging ideas, information, and opinions with others to formulate policies and programs and/or arrive jointly at decisions, conclusions, or solutions.

_____ *Instructing:* Teaching subject matter to others, or training others (including animals) through explanation, demonstration, and supervised practice, or making recommendations on the basis of technical disciplines.

_____ *Supervising:* Determining or interpreting work procedures for a group of workers, assigning specific duties to them, maintaining harmonious relations among them, and promoting efficiency; a variety of responsibilities is involved in this function.

_____ *Diverting:* Amusing others (usually accomplished through the medium of stage, screen, television, or radio).

_____ *Persuading:* Influencing others in favor of a product, service, or point of view.

_____ *Speaking; signaling:* Talking with and/or signaling people to convey or exchange information; includes giving assignments and/or directions to helpers or assistants.

_____ *Serving:* Attending to the needs or requests of people or animals or the expressed or implicit wishes of people; immediate response is involved.

_____ *Taking instructions; helping:* Helping applies to "nonlearning" helpers; no variety of responsibility is involved in this function.

☐ Total Checked

Things

Inanimate objects as distinguished from human beings, substances, or materials: machines, tools, equipment, and products. A thing is tangible and has shape, form, and other physical characteristics.

_____ *Setting up:* Adjusting machines or equipment by replacing or altering tools, jigs, fixtures, and attachments to prepare them to perform their functions, change their performance, or restore their proper functioning if they break down; workers who set up one or a number of machines for other workers or who set up and personally operate a variety of machines are included here.

_____ *Precision working:* Using body members and/or tools or work aids to work, move, guide, or place objects or materials in situations where ultimate responsibility for the attainment of standards occurs and selection of appropriate tools, objects, or materials and the adjustment of the tool to the task require exercise of considerable judgment.

_____ *Operating; controlling:* Starting, stopping, controlling, and adjusting the progress of machines or equipment; operating machines involves setting up and adjusting the machine or material(s) as the work progresses; controlling involves observing gauges, dials, etc., and turning valves and other devices to regulate factors such as temperature, pressure, flow of liquids, speed of pumps, and reaction of materials.

_____ *Driving; operating:* Starting, stopping, and controlling the actions of machines or equipment for which a course must be steered, or which must be guided, in order to fabricate, process, and/or move things or people; involves such activities as observing gauges and dials, estimating distances and determining speed and direction of other objects, turning cranks and wheels, pushing or pulling gear lifts or levers; includes such machines as cranes, conveyor systems, tractors, furnace charging machines, paving machines, and hoisting machines; excludes manually powered machines, such as handtrucks and dollies, and power assisted machines, such as electric wheelbarrows.

_____ *Manipulating:* Using body members, tools, or special devices to work, move, guide, or place objects or materials; involves some latitude for judgment with regard to precision attained and selecting appropriate tool, object, or material, although this is readily manifest.

_____ *Tending:* Starting, stopping, and observing the functioning of machines and equipment; involves adjusting materials or controls of the machine, such as changing guides, adjusting timers and temperature gauges, turning valves to allow flow of materials, and flipping switches in response to light; little judgment is involved in making these adjustments.

_____ *Feeding; offbearing:* Inserting, throwing, dumping, or placing materials in or removing them from machines or equipment which are automatic or tended or operated by other workers.

_____ *Handling:* Using body members, hand tools, and/or special devices to work, move, or carry objects or materials; involves little or no latitude for judgment with regard to attainment of standards or in selecting appropriate tools, objects, or material.

Total Checked

Write in the total number of skills checked for each functional skill area below:

Total	Skill Area
_____	Data
_____	People
_____	Things

How do your results on the survey compare with your scores on the self-assessment inventory of your preferences, interests, and skills? Do the two surveys reveal a similar pattern or do they differ in substantial ways? If they do differ, how do you explain the differences?

OCCUPATIONAL EDUCATION AND TRAINING REQUIREMENTS CATEGORIES

What level of work suits you now? Place an "X" next to the level that best applies to you now. Then, place an "O" next to the level you'd like to be at in ten years. What do you need to do to achieve your long-term goal?

_____ **First professional degree.** *Occupations that require a professional degree.* Completion of the academic program usually requires at least 6 years of full-time equivalent academic study, including college study prior to entering the professional degree program.

_____ **Doctoral degree.** *Occupations that generally require a Ph.D. or other doctoral degree.* Completion of the degree program usually requires at least 3 years of full-time equivalent academic work beyond the bachelor's degree.

_____ **Master's degree.** *Occupations that generally require a master's degree.* Completion of the degree program usually requires 1 or 2 years of full-time equivalent study beyond the bachelor's degree.

_____ **Work experience, plus a bachelor's or higher degree.** *Occupations that generally require work experience in an occupation requiring a bachelor's or higher degree.* Most occupations in this category are managerial occupations that require experience in a related nonmanagerial position.

_____ **Bachelor's degree.** *Occupations that generally require a bachelor's degree.* Completion of the degree program generally requires at least 4 years but not more than 5 years of full-time equivalent academic work.

_____ **Associate degree.** *Occupations that generally require an associate degree.* Completion of the degree program usually requires at least 2 years of full-time equivalent academic work.

_____ **Post-secondary vocational training.** *Occupations that generally require completion of vocational school training.* Some programs last only a few weeks while others may last more than a year. In some occupations, a license is needed that requires passing an examination after completion of the training.

_____ **Work experience.** *Occupations that generally require skills obtained through work experience in a related occupation.* Some occupations requiring work experience are supervisory or managerial occupations.

_____ **Long-term on-the-job training.** *Occupations that generally require more than 12 months of on-the-job training or combined work experience and formal classroom instruction for workers to develop the skills needed for average job performance.* This category includes formal and informal apprenticeships that may last up to 4 years and short-term intensive employer-sponsored training that workers must successfully complete. Individuals undergoing training are generally considered to be employed in the occupation. This category includes occupations in which workers may gain experience in nonwork activities, such as professional athletes who gain experience through participation in athletic programs in academic institutions.

_____ **Moderate-term on-the-job training.** *Occupations in which workers can develop the skills needed for average job performance after 1 to 12 months of combined on-the-job experience and informal training.*

_____ **Short-term on-the-job training.** *Occupations in which workers generally can develop the skills needed for average job performance after a short demonstration or up to 1 month of on-the-job experience and instruction.*

EXPLORING APPEALING ENTERPRISES

Circle three types of enterprise that most appeal to you as possible work settings when you graduate.

a. agriculture
b. mining
c. construction
d. manufacturing
e. utilities
f. transportation

g. communication
h. trade
i. finance
j. service
k. government

In the spaces that follow, list the enterprises you have circled, tell why you selected them, and list the functional skills you have that may be used in each setting. Also list where you acquired those skills (for example, "part-time work at a fast-food restaurant after school and summer vacations"). Use the functional skills list from the Functional Skills Survey (pp. 115–118) to help you respond.

1. Type of enterprise: _____

   a. My reasons for selecting this enterprise are _____

   _____

   _____

   b. The functional skills I may use in this enterprise are _____

   _____

   _____

   c. I learned these skills through _____

   _____

   _____

2. Type of enterprise: _____

   a. My reasons for selecting this enterprise are _____

   _____

   _____

   b. The functional skills I may use in this enterprise are _____

   _____

   _____

   c. I learned these skills through _____

   _____

   _____

3. Type of enterprise: _____

   a. My reasons for selecting this enterprise are _____

   _____

   _____

   b. The functional skills I may use in this enterprise are _____

   _____

   _____

   c. I learned these skills through _____

   _____

   _____

Table 6-2 Matrix of Occupations Listed by Education and Training Category[1]

First professional degree

Chiropractors
Clergy
Dentists

Lawyers
Ophthalmologists
Physicians

Podiatrists
Veterinarians and veterinary
  inspectors

Doctoral degree

All other life scientists
Biological scientists
College and university faculty

Mathematicians and all other
  mathematical scientists
Medical scientists

Physicists and astronomers

Master's degree

All other social scientists
All other teachers and instructors
Counselors
Curators, architects, museum
  technicians and restorers

Librarians, professional
Management analysts
Operations research analysts
Psychologists

Speech language pathologists and
  audiologists
Urban and regional planners

Work experience plus bachelor's or higher degree

Administrative services managers
All other managers and
  administrators
Artists and commercial artists
Communications, transportation,
  and utilities operations
  managers
Education administrators

Engineering, mathematics, and
  natural science managers
Farm managers
Financial managers
General managers and top
  executives
Government chief executives and
  legislators

Judges, magistrates, and other
  judicial workers
Marketing, advertising, and public
  relations managers
Personnel, training, and labor
  relations managers
Purchasing managers

Bachelor's degree

Accountants and auditors
Actuaries
Aeronautical and astronautical
  engineers
Agricultural and food scientists
All other computer scientists
All other engineers
All other management support
  workers
All other physical scientists
All other professional workers
All other therapists
Animal breeders and trainers
Architects, except landscape and
  marine
Budget analysts
Chemical engineers
Chemists
Civil engineers, including traffic
  engineers

Claims examiners, property and
  casualty insurance
Clinical laboratory technologists
  and technicians
Computer engineers
Computer programmers
Construction managers
Credit analysts
Designers, except interior
Dietitians and nutritionists
Directors, religious activities and
  education
Economists
Electrical and electronics
  engineers
Employment interviewers, private
  or public employment service
Farm and home management
  advisors
Foresters and conservation scientists

Geologists, geophysicists, and
  oceanographers
Industrial engineers, except safety
  engineers
Industrial production managers
Interior designers
Landscape architects
Loan officers and counselors
Mechanical engineers
Metallurgists and metallurgical,
  ceramic, and materials engineers
Nuclear engineers
Occupational therapists
Personnel, training, and labor
  relations specialists
Petroleum engineers
Pharmacists
Physical therapists
Physician assistants

(continued)

Table 6-2   Matrix of Occupations Listed by Education and Training Category[1] *(continued)*

Bachelor's degree *(continued)*

Property and real estate managers
Public relations specialists and publicity writers
Purchasing agents, except wholesale, retail, and farm products
Recreation workers
Recreational therapists
Reporters and correspondents

Residential counselors
Social workers
Statisticians
Systems analysts
Tax examiners, collectors, and revenue agents
Teachers, elementary school

Teachers, preschool and kindergarten
Teachers, secondary school
Teachers, special education
Underwriters
Wholesale and retail buyers, except farm products
Writers and editors, including technical writers

Associate's degree

All other engineering technicians and technologists
All other health professionals and paraprofessionals
All other legal assistants, including law clerks
Cardiology technologists
Dental hygienists

Electrical and electronic technicians and technologists
Medical records technicians
Nuclear medicine technologists
Paralegals
Psychiatric technicians
Radiologic technologists and technicians

Registered nurses
Respiratory therapists
Science and mathematics technicians
Veterinary technicians and technologists

Postsecondary vocational training

Aircraft engine specialists
Aircraft mechanics
All other communications equipment mechanics, installers, and repairers
All other electrical and electronic equipment mechanics, installers, and repairers
Barbers
Broadcast technicians
Central office and PBX installers and repairers
Dancers and choreographers
Data entry keyers, composing

Data entry keyers, except composing
Data processing equipment repairers
Drafters
Electronic home entertainment equipment repairers
Electronics repairers, commercial and industrial equipment
Emergency medical technicians
Hairdressers, hairstylists, and cosmetologists
Legal secretaries
Licensed practical nurses

Manicurists
Medical secretaries
Radio mechanics
Sales agents, real estate
Secretaries, except legal and medical
Station installers and repairers, telephone
Stenographer
Surgical technologists
Surveyors
Travel agents
Welders and cutters

Work experience in a related occupation

Aircraft assemblers, precision
All other precision assemblers
All other service workers
Blue-collar worker supervisors
Brokers, real estate
Captains and other officers, fishing vessels
Captains and pilots, ship
Clerical supervisors and managers
Construction and building inspectors

Cost estimators
Custom tailors and sewers
Electrical and electronic equipment assemblers, precision
Electromechanical equipment assemblers, precision
Fire fighting and prevention supervisors
Fire inspection occupations
Fitters, structural metal, precision
Food service and lodging managers

Inspectors and compliance officers, except construction
Inspectors, testers, and graders, precision
Institutional cleaning supervisors
Instructors, adult (nonvocational) education
Lawn service managers
Locomotive engineers
Machine builders and other precision machine assemblers

Table 6-2 Matrix of Occupations Listed by Education and Training Category[1] *(continued)*

Work experience in a related occupation (continued)

Marketing and sales worker
  supervisors
Mates, ship, boat, and barge
New accounts clerks, banks
Nursery and greenhouse managers
Police and detective supervisors
Police detectives and investigators

Programmers, numerical, tool, and
  process control
Rail yard engineers, dinkey
  operators, and hostlers
Railroad brake, signal, and switch
  operators
Railroad conductors and yardmasters

Real estate appraisers
Ship engineers
Supervisors, farm, forestry, and
  agriculture-related occupations
Teachers and instructors, vocational
  education and training

Long-term on-the-job training

Air traffic controllers and airplane
  dispatchers
Aircraft pilots and flight engineers
All other mechanics, installers, and
  repairers
All other plant and system
  operators
All other precision food and
  tobacco workers
All other precision metal workers
All other precision textile, apparel,
  and furnishings workers
All other precision woodworkers
All other precision workers
All other printing workers,
  precision
Athletes, coaches, umpires, and
  related workers
Automotive body and related
  repairers
Automotive mechanics
Boilermakers
Bricklayers and stone masons
Bus and truck mechanics and
  diesel engine specialists
Butchers and meatcutters
Cabinetmakers and bench
  carpenters
Camera operators
Carpenters
Chemical plant and system
  operators
Coin and vending machine
  servicers and repairers
Compositors and typesetters,
  precision
Concrete and terrazzo finishers
Cooks, institution or cafeteria

Cooks, restaurant
Correction officers
Dental laboratory technicians,
  precision
Electric meter installers and
  repairers
Electric powerline installers and
  repairers
Electricians
Electromedical and biomedical
  equipment repairers
Electronic pagination systems
  workers
Elevator installers and repairers
Farm equipment mechanics
Farmers
Fire fighters
Flight attendants
Funeral directors and morticians
Furniture finishers
Gas and petroleum plant and
  system occupations
Glaziers
Hard tile setters
Heating, air-conditioning, and
  refrigeration mechanics and
  installers
Home appliance and power tool
  repairers
Industrial machine mechanics
Insurance adjusters, examiners, and
  investigators
Insurance sales workers
Jewelers and silversmiths
Job printers
Machinists
Maintenance repairers, general
  utility

Millwrights
Mining, quarrying, and tunneling
  occupations
Mobile heavy equipment mechanics
Motorcycle repairers
Musical instrument repairers and
  tuners
Musicians
Office machine and cash register
  servicers
Optical goods workers, precision
Opticians, dispensing and measuring
Paste-up workers
Patternmakers and layout workers,
  fabric and apparel
Photoengravers
Photographic process workers,
  precision
Plasterers
Platemakers
Plumbers, pipefitters, and
  steamfitters
Police patrol officers
Power distributors and dispatchers
Power generating and reactor plant
  operators
Precision instrument repairers
Producers, directors, actors, and
  entertainers
Radio and TV announcers and
  newscasters
Riggers
Securities and financial services sales
  workers
Sheriffs and deputy sheriffs
Shipfitters

(continued)

Table 6-2   Matrix of Occupations Listed by Education and Training Category[1] *(continued)*

Long-term on-the-job training *(continued)*

Shoe and leather workers and repairers, precision
Small engine specialists
Stationary engineers
Strippers, printing

Structural and reinforcing metal workers
Telephone and cable TV line installers and repairers
Tool and die makers

Upholsterers
Watchmakers
Water and liquid waste treatment plant and system operators
Wood machinists

Moderate length on-the-job training

All other adjusters and investigators
All other communications equipment operators
All other construction trades workers
All other extraction and related workers
All other machine operators, tenders, setters, and set-up operators
All other machine tool cutting and forming setters and set-up operators
All other material moving equipment operators
All other metal and plastic machine setters, operators, and related workers
All other oil and gas extraction occupations
All other printing press setters and set-up operators
All other printing, binding, and related workers
All other sales and related workers
All other technicians
All other transportation and material moving equipment operators
Bakers, bread and pastry
Bakers, manufacturing
Bicycle repairers
Bindery machine operators and set-up operators
Boiler operators and tenders, low pressure
Bookbinders
Bookkeeping, accounting, and auditing clerks
Bus drivers, except school

Camera and photographic equipment repairers
Camera operators, television, motion picture, and video
Carpet installers
Ceiling tile installers and acoustical carpenters
Cement and gluing machine operators and tenders
Central office operators
Chemical equipment controllers, operators, and tenders
Coating, painting, and spraying machine operators, tenders, and setters
Combination machine tool setters, set-up operators, and operators
Computer operators, except peripheral equipment
Cooking and roasting machine operators and tenders, food and tobacco
Cooks, private household
Crane and tower operators
Crushing and mixing machine operators and tenders
Cutting and slicing machine setters, operators, and tenders
Dairy processing equipment operators, including setters
Dental assistants
Detectives, except public
Directory assistance operators
Dispatchers, except police, fire, and ambulance
Dispatchers, police, fire, and ambulance
Drilling machine tool setters and set-up operators, metal and plastic

Drywall installers and finishers
EKG technicians
Electrolytic plating machine operators and tenders, setters and set-up operators
Electroneurodiagnostic technologists
Electronic semiconductor processors
Excavation and loading machine operators
Extruding and forming machine operators and tenders, synthetic fiber
Extruding and forming machine setters, operators and tenders
Foundry mold assembly and shakeout workers
Furnace operators and tenders
Furnace, kiln, or kettle operators and tenders
Grader, dozer, and scraper operators
Grinding machine setters and set-up operators, metal and plastic
Head sawyers and sawing machine operators and tenders
Heat treating machine operators and tenders, metal and plastic
Hoist and winch operators
Housekeepers and butlers
Human services workers
Instructors and coaches, sports and physical training
Insulation workers
Insurance claims clerks
Insurance policy processing clerks
Lathe and turning machine tool setters and set-up operators, metal and plastic

Table 6-2 Matrix of Occupations Listed by Education and Training Category[1] *(continued)*

Moderate length on-the-job training (continued)

Laundry and drycleaning machine operators and tenders, except pressing
Letterpress operators
Locksmiths and safe repairers
Log handling equipment operators
Logging tractor operators
Machine forming operators and tenders, metal and plastic
Machine tool cutters, operators, and tenders, metal and plastic
Medical assistants
Metal fabricators, structural metal products
Metal mold machine operators and tenders, setters and set-up operators
Numerical control machine tool operators and tenders, metal and plastic
Occupational therapy assistants and aides
Offset lithographic press operators
Operating engineers
Other law enforcement occupations
Packaging and filling machine operators and tenders
Painters and paperhangers, construction and maintenance

Painters, transportation equipment
Paper goods machine setters and set-up operators
Paving, surfacing, and tamping equipment operators
Peripheral EDP equipment operators
Pest controllers and assistants
Pharmacy technicians
Photoengraving and lithographic machine operators and tenders
Photographers
Physical and corrective therapy assistants and aides
Pipelayers and pipelaying fitters
Plastic mold machine operators and tenders, setters and set-up operators
Pressing machine operators and tenders, textile, garment, and related materials
Printing press machine setters, operators, and tenders
Punching machine setters and set-up operators, metal and plastic
Roofers
Screen printing machine setters and set-up operators
Separating and still machine operators and tenders
Sewing machine operators, garment

Sewing machine operators, non-garment
Sheet metal workers and duct installers
Shoe sewing machine operators and tenders
Soldering and brazing machine operators and setters
Sprayers and applicators
Statistical clerks
Subway and streetcar operators
Textile bleaching and dying machine operators and tenders
Textile draw-out and winding machine operators and tenders
Textile machine setters and set-up operators
Tire building machine operators
Title examiners and searchers
Typesetting and composing machine operators and tenders
Typists and word processors
Welding machine setters, operators, and tenders
Welfare eligibility workers and interviewers
Woodworking machine operators and tenders, setters and set-up operators

Short-term on-the-job training

Able seamen, ordinary seamen, and marine oilers
Adjustment clerks
Advertising clerks
All other agriculture, forestry, fishing, and related workers
All other assemblers, fabricators, and hand workers
All other cleaners and building service workers
All other clerical and administrative support workers

All other food preparation and service workers
All other health service workers
All other helpers, laborers, and material movers, hand
All other material recording, scheduling, and distribution workers
All other motor vehicle operators
All other protective service workers
All other timber cutting and related logging workers

Ambulance drivers and attendants, except emergency medical technicians
Amusement and recreation attendants
Animal caretakers, except farm
Baggage porters and bellhops
Bank tellers
Bartenders
Bill and account collectors
Billing, cost, and rate clerks

(continued)

Table 6-2   Matrix of Occupations Listed by Education and Training Category[1] *(continued)*

Short-term on-the-job training *(continued)*

Billing, posting, and calculating machine operators
Brokerage clerks
Bus drivers, school
Cannery workers
Cashiers
Child-care workers
Child-care workers, private household
Cleaners and servants, private household
Coil winders, tapers, and finishers
Cooks, short order and fast food
Correspondence clerks
Counter and rental clerks
Court clerks
Credit authorizers
Credit checkers
Crossing guards
Customer service representatives, utilities
Cutters and trimmers, hand
Dining room and cafeteria attendants and bartender helpers
Driver/sales workers
Duplication, mail, and other office machine operators
Electrical and electronic assemblers
Fallers and buckers
Farm workers
File clerks
Fishers, hunters, and trappers
Food counter, fountain, and related workers
Food preparation workers
Forest and conservation workers
Freight, stock, and material movers, hand
Gardeners and groundskeepers, except farm
General office clerks
Grinders and polishers, hand

Guards
Hand packers and packagers
Helpers, construction trades
Highway maintenance workers
Home health aides
Hosts and hostesses, restaurant, lounge, and coffee shop
Hotel desk clerks
Industrial truck and tractor operators
Interviewing clerks, except personnel and social welfare
Janitors and cleaners, including maids and housekeepers
Lawn maintenance workers
Library assistants and bookmobile drivers
Loan and credit clerks
Loan interviewers
Machine assemblers
Machine feeders and offbearers
Mail clerks, except mail machine operators and Postal Service
Meat, poultry, and fish cutters and trimmers, hand
Messengers
Meter readers, utilities
Motion picture projectionists
Municipal clerks
Nursery workers
Nursing aides, orderlies, and attendants
Order clerks, material, merchandise, and service
Order fillers, wholesale and retail sales
Painting, coating, and decorating workers, hand
Parking lot attendants
Payroll and timekeeping clerks
Personal and home care aides
Personnel clerks, except payroll and timekeeping

Pharmacy assistants
Photographic processing machine operators and tenders
Postal mail carriers
Postal Service clerks
Pressers, hand
Procurement clerks
Production, planning, and expediting clerks
Proofreaders and copy markers
Pruners
Psychiatric aides
Real estate clerks
Receptionists and information clerks
Refuse collectors
Reservation and transportation ticket agents and travel clerks
Roustabouts
Salespersons, retail
Service station attendants
Sewers, hand
Shampooers
Solderers and brazers
Statement clerks
Stock clerks
Switchboard operators
Taxi drivers and chauffeurs
Teacher aides and educational assistants
Technical assistants, library
Tire repairers and changers
Traffic, shipping, and receiving clerks
Truck drivers, light and heavy
Ushers, lobby attendants, and ticket takers
Vehicle washers and equipment cleaners
Veterinary assistants
Waiters and waitresses
Weighers, measurers, checkers, and samplers

[1]Source: U.S. Department of Labor, 1996c, pp. 7–9.

Table 6-3 America's Most and Least Admired Occupations

Top 20: Occupations Americans Most Admire	Bottom 20: America's Sleaziest Ways to Make a Living
1. fireman	1. drug dealer
2. paramedic	2. organized crime boss
3. farmer	3. TV evangelist
4. pharmacist	4. prostitute
5. grade school teacher	5. street peddler
6. mailman	6. local politician
7. Catholic priest	7. congressman
8. housekeeper	8. car salesman
9. babysitter	9. rock and roll star
10. college professor	10. insurance salesman
11. airline pilot	11. labor union leader
12. rabbi	12. Wall Street executive
13. scientist	13. real estate agent
14. chef/cook	14. TV network executive
15. flight attendant	15. oil company executive
16. dentist	16. lawyer
17. engineer	17. soap opera star
18. accountant	18. motion picture star
19. Protestant minister	19. investment broker
20. medical doctor	20. prison guard

Patterson and Kim, 1991, pp. 143–144.

A Test of Your Knowledge and Imagination

Here's a challenge you can take on by yourself, with a classmate, or with family and friends. Your task is to identify as many different occupations and professions you can that have been involved in creating this book and placing it in your hands.

Use your imagination. There are a lot of possibilities!

REFERENCES AND RESOURCES

American College Testing Program. (1993). *A guide to the world of work.* Iowa City, IA: Author.

Cosgrave, G. P. (1973). *Career planning: Search for a future.* Toronto: University of Toronto Press.

Dale, R. V. N. (1948, April). To youth who choose blindly. *Occupations,* p. 419.

Holland, J. L. (1992). *Making vocational choices: A theory of careers.* Odessa, FL: Psychological Assessment Resources.

Naisbitt, J., & Aburdene, P. (1991). *Megatrends 2000.* New York: Avon.

Patterson, J., & Kim, P. (1991). *The day Americans told the truth.* Englewood Cliffs, NJ: Prentice-Hall.

U.S. Department of Labor. (1977). *Dictionary of occupational titles: Vol. 2. Occupational classifications* (Appendix A). 4th ed. Washington, DC: U.S. Government Printing Office.

U.S. Department of Labor. (1991). *Dictionary of occupational titles.* Washington, DC: U.S. Government Printing Office.

U.S. Department of Labor. (1996a). *Occupational outlook handbook.* Lincolnwood, IL: VGM Career Horizons.

U.S. Department of Labor. (1996b, Summer). *Occupational outlook quarterly.* Washington, DC: U.S. Government Printing Office.

U.S. Department of Labor. (1996c). *Occupational projections and training data,* Bulletin 2471. Washington, DC: U.S. Government Printing Office.

CHAPTER 7

JUST THE FACTS, PLEASE: CONDUCTING A CAREER INFORMATION SEARCH

In a world so shrunken, that certain people refer to "the global village," the term "explorer" has little meaning. But exploration is nothing more than a foray into the unknown, and a four-year-old child, wandering about alone in a department store, fits the definition as well as the snow-blind man wandering across the Khyber Pass. The explorer is the person who is lost.

When you've managed to stumble directly into the heart of the unknown—either through the misdirection of others or, better yet, through your own creative ineptitude—there is no one there to hold your hand or tell you what to do. In those bad moments, in the times when we are advised not to panic, we own the unknown, and the world belongs to us. The child within has full reign. Few of us are ever so free.

—*Tim Cahill*

VISUALIZING YOUR CAREER INFORMATION SEARCH

Before you begin your information search, we want to offer you an opportunity to create a visual presentation of how you'll go about obtaining and using information about an occupation that interests you. We offer you two ways of creating your representative display. The first approach is to draw a spider's web. Imagine yourself at the center of the web, surrounded by different sources of career information. Such sources may include people, books, Internet resources, hands-on learning activities and so on. Next, fill the spaces of your web with all of the resources you've used in conducting your search for information about an occupation. Then, write the titles of the occupations on the outer edges of the web.

The second approach is to create an imaginary tree. On the roots of the tree, list members of your family and their professional backgrounds. This will help you gain insight into how your family history affects you in the present. The trunk of the tree represents you as you grow from your family roots and reach out for your future. Use the branches to represent the occupations that interest you. Use the leaves of the tree to represent the resources you could find, people who could help you, and volunteer or intern jobs that might open doors. Also list perceived feelings, strengths, and limitation; pros and cons; and challenges and opportunities.

CAREER INFORMATION RESOURCES

In exploring the world of work, you'll need to identify resources for obtaining *career information*—information about educational and occupational opportunities. You'll need to know what to read, where to visit, and with whom to talk. How thoroughly you can explore careers will depend on how much time you can invest in the process and on the kinds of resources available in your community.

Written Resources

The easiest place to start is with written materials. Most libraries and high-school or college counseling offices contain books and pamphlets about different fields. The most frequently used resource is the *Occupational Outlook Handbook*. Published yearly by the U.S. Department of Labor, the *Handbook* contains general occupational projections for the United States as a whole and information about some 300 occupations, arranged by their common characteristics. Each occupation is described in terms of the nature of the work, place of employment, training and qualifications for advancement, employment outlook, earnings, and working conditions. The book also provides addresses for trade associations and state employment agencies you can visit or correspond with to obtain additional information (see Appendix C). You can also find addresses of organizations relevant to people with special interests and needs such as women, the physically challenged, youths, and older workers.

Here is a list of other books worth exploring:

Bell, A. H. (1997). *Great jobs abroad*. New York: McGraw-Hill.

Farr, J. M. (1997). *America's fastest growing jobs*. Indianapolis, IN: Jist Works.

Henahan, M. (1997). *Networking*. New York: Random House.

Jandt, F. E., & Nemnich, M. B. (1997). *Using the World Wide Web in job search*. Indianapolis, IN: Jist Works.

Johnston, J. W. (1997). *The post-college survival guide*. New York: McMillan Specrum Alpha.

Krantz, L. (1997). *The jobs rated almanac*. New York: World Almanac.

Wright, J. W. (1996). *The American almanac of jobs and salaries*. New York: Avon.

Other useful printed resources include the *Guide to American Directories*, the *Directory of Directories*, and the *Encyclopedia of Associations*. Periodicals you may find useful include *Changing Times, Working Woman, Glamour, Journal of College Placement, Career World, Mademoiselle*, and two government publications: *Monthly Labor Review* and the *Occupational Outlook Quarterly*. You can find these resources in the career planning and placement office at your college or university, your local library, or a bookstore.

Finally, see Appendix C, for a description of the factors that affect the utilization of occupations within industries. This may help you "see into the future" regarding the longevity of certain types of jobs.

Internet Resources

If you have access to an Internet link at home, at work, at the career development office on your campus, or at your public library, you may be able to track down career information from a variety of net links and institutional home pages by entering descriptors such as the following:

employment	find a job
employers	intellimatch
about work	job center employment services
America's employers	job digger
business job finder	job fair
career(s)	job search
career city	job web
career exploration links	MBA job
career file	monster board
career Mosaic	phone number
career placement service	post your resumé online
career web	resumé
career zone	resumé service
company job offers	self-employment
e-span	telecommuting

Also explore the U.S. Department of Labor's "hot jobs" browser. Through careful searching, you may also find the names of corporate, government, or other settings you want to learn about. Be mindful that some of the private servers charge for their services, so ask about a fee before you sign on the provider.

To get you started, here's a list of helpful Web sourcebooks. See also Table 9-1 for a list of job-search sites.

Farrell, D. (1997). *Cyberhounds web guide*. Detroit: Visible Ink Press.

Fowley, D. (1997). *New Rider's official Internet yellow pages*. Indianapolis, IN: New Riders.

Gagnone, E. (1997). *What's on the Web*. Emeryville, CA: Internet Media.

Maloy, K. (1996). *The Internet research guide: A concise, friendly and practical handbook for anyone researching the Web*. New York: Allworth.

Wolf, M. (1997). *Your personal Net guide*. New York: Dell.

Human Resources

The information you obtain from the Internet and written materials will come to life when you take the time to talk with people about their jobs, observe them at work, or read autobiographical sketches of people in professions that interest you.

Some people express dismay at the suggestion that they talk with people about their work. They say that don't know anyone in the field they're considering, and that if they found such a person, he or she wouldn't want to talk to them. A bit of detective work will solve the first problem, and a bit of self-confidence will solve the other.

Checking around   Let's start with detective work. Suppose you were interested in talking to an automobile insurance claims adjuster who happens to be a woman. We've specified the person's gender to offset the belief of some that the

"No, you can't pull a job with me on Career Day!"

Grin and Bear It, © 1993. Reprinted with special permission of North America Syndicate.

field provides limited opportunities for women. If you already know such a claims adjuster, you're in luck. All you need to do is call her to set up a visit. But let's make the problem more realistic and assume you don't know such a person. One simple way of locating a female claims adjuster is to look through the yellow pages under "insurance companies." Each insurance company will list its claims adjustment centers, so all you do is call several companies and ask if they have a female auto claims adjuster you can talk to. If a company doesn't have one, you might ask the person on the other end if he or she knows of a company that does. Your school or college placement officer may also be able to help by providing the names of graduates in your area who could assist you in your search.

Another way of approaching the problem is to develop your own informational network. The social psychologist Stanley Milgram noted that we can contact anybody in the world with a few phone calls, even if we don't know the person. All we need to do is come up with a list of qualities the person must possess, including such characteristics as gender, place of residence, and occupation, and then plan a strategy for contacting that person. For example, if you want to contact a female claims adjuster in Boise, Idaho, you might start calling relatives or friends who live in or have visited Boise to get their ideas about whom you could contact there. Or, you might call your family's insurance agent about whom to contact. You could then call the people your local resources suggest, and use their advice to whittle your search down a bit further. Milgram suggests that by the time you've made six such phone calls, you should be in touch with the female claims adjuster from Boise. Needless to say, your task will be easier if you're looking for a person in your own community. In either case, the basic method of investigation remains the same.

Does this strategy really work? The experience of the former athletic director at Kenyon College found out that it does, but not always with five phone calls. To celebrate the swimming team's success in the national championships several years ago, the director decided to see if he could arrange for the team a visit to the White House. Twenty calls later, he reached a Kenyon Alumnus working in the lower ranks of the White House staff. Glad to help his alma mater, the former student arranged for the team to meet the president. So, persistence does pay!

Gaining confidence   The second problem, that of overcoming emotional reservations about talking to people about their professions, also has several solutions. Although many students believe that professional people are too busy to bother with students, our experience proves otherwise. Most people love to talk about what they do. Sure, there will be some who can't be bothered with talking about themselves, but if you persist and use your network of friends and relatives effectively, you will most likely locate several people willing to spend some time discussing their work with you. We've also found that many graduates will let students spend a day observing them at work. Locating helpful people is usually not much of a problem.

Students often stumble in this process because they don't have a clear set of questions they want answered. You need to clarify your lifestyle needs and use them as a framework for asking others about their careers. If you are still anxious about what to ask and how to ask it, you could develop a list of specific questions and find a friend or relative who will let you "practice" by interviewing them. You might also observe television journalists as they interview people, especially interviewers with engaging and nonthreatening ways of inviting people into open conversation. In these ways, you can refine your questions, overcome some of your fears, and sharpen your interviewing skills.

Here are some questions you might ask in an interview:

1. Tell me a bit about your work history, the subjects you studied in high school or college, and the work experiences that have led you to your present position.
2. How long have you been in your present occupation and position?
3. What attracted you to your position?
4. Describe a typical day on your job.
5. What does it take to be a success in your field?
6. What do you enjoy most about your position?
7. What do you dislike about your position?
8. Does your position require specific skills? What other fields require the same skills?
9. Do the rewards of your position offset its demands?
10. How does your job affect your home and leisure life? Does your work take you away from your other pursuits more than you'd like?
11. What does the future look like for someone in your professional specialty? What new areas do you see emerging in your field?

12. Do you have any specific advice for me as I consider entering your profession? What courses should I take? What types of internship or work experience should I pursue? Are there professional journals in the field I should read or a local professional organization I might join to stay current in my knowledge of your field?

One final point: If you decide to use the interviewing-for-information approach, remember to send each person you interview a thank-you note.

Visiting, Volunteering, Working

Reading about an occupation and talking with people about it are two important ways to gather career information. If you really want to explore an occupation, however, we encourage you to get some hands-on experiences. Some corporations provide tours for the public to explain how their products are produced. You may be able to arrange a tour in a setting that employs people in your field of interest.

If you have the time and the motivation, you may be able to persuade an employer to allow you to work as a volunteer apprentice for a day or longer as a way of finding out about an occupation and your reactions to it. You might also find part-time or summer work in an interesting field or related ones. Finally, you can take advantage of any cooperative education, internship, and externship opportunities available on your campus. Through such programs, you can work part-time in settings that relate to your degree program.

An advantage of any actual experience is that in addition to gathering career information, you'll acquire skills for securing a full-time job at graduation. In fact, many employers use volunteer and internship programs to evaluate and groom potential employees.

EVALUATING CAREER INFORMATION

"Caution! Occupational information may be hazardous to your career." As far-fetched as this statement may seem, it has some truth. Occupational information may convey hidden biases. Labor projections are based on two premises—no war and no depression. Optimistic projections from some sources may represent an attempt to sell an unstable field. Be sure that your enthusiasm for a field with "opportunities for well-qualified applicants" doesn't blind you to its disadvantages; every field has some.

We noted earlier that until recently, participation in the U.S. labor force was restricted for women and minorities, who traditionally have had access only to a limited number of service-oriented occupations. Although recent surveys indicate that this picture is changing, women and minorities are still underrepresented in many professions and continue to receive relatively low levels of compensation for their efforts. One consequence of discriminatory practices has been a flight of women and minorities from traditional corporate settings.

Sexual, ethnic and racial biases associated with economic discrimination sometimes appear in sources of career information. Pictures that show a person of a particular group working at a given profession tend to project the image that the field is for them only, thus confirming widespread and inaccurate beliefs about who should work where. Though people who create informational materials don't necessarily want to exclude some groups from certain occupations, you should be mindful of how cultural stereotyping has restricted the availability of potential role models for people wishing to explore certain fields. This lack of role models can be discouraging, if you let it.

Be thorough. Use a wide variety of informational resources. Explore groups of related occupations and their different levels. Make sure the information you obtained is current. Check the date of each publication you read and compare the information it contains with the information from the most recent edition of the *Occupational Outlook Handbook*. And be sure that the information is accurate (and reasonably objective) by noting how the information was gathered, how many people were surveyed to obtain it, and who published it. Also, compare national trends with local ones. You may find that a locally tight field is more open in other geographical areas.

YOUR IDEAL JOB DESCRIPTION

> Remember, you have to work . . . So find out what you want to be, and do, and take off your coat, and make a dust in the world.
>
> —*Charles Reade*

To explore various occupations with a sense of direction and purpose, you'll find it useful to have your needs and priorities in mind before setting out to gather information. Imagine your ideal job, a job that uniquely fits you and the way you want to live. Take several sheets of paper and, using the information you've gathered about yourself so far, create a written sketch of the way you would most like to spend your life in the future. You can do this by answering five basic career-planning questions:

1. *Who am I?* Start with the life stage that most describes where you are today. What needs and pressures are affecting you right now? How are you dealing with them? What choices will you be making during the next 5 years?

Recall the personal characteristics that seem most descriptive of you in the self-assessment activities found in Chapters 3, 4, and 5. Identify three or more preferences, interests, and skills you would like to express through work. Explain in several sentences why you selected these preferences, interests, and skills and how they fit into your career objectives.

Identify three values you want to express at work. Briefly explain the reasons you selected them and discuss their implications for your future. Consider how much and what kind of decision-making and supervisory responsibility you want and the effect this preference will have on the level of work you choose.

2. *How do I want to live?* Use the wellness wheel (Chapter 1) to describe the lifestyle you prefer. How would you ideally balance the time you spend at work, the time you spend at leisure and recreation, and the time you spend with family and friends? Where do your spiritual and religious beliefs fit into your lifestyle? What kinds of things do you enjoy doing outside of work? What important needs will you be meeting through those activities? What salary will you need to support your lifestyle?

3. *Where do I want to live?* If you have a geographical preference, state it and explain what makes it ideal for you.

4. *What will I do for a living?* Avoid giving your job description a title such as "accountant" or "nurse," especially if you already have an idea about what you want to do. Try to look at the ideas you're including from a fresh perspective. Make the answer to this question a description of you doing what you want to do (and not doing what you don't want to do) rather than a description of a job you think is realistic and available. Make the component activities, pleasures, and problems clear and identifiable so that you can discover fields or settings where you might use them.

5. *Who will I be spending my time with?* Describe the kinds of people with whom you will be taking classes, working, and engaging in leisure/recreational and social pursuits. Describe these people in terms of what their interests and values would be like, the kinds of topics you would talk about, the things you would be doing together, their gender, age, and so on.

After you've answered these questions, elect at least two occupations you'd like to explore in depth. Be sure they're consistent with the information you've gathered about yourself so far. Write the occupations in the spaces provided on the pages that follow and identify the informational resources you plan to draw on while exploring each occupation. You may wish to write to some professional associations for information. Also, indicate when you plan to use these resources you've listed.

After you've identified the resources for each occupation, turn to the P.L.A.C.E. activity in the next section for guidelines on how to pull together the information you've gathered about the different occupations. By comparing your ideal job description with information about specific occupations from the P.L.A.C.E. activity, you'll begin to get a sense of which occupations would most meet your needs and preferences.

Occupation 1: _____

I will *read* the following materials about this occupation by _____
(date)

1. _____

2. _____

3. _____

I will *talk* to the following people about this occupation by ————————————
(date)

1. ——————————————————————————————————

2. ——————————————————————————————————

3. ——————————————————————————————————

I will *visit* the following places that employ people in this occupation by ——————
(date)

1. ——————————————————————————————————

2. ——————————————————————————————————

3. ——————————————————————————————————

If possible, I will *volunteer* some time to work alongside someone in this occupation.

I will do so by ————————————————
(date)

The person I will contact to see about volunteer opportunities is ————————————

——————————————————————————————————

Occupation 2: ————————————————————————————

I will *read* the following materials about this occupation by ——————————
(date)

1. ——————————————————————————————————

2. ——————————————————————————————————

3. ——————————————————————————————————

I will *talk* to the following people about this occupation by ——————————
(date)

1. ——————————————————————————————————

2. ——————————————————————————————————

3. ——————————————————————————————————

I will *visit* the following places that employ people in this occupation by ——————
(date)

1. _____
2. _____
3. _____

If possible, I will *volunteer* some time to work alongside someone in this occupation.

I will do so by _____
                        (date)

The person I will contact to see about volunteer opportunities is _____

_____

Occupation 3: _____

I will *read* the following materials about this occupation by _____
                                                                        (date)

1. _____
2. _____
3. _____

I will *talk* to the following people about this occupation by _____
                                                                      (date)

1. _____
2. _____
3. _____

I will *visit* the following places that employ people in this occupation by _____
                                                                                  (date)

1. _____
2. _____
3. _____

If possible, I will *volunteer* some time to work alongside someone in this occupation.

I will do so by _____
                        (date)

The person I will contact to see about volunteer opportunities is _____

_____

P.L.A.C.E.: A Guide for Exploring and Evaluating an Occupation

As you explore different occupations, you'll want to organize the information you gather so that you can assess the various alternatives individually and compare them with one another. A helpful system for organizing occupational information follows. This system requires that you look at each occupation in terms of five variables:

> P. Position description, including general duties, occupational level, and associated enterprises
> L. Location, including geographical area and physical environment
> A. Advancement opportunities and job security
> C. Conditions of employment, including salary, benefits, hours, and special demands such as dress codes
> E. Entry requirements, including required educational and training experiences

The following worksheets will help you to pull together the P.L.A.C.E. information about each occupation you explore and to evaluate it in terms of how it fits the description of your ideal job. Use the five P.L.A.C.E. boxes on the left side of the page to make notes about the occupation. You can use the comments section to jot down your reactions to the occupation's characteristics. In making your comments, you may wish to focus on how the demands and rewards of the occupation will affect your leisure/recreation and kinship/friendship pursuits. You can indicate how much the occupation appeals to you by circling one of the five numbers in the box across from each characteristic, according to the following criteria:

> Circle "5" if the occupation has a definite or very strong appeal to you.
> Circle "4" if the occupation is generally appealing to you.
> Circle "3" if the occupation has some appeal to you.
> Circle "2" if the occupation is somewhat unappealing to you.
> Circle "1" if the occupation is generally unappealing to you.
> Circle "0" if the occupation is very unappealing to you.

After you've rated the occupation in each of the five areas, total the circled numbers and write the figure you obtained in the box at the bottom of the page as the "total rating." This score will provide you with a sense of the occupation's overall appeal to you—or its lack of appeal. You can later compare this figure with the totals you obtain from rating other occupations. This will give you an idea of which occupations appeal most to you.

Occupational Evaluation Worksheet

Position title _____

Characteristics of the occupation	Comments	Rating
P. Position description *Notes:*		0 1 2 3 4 5
L. Location *Notes:*		0 1 2 3 4 5
A. Advancement opportunities *Notes:*		0 1 2 3 4 5
C. Conditions of employment *Notes:*		0 1 2 3 4 5
E. Entry requirements *Notes:*		0 1 2 3 4 5

Total rating =

Occupational Evaluation Worksheet

Position title _____

Characteristics of the occupation	Comments	Rating
P. Position description *Notes:*		0 1 2 3 4 5
L. Location *Notes:*		0 1 2 3 4 5
A. Advancement opportunities *Notes:*		0 1 2 3 4 5
C. Conditions of employment *Notes:*		0 1 2 3 4 5
E. Entry requirements *Notes:*		0 1 2 3 4 5

Total rating =

Occupational Evaluation Worksheet

Position title _____

Characteristics of the occupation	Comments	Rating
P. Position description *Notes:*		0 1 2 3 4 5
L. Location *Notes:*		0 1 2 3 4 5
A. Advancement opportunities *Notes:*		0 1 2 3 4 5
C. Conditions of employment *Notes:*		0 1 2 3 4 5
E. Entry requirements *Notes:*		0 1 2 3 4 5

Total rating =

A PLACE FOR YOUR VALUES

We have already explored how your personal values have emerged and changed over time and how they influence your decisions. This activity provides you with an opportunity to examine how well the different occupations you're currently exploring match your values. In this activity, you'll identify values and use them as criteria for assessing occupations. Use the worksheets to compare as many as three occupations.

Step 1: Indicate the occupations you're considering. Write the name of the occupation you're considering in the space provided at the top of the page.

Step 2: Identify your values. Read through the list of values provided on the left side of the page and check the boxes next to the values most important to you—those you must have the opportunity to express if you are to be happy with your major or work.

Step 3: Gather information about the occupation. Use the same procedures you used in the P.L.A.C.E. activity for gathering information about an occupation. Write your observations in the comments section of the grid on the worksheet next to the values you decided are most important to you.

Step 4: Rate the occupation. Rate the occupation according to the following scale. Circle the appropriate rating next to each of the values you checked as being important to you.

Circle "5" if the occupation is very consistent with your values.

Circle "4" if the occupation is generally consistent with your values.

Circle "3" if the occupation is somewhat consistent with your values.

Circle "2" if the occupation has some qualities that are consistent with your values and some that are not.

Circle "1" if the occupation is generally inconsistent with your values.

Circle "0" if the occupation is very inconsistent with your values.

Step 5: Total value rating. After you've rated the occupation for each of your values, total the circled numbers and write the figure you obtained in the space on the grid labeled "total rating." This score will provide you with a sense of the occupation's value to you. You can later compare the figures of several occupations or majors to get a clear idea of which areas appeal most to you.

Occupational Evaluation Worksheet:
Identify Your Values and Lifestyle Preferences

Occupation —————————————————————————

My ideal job would provide me with	*Comment*	*Rating of occupation*
___ *Achievement, recognition, status or approval* from others		0 1 2 3 4 5
___ Opportunities and time to appreciate *beauty* in people, art, and nature		0 1 2 3 4 5
___ *Challenging* opportunities to use my creativity, training, intelligence, and talents		0 1 2 3 4 5
___ Opportunities to experience *good health physically and mentally* by being free of anxiety and stress		0 1 2 3 4 5
___ An opportunity to improve my *financial position* significantly		0 1 2 3 4 5
___ *Independence* to be free to do my own thing, independent of others		0 1 2 3 4 5
___ Time to devote to *close personal relationships* with my peers and family		0 1 2 3 4 5
___ An opportunity to work in settings that agree with my *moral, religious, or spiritual values*		0 1 2 3 4 5
___ Time for *pleasure and fun*		0 1 2 3 4 5
___ Opportunities to *influence or control* the activities of others		0 1 2 3 4 5
___ Compatibility with my emotional needs		0 1 2 3 4 5

Total rating: —————————————————

Occupational Evaluation Worksheet:
Identify Your Values and Lifestyle Preferences

Occupation ——————————————————————

My ideal job would provide me with	*Comment*	*Rating of occupation*
___ *Achievement, recognition, status or approval* from others		0 1 2 3 4 5
___ Opportunities and time to appreciate *beauty* in people, art, and nature		0 1 2 3 4 5
___ *Challenging* opportunities to use my creativity, training, intelligence, and talents		0 1 2 3 4 5
___ Opportunities to experience *good health physically and mentally* by being free of anxiety and stress		0 1 2 3 4 5
___ An opportunity to improve my *financial position* significantly		0 1 2 3 4 5
___ *Independence* to be free to do my own thing, independent of others		0 1 2 3 4 5
___ Time to devote to *close personal relationships* with my peers and family		0 1 2 3 4 5
___ An opportunity to work in settings that agree with my *moral, religious, or spiritual values*		0 1 2 3 4 5
___ Time for *pleasure and fun*		0 1 2 3 4 5
___ Opportunities to *influence or control* the activities of others		0 1 2 3 4 5
___ Compatibility with my emotional needs		0 1 2 3 4 5

Total rating: ————————————————

Occupational Evaluation Worksheet:
Identify Your Values and Lifestyle Preferences

Occupation ―――――――――――――――――――――――――

My ideal job would provide me with	*Comment*	*Rating of occupation*
___ *Achievement, recognition, status or approval* from others		0 1 2 3 4 5
___ Opportunities and time to appreciate *beauty* in people, art, and nature		0 1 2 3 4 5
___ *Challenging* opportunities to use my creativity, training, intelligence, and talents		0 1 2 3 4 5
___ Opportunities to experience *good health physically and mentally* by being free of anxiety and stress		0 1 2 3 4 5
___ An opportunity to improve my *financial position* significantly		0 1 2 3 4 5
___ *Independence* to be free to do my own thing, independent of others		0 1 2 3 4 5
___ Time to devote to *close personal relationships* with my peers and family		0 1 2 3 4 5
___ An opportunity to work in settings that agree with my *moral, religious, or spiritual values*		0 1 2 3 4 5
___ Time for *pleasure and fun*		0 1 2 3 4 5
___ Opportunities to *influence or control* the activities of others		0 1 2 3 4 5
___ Compatibility with my emotional needs		0 1 2 3 4 5

Total rating: ―――――――――――――――

Guidelines for Your Occupational Report

Prepare a written "occupational report" to help you pull together and compare information you've generated about yourself with information you've gathered about an occupation that interests you.

The first important aspect of the occupational report, your description of your ideal job, helped you characterize your preferred lifestyle. The second step, the P.L.A.C.E. occupational rating activity, allowed you to compare a specific occupation or several occupations with these ideal requirements. The occupational report will allow you to summarize this information in narrative form and to project yourself into the future in the occupation that most appeals to you.

Plan on covering the following steps in preparing your occupational report.

1. Select an occupation from the P.L.A.C.E. activity you would like to describe in depth. _____

    _____

2. Identify the resources you've used in exploring that occupation.

    Conversations _____

    _____

    Places visited _____

    _____

    Volunteer work _____

    _____

    People visited _____

    _____

    Reading and films _____

    _____

3. Compare the information you've obtained with the requirements of your ideal job.

    In this occupation, how frequently will I be able to exercise my ideals? In what ways? _____

    _____

    _____

    _____

    _____

    Use the following information to assess your "fit" with the occupation you're considering.

    Title of occupation _____

Job family and cluster the occupation falls into (Figure 3-2, World of work map) ——————

——

——

Functional skills (data, people, things) required

Skills I possess ————————————————————————————————

——

Skills I need to acquire ————————————————————————————

——

Using the results of the Self-Assessment Inventory (Appendix A) indicate how compatible your occupational preferences, skills, and interests are with the requirements of the occupation.

Preferences ——————————————————————————————————

——

——

Skills ———————————————————————————————————————

——

——

Interests ————————————————————————————————————

——

——

Using the 11 steps of the occupational ladder (see Chapter 5), indicate the level at which the occupation is located. ——————————————————————————————————

Indicate the types of enterprise the occupation is most frequently associated with.

——

——

——

Identify and briefly describe those occupations related to the one you've explored that you'd consider as alternatives to your primary occupation.

——

——

——

Based on what you know about yourself now, the occupation you've explored in your occupational report, and what you've learned about how individuals continue to develop in their adult years, write four "notes to yourself" in the future. The notes should portray what matters to you and the choices you'll be making at the following points in time:

The remainder of this year _____

_____

_____

Shortly after college graduation _____

_____

_____

Ten years from now _____

_____

_____

At your retirement _____

_____

_____

By completing these steps, you'll gain a clearer perspective on what matters most to you in your life and work. You'll also see how well each occupation you explore fits into your most preferred way of living.

Before we close this chapter, here's a word on one "alternative" lifestyle, or prison versus work.

IN PRISON you spend the majority of your time in an 8-by-10 cell.

AT WORK you spend most your time in a 6-by-8 cubicle.

IN PRISON you get three meals a day.

AT WORK you only get a break for 1 meal and you have to pay for it.

IN PRISON you get time off for good behavior.

AT WORK you get rewarded for good behavior with more work.

IN PRISON a guard locks and unlocks all the doors for you.

AT WORK you must carry around a security card and unlock and open all the doors yourself.

IN PRISON you can watch TV and play games.

AT WORK you get fired for watching TV and playing games.

IN PRISON you get your own toilet.

AT WORK you have to share.

IN PRISON they allow your family and friends to visit.

AT WORK you cannot even speak to your family and friends.

IN PRISON all expenses are paid by taxpayers, with no work required.

AT WORK you get to pay all the expenses to go to work, and then they deduct taxes from your salary to pay for prisoners.

IN PRISON you spend most of your life looking through bars from the inside wanting to get out.

AT WORK you spend most of your time wanting to get out and inside bars.

IN PRISON there are wardens who are often sadistic.

AT WORK they are called managers.

REFERENCES AND RESOURCES

Milgram, S. (1967). The small world problem. *Psychology Today, 1,* 62–67.

U.S. Department of Labor. (1996a). *Employment outlook: 1994–2005. Job quality and other aspects of projected employment growth,* Bulletin 2472. Washington, DC: U.S. Government Printing Office.

U.S. Department of Labor. (1996b). *Occupational outlook handbook.* Lincolnwood, IL: VGM Career Horizons.

CHAPTER 8

INSIDE/OUTSIDE

"Joey, you're going to be you for the rest of your life, so you'd better get used to it."

Dennis the Menace® used by permission of Hank Ketcham and Copyright © 1991 by North American Syndicate.

Be brave enough to live life creatively. The creative is the place where no one else has ever been. You have to leave the city of your comfort and go into the wilderness of your intuition. You can't get there by bus, only by hard work and risk and by not quite knowing what you're doing. What you'll discover will be wonderful. What you'll discover will be yourself.

—*Alan Alda, "Hawkeye" on* M*A*S*H *(advice to his daughter)*

It's the end of career day at Edgewood High School. The students had prepared, with reports and research, to get the most out of meeting adults from the community and a nearby college who came to speak and answer questions about various careers and professions. Now, full of fears and conclusions, the students argue among themselves in a meeting with their guidance counselor. Bret has his mind made up. As the son of a professor, and from a family of educators, he feels that teaching is the only road. He dismisses information about sales, small business ownership, and vocational training with a slightly superior air, but inside he feels defensive. Gino tells Bret rather heatedly that there's more than one career. Gino's father founded a successful construction company. Gino could enter the family business right away, but his father would be really proud if he went to college and maybe to law school. Though glad to have choices, Gino feels pulled in two directions. Gino talks about his older brother, Tony, who has "stopped out" of college to work in a construction company owned by one of their father's rivals. His father's angry, and Gino thinks Tony's courageous but maybe crazy. Tony says their dad doesn't have all the answers and that he wants to explore on his own. He's doing what he believes in, but he's a little scared. The guidance counselor reminds the students about John Hayes, a speaker they heard earlier in the day. John's company designs and manufactures artificial limbs and medical equipment. His father, a prominent physician, had pressured John to go to medical school. John talked about his not wanting to go to medical school, having arguments with his dad, feeling guilty, and searching for and finally finding a way to combine his mechanical and engineering interests with the medical ideals he had admired while growing up. John feels good about his career, but he made it clear that finding and starting out on his own path was not easy.

Growth toward a career choice and toward a vocational self-image is a specialized part of a larger whole—the development of an identity as an interdependent adult. As we saw in previous chapters, developing from a dependent infant into an interdependent adult is a process that continues in various forms throughout life. Although career exploration and career choice may occur at different ages and times in the life cycle, we create the foundation for earning a living in early adulthood, when we start the larger task of separating physically from our family and becoming financially independent.

To lay the groundwork for successful interdependent lives and individual identities, young adults in our society are expected to separate themselves intellectually and emotionally from their parents and significant others. As children or even as adolescents, most of us relied greatly on others' opinions in determining what to do and even how to do it. Because the rules and demands of school and home have guided our lives for at least 18 years, some of us may be bewildered when we're suddenly told to figure out what we want to do with the rest of our lives. Faced with these decisions, some people may be tempted to rely on someone else's feelings or ideas, sometimes without even realizing what they're doing. Others, whose families always assumed they would follow a particular path, such as becoming a doctor or taking over the family business, encounter a different problem. Instead of too many options, they believe they have none. Although they may know of other attractive alternatives, they feel they can't disappoint their families. Most people who change careers in their 30s or 40s often do so because they've realized that their first career was not really *their* choice but a choice made by or for someone else.

Thus, learning to separate your own ideas and feelings about your future from those of others who've helped shape and influence you is crucial. Of course, complete separation is not possible—nor would we want it. We have learned important skills, attitudes, and values from our families, and we continue to learn from friends, employers, teachers, life partners, and others. What matters is being able to listen to and weigh these external opinions and feelings and decide whether they're comfortable or fit with our own feelings and plans. We've been taught from the time we were small not to let ourselves be pressured into doing things not in our best interest. ("Don't talk to strangers." "Say no to drugs.") In career choice, this principle means we need to learn how we can best use our interests, talents, and values in the world of work and how to consider the views and demands of others without turning choices over to them. Keeping this perspective can sometimes be difficult. It requires us to know ourselves, to be aware of but not totally guided by others' wishes, and to find ways to express ourselves successfully through a specific major or occupation.

Part of the process of separation involves knowing what and who is controlling our feelings and influencing our options. We all start life as helpless infants, with what psychologists call an external locus of control. We are totally dependent, and our behaviors and later our attitudes are determined by what others tell us is good or bad and by the consequences that people and situations impose on us. As we grow into and through adulthood, our main developmental goal is to learn to be physically and psychologically independent, as well as interdependent with (rather than dependent on) others. In this process we develop an *internal* locus of control—the ability to control our impulses and feelings, to act rather than react, and to examine and refine our goals, values, and beliefs to ensure that they fit us and that they aren't "swallowed whole" from a source outside ourselves. As we progress in the task of defining our identity, we can arrive at a decision by weighing our intellectual and emotional reactions, our priorities and values, and the realities that affect our choices. We can reward ourselves internally and be comfortable when we've done something we believe in, regardless of its popularity. Of course, we should not be insensitive to others' feelings. But our first and biggest responsibility is to do a constructive job of living our own lives.

DEVELOPMENT IN SOCIETY—INTEGRATING INSIDE AND OUTSIDE

In Chapter 1 we examined three reasons we work. We can also view these reasons as ways of looking at the goals of growth and development. Our goal in becoming effective adults is to be able to fulfill our needs (inside) by learning how to fill personal and social roles (inside and outside) and to complete life tasks and master the environment (outside).

Needs: Maslow

The theory we used to describe human needs, Maslow's hierarchy, begins with the most basic needs we fill through work—food, clothing, and shelter, then safety and security (see Chapter 4). Even in a financially secure family, as teens we often start working early to help fill precisely these needs. We usually spend our first paychecks on food and clothing of our choosing. If our family is less well-off, we may save our first income to ensure the security of our future plans, such as college or a deposit on our own apartment. Beyond these physical needs, Maslow lists three less concrete needs: to belong, to have self-esteem, and to reach self-actualization.

The feeling of belonging should start within our own family, although this does not always happen for people whose families have problems. During adolescence and into young adulthood, we all move away from our families and face the task of forming new relationships—making friends; forming love relationships; finding "parental figures" in advisors, mentors, or older friends; and joining groups we have something in common with. In these ways we can satisfy our need to belong.

Maslow's fourth level—the need for self-esteem—is met as we work to develop our identities. Certain parts of our "core," such as values and beliefs, develop from our earliest years. Others come later and require more active work on our part. To become competent at new tasks and feel worthwhile, we must first choose goals and priorities and then pursue and achieve them. This means making mistakes, meeting unexpected challenges, and sometimes changing direction or starting over.

It's really during and after this process that we have opportunities for what Maslow considers the "peak experience" of human beings—self-actualization. This happens when we realize our full potential, or experience what's called *synergy*—when everything we do or contribute "comes together" and the result is greater than the sum of the parts. Sometimes this is planned, but often it happens when we're hard at work, giving our best to something we believe in, and it takes us by surprise. Like happiness, self-esteem and self-actualization can't be pursued directly but result from effort invested in various steps of the growth process—self-understanding, decision making, exploration and risk taking, setting goals and priorities, living out our values, and balancing our lives. Think about things you've enjoyed or worked hard at—in school, in sports, at work, with friends. Have you ever had a "peak experience" of being thrilled by your competence or results? Was it a surprise? How did it affect your view of yourself?

Stages: Erikson

We work not only to meet personal needs but also to fill roles through which we can be part of society and of other people's lives. According to Erik Erikson, in our preschool years within our family we face three important tasks. The first, learning to trust, is often seen as external—we choose people and situations we think will be safe. But Erikson uses a concept he calls "basic trust," which means "I trust myself to be able to handle what happens to me." Our level of learning in this area shows in our ability to take risks, make mistakes, and believe in ourselves. The next two stages—having the autonomy to be true to ourselves even in the face of disapproval, and taking the initiative to express and fill our own needs—in later years are equally important for developing our individuality and sense of self-worth. These three steps form the foundation of our ability to cooperate, compromise, and keep our "self" in jobs and relationships. As we grow, we may notice uncomfortable feelings such as anger at authority, fears about intimacy, fear of being wrong, anxiety about the approval of others, or defensiveness and rebelliousness. If you notice feelings like these as you work at defining your career choice, you may find it helpful to revisit Erikson's first three stages and check for "unfinished business." We all need to do this from time to time, since our growth in any area never really ends.

Erikson's fourth stage, which starts with grade school and ends at puberty, is "industry." Play, household jobs, piano practice, Scout meetings, and other obligations and commitments all teach us about work—doing, achieving, following through, and "acting adult." Thinking about yourself in relation to work and career, review some of those childhood activities in your memory. How did you feel about them then, and how do they appear as you look back? According to Erikson, the opposite of industry is inferiority. We will not have good self-esteem or confidence unless we feel we know how to tackle a job and get results—in short, to work.

Puberty and adolescence mark the beginning of Erikson's fifth stage—the moment we begin to individuate and form our own identity. We face many tasks during these years that revolve around the question "Who am I?" They include starting a vocational identity and (for many of us) our first paid job, discovering who we are as a male or female individual, developing friendships and discovering love, breaking away from the family, forming our own values and beliefs, and trying out the role of leader and adult. Erikson's "job" for young adults at the end of adolescence is to continue building skills for intimacy. At that point we must build a social network, and eventually a family, separate from our parents and siblings. We also move into the action stage of our career—choosing, training for, and finding our first job. At this point we need the skills we've developed in all of Erikson's earlier stages—trust, autonomy, initiative, industry, and a sense of identity.

Erikson has identified two additional stages we encounter as we progress through our adult years. First is "generativity"—giving to others from our experience through parenting, mentoring, coaching, or whatever fits our interests and skills. The last stage, "ego integrity," comes as our work lives draw to a close. As we look back on what we've done, we need to see how our contribution fits into the larger framework of our personal history and our society. Looking ahead to these stages throughout our work lives sometimes helps guide us when we're confused.

Life Tasks: Covey

The third reason we work has to do with completing life tasks, including individual tasks we set as part of our own goals and values, as well as universal tasks, ones that we all have to learn, such as working with our environment effectively. The importance of the large challenges in our lives, such as jobs and relationships, is obvious. What we might overlook, though they're crucial to our happiness and self-esteem, are the smaller skills—the building blocks that lead to daily successes and eventually allow us to meet our larger goals. These are the ways we grow so we can meet new challenges: the willingness to experiment, to proceed by trial and error, to start over after a mistake or a failure, to take initiative, and to take responsibility for our actions and our lives even when we wish someone else would step in and do it. As we work at these things, we develop the resilience to go on in the face of stress or adversity, to persevere in spite of discouragement, to face our fears and do what we must in spite of them, and to stand up for what we believe. In relationships, we work to develop the courage to be honest even when it hurts, vulnerable and open even when we feel defensive, patient when we're frustrated, willing to communicate clearly even in anger, and true to our word even when it's not convenient. We ultimately learn to respect the individuality and rights of others and to demand the same respect for ourselves.

How do we do all this? Where do we start? Hard work and perseverance are only helpful if we are approaching life's tasks in ways that are effective and heading in the direction that we want to go. Stephen Covey, in *The 7 Habits of Highly Effective People* (1989), presents an overview of this process. Covey sees our development as a learning process that takes us from *dependence* (as infants and children) to *independence* (as we establish our identities and learn to take care of our own needs) to *interdependence* (as we learn how to interact constructively, form relationships, and contribute to the greater good).

Covey's first three habits take us from dependence to independence. First, he suggests we be proactive. He emphasizes focusing energy on the things we can influence and taking responsibility for doing what we can instead of worrying and blaming. And, like the famous Jewish psychiatrist and prisoner of war Victor Frankl, he reminds us that while we often can't choose our circumstances, we have the power to choose our responses and attitudes. Covey's second principle involves staying focused on our goals and long-term priorities—who we want to be and where we want to end up over our lifetime. The third habit is "First Things First." Here he points out the difference between what is important and what is urgent. This makes it clear why priorities are so necessary. Many important things that lead to valued long-term goals—nutrition and exercise, time invested in relationships, time for emotional and spiritual health—don't seem urgent: crises or deadlines can push them aside. Some of these urgent activities (such as study or work) are also important, but many are not. If we allow circumstances or other people to convince us that unimportant things are urgent, we may feel frantic and overloaded while neglecting the things that matter most. In summary, being proactive, keeping our life goals in mind, and putting important priorities first all promote independence.

> [Don't] spend ten dollars' worth of energy on a ten-cent problem. . . .
> There are millions of want-to's and have-to's in life. Ultimately, these
> pressures create stress only when your time and energy-spending deci-
> sions aren't consistent with your goals, beliefs, and values.
> —*Donald A. Tubesing*

Covey's next three habits involve relating well to others and take us from independence to interdependence, which is essential for living in the world with other people. The fourth habit involves approaching interpersonal situations from a win/win perspective. Covey points out that other ways of interacting ultimately result in "winning the war" but damaging the self or the relationship. Win/win means having the maturity and foresight to be nice but tough—to balance our own needs with empathy for others. It requires that we be high on both courage and consideration. Habit five is "Seek First to Understand, Then to be Understood." This defines the practice of empathetic listening, which is much more difficult than it may appear. It's hard to put aside our own views and hear someone else's, particularly if we're impatient, defensive, or angry. However, this lets us avoid making assumptions and allows us to collect accurate data. For others to understand us, we must communicate with integrity, honesty, respect, clarity, and logic—regardless of other people's responses. The sixth principle says that we must work toward synergy—a process in which the resulting whole exceeds the sum of its parts. Synergy empowers and unifies in any area—whether it means that two people can eventually create a family of five or that three entrepreneurs with different skills can start a huge computer company. Valuing the differences among people and their views is essential. Covey points out that this process is always creative, a process of letting go of the known and making a leap of faith. These three skills—a win/win outlook, effective listening and communicating, and a synergistic approach—lead to successful interdependence.

The seventh habit is renewal. In the spirit of our wellness wheel (Chapter 1) Covey suggests we must keep working to maintain a balance that will fuel us and make our lives rewarding.

A Few Good Web Sites

- Blonz Guide to Nutrition, Food, Science, and Health (*Note:* This site contains some crude humor.)
- Health Resource
- International Health News
- Whole Living

http://www.blonz.index.html/

http://www.coolware./com./health/joel/health/html
http://www.perspective.com/health/index.html
http://www.wholeliving.com

We hope the theories and diagrams we've introduced will help you give the world and your inner self a greater sense of structure or organization, so that you can see things more clearly and have a framework into which you plug new information as it accumulates. Choose whatever outlook makes sense or appeals to you, whether a classic theory such as that of Maslow or Erikson, a newer offering such as Covey's book, the wellness wheel or decision cycle, or something else you've learned. The important thing is to have a way of viewing yourself and your world that creates meaning and clarity for you. See the box on helpful Web sites for more wellness resources.

SOCIAL AND ENVIRONMENTAL INFLUENCES

The various sociological and cultural events that occur during our lives have the power to influence and shape our attitudes. Such changes also affect the institutions around which we build our lives, such as work organizations and the family. Major changes affect even larger areas of our environment, such as the economy, the government, and our relations with other nations. Social changes impact us when we're particularly vulnerable, such as when we're developing our own identities, choosing our careers, or establishing our independence.

An interesting finding, focused on the personal development of women (Stewart & Healy, 1989), suggests that a major social event causes changes that differ according to a person's life stage. For example, women making the transition to adulthood during the women's movement developed a strong vocational identity, and now a high number of them are employed. However, women who were mature adults during this period were affected differently. Although many of them have gone to work, their basic belief system and identity still centers on family and motherhood. So, parental models apparently exert less influence on an adolescent's identity formation than do sociological changes occurring at the same time. Clearly, from what we can observe about the adult development of "boomers" and "generation X," this research may apply widely to both genders. So, during the years when we are forming our own identities and are sometimes mightily preoccupied with what is inside, events and trends in the larger society (the outside) still have a strong and lasting effect on all aspects of our developing selves.

Social Change and Development

Now we'll see how social change affects each aspect of the wellness wheel. Social change itself will not affect our physical development, but how we experience such change will. For example, in the 1990s it's attractive and sexy to be healthy, dress casually, and like the outdoors. Everyone owns running shoes. In past decades a man on a bicycle or a woman involved in sports might have been ridiculed. At one time it was "in" to smoke or be very tan—things that we now know to be unhealthy. What we learn and what our peers believe help set our developing physical self-image. We must examine whether exposure to social messages might have caused us to absorb negative feelings and beliefs ("I should be taller, thinner . . .") which may not be valid.

Influenced by a blitz of information from media and technological advances, intellectual development in the closing decades of the 20th century is changing rapidly. Computer literacy is now a must for school-age children. To succeed in educational and intellectual environments, people need new types of skills and the ability to process ever-increasing amounts of information. And, as science constantly expands our frontiers and solves problems, it raises new questions. With genetic testing and cloning now a reality, we must resolve complex ethical dilemmas. While Pathfinder walks on the surface of Mars, we are discovering new life forms in the depths of the ocean and working to keep our old environment— Planet Earth—healthy and renewed. Intellectual advances raise new challenges and opportunities, new areas of research and learning, and new perceptions and uncertainties for people now entering adulthood.

Changes in the larger society certainly influence social development. In the late 1960s, the "hippie" ideal of peace and love translated into values and relationships that were "laid back," more sexually open, less conforming, and less structured. The "baby boomers" carried this forward, adding conflict with many types of authority and protests against U.S. involvement in Vietnam. Their motto, "Don't trust anyone over 30," seemed to translate into rebellious behavior that included a high level of idealism, insistence on being heard, and liberal attitudes about many rigidly held ideas of former generations.

Emotional influences resulting from social change are a bit more difficult to see. Though experienced as personal and internal, emotions are often influenced by our environment or by others in ways we may not immediately recognize. For example, in the 1950s the new horror of the impact of nuclear weapons caused many young people nightmares and anxiety about the future, which they combated by focusing on peace and love. People growing to adulthood in the 1960s saw the Berlin Wall, the assassination of John F. Kennedy and others, and the Vietnam War. They often felt cynical, angry, and unable to trust, feelings they made known by protesting and refusing to "go along." It appears that generation Xers—albeit more quietly—are also refusing to "go along," and are finding new and creative ways of doing things. Each succeeding generation has been bombarded with increasing amounts of information brought into their homes and schools. When you can see the explosion of an atomic bomb on film, the Vietnam War in your living room on TV, or games, fantasies, and human struggles in virtual reality on your computer screen, it's impossible not to become emotionally involved—sometimes against your will. When you're making decisions and determining how you feel about your future, pay attention to the messages you receive from the larger society. This will help you to gather useful information about yourself and the future and to keep your personal feelings clear and separate from feelings generated by external events. Social landmarks and trends during the years you enter adulthood will certainly influence your perceptions of the world, but you can be aware of these and make choices about their impact on your beliefs and character.

Spiritual development may mean different things to different people. For some, it involves a commitment to a particular religious (and sometimes family and ethnic) background. That kind of social context may influence its members greatly, often even more strongly than what occurs in the larger society. Other people may see spirituality as a set of beliefs and values about the meaning and purpose of life that each of us individually choose. Their level of comfort may depend on whether their view of life fits with their community or with current social beliefs. A community or reference group that confirms our pride in our beliefs can help us feel a sense of belonging; one that does not can leave us feeling isolated or discriminated against. Today, we see conflicts regarding whether or what religious observances have a place in public education. At differing times and geographical locations (and sometimes nationally), we have seen controversy about the teaching of evolution and creationism, personal values versus biblical values, sex education, and the inclusion of prayer.

The larger social context can affect occupational development in many ways. As we grow into adulthood, our career is one of the primary choices we must make. We look around at our world to see what seems to be important or valued, what our peers (our friends and our competition) are thinking or doing, and how it all fits with what we believe and what we know of ourselves. We do research to learn what jobs we like and what skills will be in demand when we finish our education or training as well as 10, 20, and 30 years from now. What direction our society is moving (for example: more money for medical research, more emphasis on environmental cleanup) tells us a lot about what expertise or credentials future job markets will value. Women and minorities particularly need to look at social change and occupational development, to remember how recently and how much change has occurred in society in general, in the family structure, and in the workplace. Female and minority workers need to be alert (but not hypersensitive) to "traditional" situations or attitudes and be prepared to handle them assertively but carefully. (More about this in Chapter 10.) So we learn about how we may fit in the workplace of the future by looking at how the social environment of these formative years has shaped us with regard to all sides of the wellness wheel.

With regard to our future development, the research on social change mentioned earlier (Stewart & Healy, 1989) suggests that, like those developing their identities in late adolescence, older adults (who may be reevaluating) are once again vulnerable to reconstruction of their views and values if a major social change affects them.

Myths

Although social change makes it difficult enough to gather accurate and current information for an informed career decision, we must also consider another category of external distractions more predictable but still confusing and hard to evaluate. These are the many myths we encounter—and believe—about careers and career decisions. Some of these may be hard to recognize as myths. Any idea based on the values, beliefs, and attitudes we learned from our families feels like a part of us—we've internalized it. A long-held belief can feel like it comes from inside us when it's really someone else's, or it can look like a reality from the outside world though it's really a myth or fear we've inherited. This is why we must look carefully at whether our beliefs match both our identities and reality.

For example, examine the following statements:

1. Everyone must climb the ladder of success, even if other areas of life suffer.
2. If I have a good job and make money, I can't make a change just because I don't like it.
3. Go where the money is, regardless of what kind of work it involves.
4. Work is the only route to personal fulfillment/self-esteem/contributing to society.
5. Financial support is the most important thing a man can do for his family.
6. If I lose a job or get downsized, I've failed in my career.
7. If my spouse has to go to work or keep working, I've failed as a husband.
8. If I limit work hours to enjoy my family, hobby, exercise or friends, I'm not a "go-getter."
9. We should respect tradition and maintain different types of work for men and women.
10. Women shouldn't compete for or be promoted into management or decision-making jobs.
11. Women are passive, emotional, and intuitive, so they don't do well in analytical or logical fields.
12. Women have to choose between a *real* career and having a family.
13. If I say no to what others expect of me, I am insensitive and selfish.
14. My family has planned my career choice and counted on it. I can't disappoint them.

Messages our families send us about work—such as what meanings and rewards work should bring, or what gender (or other group) should do what job—need to be recognized and examined for what they are: someone else's ideas. If we subject these messages to the light of our own personal questions, conclusions, feedback from others, and information about the world of work and still feel comfortable with them, then we may want to incorporate them into the set of beliefs we hold. In other words, we accept these messages out of choice, not because we feel we must conform to outside expectations. Developing our own choices and ideas is central to becoming an independent adult. We can't always do what others expect and still remain true to ourselves.

The current workplace reflects the reality that, by using other skills, women can do many jobs once thought to require physical strength. While not usually equal to men in certain kinds of physical strength, women have other strengths to offer and now work in many jobs once reserved for men, such as firefighting, operating heavy equipment, and police work on the beat.

Current surveys suggest that work satisfaction and success at work mean different things to different people. Many people indicate that the recognition and satisfaction gained from work matter more to them than money. Surveys about work satisfaction reveal another group of people who say they work only for a living and that their primary satisfaction in life comes from leisure activities or family. Clearly, there is no right answer.

Other myths that emerge from our early years come from dependent ways of looking at situations. Such myths include these:

1. The choice of a major or occupation is irreversible. Once I make it, I can't change my mind.
2. There is a single right career for everyone.
3. It's not OK to be undecided, because it's a sign of immaturity.
4. Nobody else is undecided. I'm all alone.
5. I know other people who have known what they wanted to be since childhood. Something's wrong with me because I didn't know.
6. Life is always fair.
7. Life is always unfair.
8. Somewhere there's a test that can tell me what to do with the rest of my life.
9. Others know what's best for me.
10. An expert can tell me what to do.
11. If I can find out what I'm interested in, that means I'll do well at it.
12. If I'm especially skilled at something, I should want to choose it as a career.

Most of these myths stay alive when people cling to old views out of fear of change and do not gather more information. These myths suggest that everything is black or white and that the one right career is out there to be discovered. To move beyond these paralyzing myths and believe in our own decision-making abilities, we must do enough communicating, observing, and information gathering to open our eyes to the reality of numerous options. Nothing is black and white: different things are right for different people—even for the different people each of us is at different stages throughout our lives.

As mentioned in Chapter 7, some 30 to 75 percent of college students change their majors at least once by graduation. Changing majors may cause some short-term hassles, but it prevents much long-term dissatisfaction. A choice is not irreversible; it's all right and even common to be undecided. Undecidedness and change are a natural part of life, because we continually grow and acquire new information. Sometimes the wisest decision a person can make is not to decide—temporarily.

There are 20,000 occupations in the U.S. Department of Labor's *Dictionary of Occupational Titles,* grouped according to skills. Skill and interest inventories confirm that many jobs can be grouped together in different ways because of aspects they have in common. This suggests what's actually happening more and more in the world today: As individuals grow and the economy changes, many people will later move into areas related to their original jobs. Some even find jobs far afield from their original career path. We need to remain open to expanding our list of interests and options if we want to continue to grow in our careers.

This complexity makes it impossible for any test or expert to tell us what's right for ourselves. At best, these external aids can help us discover our interests, skills, and attitudes and how they may relate to particular career directions. In spite of continued improvements in vocational testing and in research on career choice, statistics show that the best predictor of what occupation a person will choose is what that person has said he or she will do. Our best path is to explore how realistic our wishes and interests are and whether our skills and interests match. Interest does provide motivation to acquire skills, but it doesn't guarantee that we will acquire those skills. A satisfying career blends our skills and interests with other aspects of ourselves, including a lifestyle that balances our needs and feelings, our dreams and aspirations, and our values and beliefs.

Sometimes it's tempting to cling to myths because they give us an excuse to avoid the effort and responsibility involved in researching and making our decisions. Still other myths persist because they strongly influence our feelings about ourselves. They are easy to hide behind when reality frightens us. For example:

1. If things don't go the way I expect, it means that I'm a failure.
2. In order to have a feeling of worth, I must be thoroughly competent, intelligent, and achieving in all possible respects.
3. People are either successes or failures in their career pursuits. There's no in-between.
4. Changing my mind after I start one career means I've failed or wasted my time.
5. When I think about selecting a career goal, my discomfort comes from something external to me.
6. I should be totally in control of my career.
7. I must thoroughly analyze all aspects of a choice before I implement it; otherwise I'm not really prepared.
8. The world of work is changing so rapidly that I can't really plan for the future.
9. If I get away from the pressure to decide—if I take a year or two off from college—I'll be able to make a better decision.

Like many of those already mentioned, these myths feed on our self-doubts and unrealistic expectations. The world is unpredictable. The only thing we really have control over is ourselves. We must learn by trial and error. If we can't bounce back and learn from problems, if we run away from our problems or blame them on external factors, we can't grow. Of the myths just listed, the last three are especially handy rationalizations for avoiding the risk that comes with making a commitment. We can know or control only so much. Allowing time to pass may build motivation or increase our store of information, but time alone won't work any magic. We still need to make and implement a decision, however uncertain, in order to move forward.

INTERPERSONAL INFLUENCES

The problems most of us encounter as we grow into our own lifestyles and separate from our families are not usually great problems of moral principle but rather the daily discomforts that come with exercising independent thinking, feelings, and behaviors. Anxiety accompanies examining ourselves and our realistic opportunities; we may find problems or limitations we would prefer to ignore. Change, trying new things, committing ourselves to a decision with an uncertain outcome—all involve risks. Finally, we have the burden of responsibility for the choices we make and their consequences.

An independent choice, perhaps scary in itself, may seem especially difficult if others we care about disagree with our views. Although it is a much smaller source of outside influence than society as a whole, the family can assert an intimidating emotional influence. If our tentative plans generate familial conflict or disapproval, we may find it difficult to stick with them. Most of us have loved ones who want to be supportive but who nonetheless hold definite values and hopes for us—for example, that we be in a certain business or profession, mix with certain kinds of people, support a family, or take care of one at home. Our loved ones may have beliefs about what makes a "successful" adult—making money, helping others, or acquiring education or prestige. If we have a family of our own creation—a spouse and/or children—the problem becomes more complex, both financially and emotionally. We may experience conflict or guilt about taking time and money away from the family to pursue or change a career. Many times these loved ones feel let down by our choices. They don't realize that they may really be expecting us to meet their needs at the price of meeting our own. However unpleasant, we must sometimes fight it out with those we love in order to resolve our discomfort and help them understand our reasoning and goals. Resolution may mean acceptance or compromise.

If your initial announcement of career choices or interests causes consternation or conflict, you may need some time to think things through. Instead of perceiving the disagreement as a criticism of you or your judgment, try to understand the point of view of the others involved.

1. They may lack information about you or your choice.
2. They may think you're bucking an important family tradition.
3. Your choice may not fit their image of you.
4. They may think they have a better understanding of you or the world of work than you do.

5. Even though you've changed, they may still view you the way you were before.

6. They may believe you should engage only in certain kinds of work because of your gender or ethnic background.

7. They may be disappointed because they think your goals are either too low or unrealistically high.

8. They may be afraid of losing you because you are becoming independent and are changing your views of life.

9. They may be concerned about the costs associated with your choice, because they are footing the bill for your education or training.

10. They may depend on you financially or emotionally and fear your plan will jeopardize their current way of living.

11. They may be upset about the time or attention this choice will take away from the family.

Then consider your own feelings and attitudes. If you respond defensively, you may want to take some time out or talk with someone supportive to get yourself calmed down and more confident before renewing discussions with your loved ones. When you do return to your significant person or group to work at resolving the differences, try to do the following:

1. *Select a comfortable place to discuss your plan.* A public setting such as a park or a restaurant can be a good place to share your decision. It can help you feel relaxed, create the atmosphere of a special occasion, encourage a sense of mutual understanding, and discourage raised voices.

2. *Be positive, clear, and calm in presenting your choice.* Know yourself and what you want to do and can do. Use accurate, current, and unbiased career information to back up your decision and show that it's realistic and carefully thought out. Express your views enthusiastically.

3. *Be open to learn from what others say.* Invite their reactions without losing sight of your own objectives. Be willing to consider their views or change your mind if you find that you haven't seen things as fully or clearly as you had first thought.

4. *Be willing to listen to others.* Acknowledge others' feelings and interpretations before challenging them. Try to see the situation from other people's perspectives and let them know that you're trying to understand their point of view without compromising your own objectives.

5. *Be patient.* Others may take a while to change their views. Plant the seed of your view and nourish it over time with additional facts and observations. Knowing how these others usually behave can help you understand their challenge until they're willing to see your side.

6. *Build on your commonalities and agreements; minimize your differences.* This should be done honestly and openly, not in a shallow, camouflaging way. Show that you do not disagree about everything.

7. *Accept responsibility for your part of the conflict.* If conflict arises, don't blame or placate others—talk about it instead.

8. *Act assertively.* Express your needs and feelings in a nonjudgmental, responsible way. Identify the source(s) of disagreement (probably where interpretations differ) and discuss strategies for moving beyond them. For example, the pressure to live up to a family tradition may make you feel angry and disappointed. Stating what you feel and what causes you to feel that way, and asking that the family not have such fixed expectations of you, is an assertive way of dealing with the situation. Another assertive technique is to keep the discussion focused on the choice to be made, rather than letting it drift into an argument about personalities or past disagreements. If you have a job, a family of your own, or both, you can suggest acceptable compromises. You may be able to do what you want to but change your job, timetable, or other plans to minimize time and money pressures on yourself and on others.

The flowchart in Figure 8-1 gives a step-by-step example of how a hypothetical student, Suzanne, might deal with her family's reactions. Of course, not all such situations have an ideal outcome. If you think you're falling into self-defeating behaviors or avoiding conflict, you can turn to someone more objective to help sort things out. If you believe you've said and done all you can to resolve the issue and find that people important to you are still upset, you may feel that you must choose between a harmonious relationship and your career. At this point, you also have some sorting to do and may need help to see all sides of the problem. It's important to consider the feelings of people you love, especially those who may have to share directly in the results of your decision. But if you're thinking of compromising in your decision because of someone else's opinions, you must examine both yourself and the other person's feedback carefully. To

10-16
©1996 Bil Keane, Inc.
Dist. by Cowles Synd., Inc.

"Have you and Mommy decided which college I'll be workin' my way through?"

Family Circus, © 1996. Reprinted with special permission of King Features Syndicate.

Behavior →	Interpretation →	Feelings
Suzanne announces at a family dinner that she is leaving teacher education to major in business.	Her father and husband are both college professors with Ph.D.s. They feel she is abandoning a family tradition of careers in education. Her mother and her husband feel that a business career won't combine well with motherhood.	Family members feel hurt, angry, disappointed, worried that Suzanne is making the wrong choice. She is experiencing the same feelings.

Behavior →	Interpretation →	Feelings →	Behaviors →	Outcomes
Her family tells her she is making a mistake. Her father tells her she is choosing a material-istic career that won't benefit society. Her mother and her husband warn that she will not have the time or energy to spend with her children that a teacher would.	Suzanne may make several interpretations, leading to different feelings and behaviors:	She feels:		
	(a) I'm letting my family down.	Guilty, selfish.	Continues with education but is unhappy.	Trains for a career she doesn't like, resents her family's inter-ference, and later has to change careers.
	(b) My judgment is bad.	Self-doubt, anxiety.	Worries, vacillates, asks for advice.	Loses valuable time and confidence, is uncertain about whatever decision she makes.
	(c) Motherhood is compatible only with certain careers.	Trapped, fearful about future.	Avoids a decision, studies less, and goes out more.	Loses time, grades drop, ends up on probation, and cannot change majors.
	(d) My family doesn't care what I want.	Angry, hurt.	Rebelliously changes her major and remains angry at the family.	Goes into business at the cost of anger and strained relation-ships. Unresolved resentments later interfere with her career.
	(e) I need to work at clearing this up.	Hopeful, but worried.	Thinks and does research to confirm and improve her ability to explain her decision.	Talks out decision, listens to family arguments, works out compromises. She will try business but keep them informed and be alert for problems.

Figure 8-1   Sharing a decision with others: what can happen

avoid long-term problems with your career satisfaction you must make your choice not because you fear someone else's reaction but because the choice is in your best interests and is comfortable for you.

INTERNAL INFLUENCES

Successfully confronting and dealing with the concerns and barriers that come from within us is sometimes more difficult than coping with the outside factors—social and interpersonal—that we've just discussed. Our fears, prejudices, attitudes, and expectations can influence our view of the world of work in ways we don't even realize. For this reason, it's especially important to examine the myths and learned perspectives just mentioned to be sure they haven't contaminated the research you've done and the conclusions you've drawn. Many people look back at their career choices later in life and see that options they believed were closed to them because of something external were really blocked by their own fears or lack of confidence.

The good news about internal barriers is that, unlike external realities, we can control them. If we can uncover and face our fears, we can learn to deal with them, increase our confidence, and change our perspectives on ourselves and our career options.

Fears

In addition to the fears generated by conflict or misunderstandings with loved ones, we can feel completely (although usually temporarily) blocked by self-doubt, difficulty in trusting, lack of self-esteem, or fears about change, humiliation, or failure. For example, researchers (Belenky et al., 1986) have noted a problem for one particular group lay not in the workplace but inside them. They found that advantaged college women (who might seem to have everything) may still retreat into the "good girl" mentality when faced with diversity of opportunity. Women who follow this pattern prefer to observe, listen, and try to find identity in their relationships with others. These researchers conclude that neither families nor society seem to support risk taking in women. Unfortunately, people close to us may not give encouragement or permission for us to strike out on an unfamiliar or risky path. With no one handing us a right answer, making an autonomous decision often means that in spite of both our fears and external obstacles, we must give ourselves permission to go ahead with our choice.

Here's a list of questions generated by common fears, along with responses designed to help you gain perspective (adapted from Figler, 1994):

1. *Will my major prepare me for the job I want?* After several years of work, 50 percent or more of us hold jobs unrelated to what we studied in school.
2. *Will my education provide competitive credentials?* Research suggests that many factors other than credentials are important to being competitive. Among these are persistence, level of motivation, geographic flexibility,

background and experience, people skills, communication skills, and, of course, continued willingness to learn, grow, and adapt.

3. *Will jobs be available in my field? Will my skills become obsolete? Will I have job security?* To avoid obsolescence, we must pay attention to trends in our fields, keeping options open and skills updated, and forming contingency plans. Our vocational survival depends on a commitment to continued growth. Job security lies in preparedness, confidence, hard work, and the flexibility to change with the times. Holding multiple jobs no longer suggests instability; indeed, many people have several different careers, let alone multiple jobs, during their lives.

4. *Will I have good enough skills to succeed? Will I have the right skills to succeed?* Employers don't expect new hires to know everything. Often, they prefer someone with no bad habits whom they can train as they prefer. On-the-job training is common. In addition, job advancement hinges to a large degree on more generalized skills we all can acquire through experience, such as written and oral communication, analysis and planning, and cooperation with co-workers.

5. *Can current or past skills be converted into assets for a career change?* One discouraging thing about interest tests is that you often come out high in areas where you've had previous work experience, because of skills and attitudes you've acquired. Don't forget that most skills can be generalized. For example, teaching occurs in school settings, but also in counseling, corporate training, marketing, community activities, and so on. Interests, skills, and knowledge that you now have may allow you to find a job that brings you in contact with new areas of interest, or one where you can apprentice yourself to someone who will train you in exchange for your present skills.

6. *Will my field offer sufficient financial rewards?* Financial rewards in many fields may seem disappointing in the short run. Entry-level salaries are often modest, and new businesses require sacrifice. The key to a financially rewarding career is to look ahead. We must remain aware of changes and trends in our fields, keep old skills fresh, and build on present challenges to acquire new skills and to take advantage of new opportunities.

7. *What if I get good training and a good job and fail?* The fear of failure is something we all struggle with, no matter how confident or competent we are (or seem to be). Our fears take many forms: "I'll humiliate myself." "I'll disappoint myself." "I'll disappoint others." "I'll be exposed as a fraud." We fear we'll never recover from such a catastrophe, when in fact trial and error is the most effective kind of learning. We learn that we can indeed deal with setbacks and that they teach us grace under pressure. In fact, they help us to evaluate our strengths and limitations, as well as our decisions, and often spur us on to greater risk taking and bigger successes.

This brief look at some fears shared by everyone seeking a job or launching a career makes it clear that whatever our fears, they're probably more common, more manageable, and less catastrophic than we imagine. It's important to acknowledge and deal with them, since suppressing feelings takes energy and interferes with our effectiveness, even if we think they're well hidden. Searching for a career and a job can be scary and confusing, and we need all the confidence we have. To stick with our career exploration and job hunt, we must believe we can succeed. To do so, we need to confront and resolve or put into perspective our fears and potential problems. As Satchel Paige once put it:

- Avoid fried meats which angry up the blood.
- If your stomach disputes you, lie down and pacify it with cool thoughts.
- Keep the juices flowing by jangling around gently as you move.
- Go very light on the vices, such as carrying on in society. The social rumble ain't restful.
- Avoid running at all times.
- Don't look back. Something might be gaining on you.

INTEGRATED CAREER CHOICES

Assembling information from all significant internal and external sources and fitting feelings, data, and realities together to form a coherent picture of a career option (or more than one) is one of life's most challenging developmental tasks. It's hard work intellectually and emotionally. We encounter conflicts, doubts, and surprises as we learn about ourselves and the world of work, and we often change in the process—another surprise that may in turn alter our perspectives and require adjustments in our lives or goals. Letting go of old ideas, myths, expectations, and dependent decisions may be difficult but it is not negative. Moving ahead requires such changes and feelings—necessary vehicles for growth. We must move beyond our early view of the world as a place of right and wrong answers toward learning how to live with confusion and shades of gray. Only through our ability to tolerate ambiguity and anxiety can we follow Alan Alda's advice to "leave the city of your comfort and go into the wilderness of your intuition," where we will find the pathway from the jumble of feedback, information, advice, expectations, and dreams to the realization that we create our own options and answers by choosing from available alternatives those that fit us. To do this, we must examine our values, beliefs, interests, abilities, opportunities, and relationships. In developmental terms, integration means taking the internal (self-knowledge—attitudes, values, needs, feelings, interests, and abilities) and the external (the realities of the workplace, the opinions of others, the changing environment) and making them work together. In other words, integration means acting interdependently.

If this process, represented in Figure 8-2, gets short-circuited, we lose the ability to make (and appropriately change) decisions and commitments. Going through all the steps of gathering information about ourselves and the world of work and considering all the elements is difficult and sometimes discouraging. Doing so while still holding on to our dreams and ideals, being realistic without being cynical, accepting external limitations gracefully, and managing our own

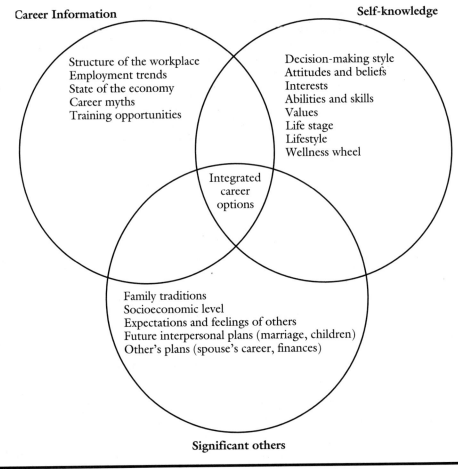

Figure 8-2 Self-knowledge, career information, and the dreams of significant others: three factors to consider in developing integrated career options

Career Information

Structure of the workplace
Employment trends
State of the economy
Career myths
Training opportunities

Self-knowledge

Decision-making style
Attitudes and beliefs
Interests
Abilities and skills
Values
Life stage
Lifestyle
Wellness wheel

Integrated
career
options

Family traditions
Socioeconomic level
Expectations and feelings of others
Future interpersonal plans (marriage, children)
Other's plans (spouse's career, finances)

Significant others

feelings requires courage and consistent effort. But when we've completed this process of integration, we'll be able to make and enjoy our best adult decisions and commitments.

CAREER ROADBLOCKS

Read the following vignettes. For each situation, brainstorm ideas for solutions and write them down. (Remember, brainstorming means just throwing in all ideas without evaluating them.) Then take the ideas and evaluate their pros and cons. Note who is influencing the decision maker and whether you think that influence is legitimate. See whether you can spot any ideas based on career myths.

See what values are being exercised and which of these might be in conflict. Where appropriate, consider possible legal ramifications or the effect on the economy. Try to determine what you think is the best solution and why.

1. Paget has taught physical education at a teacher's college for years. After a serious auto accident and months of physical therapy and rehabilitation, she can walk with two canes, but she can't do many things she did before. The staffing committee at her school is split over renewing her contract. Some feel she should be able to participate in all the activities she used to with students. Others feel that since she's not really teaching phys. ed. but teaching others how to teach it, she would do fine with a student assistant to help demonstrate and lead various sports. The staffing committee members would all like to support Paget's return to work, but they want to maintain the high quality of their teaching.

2. Leland wants to return to school and retrain himself in order to get out of a job he doesn't like. However, the program he wants is full-time for 2 years, which means that he, Candy, and their son would have to live on her income as a secretary. This would result in big lifestyle changes and a smaller place to live, among other sacrifices. Though Candy wants Leland to be happy, she's upset about these drastic changes. She doesn't understand why he took the job in the first place if it wasn't the right job for him.

3. Dennis and Susan are married and have just finished graduate school. Susan is a veterinarian specializing in large animals and has two likely offers, both in wonderful rural settings in the Midwest. Dennis is an expert in high-tech electronics, and his best opportunities lie in highly populated coastal areas such as New York or Los Angeles.

4. Tanya is a senior in college who has won a fellowship to go on in school. Surprised but thrilled, she feels that under the circumstances she can postpone her family until she is established in her career—say, age 32 or so. Her fiance, Harley, is against this. His parents were older when he was born, and he's always planned to have his children while he's young. He's hurt because he believes that a family should come first; he feels that Tanya can return to school when the children are older.

5. Jay was recently passed up for a promotion at age 46. He makes good money but realizes that he'll never go any higher in the company. He doesn't get along with his new boss. He wants to quit and turn his hobby of toymaking into a mail-order business. His wife, Glenda, fears the financial risk. She thinks she's too old now to start working, and they'll soon have two children ready for college.

6. Pearl heads a large data-processing department facing cutbacks. She must lay off one of the following employees. Which one should she let go and why?
   a. A recently hired college graduate who catches on quickly but has no experience.
   b. A 59-year-old woman who has been there 30 years. Though not energetic, she's careful and thorough.
   c. A 32-year-old woman who's a good worker but who is absent frequently (from a crucial job) because of a handicapped child.

    d. A 33-year-old man who has one of the less essential jobs in the department but is a close friend of the company's owner.

    e. A new immigrant who has some valuable technical expertise but takes extra time because of difficulty with the English language.

LETTER TO YOUR SIGNIFICANT OTHERS

Prepare a letter about your career plans to the person or people most important to you—your parents, spouse, fiancé, children, or friends. Use the following points as guidelines:

1. What I've learned about myself—interests, abilities, values, and what I need and want from a career.
2. What I've learned about the world of work and how it applies to me.
3. What career alternatives I've chosen and why.
4. What questions I have about how others might perceive my choice.
5. What myths or prejudices I think my loved ones and I might be subject to.
6. Why I might be nervous about sharing my feelings and ideas.
7. What kind of response I hope for.
8. Areas in which I would welcome advice.
9. What I plan to do next.

Since the relationships you value are an important part of your life, communicating your goals and hopes clearly is worth the effort. This will help you to think out and clarify your plans and to be aware of input that might be valuable. You can learn to listen without feeling pressured.

IDENTIFYING PATHWAYS AND ROADBLOCKS

To make a balanced career decision, you need to consider three sources of information and potential interference. These three (see Figure 8-2) are career information, significant others, and self-knowledge. Use the following exercise to evaluate where you stand on each of these.

1. Which of the three areas do I know the most about? _____

_____

What in this area do I still need to work on to increase my understanding? _____

2. Which of these areas do I feel best or most confident about? (This question is not necessarily the same as question 1. Consult your feelings, not your knowledge base.)

_____

_____

Why do I feel good about this? _____

_____

3. Which area do I know the least about? _____

_____

What things can I do to learn more about it? _____

_____

_____

How do I plan to do this? _____

_____

_____

_____

4. What area do I feel most scared or uncertain about? _____

_____

Why? _____

_____

What can I do to feel better about this? _____

_____

5. What one thing, if changed, would help me the most? _____

_____

What (if anything) can I do about it now? _____

_____

6. What strengths do I have that I can fall back on? _____

_____

_____

How can I use these to help in areas where I have problems or limitations? _____

_____

_____

MESSAGES FROM WITHIN

In our childhood, our parents try to socialize us—to teach us socially acceptable behavior. We learn (to different degrees) to be quiet, courteous, and obedient. Many of us learn to put the lid on tantrums, crying, hysterical excitement, or eagerness—in short, not to make any excessive emotional displays. By adulthood, many of us are unaware of, unfamiliar with, or afraid of our feelings. Being out of touch with feelings is a problem in making personal decisions and choices, because although feelings are nonrational and not very efficient, they are the source of much information about who we really are and what will make us happy. In this exercise, use the questions to recognize and assess feeling messages from your experiences that may reveal clues to your vocational identity.

Read these questions adapted from Figler (1994) and answer by describing one or two jobs, activities, situations, or ages or stages in your life that seem to fit. These can be from last week or from childhood. Then consider and discuss how this information fits your possible vocational skills, interests, or goals.

1. When have you felt most energized? Can you remember a time when you felt a high, as if the activity or situation gave you more energy than it took?

_____

_____

_____

2. When have you felt highly motivated? That is, when do you look forward to doing something and don't feel you must force yourself to get started?

_____

_____

_____

3. When have you felt fully involved in something, with no room for boredom or second thoughts?

_____

_____

_____

4. When have you felt the most respected and valued, or the greatest self-respect and pride?

_____

_____

_____

5. When have you felt the most challenged, anxious to better your previous performance or that of others?

  _____

  _____

  _____

6. When have you felt most comfortable with yourself? When can you be yourself, having no need to think about making an impression?

  _____

  _____

  _____

7. When have you felt most "in the groove"—as if you were a natural for some activity or situation?

  _____

  _____

  _____

8. Have you ever had feedback from others that you seem especially gifted in something? Did you know this about yourself, or were you surprised?

  _____

  _____

  _____

9. What do you believe in? Whether or not you are good at sales, what products, services, or ideas could you sell comfortably because of your convictions about their value?

  _____

  _____

  _____

10. Keeping in mind your current vocational interest (or one that you have wondered about), review your answers to the previous questions to see what clues they provide that might shed new light on your career search.

  _____

  _____

  _____

***

REFERENCES AND RESOURCES

Bandura, A. (1982). Self-efficacy theory in human agency. *American Psychologist, 37,* 122–147.

Belenky, M. F., Clinchy, B. M., Goldberger, N. R., & Tarule, J. M. (1986). *Women's ways of knowing: The development of self, voice and mind.* New York: Basic Books.

Carney, C. G., and Reynolds, A. (1985). *When others challenge your career choice: Strategies for conflict resolution.* Columbus: Ohio State University, Counseling and Consultation Service.

Covey, S. (1989). *Seven habits of highly effective people.* New York: Simon & Schuster.

Figler, H. (1994). Give yourself permission to pursue the career you really want. *Planning job choices, 1994* (37th ed., pp. 4–11). Bethlehem, PA: College Placement Council.

Knefelkamp, L. L., and Slepitza, R. (1976). A cognitive-developmental model of career development: An adaptation of the Perry scheme. *Counseling Psychologist, 6*(3), 53–58.

Matteson, D. R. (1975). *Adolescence today: Sex roles and the search for identity.* Homewood, IL: Dorsey Press.

Perry, W. G. (1970). *Forms of intellectual and ethical development in the college years.* New York: Holt, Rinehart, & Winston.

Stewart, A., & Healy, J. M., Jr. (1989). Linking individual development and social changes. *American Psychologist, 44,* 30–42.

CHAPTER 9

FINDING A JOB IS A JOB!

"Does this mean I have to go to work?"

Grin and Bear It, © 1993. Reprinted with special permission of North America Syndicate.

Before you begin a thing, remind yourself that difficulties and delays quite impossible to foresee are ahead. If you could see them clearly, naturally you could do a great deal to get rid of them but you can't. You can only see one thing clearly and that is your goal. Form a mental vision of that and cling to it through thick and thin.

—*Kathleen Norris*

5:30 P.M. "It's been a long and frustrating afternoon," Mr. Stranges thought as he picked up his briefcase and left the interviewing room of the college placement office. He'd interviewed five students since he'd arrived on campus that morning, but he hadn't found the right combination of enthusiasm, style, goal direction, well-roundedness, and experience essential for the position. To make matters worse, one of the candidates had presented a poorly prepared résumé, another was overly anxious, and the candidate who was best prepared didn't want to relocate.

As he walked to his car, his mind drifted to words from the legendary football coach Vince Lombardi: "If you aren't fired with enthusiasm you will be fired with enthusiasm." Mr. Stranges decided to put it another way: "If you aren't fired with enthusiasm, you won't be hired with enthusiasm." His train of thought continued: "I just wish they'd prepare earlier and think more about what they want ahead of time. It would save them a lot of disappointment and me a lot of time. I hope things will improve tomorrow."

As he found out later that night during dinner with some interviewers, every profession has its quirky and humorous side; employment interviews boast their share of strange twists of events. The conversation turned to a national survey of one hundred vice presidents and personnel directors, who were asked to describe their most unusual experiences interviewing job applicants. In one story, an applicant challenged the interviewer to arm wrestle. In another, an applicant fell asleep during the interview. When asked about his academic and work experience, another candidate said he never finished high school, because he had been kidnapped and kept in a closet in Mexico. One poor fellow fell and broke his arm during the interview (do you think he was the arm wrestler?). Another fell over when he stood up at the end of the interview because his foot had fallen asleep.

Other stories included a candidate who brought a dog to the interview (it wasn't a seeing-eye dog). And there were stories of a woman who kept her raincoat on during the interview because she had forgotten to put on her skirt, a man who had forgotten to zip his fly, and a bald man who had forgotten to put on his hairpiece (Harden, 1989; Laugh of the Day, 1996).

The stories climaxed with a joke:

Reaching the end of a job interview, the human resources (HR) person asked the M.B.A. fresh out of graduate school, "And what starting salary were you looking for?" The candidate said, "In the neighborhood of $125,000 a year, depending on the benefits package." The HR person said, "Well, what would you say to a package of 5 weeks of vacation, 14 paid holidays, full medical and dental, company matching retirement fund to 50 percent of salary, and a company car leased every 2 years—say, a red Corvette?" The engineer sat up straight and said, "Wow!!! Are you kidding?" And the HR person said, "Certainly, but you started it."

Although he laughed at the stories, Mr. Stranges realized that the students he'd interviewed that day would be disappointed when they received a letter of rejection from his firm.

All these stories about interviewing disasters share a common theme: A primary reason why students have difficulty in securing a job is their inability to communicate their interests and talents effectively to an employer. To avoid this pitfall, preparation for a job search should begin well in advance of the senior year—ideally, during the first year of college, when part-time and summer jobs are sought. Although a temporary job may involve less personal investment than a long-term job, the two share some important similarities. By capitalizing on these similarities, job seekers tend to pursue their career goals more effectively.

To be fair to the applicants in the interviewing stories, we should point out that job applicants also tell many quirky and humorous stories. *Worksearch,* a Web guide for applicants seeking employment, asks its readers about their worst interviewing experiences. Here's what some of the respondents disclosed:

- A person applying for a marketing job at a junior college was asked, "Why did you give up teaching?" He had never been a teacher. It turned out that someone had stapled part of another applicant's résumé to his.
- One boss told a candidate that she'd be hired if she painted her toenails red.
- Some of the questions that applicants were asked include

  "Discuss morals."

  "How would your epitaph read?"

  "If we don't hire you, can we still have your ideas?"

  "If you were a vegetable, which one would it be?"

  "We don't pay anyone what they are worth."

  "How will you motivate yourself to excel and improve company profits without personal financial incentive?"

  "I can't see you and you can't see me. We're on the phone. Now, tell me how to tie my shoelaces."

  "Do you have any problems with someone calling you 'Shorty'?"

- Another applicant was told, "We like people with strong communications traits. Do you have the ability to lie?"

- Other stories include a candidate told that she was exactly what the employer wanted, but there was "no way" he could put "someone as good-looking as you on a shop floor with 300 men."
- One interviewer was swaying back and forth on his chair asking questions. His chair fell backwards and he landed on the floor. The applicant was so tense she couldn't stop laughing. The interviewer got up and finished the interview. The interviewee was not hired.

PROFITING FROM EXPERIENCE

Temporary and long-term work provide excellent opportunities to learn and demonstrate new skills. For example, a newspaper route provides a young person a chance to learn how to deal with the public, to sell a product, to manage money, and to organize time around work tasks. It's wise to investigate and consider any appropriate volunteer or cooperative educational experiences available through your college or other sources. Such experiences provide a rich source of occupational information, as well as opportunities to confirm and develop your skills and to build an informational network.

If you begin the process of refining your job search skills during college, you can take advantage of your personal support and easily attainable resources of your campus placement office. This chapter will help you learn formal job-search skills you can use while applying for temporary or volunteer work during college, as well as for permanent jobs after graduation.

> Learning—a kind of natural food for the mind.
>
> —*Cicero*

THE TRADITIONAL JOB CAMPAIGN

To conduct an effective job campaign, you'll need to answer four questions:

1. What do I want to do?
2. When will I begin my job search?
3. Where do I want to work?
4. How will I go about getting a job?

What Do I Want to Do?

Learning about possible answers to this question, as well as narrowing down ideas, has been our focus up to this point. As you know, this decision stems from your personal qualities and self-image. These include your preferences, attitudes, beliefs, values, interests, and skills. You express them in your work history, self-assessment activities, work orientation, ideal job description, lifestyle preferences, daily decisions, and interactions with others. Personal qualities and self-image are in turn affected by your history, experience, decision and planning style, life stage, and choice of lifestyle. When you make and implement tentative commitments, you must pay attention to specific preferences, such as work location, environment, and level; to the training and experience needed; and to the balance between what you must give to the job and what you'll get out of it. The search for occupational information and opportunities can clarify many of these issues.

When Will I Begin?

This question has two parts: (1) When should I start work? and (2) When do I begin my job campaign? Coming up with a date for starting work will allow time to plan a thorough job campaign, one that will let you explore many options with little time pressure. Although we have no precise rules about how much time to spend preparing for and conducting a job campaign, a good rule of thumb is this: A typical job campaign takes 15 hours a week for 4 to 6 months. Planning ahead will produce better, and perhaps quicker, results. For example, say you're thinking about working at a national park for the summer. You might start writing for information during the preceding fall. That gives you at least 5 months to explore options and another 5 months to conduct a formal job search.

Where Do I Want to Work?

Getting started   Having clarified a personal direction and decided how much time you need for a job campaign, you can begin the task of identifying and evaluating specific work opportunities. Be creative. Cast your job information net as far and wide as you can. Use the informational resources that are close to home, such as your friends' parents, friends of your parents, and your relatives. About 60 percent of jobs are found through such forms of networking. Also, use the help-wanted and business sections of newspapers and trade journals (20 percent of jobs are found in this way), professional associations, government employment services, private personnel recruiting firms, temporary employment agencies, direct contact with employers, and, of course, the internet.

Take advantage of the placement office on your campus. Placement professionals can help you locate jobs, help you polish written application materials and interviewing skills, and match you with employers recruiting on your campus. Another potential resource is the college alumni office. The staff there may provide a list of alumni in jobs or work settings that appeal to you. They may also know people who can help you in other ways. Finally, seek the assistance of your academic adviser and other faculty members who teach in areas related to your career interests.

Don't be afraid to respond to blind advertisements in the newspaper—the ads that ask people to send their credentials to a post office box. Marvin Walberg, the author of many helpful newspaper articles on the job-search process (1993), has pointed out that firms may use blind ads for legitimate reasons. For example, if a company is highly visible in the local community, recruiters for the company may not wish to be overwhelmed with applications for the position. Or, the company could be exploring the feasibility of relocating to a new community and use an ad to see whether a qualified applicant pool exists. A company thinking about restructuring its operations may look for new faces for key new positions while trying to avoid unduly upsetting the current staff.

Avoid restrictive thinking! James E. Challenger (1992) has pointed out several myths people need to avoid during a job campaign. The first myth is that you should limit your job search to large companies because they have more people and pay more than smaller firms. Actually, the opposite is true. In today's economy, the small and medium-sized organizations are doing the hiring. They also offer salaries and benefit packages that compete with those of larger companies.

Another myth is that one should stay away from companies that are downsizing. Though such companies may cut back staff in product areas that no longer sell, they may simultaneously add staff in more profitable product lines. Further, they may be entering new market areas that require new employee skills. Finally, they could be offering buyout or early retirement packages for older and more highly paid employees and seeking to replace them with entry-level staff.

Challenger has also advised people to avoid time-trap myths, such as the belief that you shouldn't look for a job during holiday and vacation seasons. Another time-trap myth is the notion that employment interviews can only take place between 8 A.M. and 5 P.M. on a weekday. Neither myth is true. Employers hire throughout the year, and many of them will schedule after-hours appointments if the situation warrants it.

In reviewing help-wanted ads, you may find yourself scratching your head and wondering what demented mind in the personnel office came up with buzzwords and phrases such as *facilitation skills* and *product specialist*. And, exactly, what kind of "room to grow," "excellent benefits," and "job security" can you expect? Al Sicherman, a writer for the *Minneapolis–St. Paul Star Tribune*, has offered some humorous insight into the clichés of the personnel office (see the box, "Translations Tell Story. . .).

The next steps   Having cultivated informational resources and learned a bit more about the mythologies and code language associated with the job search process, you will pull in your informational net to see how many employment prospects you have. A bit of preliminary research on each organization you're thinking of contacting can help you in subsequent job interviews. Gather as much information as possible about employers. Use company brochures, trade and professional newsletters, public financial information (including salary information, which is vital in negotiating employment conditions), internet sites such as those in Table 9-1, and word-of-mouth insights from friends, family, college faculty, and placement-office staff. All these sources can help provide a picture of a firm's economic stability and growth potential.

Most job applicants use a mass-mailing procedure, sending the same résumé and cover letter to all employers, however they may differ. This approach can have some success, but it will not catch an employer's eye as effectively as a cover letter showing that you know about the employer's enterprise. The background

Translations Tell Story Between the Lines of Help-Wanted Ads

By Al Sicherman
Minneapolis–St. Paul Star Tribune

If you've answered a help-wanted advertisement any time recently, you might well have discovered that the job didn't bear much resemblance to the description in the advertisement.

This is because many employers, knowing that no sane person would willingly apply for some of the jobs they offer, tend to place somewhat obscure ads, hoping to sway you with a cup of vending-machine coffee when you turn up to interview.

The startling truth is that in generating these cloudy ads, employers make use of a set of code words even more closely guarded than that employed in the real estate advertising profession.

As a public service, and at no small danger to myself, I have obtained translations of the most-common such words and phrases.

Product specialist: Phone sales.

Marketing specialist: Phone sales to people who have already said no.

Career opportunity: Starting salary would not support a large dog.

Competitive pay: We pay the minimum wage, just like our competitors do.

Competitive compensation: We pay the minimum wage, just like our competitors do, and you have to wear a suit.

Entry-level position: Minimum wage, unpleasant conditions, advancement impossible.

Room to grow: Minimum wage, unpleasant conditions; you get to fill in at next-level job at no higher pay.

Job security: We won't fire you unless we want to.

Prestige: You may purchase a bowling shirt and/or hat carrying the company logo.

Source: Sicherman, 1992.

Excellent benefits: The company nurse is experienced in dealing with lacerations caused by plant machinery.

Major medical coverage: You pay 100 percent of everything short of triple bypass surgery.

Challenge: Your desk has no chair.

Supervisory skills: You will search arriving employees for weapons.

Interpersonal skills: Employees and management do not speak to each other.

Coordination skills: Employees and management do not even write to each other except through third parties.

Facilitation skills: Employee-management disputes now involve permanent howitzer emplacements.

Report directly to board of directors: President, CEO and all department heads have quit.

Team player: Last person to push a new idea was shot.

Stable working situation: Nothing has changed here since McKinley was assassinated.

Able to work in a changing environment: Boss is unable to decide what he wants.

Sunny personality: You are expected to provide doughnuts.

Flexible schedule: You will never work the same shift twice.

Management position: Lots of overtime, no extra pay, everybody hates you.

Self-starter: Nobody knows what you're supposed to do.

Function independently as part of a team: Even you will never figure out what you're supposed to do.

Table 9-1   Web Site Job-Search Sources

America's Job Bank	http://www.ajb.dni.us/
Career Mosaic	http://www.careermosaic.com
Careernet	http://www.careers.org/
CareerPath	http://www.careerpath.com
Career Web	http://www.cweb.com/
Fedworld (U.S. Government)	http://www.fedworld.gov/
Government Information Exchange	http://www.info.gov/
Jobsmart (Northern California)	http://www.jobsmart.org
Mainstream Worklife Center	http://www.worklife.com/
Monster Board	http://www.monster.com/
Online Career Center	http://www.occ.com/
Riley's Guide	http://www.jobtrak.com/jobguide
USA Federal Jobs	http://www.usajobs.opm.gov/

information you've gathered to identify potential employers will help you tailor a cover letter to an employer's needs. Some students use the same résumé with different cover letters for different employers, while others—especially with access to word processors and computers—create a cover letter and résumé for each employer.

The knowledge you've gathered about employers can also help you decide which applications to send out in the first place. After all, employees hire employers too! In making such initial decisions, it's helpful to prepare a list of criteria for evaluating employers. Such criteria might include the size of the organization, its location, its history and image, its products or services, its administrative and promotional structure, its atmosphere and attitudes toward employee wellness, and its future prospects. We provide specific guidelines for preparing a cover letter and résumé later in this chapter.

A NOVEL APPROACH TO JOB CAMPAIGNING

Richard Bolles (1997) has created an alternative approach to the traditional job search just discussed. He advocates starting a job campaign in the traditional way: Identify the skills and interests you want to make use of through work. After you determine what you want to do, identify the specific geographical location where you want to live. Do this by making up a list of criteria for an ideal living and working environment (size of community, weather preference, terrain, leisure and cultural opportunities) and then identifying the place or places that most closely match those criteria. Then have local telephone companies send you directories for communities that interest you. Directories can also be used to explore community resources and to identify and contact potential employers. The internet may have some of this information as well.

Tips for Advertising Yourself in Cyberspace

If you create your own web page to advertise your availability for employment, keep the following points in mind:

- Surf the web and printed employment sources for information about the types of employer that interest you.
- Look at the web pages of other applicants to get ideas for your own presentation, but respect their right not to have their ideas used without their permission.
- Use the information that you've gathered to prepare your home page.
- Remember that simplicity and clarity are essential if you want to attract and keep an employer's attention.
- Sell yourself as you are, not as an artificial image of who you think you should be to get a job.

Once you decide on a particular place, visit it to conduct a job-information campaign. Contact the Chamber of Commerce in each area for information about community resources and the quality of life in that setting. Though visiting different areas can be expensive, you can offset the cost by using the job campaign as a working vacation—visiting areas of interest during free time prior to a job search.

You can take two steps in contacting employers in a preferred environment: conduct a community survey and submit a prospectus. To canvass a community, locate at least one work setting where you can use your talents, and then attempt to set up an information-gathering interview with the person who makes decisions about hiring in that setting. Such people might include vice presidents, managers, and personnel directors but not clerks and receptionists, who simply implement decisions. Through the information-gathering interview, you can explore in a personal way the atmosphere of the company, its plan for the future, and the specific needs of the employer. The idea is to gather and share information, not secure a job. Remembering this can alleviate anxieties about applying for a job and provide valuable insights into the organization. At the end of the information-gathering interview, ask the person for names of other individuals in similar positions you can contact for additional informational interviews. Contact and interview these people in a similar manner until you've canvassed the entire community.

A thorough informational-interviewing campaign will cover most of the employers who may have jobs of the type you wish to pursue. The campaign can lead to three important outcomes: (1) you'll know where the potential but hidden jobs are (up to 80 percent of the jobs in the United States are hidden); (2) you'll know which companies offer the work atmosphere that most appeals to you; and (3) you'll be more confident about what you want to do and be able to sell yourself better.

Dilbert reprinted by permission of United Feature Syndicate, Inc.

In the second step—developing a prospectus to submit to desired employers—your prospectus should include your observations of the positive aspects of the employer's setting, your projections of the employer's needs, and the special qualities you have to offer to fill those needs. In essence, you're writing your own job description—a contract open to mutual negotiation. After the employer has had time to read your prospectus, you should recontact him or her and set up an interview to present your case, a task that requires a considerable amount of self-confidence and sensitivity to others.

CONTENTS OF A RÉSUMÉ

Let's try an experiment. Stop reading! Put this book down. Look at your watch and let a minute pass by. One minute—60 seconds. When we're rushed, a minute passes too fast; when we're waiting, it can seem like a lifetime!

Now, imagine that you're an employment interviewer hurriedly reading through a stack of student résumés in a college placement office. Your time is limited, and you must work fast. How fast? You guessed it. According to Tom Jackson (1993), author of *Guerilla Tactics in the New Job Market,* 1 minute is the average amount of time employment interviewers spend reviewing a résumé. During that brief period, a decision will be made about whether or not an applicant will get an employment interview.

Preparing an effective résumé takes creativity. The résumé must immediately capture the reader's interest through its clear and crisp language, logical format, and brevity. For most students, a one-page résumé will do. Two pages are warranted for people who possess considerable work experience and seniority. Write several drafts of your résumé and cover letter. Experiment with different formats to develop an approach that best suits you. An outline of the contents of a résumé and examples of the different types follow. And always keep in mind what William James once said:

> The art of being wise is knowing what to overlook.
>
> —*William James*

Identifying information   Include here your name, address, telephone number, and e-mail address. You can also present permanent and temporary addresses, if helpful.

Job or position objective   The job or position objective identifies the responsibilities, challenges, and work activities you wish to assume. Use job titles (for example, medical laboratory technician, marketing representative, elementary school teacher) or descriptive phrases to specify the kind of job you seek. The *Dictionary of Occupational Titles* and the *Occupational Outlook Handbook* may help you locate appropriate job titles and articulate the range of duties being sought. Position descriptions posted in newspaper ads, trade journals, and college placement offices are also good sources of such information.

An alternative to the job or position objective is the summary statement. It requires you to use a maximum of three sentences to summarize your years of work experience, when you gained that experience, and how you can benefit the employer.

If you're not clear about the type of work you wish to pursue, want to leave your options open, or have limited work experience, you may wish to eliminate this section from your résumé. Your college placement officer or the personnel offices at the places you're contacting can tell you if the employer expects a job objective or summary statement.

Educational background   List schools attended, dates, degrees, diplomas, and certificates, with emphasis on the highest level achieved and relevant special training pertinent to your job objective.

Experience or work history   Provide a summary of your work experience describing the nature of the work, job titles, name of employer, and inclusive dates of employment. Emphasize the work experience relevant to your job objective or summary statement. Be sure to list all summer, part-time, and significant volunteer positions.

Military record   Summarize your service obligations, if any, or your service experience, if your tour of duty is completed. If your work history and educational background are mostly military, include your military experience and training under the previous headings.

References   Simply state that references will be supplied on request. If you're registered with a placement office and have a complete credential/job-placement file, indicate how to get your confidential data from that office, noting its full address and telephone number. Before this point, you should have already done three things: identified people who will provide references for you, asked permission to use their names, and obtained their complete addresses, phone numbers, and e-mail addresses.

Personal data   Include early background (if significant), hobbies, and other activities. Do not include personal characteristics such as age, gender, marital status, or physical disabilities. Your employer will ask for this information after you are hired.

Date, statement of availability   These items are optional, but it is desirable to date each résumé as you distribute it and to mention when you can begin work.

Résumé Suggestions

Here are some ideas on how to create a successful résumé (items 1–11 from Dunphy, 1973, pp. 89–90).

1. Confine a résumé to one page, if possible. Few college students have had enough experience to justify more than that. If you are one of those few, don't hesitate to use the space you need to tell your story, but don't go beyond two pages.

2. Experiment with the arrangement of headings and text so as to find the best total appearance and readability. Use capital letters and underlining sparingly. You can use indentation as a means of identifying separate items. Organize material so that the reader can easily find facts and categories.

3. Balance the material on the page so that the total effect is pleasing to the eye. Leave sufficient margins so that the page doesn't look crowded. Fill the page to eliminate excessive space at the bottom.

4. Be consistent in the use of graphic display techniques. For example, don't use indentation in one section and underscoring in the next.

5. As you edit your material, keep in mind your intended purpose. Eliminate unimportant details; stress accomplishments you're proud of. Write and rewrite until you feel you've provided factual and positive statements of your experience that promise potential and continued growth.

6. As long as your meaning is clear, you may write in complete or partial sentences. The test is whether your text is readable and understandable. Use simple words that convey exactly what you mean. Use punctuation marks intelligently.

7. You don't need to use the first-person pronoun unless the text doesn't make sense without it. Since you're writing about yourself, verbs will imply the "I" as the subject of your sentences. Do not use the third person to refer to yourself unless it's contained in a quote from another person.

8. Use the present or active tense when you refer to current activities (for example, supervise, manage, develop), but use past tense for anything previous.

9. Avoid the use of slang, professional jargon, and clichés. Do not abbreviate. Employers who have to take time to interpret what you're saying will probably not bother.

10. Consult a dictionary or use your word processor's spelling checker for correct spelling. Mistakes reflect on your education and therefore on your qualifications.

11. Before you type your final copy, have someone else read your résumé. Your family and friends or your college placement officer may offer helpful suggestions. Consider your own reaction after setting it aside for a day or two. Would you hire the person described in this résumé?

12. Have your résumés reproduced by a reputable copy or printing service.

13. When contacting an employer through the mail, always enclose a résumé with a typed letter of introduction. (See the section on cover letters that follows.)

RÉSUMÉ ORGANIZATION

If your most recent educational or work activity is your most important, place it first in the résumé. Other experiences should then be listed in order of occurrence. Start with the most recent and end with the most distant. Include the starting and ending dates of each.

Before you begin writing, jot down all your educational and work experiences. Then go back and select those directly related to the job you're applying

Daffy's résumé
The Far Side, copyright Farworks, Inc. Dist. by Universal Press Syndicate.
Reprinted with permission. All rights reserved.

for. In this way you'll avoid the common pitfall of losing the most significant aspects of your work history in a Web of unessential facts and dates and unimportant jobs.

The chronological format is probably the most common, especially for job seekers with limited experience. Its logical sequence makes it easy to follow and allows the reader to trace your educational and work history rapidly.

The functional approach highlights the function or title of the positions you held. In this type of résumé, you place your most significant work experience immediately before the employer. Job titles and specific duties are highlighted to support your qualifications for the job. Although you should include names of employers and dates of employment with each description, remember that they come in second to the functions or positions you wish to emphasize.

This approach will be especially useful as you gain more experience. It allows you to highlight part-time, temporary, and volunteer work in your career field more effectively than you could do in a chronological résumé.

The combination résumé tends to be more focused than the other types of résumés. It minimizes employment dates and job titles and stresses transferrable skills, accomplishments, and work experiences. Because it focuses on skills and accomplishments, it makes the applicant appear focused on his or her skills, experiences, and accomplishments.

The sample résumés that follow highlight the career path of Virginia Romfh, Robert Milt, and Ginny Hillier. As you read their résumés, notice how Virginia and Robert use different types of résumés to accomplish different job objectives. Note also how they emphasize different aspects of their work histories in each résumé, thus demonstrating to employers that they have the skills and experience required to succeed in the positions they're applying for.

COVER LETTER AND FOLLOW-UP CALLS

Each time you send a résumé, you need to include a cover letter as well. The cover letter introduces you to the employer by indicating why you're writing and what you can do for his or her organization. The cover letter briefly highlights your qualifications for the position and suggests a follow-up interview so you can fully present your background experiences. Suggestions for preparing a cover letter and a sample cover letter follow. Typed cover letters always look more professional and present a résumé better than handwritten letters do.

Unless you've been advised to correspond directly with your potential supervisor through referral, it's best to direct initial correspondence to the company's director of personnel. Even though some popular books suggest going around the director, surveys conducted by the Administrative Management Society have shown that most employers still prefer that applicants start with the personnel office.

Pay attention to the smallest details! Marvin Walberg (1997) advises that when you begin the process of sending out your application materials, to give some thought to the hidden or mixed messages you may be sending to potential employers. For example, listen to the message you've placed on your telephone

Chronological Format

Virginia A. Romfh
P.O. Box 1607
Gambier, OH 43022
555/555-5555

EDUCATION

Kenyon College: Bachelor of Arts Degree   May 1994
Major: Classics   Minor: Anthropology/Archaeology   GPA: 3.0

WORK EXPERIENCE

January–May 1994	Writing center assistant, Kenyon College
Summer 1993	Temporary help, employed by Express Services, The Job Team, and Kelly Temporary Services, Bellingham, WA
Summer 1992	Waitress. Chief Enterprises, Custer, SD
Summer 1991	Administrative assistant. Civil Service Career Development Center, U.S. Department of State, Washington, DC
Summer 1990	Summer clerical intern. Department of State, Washington, DC

STUDY AND TRAVEL ABROAD

August–December 1992	College Year in Athens: College Study in Greece
August 1989–June 1990	Open Door: 13th Year Abroad Program in Germany
Summer 1987	German American Partnership Program (GAPP) Additional travel to Australia, Turkey, Hungary

INTERESTS AND ACTIVITIES

Creative writing:	Poetry, short stories, and a novel Since 1984
Xenophilia:	Student multicultural journal 1993–1994

Functional Format

Virginia A. Romfh
P.O. Box 1607
Gambier, OH 43022
555/555-5555

WORK EXPERIENCE

Writing Center Assistant	Kenyon College	January–May 1994
Temporary Clerical Helper	Express Services, The Job Team, and Kelly Temporary Services, Bellingham, WA	Summer 1993
Waitress	Chief Enterprises, Custer, SD	Summer 1992
Administrative Assistant	Civil Service Career Development Center, U.S. Department of State, Rosslyn, VA	Summer 1991

- Managed the Center two days a week and during counselor's vacation.
- Wrote handbook for administrative assistant position, created entries for an annotated bibliography of the resources, and drafted instructions for the equipment.
- Word processed, compiled statistics, inventoried, and ordered supplies.
- Invented and installed the Center's resource checkout system, thus increasing the number of resources checked out and returned.
- Designed advertising for Center's workshops and seminars.
- Introduced Civil Service employees to the Center and resources.

Summer Clerical Intern	U.S. Department of State, Washington, DC	Summer 1990

- Eliminated office backlog of filing; tracked down and retrieved missing personnel files.
- Edited office secretarial handbook and compiled a list of offices worldwide and their location codes.
- Drafted telegrams, entered data into computer, and typed memos.

EDUCATION

Kenyon College	Bachelor of Arts Degree May 1994
	Major: Classics Minor: Anthropology/Archaeology GPA: 3.0

STUDY AND TRAVEL ABROAD

August–December 1992	College Year in Athens: College Study in Greece
August 1989–June 1990	Open Door: 13th Year Abroad Program in Germany
Summer 1987	German American Partnership Program (GAPP) Additional travel to Australia, Turkey, Hungary

INTERESTS AND ACTIVITIES

Creative writing: *Xenophilia*	Poetry, short stories, and a novel Since 1984 Student multicultural journal 1993–1994

Analytical Format

Virginia A. Romfh
P.O. Box 1607
Gambier, OH 43022
555/555-5555

EDUCATION

Kenyon College

Bachelor of Arts Degree   May 1994
Major: Classics   Minor: Anthropology/Archaeology   GPA: 3.0

EXPERIENCE

Administrative

Administrative assistant for newly opened Civil Service Career Development Center, U.S. Department of State, Rosslyn, VA, Summer 1991.

- Managed the center two days a week and during career counselor's vacation.
- Wrote handbook for administrative assistant position, created entries for an annotated bibliography of the resources, and drafted instructions for the equipment.
- Used word processor, compiled statistics, inventoried and ordered supplies.
- Invented and installed the center's resource checkout system thus increasing the number of resources checked out and returned.
- Designed advertising for center's workshops, seminars.
- Introduced civil service employees to the center and resources.

Clerical

Summer clerical intern in charge of personnel files for foreign service employees working in Latin and South America, U.S. Department of State, Washington, DC, Summer 1990.

- Eliminated backlog of filing, tracked down and retrieved missing personnel files.
- Edited office secretarial handbook, compiled list of offices worldwide and their location codes.
- Drafted telegrams, entered data in computer, typed memos.

Temporary office helper employed by Express Services, The Job Team, and Kelly Temporary Services, Bellingham, WA, Summer 1993.

*Teaching/
Service*

Writing Center assistant helping college students improve their writing skills, Kenyon College, January to May 1994.
Waitress, Chief Enterprises, Custer, SD, Summer 1992.

INTERESTS AND ACTIVITIES

*International
Travel*

- College year in Athens: College Study in Greece, August–December 1992
- Open Door: 13th Year Abroad Program in Germany, August 1989–June 1990
- German American Partnership Program (GAPP), Summer 1987
- Additional travel to Australia, Turkey, and Hungary

Writing

Presently writing a novel. Have submitted poetry and short stories to student publications at Kenyon College.

Robert A. Milt
P.O. Box 1257
Gambier, OH 43022
(555) 555-5555

Education	Kenyon College B.A. History candidate May 1998
Research Experience	**National Endowment for the Humanities Younger Scholar,** Summer 1996

—Presented findings of intensive scholarly research at the National Conference on Undergraduate Research at the University of North Carolina at Asheville.

Family Farm Project Student Participant, Kenyon College, 1995 - 1996
—Interviewed members of the Knox County, Ohio, community to assess and discuss the changes occurring in the local farm economy.
—Designed and authored Family Farm Project Web-Site (www.kenyon.edu/projects/famfarm). Won 1996 Ohio Association of Historical Societies and Museums' Outstanding Achievement Award and the Ohio Academy of History Public History Award.

Oral History Archives Intern, Washington, DC, Spring 1997
—Produced archival records for the United States Holocaust Memorial Museum's Research Institute.

Course Development Opportunity and Pew Charitable Trusts' Institute Participant, Kenyon College, Summer 1994
—Aided in the design of an introductory physics computer program for the Kenyon Physics Department.
—Participated in Institute to facilitate the increased usage of information technologies by first- and second-year undergraduates.

Leadership

Search Committee Member, Kenyon College, 1995, 1996
—Chosen as one of two students for the Dean of Residential Life search committee.
—Interviewed and selected the Director of the Career Development Center.

House Manager, Kenyon College, 1995 - 1996, 1997 - Present
—Coordinated, supervised, and was responsible for all social and educational programs for up to 80 students in a residence hall.
—Analyzed challenges and developed dynamic solutions for a diverse student population with members of the student affairs team.

Civil Involvement

Research and Archival Services Intern, The History Factory, Chantilly, VA, 1997
—Participated in weekly strategy meetings.
—Consulted with the International Paper 100th Anniversary planning committee.
—Organized and cataloged International Paper's artifact and document collection.
—On-site researcher for Kimberly-Clark Corporation archives in Neenah, WI.

Robert A. Milt

P.O. Box 1257
Gambier, OH 43022
(555) 555-5555

miltr@kenyon.edu

36 Warren Ave.
Plymouth, MA 02360
(555) 555-5555

Education
Kenyon College, Gambier, OH
  B.A. History candidate   May 1998

Employment/Internships
The History Factory, Chantilly, VA, Summer 1997
  Processed and cataloged International Paper 100th Anniversary collection.
  On-site reference archivist for Kimberly-Clark Corporation in Neenah, WI.

Oral History Archives Intern, United States Holocaust Memorial Museum, Washington, DC,
Spring 1997
  Produced a fully cataloged collection consisting of oral history interviews with Holocaust survivors
  and liberators accessible via the Internet.

Archive Intern, Chicago, IL, Fall 1996
  Interned at the archives of the College of American Pathologists, Motorola Corporation, and
  Loyola University. Processed documents and images.

Office Assistant for the Dean of Academic Advising, Kenyon College, Summer 1996
  Organized and coordinated mailings and files for the incoming class, faculty advisors, upperclass
  counselors, and resident advisors.

Pew Charitable Trusts' Course Design Opportunity, Kenyon College, Summer 1994
  Participated in the design of an introductory physics computer program for the Kenyon Physics
  Department.

Community Service and Volunteer Activities
Search Committee for Dean of Residential Life, Kenyon College, Spring 1996
Search Committee for Director of the Career Development Center, Kenyon College, Spring 1995
  Interviewed prospective candidates through phone interviews.
  Conducted on-site interviews and made final selection for the position.

House Manager, Kenyon College, 1995 - 1996, 1997 - Present
  Upperclass resident advisor for residence hall. Coordinated, supervised, and was responsible for all
  social and educational programs for students.

Family Farm Project, Kenyon College, 1995 - 1996
  Designed and authored Family Farm Project World Wide Web Site
  (www.kenyon.edu/projects/famfarm).

Awards and Distinctions
Family Farm Project, Kenyon College, 1996
  Won 1996 Ohio Association of Historical Societies and Museums' Outstanding Achievement Award
  and the Ohio Academy of History Public History Award.

National Endowment for the Humanities Younger Scholar, Summer 1995
  Proposal chosen by National Endowment for the Humanities under highly competitive selection
  process.

National Conference on Undergraduate Research, University of North Carolina at Asheville,
April 1996
  Presented research entitled "Scenes of Old and New New York: *The Mural Cycle of Brooklyn's Public
  School 164.*"

Pew Charitable Trusts' Summer Institute, Summer 1994
  Participated in Institute to facilitate the increasing usage of information technologies by first- and
  second-year undergraduates.

GINNY LYNNE HILLIER
118 Ringold St.
Mt. Vernon, OH 43050
(555) 555-5555
HILLIERG@KENYON.EDU

EDUCATION

KENYON COLLEGE, Gambier, OH   Graduated May 1997
Psychology Major, Anthropology Minor   GPA 3.43
Women and Gender Studies Concentration   Cumulative GPA 3.08
Additional Courses of Study: Religion, Legal Studies, Sociology, History, Drama

WORK IN MAJOR

RESIDENT ASSISTANT   **SUMMER 1997–PRESENT**
Currently working at Karrington Place, a facility that specializes in the care of 30 residents who have been diagnosed with Alzheimer's disease, all of whom are in various stages of the disease. Duties include assisting with activities in daily living, recreational activities and exercises, keeping a daily log of resident progress and needs. Act as a liaison between the residents and Administration, Activities Director, and family members to ensure needs and interests of residents are being met.

DRUG AND ALCOHOL COUNSELING APPRENTICE   **FALL 1996–SPRING 1997**
Learned techniques in assessment and helped to prepare and facilitate discussions regarding prevention on campus.

PSYCHOLOGY DEPARTMENT STUDENT WORKER   **SPRING 1996–FALL 1997**
Worked closely with faculty and their current research projects by soliciting subject participation, running experiment sessions, and executing data entry.

SUMMER SCIENCE RESEARCH SCHOLAR   **SUMMER 1996**
Prepared budget, set up timeline, researched topic and solicited subjects for participation, collected and analyzed computer data, compiled findings, and presented results to Board of Trustees and community.

UPPER-CLASS COUNSELOR   **FALL 1996**
Helped with orientation by being paired with five freshmen. Advised them in course selection, acquainted them with faculty and administrators, and answered questions/problems regarding their adjustment as first-year students.

PSYCHOLOGICAL COUNSELING EXTERN   **SUMMER 1995**
Worked in Dublin, OH, school system with students in Quest Program. Studied assessment techniques. Also externed with licensed professional counselor and personnel at the Dublin Counseling Center.

OTHER WORK EXPERIENCE

ASSISTANT SUMMER CONFERENCE COORDINATOR   **SUMMER 1994 & 1995**
Provided tours, worked in collaboration with other campus departments to ensure customer satisfaction and safety. Staffed office in Coordinator's absence. Liaison in scheduling food-service and security efforts. Handled conference housing questions on round-the-clock basis.

STUDENT HOUSING OFFICE INTERN   **SUMMER 1994–SPRING 1997**
Answered phones and housing questions, gave tours, scheduled appointments, performed data entry, and coded dorm key system.

COMPUTER EXPERIENCE

*Windows 95 *Windows NT *Wordperfect *SPSS *Authorware-Pro *Excel *Microsoft Word *WWW
*E-Mail *Windows *AmiPro *Lotus 123 *Scanning

Things Noted on Real Resumés

REASONS FOR LEAVING THE LAST JOB:

- Responsibility makes me nervous.
- They insisted that all employees get to work by 8:45 every morning. Couldn't work under those conditions.
- Was met with a string of broken promises and lies, as well as cockroaches.
- I was working for my mom until she decided to move.
- The company made me a scapegoat—just like my three previous employers.

JOB RESPONSIBILITIES:

- While I am open to the initial nature of an assignment, I am decidedly disposed that it be so oriented as to at least partially incorporate the experience enjoyed heretofore and that it be configured so as to ultimately lead to the application of more rarefied facets of financial management as the major sphere of responsibility.
- I was proud to win the Gregg Typting Award.

SPECIAL REQUESTS AND JOB OBJECTIVES:

- Please call me after 5:30 because I am self-employed and my employer does not know I am looking for another job.
- My goal is to be a meteorologist. But since I have no training in meteorology, I suppose I should try stock brokerage.
- I procrastinate—especially when the task is unpleasant.

PHYSICAL DISABILITIES:

- Minor allergies to house cats and Mongolian sheep.

PERSONAL INTERESTS:

- Donating blood. Fourteen gallons so far.

SMALL TYPOS THAT CAN CHANGE THE MEANING:

- Education: College, August 1880–May 1984.
- Work Experience: Dealing with customers' conflicts that arouse.
- Develop and recommend an annual operating expense fudget.
- I'm a rabid typist.
- Instrumental in ruining entire operation for a Midwest chain operation.

Source: Internet

Correct Style and Content for Cover Letter

Box 1945
The Ohio State University
Columbus, Ohio 43204
October 25, 1997

(allow 2 or 3 spaces)

Mr. George McCormick
Director of Personnel
American Manufacturing Company
124 North Evans Avenue
Chicago, Illinois 60645

Dear Mr. McCormick: (use name)

Opening Paragraph State why you're writing, name the position or type of work for which you're applying, and mention how you heard of the opening.

Middle Paragraphs Explain why you're interested in working for this employer and specify your reasons for desiring this type of work. If you've had experience, be sure to point out your particular achievements or other qualifications in this field or type of work.

Middle Paragraphs Refer the reader to the enclosed résumé summarizing your qualifications, and/or to whatever media you're using to illustrate your training, interests, and experience.

Closing Paragraph Prepare an appropriate closing that paves the way for an interview by asking for an appointment, by giving your telephone number, or by offering some similar suggestion that will facilitate an immediate and favorable reply. Ending your letter with a question encourages a reply.

Very truly yours,

(always sign)

Juan Martinez

Enclosure *(if enclosing a résumé, note it)*
          (top and bottom margins should be equal)

Sample Cover Letter

2707 South Standard Avenue
Columbus, Ohio 43214
November 1, 1997

Ms. Jane R. Jones
Personnel Officer
Burke Technological Center
6401 Laughton Street
Los Angeles, California 90103

Dear Ms. Jones:

This morning's *Los Angeles Times* carried your advertisement for a "college student who is looking for a challenging and interesting summer position in a national park." With my educational background, practical experience, and willingness to work in an interesting position that offers a real challenge, I am sure I can be of value to your service.

Next February I shall receive my Bachelor of Science degree from The Ohio State University, where I have majored in public recreation.

For the last six years I have worked at a variety of part-time jobs: waiter, customer service assistant, and assistant activities coordinator for the local YMCA. During the past two years, I have gained working experience that will be very valuable to your organization. Details of these jobs, my education, and other information may be found on the enclosed resume.

I know that I can fill the challenging position you have open, and I would appreciate an opportunity to meet with you at your convenience to discuss in detail my qualifications and future potential with your company. I may be reached every afternoon at (614) 267-9200, extension 32; or any evening at (614) 261-1282.

Sincerely yours,

(signature)

Scott Donaldson

answering machine. Is it a message that an employer will hear as professional or is it too cute or potentially offensive to an employer? Ditto with any postings you may place on your internet Web page.

If you feel shy or unsure about how to manage follow-up telephone contacts after you've sent in your written material, Walberg suggests that you use a script like the following to guide you in your conversation:

> Hello, Mr. Adamson, this is———. I sent a copy of my résumé to you last week and wanted to follow up with you to see if you have received it or had any questions about it. I would like to meet with you to talk about the possibility of my becoming a member of your staff. Would next Tuesday, the 23rd, be a good day? I can come in during the morning or the afternoon. (Adapted from Walberg, 1997)

He also suggests that you not let the employer turn your phone conversation into an interview. You would say something like "I'm on a tight time schedule today, but I do want to meet with you soon, perhaps even tomorrow. When would it be best for me to stop by your office?"

THE EMPLOYMENT INTERVIEW

Whether you use the traditional or nontraditional approach in establishing job leads, the step that follows is the same: the employment interview. This interview provides an opportunity for you and an employer to meet, exchange information, and evaluate what each has to offer the other. As in any conversation between people, no two interviews are identical. Nevertheless, four common stages or components of an interview have been identified by the College Placement Council—the opening, inquiry, matching, and closing.[1]

The Opening

Have you ever met someone for the first time and felt strange, negative vibes about that person? You may not be able to pinpoint exactly why you reacted that way. It's like a chemical reaction—strong, rapid, direct, and lasting. And it sets up an immediate barrier between you and the other person that is not easily overcome.

Such quick and deep impressions often occur during the opening phase of the job interview. In fact, Walberg (1992, Oct. 18) suggests that impressions formed during the first 20 seconds of an interview may determine whether you're hired. So, your appearance and attitude—the look and feel of a true professional—must be positively conveyed at the first "hello" and introductory handshake with the interviewer.

During the remaining minutes of the opening phase, small talk that appears unrelated to the business of securing employment may occur. This stage will allow

---

[1]Adapted from *The Campus Interview—Are You Ready?* (audiotape). With the permission of the College Placement Council, Inc., copyright holder.

you to relax, get accustomed to the interviewing situation, and develop some initial impressions of the interviewer's style. This part of the interview is usually brief.

The Inquiry

A great number of questions are asked during this stage of the interview. The interviewer will try to obtain a clear understanding of your education, previous experience, achievements, short-term goals, and long-term aspirations. He or she will ask a variety of questions to secure this information. Some may be direct and require specific responses, but others may be more open-ended, providing you with an opportunity to emphasize your skills and interests. Although you'll receive many questions during this phase of the interview, you should plan to ask some questions of your own. You'll need to clarify with whom and for whom you'll be working, what you may be expected to do, and where. Your questions will also demonstrate how much research and thinking you've done concerning the position and the organization. A useful guide in choosing questions is not to ask questions that you yourself would be unwilling to answer.

The Matching

Matching occurs in two ways. The first screens you into a company by accentuating the skills, interests, and needs you have that are consistent with what a potential position demands and provides. The second screens you out of a company by identifying factors that reflect differences between what you want and what the employer has to offer. Both types of matching operate during the interview. The purpose of both is to recognize and project how your specific skills and goals might relate to specific job responsibilities and opportunities.

The Closing

Interviews may last for a few minutes or for several hours. Initial interviews will often be brief, with follow-up interviews taking considerably more time. Regardless, the main purpose of this last part of the interview is to specify the next steps in the selection process and who will take the initiative. At times you may be asked to take additional placement tests, undergo a physical examination, or return for further interviewing at another time, possibly with different people or at a different location. At other times the interviewer may indicate that the selection procedure is complete and that you'll be notified as soon as a decision is reached.

According to Edgar Schein (1978, pp. 103–104), an authority on career development in organizations, the employer must learn several things about you during the interview:

1. Does the person have the *skills* and *experience* to do the job?
2. How will the person *fit* into my organization? Does he or she possess the style of work, attitudes, values, and personality that will blend with our organization? Can the person conform to the norms of our organization without sacrificing creativity and individuality?

3. Will the person easily *learn the ropes* and *make a contribution* to our setting, and possibly improve it?
4. Is the person capable of and invested in *learning* and *growing* as an independent contributor and possibly as a leader?

Schein (1978, pp. 103–104) suggests that you learn at least six things about an organization during the campus and on-site interviews:

1. Will I have the opportunity to *test myself* in the job? Is it challenging? Do I have the skills to do it? Can I take the pressure it may involve? Is it a position that I will enjoy?
2. Will I be *considered worthwhile*? Will I be given a chance to show what I can do? Will I be able to make a contribution and have it appreciated? Will I be liked and appreciated as a person?
3. Will I be able to maintain my *integrity and individuality*? Can I be part of the culture of the organization without violating my values or standards? Can I fit in without losing sight of who I am and what is important to me in life?
4. Will I be able to have a *balanced life*? Can I enjoy my leisure-recreational and social pursuits and still feel that I am working hard enough to satisfy myself and my employer?
5. Will I *learn and grow*? Will my colleagues and supervisors be the kind of people who provide me with new ideas and opportunities? Will I be supported if I decide to take classes or seminars to continue my professional growth?
6. If I become a member of the organization, will I *meet my own ideals* and *feel good about myself*? Will I be proud to be a member of the organization?

Often, the person interviewing you is not solely responsible for determining who will be hired, and other candidates may still be waiting for an interview. In either situation, the status of your application can't be decided until all the interviews are completed and the results of the selection process have been reviewed by everyone involved. Consequently, you may leave the interview with the feeling that you really don't know where you stand. The truth is, at the moment, probably nobody else does either!

Dilbert reprinted by permission of United Feature Syndicate, Inc.

Preparing for the Interview

Information about yourself and the prospective employer is only a portion of what you need for effective interviewing. What you know about yourself and the employer must be communicated confidently, clearly, and concisely. These skills can best be enhanced through practice. One way of practicing for an interview is to imagine that you are the interviewer. What kinds of questions would you ask an applicant for a position in your organization? Frank S. Endicott, a former director of placement at Northwestern University, asked this question of recruiters for 92 companies. He found that the interviewers asked 50 common questions, as follows:[2]

1. What are your long-range and short-range goals and objectives, when and why did you establish these goals, and how are you preparing yourself to achieve them?
2. What specific goals, other than those related to your occupation, have you established for yourself for the next ten years?
3. What do you see yourself doing five years from now?
4. What do you *really* want to do in life?
5. What are your long-range career objectives?
6. How do you plan to achieve your career goals?
7. What are the most important rewards you expect in your business career?
8. What do you expect to be earning in five years?
9. Why did you choose the career for which you are preparing?
10. Which is more important to you, the money or the type of job?
11. What do you consider to be your greatest strengths and weaknesses?
12. How would you describe yourself?
13. How do you think a friend or professor who knows you well would describe you?
14. What motivates you to put forth your greatest effort?
15. How has your college experience prepared you for a business career?
16. Why should I hire you?
17. What qualifications do you have that make you think you will be successful in business?
18. How do you determine or evaluate success?
19. What do you think it takes to be successful in a company like ours?
20. In what ways do you think you can make a contribution to our company?
21. What qualities should a successful manager possess?
22. Describe the relationship that should exist between a supervisor and those reporting to him or her.
23. What two or three accomplishments have given you the most satisfaction? Why?

---

[2]Reprinted by permission of Dr. Frank S. Endicott, Placement Office, Northwestern University, Evanston, IL.

24. Describe your most rewarding college experience.
25. If you were hiring a graduate for this position, what qualities would you look for?
26. Why did you select your college or university?
27. What led you to choose your field of major study?
28. What college subjects did you like best? Why?
29. What college subjects did you like least? Why?
30. If you could do so, how would you plan your academic study differently? Why?
31. What changes would you make in your college or university? Why?
32. Do you have plans for continued study? An advanced degree?
33. Do you think that your grades are a good indication of your academic achievement?
34. What have you learned from participation in extracurricular activities?
35. In what kind of work environment are you most comfortable?
36. How do you work under pressure?
37. In what part-time or summer jobs have you been most interested? Why?
38. How would you describe the ideal job for you following graduation?
39. Why did you decide to seek a position with this company?
40. What do you know about our company?
41. What two or three things are most important to you in your job?
42. Are you seeking employment in a company of a certain size? Why?
43. What criteria are you using to evaluate the company for which you hope to work?
44. Do you have a geographical preference? Why?
45. Will you relocate? Does relocation bother you?
46. Are you willing to travel?
47. Are you willing to spend at least six months as a trainee?
48. Why do you think you might like to live in the community in which our company is located?
49. What major problem have you encountered and how did you deal with it?
50. What have you learned from your mistakes?

If Endicott's list of questions isn't enough of a challenge for you, consider a list of the "ten toughest business questions" that executives ask of applicants for leadership positions. The list was developed by Joan Detz, a writer and lecturer on communication topics, for *New Woman* magazine (January 1989, p. 132). We've modified her list to suit college students entering a job after graduation.

1. *The hypothetical question:* "Suppose you were given an assignment during your first week on the job and couldn't meet the deadline. What would you do?"

   Detz suggests that you try to avoid doomsday situations like this, because they lead to an endless cycle of "what if" follow-up questions. Don't focus on what you would do if you failed; focus on what you will do to make sure that your efforts succeed.

2. *The yes-or-no question:* "Will you be able to do this job on your own, right away?"

   Detz advises that you not be hasty with a yes answer. Instead, she suggested this response: "From the information I have now, it looks like things should go smoothly. However, I may need to consult with you if the situation changes or if I need more resources to manage it successfully."

3. *The what-do-you-think-the-other-guy-thinks question:* "How do you think your supervisor will view your leaving your present position?"

   Avoid being a mind reader. Instead, you might respond, "My supervisor has agreed to write a reference letter for me, so she apparently understands my need for a change and my decision to advance in my career. If you have any questions about my performance, you might ask her directly."

4. *The ranking question:* "What do you think are the two or three most important concerns of people who are entering the type of position you are applying for?"

   This question presupposes that you have a great deal of familiarity with the position and other applicants and are able to speak with confidence regarding the careers of others. Don't answer for others; speak for yourself, and point out that opinions will no doubt vary from applicant to applicant.

5. *The nonquestion question:* "I've enjoyed reading your credentials but don't think your background matches with our needs."

   This form of resistance to your application is a challenge that should not go unanswered. Detz advises that you turn it into a question such as "You wonder how I can best serve you in the job. Let me tell you what makes me the best candidate for it. . . ."

6. *The off-the-record question:* "Between you and me, is this college really the best place for me to be looking for someone to fill this position?"

   Although such a question may seem to provide you with an opportunity to openly express your frustrations with your academic experiences at your college (if you have any), taking that opportunity could come back to haunt you in two ways. First, secrets shared in confidence have a way of getting out. Second, if you answer the question, you will be in the awkward position of gossiping about someone else and may create some doubt about your loyalty to your employer. Therefore, we advise you not to tell the interviewer anything that you wouldn't share openly in public. Instead, focus on how your background experiences benefit the employer.

7. *The A-or-B orientation question:* "What is more important to you, salary or job?"

   If you are like most students, you want a job that pays adequate salary and provides an opportunity for long-term professional growth. You need not exclude one to get the other; you should feel free to say "Both are important to me as opportunities to. . . ."

8. *The why question:* "Most college students are alike. Why should I hire you for the position?"

   Detz advises that when you hear the word *why*, begin to put yourself in the interviewer's shoes. Think about what the employer needs and what you can do to fill those needs. For example, "Judging from the job description and our conversation, I gather that you're looking for someone who is a self-starter, can set goals, and isn't afraid of a challenge. I'm that kind of person. Let me tell you a bit more about how I've demonstrated those qualities in my studies and outside employment."

9. *The false-premise question:* "I notice you've had a series of short-term positions. I wonder why. Can't you keep a job for a long period?"

   If you don't immediately challenge or correct a false-premise statement, it will continue to haunt you during the interview. Be firm in your response and say something like "In my desire to make my résumé brief and easy for you to read, I did not describe my reasons for leaving the positions I've listed. I'm sorry that it has left you with an inaccurate impression of my background and want to thank you for bringing it up so I can provide you with more complete information. Let me explain more fully why I left each position and what I gained from working in it."

10. *The open question:* "So tell me about your last job."

    Open-ended questions provide a golden opportunity to show why you're an attractive applicant for the position. Anticipate the opportunity and prepare for it by creating in advance a short summary statement of how you utilized your interests, values, and skills to complete your assignments successfully on your last job and to enrich your preparation for the job you presently seek.

    You might start your summary statement as follows: "My last job required that I be able to _____. I was successful at it because I was skillful at _____ and enjoyed _____. It also gave me an opportunity to do the following things that matter to me in a job. These are qualities I will bring to your position."

As you can see from these lists of common questions, employment interviewers cover a variety of topics, ranging from your preparation for and commitment to the job to your preferred lifestyle. As part of your preparation for the job interview, read through the list of questions, single out some that are difficult to answer as well as some that are easy, and mentally rehearse your responses to them. You may wish to write the questions down or record them on tape. Respond to them out loud. Taping your answers may help you to hear how you present yourself to others. It may also be helpful to sit down with one or two friends and practice interviewing one another. One person can serve as the employer. The other can observe the interview and critique your performance. When practicing for an interview, keep in mind that how something is said may be as important as the content. Your tone of voice, gestures, eye contact, and posture convey as much about you as what you say.

MORE INTERVIEW SUGGESTIONS

Many factors contribute to effective interviewing. Here are a few important tips. (Most are taken from Employment Supplement, 1997).

Preparation

Know yourself. Have a clear understanding of your most prominent assets and goals and how these may be communicated. Know the organization. Be familiar with its products, priorities, and problems and how your skills can contribute to its goal. Don't judge the employer before the interview! Also, avoid negative thinking about the employer and your employment prospects.

Write down the time and place of your interview and the interviewer's name on your calendar. Be sure you can pronounce the interviewer's name properly. Confirm your appointment the day before the meeting. Make sure you know where you're going. If you don't know, ask for explicit directions and, if it's a new area to you, make a practice run and time it. Add an extra 30 minutes to that time in case of an emergency or an unexpected detour. Also, look for the nearest available parking lot so you won't get caught driving in circles while the interviewer waits. Immediately call the interviewer if you will be late or can't make the appointment. Reschedule another appointment as soon as possible.

Have in mind a list of questions that you would like to have answered about the position and the firm during the interview. Try to arrive a few minutes early so you can relax and mentally rehearse your plan for the interview.

Physical Appearance

Let basic good taste determine how you dress. Wear clothing that you feel will represent you well and will convey an image of which you are proud. Above all, be neat and clean. Maintain a relaxed and alert posture. When listening or speaking to an interviewer, maintain eye contact.

Speaking Style

Be honest and be yourself. Speak clearly and with enthusiasm, at a pace and volume that can be easily heard. Emphasize your strengths and be ready to support statements with examples. Be sure you understand the question before you answer it. Listen and pause, then respond. Ask questions. Remember that the interview is a two-way street. As you approach the interview, remember that it's not meant to intimidate you or put you through an ordeal (although occasionally an interviewer will do that). The interview offers the most efficient way for you and an employer to get to know each other in a short time. Recognize that you have qualities and attributes that will make you a valuable employee and that an employer would not meet with you if he or she weren't interested in hiring you.

If you're shy, hesitant, or concerned about your speaking style—a significant problem for those who will be having a high degree of public contact in their job—here are some ideas, mostly taken from Employment Supplement (1997).

Some common speaking concerns include these:

- Speaking too loudly, softly, or quickly
- Not speaking clearly
- Running words together or slurring them
- Hesitant speech, which conveys a lack of confidence
- Using slang or clichéd phrases excessively, such as "you know" or "got it"
- Speech anxiety, which causes a person to become mute or talk in a confused manner

Recognize that many employment settings rely on their staff members to communicate with their customers in oral as well as written forms. As such, you can either look for work that involves minimal speaking or try a few simple steps to overcome the problem.

To improve your speaking style, use a tape recorder to record yourself reading a book out loud or having a conversation with someone. Listen to the recording and note the areas you think need improvement, such as the volume and tone of your voice. Jot down your ideas so you can refer to them later.

Practice speaking more clearly by standing in front of a mirror so you can see how you move your mouth and tongue when you attempt to say words that are difficult for you to pronounce. Practice saying those words more clearly and continue to record your voice and watch yourself in the mirror until you improve to a level that satisfies you.

One last point: If these strategies don't work, you may want to contact a mental health practitioner who can help you deal with speech anxiety. You could also seek out a speech pathologist who specializes in your area of concern. In any case, approaching an interview with confidence derived from an understanding of what may occur, from knowing yourself and being informed, and from prior practice will make the employment interview a valuable and rewarding experience.

Filling out Forms

In planning for an interview, remember that the interviewer may ask you to complete some application forms. Be sure to have the completed names, addresses, phone numbers, and e-mail addresses of your former employers and the people who have directly supervised your work and will speak on your behalf. Have on hand your job title(s), dates of employment, and a clear statement of why you left your job(s). A summary of your educational and training experiences will also help you.

Though a good portion of this information will already be on your résumé, put it on the job application anyway. Personnel managers tend to refer to their company form because it's standardized for their setting. If you find that you don't have all of the information required to complete the company form, let the interviewer know and indicate that you'll provide the information as soon as you can.

Sarcasm on the Side

This is an actual job application someone submitted for a fast-food establishment. Only the name has been changed, as you might have guessed.

APPLICATION FOR EMPLOYMENT

NAME: James B. Anonymous

DESIRED POSITION: Reclining. Ha ha. But seriously, whatever's available. If I was in a position to be picky, I wouldn't be applying here in the first place.

DESIRED SALARY: $185,000 a year plus stock options and a Michael Ovitz–style severance package. If that's not possible, make an offer and we can haggle.

EDUCATION: Yes.

LAST POSITION HELD: Target for middle-management hostility.

SALARY: Less than I'm worth.

MOST NOTABLE ACHIEVEMENT: My incredible collection of stolen pens and Post-it notes.

REASON FOR LEAVING: It sucked.

HOURS AVAILABLE TO WORK: Any.

PREFERRED HOURS: 1:30–3:30 P.M., Monday, Tuesday, and Thursday.

DO YOU HAVE ANY SPECIAL SKILLS? Yes, but they're better suited to a more intimate environment.

MAY WE CONTACT YOUR CURRENT EMPLOYER? If I had one, would I be here?

DO YOU HAVE ANY PHYSICAL CONDITIONS THAT WOULD PROHIBIT YOU FROM LIFTING UP TO 50 LBS? Of what?

DO YOU HAVE A CAR? I think the more appropriate question here would be "Do you have a car that runs?"

HAVE YOU RECEIVED ANY SPECIAL AWARDS OR RECOGNITION? I may already be a winner of the Publishers Clearinghouse Sweepstakes.

DO YOU SMOKE? Only when set on fire.

WHAT WOULD YOU LIKE TO BE DOING IN FIVE YEARS? Living in Bimini with a fabulously wealthy supermodel who thinks I'm the greatest thing since sliced bread. Actually, I'd like to be doing that now.

DO YOU CERTIFY THAT THE ABOVE IS TRUE AND COMPLETE TO THE BEST OF YOUR KNOWLEDGE? No, but I dare you to prove otherwise.

SIGN HERE: Scorpio with Libra rising.

Source: Internet

Bring along some blank sheets of paper in case you run out of space on the form. If you do extend your background information in this way, be brief in your presentation.

Know Your Rights and Those of the Employer

In their attempts to get answers to their questions about each other, employers and employees are expected to play fair with one another—that is, to demonstrate mutual respect and ensure that their questions relate to the job and to the applicant's skills. The problems that women, minorities, older individuals, and the physically challenged have experienced in the past, however, indicate that simple goodwill cannot overcome the problem of employment discrimination. Consequently, state and federal governments and the College Placement Council have developed a set of guidelines for employers and applicants to abide by during the job-selection process. You should know these guidelines as you enter your own job campaign.

During the interviewing and selection process, you and the interviewer are expected to treat each other fairly and with dignity and respect. The employer should fully and truthfully inform you about the organization and the particular duties and rewards of the position. Conversely, you should fully and truthfully tell the employer about your qualifications for the position and your professional plans. Although the employer may dictate the general format (relaxed and casual or stressful and highly directed) and the length of the interview, you should receive the opportunity to present your interests, talents, needs, and plans in the manner most comfortable for you. Both of you may refuse any unreasonable or inappropriate request without feeling that doing so will cause distrust or conflict. You may also expect to be screened on the basis of your abilities rather than your age, race, gender, marital status, sexual orientation, national origin, or physical disability. The employer, on the other hand, can make decisions about your fit for the job based on your job-related skills, interests, values, and plans. Finally, you should also remember that interviewing for the job guarantees neither a job offer nor an acceptance of it.

Wiley Miller, © 1998, Washington Post Writers Group. Reprinted with permission.

Table 9-2 sets out guidelines for questioning applicants for employment. These guidelines were developed by the Ohio Civil Rights Commission under the Ohio Fair Employment Practices Act. They parallel federal guidelines developed by the Department of Employment Security of the U.S. Department of Labor, so they probably apply to your state as well. Read through the guidelines carefully to get a good understanding of what questions may legally be asked of you during the selection process. Realize that although a prospective employer must not ask you certain questions, you may be required to provide such information—for example, a picture, your race, your gender, or your age—*after* you're hired, to help the employer provide affirmative action information to the government or for security purposes within the organization.

If you receive an unlawful question during the campus interview, let your college placement officer know so he or she can remind the interviewer what is and is not an appropriate question. Also, remember that you share a responsibility to keep the interview focused on your ability to do the job; don't volunteer information that is illegal or unrelated to your capabilities as a potential employee.

For further information about your rights as a job applicant, talk to your campus placement officer or contact the Civil Rights Commission in your state. Your placement officer can help you with questions about your rights and responsibilities and can suggest ways to deal with illegal questions asked during the interviewing process.

When Awkward Questions Occur

Planning and thinking about your personal as well as career goals and philosophies set the stage for a successful interview. They help you to act rather than react when faced with difficult or unexpected questions. Open-ended questions such as "Tell me a story" or "Tell me about yourself" give the interviewer a chance to see how you operate in an unstructured situation. What matters is not that you come up with the most clever response ever given but that you handle the challenge calmly, thoughtfully, and honestly—no cute answers or stuttering panic. It's perfectly acceptable to say that you need a moment to organize your thoughts.

If asked about your previous job, don't be negative or bad-mouth your former employer, even if you did have a bad experience there. Just describe your previous responsibilities and what you learned from the setting, then focus on how the job you're applying for will advance your career objectives.

Another type of question that is common (especially for women) and difficult to handle is technically illegal—that is, questioning about plans for a family, age, religion, or ethnic background. One option is to refuse to answer or to remind the interviewer that the question is illegal. Although you're in the right, such a defensive response will likely make a negative impression. When such a question is asked, you must make a quick assessment of how the situation feels to you. If the job seems attractive, you may choose to give a pleasant (and perhaps vague) response that stresses your assets, such as plans for child care or the advantages of your maturity. Or you may wish to redirect the question and answer with regard

Table 9-2   Questioning Applicants for Employment

Inquiries before hiring	*Lawful*	*Unlawful*
1. *Name*	Name	Inquiry into any title which indicates race, color, religion, sex, national origin, handicap, age, or ancestry
2. *Address*	Inquiry into place and length of current address	Inquiry into foreign addresses which would indicate national origin
3. *Age*	Any inquiry limited to establishing that applicant meets any minimum age requirement that may be established by law	a. Requiring birth certificate or baptismal record before hiring b. Any other inquiry which may reveal whether applicant is at least 40 and less than 70 years of age
4. *Birthplace or national origin*		a. Any inquiry into place of birth b. Any inquiry into place of birth of parents, grandparents, or spouse c. Any other inquiry into national origin
5. *Race or color*		Any inquiry which would indicate race or color
6. *Sex*		a. Any inquiry which would indicate sex b. Any inquiry made of members of one sex but not the other
7. *Religion/creed*		a. Any inquiry which would indicate or identify religious denomination or custom b. Applicant may not be told any religious identity or preference of the employer c. Request pastor's recommendation or reference
8. *Handicap*	Inquiries necessary to determine applicant's ability to substantially perform specific job without significant hazard	Any other inquiry which would reveal handicap
9. *Citizenship*	a. Whether a U.S. citizen b. If not, whether applicant intends to become one c. If U.S. residence is legal d. If spouse is citizen e. Require proof of citizenship after being hired	a. If native-born or naturalized b. Proof of citizenship before hiring c. Whether parents or spouse are native-born or naturalized
10. *Photographs*	May be required after hiring for identification purposes	Require photograph before hiring
11. *Arrests and convictions*	Inquiries into conviction of specific crimes related to qualifications for the job applied for	Any inquiry which would reveal arrests without convictions

Table 9-2 Questioning Applicants for Employment *(continued)*

12. *Education*	a. Inquiry into nature and extent of academic, professional, or vocational training b. Inquiry into language skills, such as reading and writing of foreign languages	a. Any inquiry which would reveal the nationality or religious affiliation of a school b. Inquiry as to what mother tongue is or how foreign language ability was acquired
13. *Relatives*	Inquiry into name, relationship, and address of person to be notified in case of emergency	Any inquiry about a relative which would be unlawful if made about the applicant
14. *Organizations*	Inquiry into organization memberships and offices held, excluding any organization the name or character of which indicates the race, color, religion, sex, national origin, handicap, age, or ancestry of its members	Inquiry into all clubs and organizations where membership is held
15. *Military service*	a. Inquiry into service in the U.S. armed forces when such service is a qualification for the job b. Requires military discharge certificate after being hired	a. Inquiry into military service in armed service of any country but U.S. b. Request military service records c. Inquiry into type of discharge
16. *Work schedule*	Inquiry into willingness to work required work schedule	Any inquiry into willingness to work any particular religious holiday
17. *Other*	Any questions to reveal qualifications for the job applied for	Any non-job-related inquiry which may reveal information permitting unlawful discrimination
18. *References*	General personal and work references not related to race, color, religion, sex, national origin, handicap, age, or ancestry	Request references specifically from clergy or any other persons who might reflect race, color, religion, sex, national origin, handicap, age, or ancestry of applicant

to your skills and your commitment to your career. If you feel sufficiently comfortable with the interviewer, you could initiate a dialogue to determine what lies behind the interviewer's questions and what the company's real concerns are. If you're seriously interested in the job, you'll probably need to discover the attitudes and feelings behind such questions. If there is truly a prejudice in the organization about working mothers or people of a certain background, you may not want to work there.

Still another difficult subject to address during the interviewing process involves salary and benefits. Ideally this issue should come up only after the employer has made it clear that you're the candidate of choice. Even then it can be a sticky topic, especially if you haven't had the opportunity to survey the local labor market regarding the relevant salary ranges. Lacking such knowledge, you may find yourself setting your salary expectations too high or too low. If your expectations are set too low, you may be viewed as lacking confidence in your talents. If you set them too high, you may be seen as overvaluing your skills relative to other employees and price yourself out of a job. So, if at all possible, conduct a market survey before you enter the interviewing process. If you do not have a clear picture of the local salary structure, be honest with the employer about your lack of knowledge and ask for a brief summary of the salary ranges in the company and where you would fit on that scale given your training and experience. Remember that when you've signed an employment contact, altering it will be extremely difficult if you believe you misjudged your value to the employer.

FOLLOW-UP CONTACT

After an interview, and especially after an on-site visit, you'll need to write a brief reply to your interviewer or host. This correspondence may include a thank-you for the interview, a brief review of reactions to information you received, a response or follow-up to any specific requests made during the interview, and a request for any additional information desired.

A major goal of this type of letter is to demonstrate your interest and initiative and to keep your name before those who may know of future job openings. See the sample follow-up letter that follows.

The employment specialist Donna Cobble (1993) advises that if you don't hear from the employer after a reasonable period of time—say a week and a half to 2 weeks after you've sent your letter—it can be beneficial to call the person you interviewed with to restate your interest in the position and the skills you can offer, and to inquire about the status of your application. You may find that the employer has not finished interviewing applicants, that funding for the position has been temporarily frozen, or that an unforeseen circumstance has called the person to whom you would be reporting away from the office for a brief period. In any case, your call will clarify your status and give you an opportunity to keep your name in the employer's mind.

WHEN YOU NEED A DETOUR

Whatever job-search methods you use and however well you prepare yourself for an interview, inexperience and an increasingly tight job market make it difficult to get the ideal job on the first try. In fact, it appears that only a few students will secure their most preferred job right after they graduate. (And many of them later discover it's not their ideal job!) Statistics show that most people change jobs within 2 years of their first employment after college. This suggests that job shopping, like selecting a major, is a normal part of the ongoing process of career development beyond college. Consequently, putting aside the idea that one should achieve the ideal job standard on the first job try may help alleviate job-search pressures. You should look at all jobs in terms of the opportunities for development

Sample Follow-Up Letter

815 N.E. Seventh Street
Hibbing, Minnesota 55746
December 2, 1997

Ms. Jeanne Clarke
Associate Director of Personnel
Allied Products
Duluth, Minnesota 55806

Dear Ms. Clarke:

Thank you for the invitation and the opportunity to discuss the marketing position available with your firm in Duluth.

I was particularly impressed by the information you provided about the in-service training opportunities with Allied Products. Likewise, your incentive and evaluation programs would provide the kind of salary, benefits, and constructive feedback that are important to me at this point in my career.

I have been giving a great deal of thought to the options you presented for starting in a regional or division office. Since I prefer to live in a larger metropolitan area, the division office assignment would be my first choice. However, the range of duties to be performed at either type of office is compatible with my experience and interest. I am attracted to both opportunities.

I understand that your recruiting process for this position will take an additional two to three weeks. I look forward to hearing from you at that time.

Sincerely yours,

(signature)

Maryann J. Olson

they provide. To maximize your opportunities for growth in a tight job market, you may need to pursue other work alternatives, at least temporarily.

The Vocational Contingency Planning (VCP) approach developed by Jeffrey Kleinberg (1976) provides an alternate route and expanded opportunities when things don't work as hoped. VCP is a useful backup to the traditional and non-traditional approaches. Like these, it begins with identification of the specific work-related skills you possess. Unlike the traditional approach, which empha-sizes matching one's skills to specific job titles, VCP resembles the nontraditional approach, which looks at how you can use specific skills in a range of work set-tings and occupational levels.

The VCP strategy assumes that, through employee turnover (retirement, death, advancement, and change), all occupations will in time have vacancies. VCP enables you to compete strongly for these openings when they become available. Essentially, it offers three strategies for obtaining a primary occupational choice at some time in the future, even if the choice is currently inaccessible. The three alternative approaches are derived from classifying occupations in terms of level, field, and enterprise, and from identifying the skills that various occupations share. To illustrate, suppose your primary vocational choice, elementary public school teaching (a social occupation), were unavailable to you in the area where you want to work. VCP offers three options for using the social skills of a teacher: the level detour, the field detour, and the enterprise detour.

The level detour   You could seek a position in the teaching field at a level of responsibility below that of a full-fledged teacher, such as assistant or day-care center aid.

The field detour   You could seek work in a field that relates in some significant way to the work of a teacher: textbook sales, audiovisual equipment maintenance, school security, or community liaison work. One way to identify field-related oc-cupations is to list occupations that a person in your primary occupation may have contact with during a normal day's activities.

The enterprise detour   You could seek a position in nonpublic school settings, such as teaching in a private, parochial, or military school, tutoring, educational activities for a private firm, or volunteer work in community or government set-tings. This detour approach depends on locating other settings with the same type of work.

All these vocational detours allow you to

1. Build up a positive work history with good, solid references in work activ-ities related to your primary occupational goal.
2. Make personal contacts with those who might eventually hire you.
3. Pursue advanced study and training concurrently with the detour work.
4. Offer a richer repertoire of skills than is typically presented by the fresh-out-of-college applicant.
5. Prepare for the detour with a minimal amount of effort and time.

6. Engage in temporary work that will support you financially as you continue to pursue your primary goal.

VCP is not a panacea for achieving your primary occupational goal in a restrictive and deflated job market. However, it can increase the odds that you'll eventually attain your occupational goal and that in the interim you'll learn about your interests and skills and be exposed to many interesting job possibilities.

In this chapter, we've presented three methods of job campaigning—traditional, nontraditional, and contingency—to illustrate the diverse ways you can conduct a job-search campaign. Each approach has advantages and disadvantages. Using aspects of each, you can develop the personal style that works best for you.

WHEN YOU'RE OUT OF WORK

Not everyone sits in the enviable position of looking for the next job while still employed. At some time, after graduation or because of certain circumstances in your life, you may find yourself unemployed. Here are some tips on how to cope with job hunting in that situation.

First and foremost, stay active! Keep yourself busy. Taking a part-time job will fill your time, bring in some money, and provide an opportunity to meet new people. Part-time or temporary work will also give you some time to spend on your job search—time to make contacts, write letters, interview, and make telephone calls. Many employers are sympathetic to the plight of the young person looking for a first job. Saying that you're working part-time on a temporary basis while you look for a good job demonstrates that you are assertive and enterprising. And if your part-time job is in a field related to your ultimate career goal, so much the better.

When you find yourself out of work, be prepared to pursue any and all leads that might land you a job. Letters, telephone calls, and personal contacts can be important parts of your job search. As a general rule, the job searcher will have to make 30 contacts with potential employers before getting a nibble. You can

Dave. © Tribune Media Services, Inc. All Rights Reserved. Reprinted with permission.

alleviate some of the anxiety by setting a goal of making 30 contacts in a month, rather than feeling that you must have a job in 2 weeks. Decide to be an active agent in your job search, not passively dependent on newspapers and employment agencies. Go out and look for a job—don't wait for a job to come your way.

If you've exhausted all your job leads, a private placement service may help. If you decide to use such a service, check it out carefully before you sign on. Pay particular attention to the kinds of assistance they provide and their expectations of you. For example, some agencies require that you pay for their assistance, whereas others expect the employer to pay. The agency may also expect payment if you take a permanent job with an employer they've placed you with.

Carefully interview the person assigned to assist you, to determine his or her commitment to helping you secure a job and how well the two of you can work together. Avoid a person or agency that tries to talk you into creating a résumé that artificially inflates your experience and skills. Remember, too, that a growing number of employers are directly hiring staff on a temporary basis to reduce their personnel costs and to screen new employees for long-term jobs. So, keep in mind that temporary employment may lead to long-term prospects, with or without the help of a temporary employment service.

Marvin Walberg (1992, Oct. 11) suggests that, when unemployed, above all you should keep a positive outlook and stay active. Specifically, he suggests several ways to do this, which we present here with some suggestions of our own.

1. Create a daily routine of getting up early and dressing to conduct the work of finding a job.
2. Develop an exercise routine and stick with it. Join a sports team and use the acquaintances you develop with your teammates to expand your informational network.
3. When you're not seeking a job, stay mentally and socially active by reading a newspaper or book, attending a lecture, creating a new and inexpensive hobby, or visiting with friends.
4. Treat yourself to an inexpensive trip or a special meal.
5. Set aside time to worry each day (no more than half an hour!). Purchase a small notebook to jot down your negative thoughts as they occur. Later, during your worry time, try to recast negative thoughts into positive self-statements: "I'm worried because I care about my family and want to use my talents to support them."
6. Join a club or support group for unemployed people. Such services are usually free and can enhance your job-search skills, expand your informational network, and help you allay your fears. Also maintain contact with your college placement office as a source of job leads and career-planning assistance. Believe that you can always learn something new to enhance your job search and professional skills.
7. Perform volunteer work for a civil or social organization. Take advantage of opportunities in the organization to expand or develop new skills and resource contacts. Such activities can also enhance your self-esteem and can be used to fill in time lapses on your résumé.

8. If you find yourself feeling depressed or having frequent arguments with your family, seek the help of a mental health professional for your own sake and others'.

9. Attend to all the dimensions of the wellness wheel (Chapter 1) so you can maintain a balanced lifestyle while you search for a job.

Finally, we suggest you keep in mind the following lessons from an item in the March 1998 issue of "Footprints," the newsletter of the Sisters of St. Francis: "All I really need to know about wellness, I learned from Noah's Ark."

- Plan ahead. It wasn't raining when Noah built the ark.
- Stay fit. When you're 600 years old, someone might ask you to do something really big.
- Remember, the ark was built by amateurs and the *Titanic* was built by professionals.
- Don't forget we're all in the same boat.
- If you can't fight or flee, float.
- No matter how bleak it looks, there's always a rainbow on the other side.

PERSONAL SKILLS REVIEW

Throughout this text we've stressed the importance of identifying and capitalizing on your work-related skills in order to identify and pursue a career objective effectively. We've also pointed out the benefits of a thorough skill assessment in developing a job-search strategy. This will allow you to pursue several work alternatives in different levels, fields, and enterprises flexibly.

Skill identification especially matters when you conduct a job campaign. It allows you to put your best foot forward through correspondence and job interviews. Employers need to know that not only are you interested in a job but you can also demonstrate that you have the appropriate skills for it.

We often think that employers will notice only those skills and experiences we can tie to formal educational, training, and work experience. Actually, we usually enjoy abundant opportunities in leisure and social pursuits to acquire solid skills that we can use in work settings. Being a member of a family, for example, can provide opportunities to observe how a minicorporation (the family enterprise) manages its resources, uses lines of communication in decision making, and negotiates differences in styles and opinions. Thus, you need to attend to the learning opportunities you've had in all dimensions of the wellness wheel. You can do so by identifying where and how you acquired the skills you noted in the self-assessment inventories provided in Appendix A. This approach can especially help you if you have limited work experience or have "stopped out" from work. Other useful approaches to identifying your skills appear in the book by Bolles and in other job-search books listed among the resources at the end of this chapter. Whatever approach you use to identify your skills, you must specify what the skill is and where and when you learned it, so that you can accurately present your qualifications to employers.

You may conclude that you learned some of your significant skills in informal settings: cooking or child care in the home, bookkeeping for a club or group, running a local hospital benefit, photography for friends or a school paper, botany learned at city park classes. Though the origins of these skills may sound unprofessional, you can often legitimize them through imaginative additions, such as statistics, samples, or letters of recommendation. The hospital bazaar experience may look more professional diagramed on paper, detailing such things as your duties, the number of people you supervised, and the amounts of money you handled. If your skill has produced a portable product, bring a portfolio of your best work. If your product is not portable, it may show off well in photographs or drawings. If you've performed a service (cooking, child care, bookkeeping, photography) for individuals or groups in the community or learned a skill from someone (the park director), ask for a letter of recommendation describing or confirming your skills.

PERSONAL SKILLS INVENTORY

The following personal skills inventory is designed to help you identify and pull together all the skills you've acquired. These include skills from your education or training and work experiences, as well as your leisure and recreational pursuits and your interactions with family and friends.

The inventory requires that you clearly describe the specific skill you wish to share with an employer and the context in which you acquired it. Examples are provided to stimulate your thinking. We also encourage you to go through the skill items in the self-assessment inventories in Appendix A to generate other skills for your list. If, for example, you indicated that you have a strong skill in operating office machines—a "Business Operations" skill—you would try to identify on the personal skills inventory where and how you acquired that skill and describe which machines you know how to operate. For each section, write several paragraphs on separate paper.

Learning context: Describe where you learned the skill.	Skills: Describe the specific skill in terms of what it is, where you learned it, and when you learned it.
From education or training	1. In my secretarial sciences curriculum at my technical college, I acquired specific skills in running a duplicating machine, a desk calculator, and a dictaphone.
	2. I took two computer literacy classes and learned to use office software.
From work experiences	1. To pay for my education, I worked part-time at night selling shoes. This gave me the opportunity to develop special and "Business Contact" skills in meeting others, assisting them in meeting a specific need, and dealing with customer complaints. It also

helped me acquire "Business Operations" skills in maintaining an inventory, exchanging money, and record keeping.

2. As a result of my being employed, I learned how to keep a balanced budget to meet my own educational objectives. Thus, I am very familiar with the skills of setting priorities and long-range planning.

From leisure/recreational pursuits

1. I like to fish, and during high school I learned how to tie flies for fishing, an "Arts" and "Technical" skill. I became so proficient at it that I soon was able to set up a profitable part-time business selling them. Through this experience I learned how to produce a quality product to meet a public demand, to manage a stock inventory, and to plan and manage a budget. I also learned how to relate to customers effectively. All these are "Business Contact" skills.

2. As captain of my YWCA baseball team, I learned how to support and encourage others, to give advice, and to present their views to people in authority (the coaches). These are primarily "Social Service" skills.

From kinship/friendship activities

1. During the summer of my junior year in high school, both my parents became quite ill for a month. Since I was the oldest child, I had to assume the responsibility for managing many household activities. Working with my relatives, I learned how to plan schedules, project a family budget, negotiate difficult situations with others, and supervise the activities of others (my younger brother and sister). These managerial skills fall into the "Social Service" and "Business Contact" categories.

2. I was in charge of the committee that planned and made decorations for our senior prom. I used "Social Service" and "Arts" skills.

ADAPTIVE SKILLS SELF-SURVEY

Listed here are personality traits you may possess that you can call on to assist you in adapting to new work settings. In fact, employment interviewers frequently ask job applicants to list the adjectives that best describe them, so this activity can be of great help to you in preparing for a job interview. Check the adjectives that you feel best describe you:

_____ achievement-oriented	_____ amusing	_____ trusting
_____ dominant	_____ idealistic	_____ gentle

_____ kind	_____ reserved	_____ assertive
_____ helpful	_____ conscientious	_____ confident
_____ efficient	_____ punctual	_____ active
_____ unconventional	_____ careful	_____ logical
_____ realistic	_____ decisive	_____ adaptable
_____ flexible	_____ compassionate	_____ competitive
_____ imaginative	_____ sincere	_____ orderly
_____ creative	_____ likable	_____ stable
_____ principled	_____ warm-hearted	_____ easygoing
_____ tactful	_____ playful	_____ dependable
_____ sympathetic	_____ friendly	_____ expressive
_____ sensitive	_____ outgoing	_____ interdependent
_____ truthful	_____ levelheaded	_____ strong-willed
_____ adventurous	_____ aggressive	_____ conventional

When you complete the survey, look over the traits that you checked and imagine how they'll benefit you and an employer in an occupation that interests you. Better yet, imagine that an interviewer has asked you to list five adjectives that best describe you and to give an example of a situation where those characteristics benefited you and someone else. How would you respond?

SOME CHALLENGING SITUATIONS FOR THE INTERVIEWEE

Imagine yourself as Leslie, Jason, or Laurie in the following situations.

1. While Leslie is in the placement office scheduling an appointment for an interview with a campus recruiter, another student interrupts. He says he can't wait for his turn to make an appointment, because he has to leave for home in 15 minutes to sing in a wedding. He also says he wants an appointment "next Monday at 10 A.M." with the employer that Leslie wants to see at that time.

2. During his meeting with a campus recruiter, Jason notices that the interviewer seems distracted. Her questions seem to have no direction and she jumps from topic to topic without paying attention to what Jason has said. When Jason asks about specific aspects of the job, the interviewer says, "I'll get to that later," but she hasn't yet.

3. Laurie made it through the campus interview and is now being interviewed at the federal agency where she wants to work. It has been a good day. She likes the people she met, and the position will be an ideal place

for her to start her career. Over lunch, the person who may be her supervisor starts asking her questions about her family background, religious practices, and marriage plans.

Review each situation. What employee rights are being violated in each case?

SOME CHALLENGING SITUATIONS FOR THE INTERVIEWER

Imagine yourself as Ms. Creps, Mr. Schermer, Mr. Smout, or Ms. Beir in the following vignettes. As a responsible interviewer, how would you respond to each situation?

1. Ms. Creps is interviewing a recent graduate for a position as an administrative assistant in a small firm. The student begins to talk about her immigrant family and the religious teachings of her college.
2. Mr. Schermer, the personnel director for a local school system, has advertised an opening for administrative assistant to the principal. His secretary has been preparing the candidates' files. As she files one candidate's résumé, she notices that it includes a picture of the person and his date of birth.
3. After a lengthy search, Mr. Smout has offered a position to a recent graduate who has considerable work experience in the field. The candidate initially accepted the position but has just called to decline it because he got a better offer elsewhere.
4. Ms. Beir just found out that an employee she has been supervising for a year lied about his criminal record during his job interview.
5. Look back over the interviewing stories described at the start of this chapter. Do any of the situations seem inappropriate or unethical to you? On what basis do you make that judgment?

REFERENCES AND RESOURCES

Bolles, R. N. (1997). *What color is your parachute? A practical manual for job hunters and career changers.* Berkeley, CA: Ten Speed Press.

Byron, W. J. (1995). *Finding work without losing heart: Bouncing back from mid-career job loss.* Holbrook, MA: Adams Publishing.

Challenger, J. E. (1992, Sept. 29). Several myths impede success of job seekers. *Columbus Dispatch* (OH), Employment Supplement, p. 2.

Cobble, D. (1993, Oct. 17). Tailor résumé: Cover letter to job opening. *Columbus Dispatch* (OH), p. 337.

Dunphy, P. (Ed.). (1973). *Career development for the college student.* 2nd ed. Carroll Press.

Employment supplement. (1997, July 23). *Columbus Dispatch* (OH).

Hanson, C. (1993, April 25). Resumes must show focus, emphasize skills. *Columbus Dispatch* (OH), p. 33J.

Harden, M. (1989, July 19). On job interview, some go far out to make impression. *Columbus Dispatch* (OH), p. 1E.

Innis, K. (Spring 1994). 10 tips: Great job-search advice you didn't learn in school. In *Managing Your Career* (pp. 21–24). New York: Wall Street Journal.

Jackson, T. (1993). *Guerilla tactics in the new job market.* New York: Bantam.

Kleinberg, J. D. (1976). Vocational contingency planning in a recession. *Vocational Guidance Quarterly, 24*(4), 366–367.

Laugh of the day. (1996, Oct. 1). *Laugh Web* (http://www.misty.com/laughweb/)

Schein, E. (1978). *Career dynamics: Matching individual and organizational needs.* Reading, MA: Addison-Wesley.

Sicherman, A. (1992, Oct. 11). Translations tell story between the lines of help-wanted ads. *Columbus Dispatch* (OH), p. 31J.

Walberg, M. (1992, Aug. 2). First 20 seconds of interview are key to hiring. *Columbus Dispatch* (OH), p. 31J.

Walberg, M. (1992, Oct. 11). Try to maintain positive attitude during job search. *Columbus Dispatch* (OH), p. 31J.

Walberg, M. (1992, Oct. 18). Got a job interview? Then get there on time. *Columbus Dispatch* (OH), p. 27I.

Walberg, M. (1992, Nov. 8). Be careful in picking agency. *Columbus Dispatch* (OH), p. 31J.

Walberg, M. (1992, Nov. 22). Consider rejection temporary when looking for employment. *Columbus Dispatch* (OH), p. 29J.

Walberg, M. (1993). Anonymous help-wanted ads can lead to job offer. *Columbus Dispatch* (OH), p. 27J.

Walberg, M. (1993, Jan. 10). Don't judge an employer before the job interview. *Columbus Dispatch* (OH), p. 39K.

Walberg, M. (1993, Feb. 14). Preparation can prevent panic. *Columbus Dispatch* (OH), p. 39K.

Walberg, M. (1997, Mar. 30). Preparation helps make follow-up call less painful. *Columbus Dispatch* (OH), Employment guide, p. 23J.

CHAPTER 10

WORK ADJUSTMENT
AND CAREER EXPANSION

"Ready to *work* at 8 o'clock, Velez! Not just *here* at 8 o'clock! Ready to work!"

Close to Home, © 1993 John McPherson. Dist. by Universal Press Syndicate. Reprinted with permission. All rights reserved.

We have a choice every day regarding the attitude we will embrace for that day. We cannot change our past . . . we cannot change the fact that people will act in a certain way. We cannot change the inevitable. The only thing we can do is play on the one thing we have, and that is our attitude.

I am convinced that life is 10% what happens to me and 90% how I react to it. And so it is with you . . . we are in charge of our attitudes.

—*Charles Swindoll*

In the cafeteria of a large corporation, three friends from the secretarial pool meet for lunch. Debbie has been angry all morning at Evelyn, whose personal call made a difficult morning worse. Though scared of losing a friend, Debbie remembers what she learned in an assertiveness training about not allowing unresolved anger to build up. So during lunch she tells Evelyn how she feels. Though a little defensive, Evelyn understands Debbie's concerns and tells her she had a fight with her husband before work. This honest exchange feels good, and it makes Marian decide to confide in her two friends. She had expected a promotion to a department that had lost a secretary, but she didn't get it. She feels it is because she is African American, and recently confronted her boss about some of his business dealings, which seemed to border on unethical. She knows she can file a claim with the personnel department or the Equal Employment Opportunity Commission but doesn't want to jump to conclusions, since this was her first try at promotion. The three friends talk it over and agree that Marian should start by going to the head of the department where she applied and expressing her disappointment. Her goal is to find out why she wasn't chosen and what she can do to improve her future chances. Doing this will help Marian and will also call attention to her ambition in a positive way. She has also decided to keep notes on situations with her boss so she can be specific with him if she needs to confront him again, or go to higher authorities of the organization to discuss her concerns. After lunch, the three friends, laughing and chatting, walk toward the south end of the building.

Meanwhile, two men have stopped in the rest room after their lunches and are sharing their experiences. Tom's unhappy with his job, which is no longer challenging, but he feels stuck. He knows he hasn't done enough to promote his success or to network within the company. He realizes that if he starts now it will take years. He's angry at himself, knowing that if he'd looked ahead 5 years ago, he could have gone to school at the company's expense. Andrew is 59 and has been asked to take early retirement because of cutbacks. The financial package is good, but Andrew fears that without his job he'll feel useless and bored. He hasn't really developed any interests or plans for retirement, because it has always seemed so far away.

Heading away from the cafeteria, a man and woman are deep in conversation. Stuart, a sales manager approaching middle age, is quite satisfied with his current progress. Though not expecting an upward move any time soon, he's been included in more meetings and golf games and feels he's moving toward the influential "inner circle" of higher executives who control the important promotions. The young woman with him, his assistant, is still learning the ropes. Stuart had originally disliked the idea of training someone fresh out of college who, he thought, would be idealistic and resist the politics, pragmatism, and tradition that make the business world different from textbooks. But Phyllis surprised him. She has good people skills and common sense. Without intending to, Stuart has become her mentor. He enjoys giving her advice and encouragement and watching her blossom. He's proud that management has noticed how she stands out.

People in work settings differ greatly. Constantly adjusting and learning, they operate at different stages of personal and career development. In fact, we're all students of one another and of our surroundings, constantly looking for clues about how others react to us and what behaviors are appropriate. This survival mechanism—no doubt a part of us at birth—helps us adapt to our environment.

Usually we only dimly realize that we're fortune telling, probably because our predictions are fairly accurate and require little conscious thought. It is the unexpected event, the situation we could not have anticipated, that reminds us that our trust often rests on mind reading and assumptions. The unexpected may appear in a minor way—someone doesn't show up as usual—or may involve major changes, such as travel to a new place. Our antennae go up regardless, looking for clues and guidelines for dealing with the new situation. Until we reach a balance again, we usually feel uneasy, even in conflict, about who and where we are.

THE ORGANIZATIONAL CLIMATE

Successful employees recognize that the workplace is really a minisociety that sends out a constant stream of information about what it expects of its members and what the rules and limits are. Some of the rules are explicit, as in a job description or a personnel handbook, but many codes manifest themselves only in subtle patterns of behavior—in the ways workers dress, how they speak, topics of conversation, informal leadership patterns, and so on. Together, these subtle clues create an *organizational climate,* a bond that maintains the stability of the work settings and allows us to learn behaviors through which we can meet our needs and achieve our goals.

Criteria for Assessing the Health of an Organization

Robert Gallagher, an administrator at the University of Pittsburgh, has identified 25 questions that you may find helpful in evaluating the social climate of an organization. These may help you assess the work environment of any organization under consideration.

1. Is there general consensus on the broad objective of the organization?
2. Is there evidence of a team effort for achieving organizational goals?
3. Are lines of authority clearly defined?
4. Is leadership flexible?
5. Do staff members participate in decision making?
6. Is there a fair and reasonable evaluation system in place?
7. Do opportunities for innovation exist?
8. Are concerns about organizational problems expressed and discussed?
9. Are there attempts to adjust to the personal needs, strengths, and styles of staff members?
10. Is problem solving pragmatic, or do other issues get in the way?
11. Does the staff pull together in times of crisis?
12. Is there a feeling of collaboration among staff members?
13. Is there room for healthy conflict?
14. Is there a willingness to give, seek, and use feedback and advice?
15. Does the organization's atmosphere facilitate personal development, growth, and wellness?
16. Are staff stimulated by their work and highly committed to the work of the organization?
17. Is there trust among staff: a sense of freedom and mutual responsibility?
18. Does loyalty to the organization go beyond the interpersonal conflicts within?
19. Are discussions of ethical issues encouraged?
20. Is attention given to staff burnout issues?
21. Do staff take personal responsibility for making things work better?
22. Do staff have an attitude of "what can we learn from our mistakes?"
23. Is there an organizational structure in place that helps people get the job done and that protects the long-term well-being of the organization?
24. Is attention paid to the personal wellness of the staff?
25. Does the environment support the family?

The Sixth Skill: Work Adjustment

The first five of the six career-planning skills mentioned earlier in this book—decision making, self-assessment, information gathering, integration, and job-search strategies—will all help you in your job performance and expansion. To use them effectively, to stay employed and grow with a job, you need a final skill: work adjustment.

In dealing with your work environment and co-workers, you'll use the same people-reading skills discussed in reference to job interviews and job choice. You'll face issues such as interpersonal conflict, responsibility, communication, time management, stress, performance appraisals, and personal harassment, all of which we discuss in the next few sections. Then, we'll talk about career development and expansion.

GETTING ALONG WITH OTHERS

Researchers have found over many years that, after "lack of specific job skills," the primary reason people are not hired (or lose their jobs) is their inability to get along with others in the work setting. To perform effectively in a new environment, you must look for and learn the hidden rules of behavior for getting a promotion and dealing with co-workers on a day-to-day basis. To be effective at work, you need to negotiate the complex maze of daily interactions with peers. This involves learning the social pecking order, dress habits, conversational customs, and individual roles. (Does your group of co-workers have a "gossip," "snitch," "mother hen," "swinging single," "scapegoat," or an informal leader?) Fitting comfortably into a changing work group involves learning to interact pleasantly with and be tolerant of all kinds of people, but it often requires much more than that. Many situations demand that each group member do part of a total job, which means that members must agree on the goals and methods of operation and be able to depend on one another. Working together requires giving and taking directions and sharing ideas and credit, which in turn require patience, kindness, tolerance, discretion, and tact—and, when all of the above fail, the ability to handle conflict.

You also need to pay attention to social protocol at celebrations, holiday parties, and company picnics. Donna Cobble (1996), who runs an employment agency in Knoxville, Tennessee, suggests that when you attend a company picnic, keep the following tips in mind:

1. Consider refraining from alcoholic beverages and stick with soft drinks. If you do drink, keep your consumption low. Careers have been threatened by off-hand comments made by someone who is drunk.
2. Keep your conversation light and fun, leave work-talk at the office. Use the gathering to make new friends and become better acquainted with employees and their families.
3. Avoid flirting even if light hearted. It can easily be misunderstood.
4. Dress appropriately. If it's a summer gathering, keep in mind that "less is not more" and dress conservatively.
5. Don't overdo the athletic activities. Enjoy yourself, but don't push yourself to the point of injury to impress your colleagues.
6. Be conscious of when the event is scheduled to begin and end. If you want to stay beyond the end of the event to help clean up, that's fine. Otherwise, leave a bit before the planned ending of the event.
7. Finally, thank the host. A note of appreciation sent the next day is also a nice touch.

When Conflict Occurs

Despite many characteristics people share in a work environment, they usually differ greatly in the ways they approach their jobs. These differences are most likely to stand out when workers face pressure, unclear responsibilities, or violations of their personal expectations or needs. Such situations offer ideal opportunities for clarifying personal differences and for team building. In fact, people sometimes unwittingly engage in conflict to bring themselves closer together.

Regardless of the origin and content of the conflict, some simple guidelines may prove helpful in dealing with a conflict at work.

1. Don't let differences build up. To avoid the risk of confusing several issues, deal with problems as they occur.
2. Deal with the other individual directly. Do not create a triangle with a third person who must carry your frustrations in secret. At the same time, avoid unnecessary stress and confusion by refusing invitations to become involved as a third party yourself, unless becoming involved is clearly a part of your job and you have the support of both parties to help them resolve their conflict.
3. Avoid personalizing the issue by placing blame or engaging in name-calling. If the conflict is related to a colleague's behavior, be sure to keep the focus on the specific behavior, not on the individual's personality. Notice, for example, the difference between the following two statements: (1) "When you extend your lunch hour without notifying me, I get frustrated because I can't live up to my commitments. In the future, please let me know when you're planning on being late so I can schedule around it." (2) "You'll never learn. You made me miss my appointment. Wait till I tell your supervisor." Which is more likely to solve the problem?
4. Have a win/win attitude. Plan ahead and try to identify at least one mutually beneficial alternative for correcting the situation, and plan on inviting other alternatives from the other person involved. Maintain a sense of control. Avoid blindly lashing out.
5. Use "I" statements, such as "I want," "I need." Don't try to strengthen your position by revealing that co-workers agree with you. Let others speak for themselves.
6. Use humor and focus on the positive aspects of personal differences as a way of relieving tension and supporting the other person's efforts to change.
7. Plan time for a follow-up review of the changes made, so that you can deal with any new problems as they arise.
8. Don't go up the chain of command unless the situation can't be resolved directly through the steps we've suggested. If you do need a superior's help, find out what the appropriate procedures are and inform the other person of your plans.

ADJUSTING TO A WORK ENVIRONMENT

In addition to learning how to get along smoothly with all kinds of people in an organization, successful work adjustment usually requires learning to handle particular aspects of your work environment and duties. A major cause of job failure is the unwillingness to accept the job as it is, versus what it was imagined to be.

Managing Conflict Sanely

Peter S. Chantilis (1997), an attorney-mediator in Dallas, Texas, offers us some useful tips in managing conflict at home or on the job:

1. Learn how to disagree without being disagreeable. It's all right to be assertive, but not aggressive, abusive, or abrasive.
2. When someone says something with which you disagree, try not to be judgmental.
3. Maintain eye contact when greeting people, and shake their hands. (Touching is important.)
4. Be kind and courteous to everyone.
5. Remember that civility is a sign of strength, not weakness.
6. Speak softly. (People tune out loud, angry voices.)
7. Saving face is important. Give your opponent the opportunity to withdraw.
8. Your attitude is more important than your aptitude.
9. Mutual respect is key in avoiding conflict.
10. Give the other person a chance to be heard without interrupting.
11. The shortest distance between two people is a smile.

The transition to a new work environment requires time and effort. You may not immediately understand why your company does something in a certain way. What works in practice may not always coincide with what you learned in college. And, of course, employers present their best side in the job interview, just as applicants do. Further, you may not have anticipated certain routines or unpleasant duties associated with the job. Some of the problems of romanticizing a job can be avoided by looking at the world of work as realistically as possible and by determining what is and isn't wanted in a job so that accurate questions can be asked about those things during a job interview. Even in the stress of a job interview, it's important to remember that *you're* also interviewing *them*.

When you begin your first job, no matter how carefully you've searched and how realistic your job choice is, you have to face the major challenge of accepting and adjusting to a work setting that differs greatly from life at home or in school. You'll probably need to modify all the things we've discussed—your relation to the environment, your personal image, and your ways of relating to others. Having an employer or supervisor overseeing and evaluating your work will be a new and at times anxiety-producing experience.

The greatest single adjustment problem new employees have is making the transition from classroom learning to job experience. Moving from taking tests, supervised lab experience, or even apprenticeship to doing what has been learned is a big step. New employees are expected to correct their own mistakes, overcome job problems, and pat themselves on the back. Criticism or reassurance from others does not come as often as it did in college. In a career, unlike the classroom, an employee will be missed if he or she oversleeps, takes a day off, or leaves early. New employees are held responsible not just for understanding the theory behind a situation but also for making it work.

In learning what responsibilities their job involves, new employees often discover that it calls for things they didn't learn in class and must now learn on the job. We've already discussed a primary example of such a skill—the art of getting along with all kinds of people. You also need patience when you don't receive a merited raise or promotion; hard work isn't always appreciated. Changes won't always come when expected or thought to be needed. Further, new employees may not have as much responsibility or voice in some matters as they like, at least at first.

A work situation can be fun, informal, and comfortable, but it's also scheduled and structured. Every member takes each person's part in an organization seriously. A first job is a world of new responsibilities.

BEING AN EFFECTIVE COMMUNICATOR

Another skill that employers mention often is effective communication. Successful employees know how to communicate at many levels. The first level involves the basic skills we all know about: reading, writing, and speaking. Almost all jobs require oral communication. Many require reading as well—correspondence, reports, memos, minutes, newsletters, and public relations information. Most settings also demand skills of clear communication: organizing ideas, using correct vocabulary and grammar, being understood, being tactful, and being persuasive. For written communications, clear and logical organization and correct spelling and punctuation are essential. To make friends and to hold one's own among colleagues, you need informal communication skills, such as confiding, confronting, using appropriate humor, and keeping confidences.

Less obvious, the second group of common skills involves self-expression—telling people what we believe, stand for, and want. This is what gives us each a distinct "personality" and attracts others. It also sets boundaries by letting others know what we value, what we won't tolerate, and how we feel. People also reveal much about themselves nonverbally, including things they may be trying to hide. Since nonverbal communication is a fact of life, you need to understand your own attitudes and feelings and be as honest as you can about yourself. Individuals who have interpersonal problems or get unexpected reactions from others often have negative feelings or attitudes that they cannot hide successfully.

One unique problem that almost everyone who works must face is the need to communicate clearly and successfully with a supervisor or boss. Problems may arise if the boss is a poor communicator or is prejudiced, angry, or incompetent. Unfortunately, the problem still belongs to the employee, who must persevere to find out what the boss wants. Many employees also create their own problems with their boss because of an anger with authority figures that originated in their relationship with their parents. If you suspect this is a problem for you, try to be aware and objective, or you may see problems in your work relationship where none exists.

The third communication arena involves transcending personal and cultural differences. Increasing numbers of women hold key management positions. As discussed in Chapter 5, many immigrants now live and work in the United States. Their backgrounds may differ from those of native-born citizens, and for many,

English is a second language. Other countries are also buying and building businesses and factories here (like Honda) and hiring U.S. citizens into jobs supervised by foreign-born managers.

Further problems arise in communications between men and women and between majority- and minority-group members. Studies show that in groups, meetings, and classes, majority-group men tend to talk more than women and minorities, talk longer, interrupt more frequently, and be validated more by discussion leaders. This problem is worst in traditionally male-dominated fields or corporations. Women and minorities need to be prepared to deal with this and to meet it with confidence and assertiveness rather than hostility. Majority-group men also need to be sensitive to these differences and change their behaviors accordingly. Career success depends on what co-workers do and don't say and how they express themselves in an increasingly diverse workplace that requires many forms of communication.

MANAGING YOUR TIME WISELY

Still another important work-adjustment skill is the wise management of time. For most employees, especially those with tight schedules, the old cliché "Time is money" rings true. When they waste time on the job, workers create problems for themselves with a time-conscious employer. Such workers are easy to identify, because they constantly socialize with other employees, make excessive personal phone calls, fake illness or take unwarranted sick days, take inordinately long lunch hours and coffee breaks, frequently arrive late or leave early, play solitaire on their office computer, and conduct personal business or engage in activities related to other employment while on the job. They also may look busy while doing nothing or create a need for overtime by working slowly during normal hours. If you find yourself engaging in such behaviors, try to find out why. Are you bored with your job and in need of a new set of challenges? Are you a victim of the "push-pause syndrome"—doing things rapidly for a brief period of time, then slowing down greatly for a long period—and in need of a more balanced work load? Do you need to transfer to a work setting that allows for more flexible use of your time and greater control of your work schedule? Have you lost track of your personal wellness? Are you losing sleep, not eating well, not exercising or relaxing? Is your personal rhythm different from what the job requires? By asking yourself these questions, you may be able to identify needed changes that you can make, perhaps with input from your supervisor, to make your time and that of your employer more productive and your life more enriched.

UNDERSTANDING AND MANAGING STRESS ON THE JOB

Stress has become a familiar term and a well-researched concept as the fast-moving 20th century moves toward the new millennium. It's easy to see stress as something caused externally, a problem, rather than what it is—a fight-or-flight reaction, an internal psychological and physiological response that living things produce when faced with change or danger. Risks and problems, including positive risks like marriage or a job promotion, often cause stress. Stress comes with meeting life's challenges; we can't avoid it. However, we can accept and manage it constructively.

Tension Equals Energy

The anxiety that accompanies new experiences, expectations, conflicts, and even happiness is a physiological message to us that we have needs or concerns that we haven't addressed. This anxiety stresses us, and our systems generate energy to deal with the challenge. Our job is to identify our needs and figure out how we can satisfy them. Sometimes the cause of our discomfort and the solutions are obvious and easily resolved ("I'm hungry; I'll eat" or "I disagree; I'll argue"). Often, however, the need or problem is hard to identify or the solution is delayed or unavailable ("I don't know why I feel angry at my boss" or "I love this work, but the pay is too low"). Then, we may need indirect strategies for dealing with anxiety, such as a relaxation exercise, jogging, a talk with a friend, reading a good novel, or meditation. Since a great deal of potential energy builds up along with feelings and concerns, we need to learn to recognize any self-defeating behaviors that may occur in our attempt to reduce this pressure (being late to work, drinking too much, kicking the dog) and find ways to convert the energy into positive action (confronting the situation, finding a "detour," planning a long-term change).

How Much Is Enough?

Another interesting and consistent finding is that the removal of all stress does not help. If too much stress is bad for maintaining our sense of well-being, so is too little. People perform best at a certain optimal (moderate) level of stress, where they are stimulated enough to be "on their toes" but not enough to be panicked or discouraged. At the optimum level of stress, they can convert the tension and energy into a creative motivator. Burnout occurs only when a person experiences too much or too little stress (Levi, 1972).

Level of stimulation is not the only determinant of stress. Personal effectiveness depends on (1) the level of stimulation or arousal, (2) our talents and capabilities, and (3) the nature or difficulty of our work (Gmelch, 1983). Stress level depends as well on our perceptions and beliefs. In other words, stress depends not only on our capabilities and job difficulty but also on our perceptions of our own abilities and of the problems that lie ahead. So, it's important for you to be self-aware and have an objective view of your job. If you do, you can more accurately answer such questions as the following: (1) Is the job too easy or too difficult for me? (2) Will I be comfortable with the people, circumstances, and rewards? (3) Do I have enough skills and experience? An unrealistic level of confidence can create a stressful situation that might have been avoided, whereas too little confidence can cause the loss of an ideal job.

Sally Forth, © 1990. Reprinted with special permission of King Features Syndicate.

Remaining aware of one's personal "stress index" takes effort and alertness, because many possibilities for falling outside of this optimal stress zone exist. For example, most people have experienced overstimulation or overwork, which results in exhaustion or illness, hasty and shortsighted solutions, and low self-esteem (feelings of failure). Interestingly, sleep deprivation is now a significant concern among employers because of lost productivity and increasing accidents on the job. Many employers do not realize how stressful understimulation is. Lack of variety, challenge, or excitement results in decreased motivation, boredom, fatigue, frustration, and dissatisfaction (Gmelch, 1983), which also adversely affect job performance and self-esteem.

To decide how closely your abilities, interests, and goals match an unknown job, you must evaluate job difficulty—both quality and quantity of work. ("Can I do this? How much can I do? Is what they're asking realistic?") You should also become aware of the kinds of things that bother you ("I hate to be indoors on nice days") and how many of these stresses are built into a particular job ("As a teacher, I'll be indoors on a lot of nice days, but I'll be out at 3:30 and all summer. And I can take the students on field trips"). The optimal level of challenges in any area of a job calls for us to reach just beyond our grasp: a stretch but not an impossibility.

Managing Stress and Promoting Wellness

Fortunately, just as there are multiple sources of stress, there are many ways of dealing with it. The prerequisites are self-understanding and an awareness of the stressors associated with the job so that you can bring the source of the problem into awareness. To convert tension into constructive action, you must know your goals and priorities.

Taking care of yourself   In any stressful situation, you need first to examine the part your attitudes, behaviors, and choices play rather than blame your discomfort on something external (the boss, the economy) that you can't change. You can maintain good health and attitudes by pursuing recreation, hobbies, relaxation techniques, proper diet, and so on. Continuing education will help avoid obsolescence, increase preparedness for career shifts, and help you remain optimistic.

To some extent, you can alleviate stress through appropriate changes in your work environment. For example you may be able to get help from a boss or transfer to another department. A feeling of being overwhelmed can be reduced by breaking a large project into smaller parts and by delegating responsibility (which can be difficult for people who need to have everything perfect). Finally, if you want a change—internal or external—in a job or career, you must take the initiative.

Taking responsibility   Avoiding stress doesn't just mean knowing your limits; it means making sure others know them as well. It means saying no and speaking up in a constructive, nonthreatening way. It means not taking responsibility for others, but instead taking responsibility for your own health, happiness, and commitments.

Part of your responsibility is to identify sources of stress so you can work with them. Doing so involves knowing where to look. We've discussed the most obvious stresses—orienting to a new job and work climate; forming new relationships; dealing with conflict and, possibly, discrimination; and pleasing superiors while being appropriately assertive when the situation calls for it. However, much subtler stresses persist throughout a person's working life. In any career, you must make decisions daily, balancing numerous factors, including your own self-interests. Effective workers constantly try to move toward new goals by learning new job skills and networking, and every new stage in a person's career development brings new challenges. Change, a constant source of anxiety, is inescapable. Other stresses come from intangibles. Some employees find that although they like a job, the company has a poor ethical climate (for example, widespread discrimination) or expects behaviors contrary to the personal beliefs of the employees. Discomfort also occurs when colleagues act in ways inconsistent with an individual's personal values or those of the organization. If you have negative feelings about your job for any of these reasons, don't talk yourself out of them; try to determine the source and what you can realistically do to change your situation.

Taking control   The bottom line of stress management is taking control. Highly stressed people do not feel in control. Staying in control means using all the strategies we've just mentioned, in addition to looking ahead and anticipating other challenges to overcome. It means knowing where you're going, why, and how you plan to get there. It means knowing what things distress you and either limiting exposure to them or learning how to deal with them; saving energy for important issues; and being clear about personal feelings, goals and values, so that you can confront and conquer disappointment, change, and conflict. It also means recognizing early warning signs of stress, understanding the problem, and making changes before it becomes a crisis (Gmelch, 1983).

In summary, stress is an unavoidable part of being human—of growth, change, and getting what we want. A moderate level of stimulation is the most comfortable. Feeling too much or too little stimulation results in stress. Stress creates energy, which we must convert to motivation and action instead of letting

---

Source Books on Health, Wellness, and Personal Development

Bloomfield, H. H., & Cooper, R. K. (1995). *The power of five.* Erasmus, PA: Rodale Press.

Covey, S. R. (1990). *The 7 habits of highly effective people.* New York: Simon & Schuster.

Weil, A. (1995). *Spontaneous healing.* New York: Fawcett Columbine.

---

it get out of control. The best way to minimize and use stress is by working in a job that provides a good personal and professional "fit" and by using stress-management techniques that emphasize personal wellness, adaptability, taking risks and responsibilities, and remaining in charge of ourselves—our feelings, priorities, goals, and choices—even when life is, well, stressful.

> Be master of your petty annoyances and conserve your energies for the big, worthwhile things. It isn't the mountain ahead that wears you out—it's the grain of sand in your shoe.
>
> —*Robert Service*

Working Well and Living Well: A Delicate Balance

Young couples tend to believe they can have it all—two challenging careers; a tidy home; gourmet meals; time to ski, golf, or travel; and many children. It's becoming clear, however, that having it all demands high energy, motivation, cooperation, strategic planning, and organization. Such a lifestyle exacts a physical and emotional price even when it's going smoothly: guilt; regret over leaving the children; less time for self, spouse, or partner; frequent exhaustion. When something goes wrong in this carefully orchestrated system—a sick child or babysitter, one person feeling overworked, cash-flow problems—the stress level can go from manageable to acute. Though these problems have no easy solutions, it does help to anticipate stress and have clear priorities for the family and its members, including communication, a long-term commitment to each other, and flexibility to combine career and family successfully with the other factors associated with living well—physical self-care, social connectedness, emotional balance, intellectual growth, and spiritual awareness.

HANDLING PERFORMANCE APPRAISALS EFFECTIVELY

Another important element in adjusting to a work setting is handling performance evaluations from superiors. Supervisors can appraise performance on the job through a variety of methods. The way they approach the evaluation may be

a matter of personal preference, organizational policy, or a combination of the two. The most informal manner is the general pat-on-the-back approach, which may or may not be tied to specific areas of performance or to merit raises. A variation is the "management by exception" method, in which staff do not receive an evaluation unless they're doing poorly.

Many organizations require relatively formal and concrete feedback about an employee's performance, most often before the end of a 6-month probationary period and yearly after that. The supervisor may be asked to rate the employee on a form used to evaluate all staff members in comparable positions. Employees are commonly evaluated on their job knowledge, achievements/accomplishments, planfulness/thoroughness, creativity/originality, problem solving/decision making, ability to get along with others, communication skills, and ability as a supervisor/leader. Companies that use this type of evaluation may ask supervisors to compare an employee's performance on these dimensions with those of other employees in a similar position or with an objective performance standard. Space is usually provided for the supervisor to summarize the employee's overall performance and suggest areas for improvement. How much input employees have into their evaluation may depend on the supervisor's personal preferences. One supervisor may simply provide a written evaluation for the employee to review and sign without much discussion. Another supervisor may ask employees to rate themselves on a form prior to the evaluation session and then spend some time with the employee comparing both ratings in an effort to reach a consensus with the employee about her or his performance. Forward-looking employees find out in advance how they will be evaluated so they can optimize their input—either by giving their supervisor needed information before the evaluation or by preparing to present their best case during it.

In another approach to performance appraisal, "management by objectives" or "management by results," employees meet with their supervisor to develop an action plan that describes what they expect to accomplish during a particular time, how they'll accomplish it and by what target date. The employees regularly review their progress, sharing the information with the supervisor. Performance evaluations focus on how effectively employees have accomplished their objectives. Try to find out early during your employment how you'll be evaluated so that you can be prepared to present your strengths, weaknesses, and accomplishments in the most constructive manner.

DEALING WITH DISCRIMINATION AND HARASSMENT

If you begin work in a company with few female or minority employees, and you're one of them, be yourself. Don't go to extremes either to blend in or to emphasize your differences. It's important to accept the existing situation if it's essentially fair. Be friendly and give your co-workers time. Some white men, for example, may resent the presence of female or minority "competition." If you encountered angry reactions, it helps not to be oversensitive. Try your best to make friends with the colleagues you like, since informal gossip and lunchtime conversation can be the best sources of important information and contacts for promotion in a large organization.

If you have a disability, you're protected from discrimination in hiring by the Americans with Disabilities Act (ADA). This law provides that qualified individuals may not be discriminated against because of disabilities. However, applicants must be able to perform the essential duties of the job once any necessary "reasonable accommodation" has been made. A disabled employee must receive the same treatment as other employees but need not be given special benefits or sick-leave arrangements. Employers must provide accessible nonwork facilities such as restrooms, drinking fountains, and food areas.

If you feel you're being discriminated against in your job, the best source of information is the Equal Employment Opportunity Commission. Before making a complaint, be sure that you have facts and dates to back up your accusations. Keep written notes of all conversations and events that you believe demonstrate discrimination against you.

In general, if you're a minority member, a woman, or an older person hired into any situation where you are a pioneer—a tradition breaker—you may need to take extra care just to "be yourself" at work. Be as responsible as you can, move cautiously, and listen and watch carefully for those clues discussed earlier that convey behavioral norms. Again, try not to be negative or defensive. By responding to your situation with care and sensitivity, you can help to open more jobs like yours to a more diverse workforce.

The workplace reflects the diversity that exists in our changing society. Consequently, organizational cultures are evolving to accommodate greater variability in individual styles of relating, personal values and lifestyles, and physical capacities. Attitudes based on stereotypes and outdated information are being challenged, and individual behaviors that reflect outmoded thinking are being called into question.

Despite the more general changes in society and in particular work settings, such as the military, that demonstrate a commitment to social diversity through organizational policies and practices, outright harassment still occurs. Sometimes the perpetrator of the harassment doesn't know that the behavior is inappropriate; often, the victim doesn't report the harassment for fear of reprisal or embarrassment.

Because of people's differences in background, upbringing, and attitude, old ideas about male and female roles and about ethnic differences may create problems. Thus, problems that women experience with sexually aggressive men during high school and college may continue in the work setting, often in more subtle ways. Someone in a position of power may promise better grades or a promotion to a person who will sleep with him or her. Suggestive comments may be made about a person's manner of dress, walk, or voice. Sexual and off-color jokes may be told to test a person's tolerance of sexual put-downs. The continuum of sexually oriented activity of this type may start with a glance or gesture, a whistle, or a comment with a double meaning, move toward a direct proposition, and end with touching, a forced embrace, or coerced intercourse.

Slurs or attempts at intimidation can also focus on a person's ethnicity, religious preference, physical capacity, or age. However it occurs, one person's attempt to assert power in the form of harassment violates another's right to work in a setting free of unwanted attention, coercion, or abasement.

Ignoring abusive behavior does not usually stop it. Confronting harassment in a constructive way can help, though. The Project on the Status and Education of Women of the Association of American Colleges has offered the following steps to confront harassment.

First, speak up and act assertively when the incident occurs. Say *no* firmly, directly, and clearly—for example, "When you say such things you offend me and make me uncomfortable." Start by giving the other person the benefit of the doubt. If he or she didn't realize that the behavior was offensive, your feedback may stop it.

Second, if it continues, keep a record of what happened, where it happened, when it happened, who was around to witness the event, and how you responded. These records will be of great help if you need to make a formal complaint later. Tell someone such as a trusted peer or colleague about the event. Harassers often make abusive comments and overtures to more than one person; you may find that you're not alone in your concern.

Third, find an advocate, such as your supervisor (if that person is not the harasser), an affirmative action officer, a personnel specialist, or a mental health professional who can support you emotionally as well as counsel you on organizational and legal procedures for managing such situations.

Fourth, write a letter to the harasser that clearly and succinctly states your case. Mary P. Rowe (1981) has provided useful guidelines for composing such a letter. She suggests that you write the letter in three parts. The first part provides a concise, factual account of what happened, as you experienced it, without any evaluation. You should focus on specific behaviors exhibited by the other person (for example, words and physical gestures such as touching), along with the time and place they occurred. The second part describes your reactions to the other person's actions: what you thought and how you felt about it. The third part briefly, clearly, and directly states how you want the other person to change—for example, "I want you to stop saying (or doing) . . ." To insure that the person receives the letter, deliver it directly or send it by registered or certified mail. Keep a copy

Dilbert reprinted by permission of United Feature Syndicate, Inc.

for your files, but don't send a copy to someone in authority, at least not at first. Give the harasser a chance to change. If that doesn't work, use the letter to document any attempt at retaliation by the other person, to file a formal complaint later, or as part of a lawsuit.

You may want to bolster your confidence by taking a course in assertiveness training or self-defense. Draw as many supportive people around you as you can (trusted family members, colleagues, or a mental health professional) to advise and counsel you in case the situation becomes complex, drawn out, and conflicted.

Keep in mind, too, that even though your employer may seem reasonable and fair, some unfair, hidden expectations may exist. Offenders in supervisory roles or other influential positions tend to have more credibility than younger employees. Some executives may believe that a subordinate who can't adjust to a supervisor's expectations has an "attitude problem" (is a "tattletale" or "paranoid") and should be transferred within the organization or fired. If you encounter such expectations, document your experiences, be patient and persistent, and follow the steps just outlined before requesting a personal action by the employer or taking your case to court.

> Don't be afraid of opposition. Remember, a kite rises against, not with the wind.
>
> —*Hamilton Wright Mabie*

AVENUES FOR CAREER DEVELOPMENT WITHIN AN ORGANIZATION

Knowing about the general structure of the world of work may suggest ideas about ways to apply one's skills, interests, and values in a variety of settings, but it does not give specific details about avenues for careers within a particular organization or across several organizations. To learn about such avenues, you can use the career cone approach or the career roles approach. As you read about each, be mindful that a person's career in today's workplace will not likely take the course of a straight line to the top. It will move about like a sailboat, controlled by the winds of economic change and zig-zagging toward its distant goal.

The Career Cone

The first approach for charting your growth within an organization was developed by Edgar Schein (1971) of the Sloan School of Management at the Massachusetts Institute of Technology. He suggests that the best way to look at career advancement within a given organization involves the "career cone" shown in Figure 10-1.

Schein's career cone illustrates the three ways of growing within an organization: inwardly, vertically, and horizontally. The first form of growth, movement toward the inner circle, is probably the least familiar of the three because it's not necessarily accompanied by a visible change in position or title. Also, unlike many other forms of growth, it may not require the development of new skills. Progress in this dimension occurs through interpersonal relationships. New employees must prove to their supervisors their trustworthiness and dedication to organizational goals. The first test for a new employee occurs when a supervisor passes on an organizational secret such as the reasons a particular decision was made or who's in with the boss and why. The sharing of this secret may precede a request for help or support in carrying out certain actions or decisions. If the employee passes this test, others will follow. The secrets shared will become increasingly important, as a staff member becomes a central member of the inner core of decision makers within the organization. Status in an organization thus depends as much on "who you know" as "what you do." Failure to pass this test of confidence may be costly: A promotion may be lost, or information affecting one's work may not be provided. But passing the test is not always the only, or even the best, choice.

Generally speaking, the higher the position, the more access one has to privileged information within the organization. Individuals at the top need more information to make decisions critical to the entire organization. Thus, movement toward the inner core is often accompanied by a promotion or a change in title. In many circumstances, however, managers may call on a trusted employee at lower levels of the organization for input into key decisions because of specialized knowledge or informal leadership status.

The second form of growth, vertical movement, is probably the most familiar. Achievement by moving up the organizational ladder is a common standard for success to most people in the United States. We are all familiar with the story of the unskilled worker who, through diligence and a willingness to acquire new skills, is eventually promoted all the way to the president's chair. A new employee's potential for promotion within the organization is measured in terms of trustworthiness and capacity to take on increasingly greater levels of responsibility for complex tasks and for supervising others. Tolerance for stress and a willingness to pursue additional professional education also play an important role in determining how successfully a person will advance in the ranks.

Figure 10-1
Schein's career
cone: a three-
dimensional model
of an organization
(Schein, 1971,
p. 404)

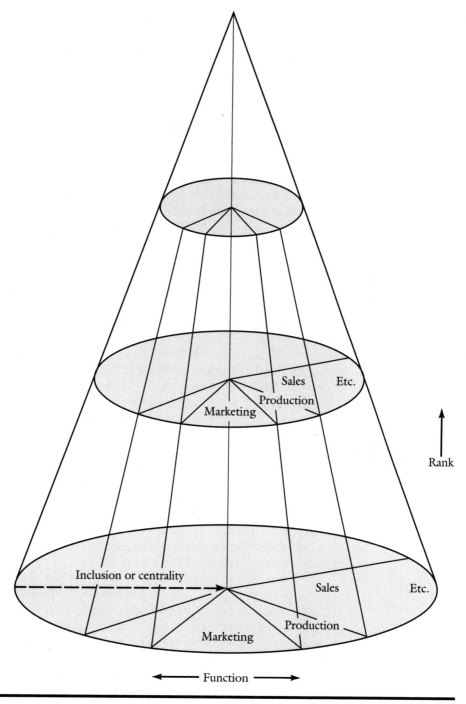

The third form of professional growth described by Schein involves a rotation across a series of functions within the organization. Rather than moving upward, an individual may move horizontally across positions at the same level. Many management-training programs use this form of growth as a means of exposing new employees to the different facets of an organization. A new sales representative, for example, may spend several weeks in the production department, then serve in several other departments until he or she has gained experience in each facet of the entire organization. For some, this short-term approach to horizontal mobility may also provide a forum for long-term growth. It's not uncommon to find an employee who has worked in several departments all at the same level of responsibility. In such situations, the employee uses the same set of transferable skills to perform related functions. Further, making a series of lateral moves may create new learning opportunities and keep an individual professionally fresh. When coupled with an active refinement of one's management skills, a broad range of experience can also be a valuable asset when one seeks a promotion or a new job.

Career Roles

We can also view growth within an organization by looking at the professional roles a person may assume during his or her career. Several writers (Dalton, Thompson, & Price, 1977; Schein, 1978; Tiedeman & O'Hara, 1963) have contributed to our knowledge of what happens to students during college and after they enter the labor force. Perhaps the easiest way of thinking about career development during college and beyond is to imagine a person moving through seven roles over time: student, applicant, apprentice/trainee, colleague, mentor, sponsor, and retiree. Table 10-1 describes each role in terms of the central tasks and activities it involves and the major psychological issues it may create. Each of the roles shown in Table 10-1 evolves over time as we gain new skills and insight into ourselves.

A person keeps the role of student for many years, through formal and informal education. This role becomes more complex over time as people must make more choices and assume greater levels of responsibility. We often base initial career choices on a fantasy or an admired person, but we later come to base them on actual work experience, better occupational information, and higher levels of awareness of what we like and want to do.

In Chapter 9, we described in great detail the role of applicant for a professional position. This role requires a shift in view from a general understanding of occupations to a more precise understanding of particular organizations and specific jobs. It also requires an assertive engagement, locating positions, applying for them and securing a position. Since the job-campaigning process may contain much stress, frustration, and disappointment, it can teach a great deal about how to cope with uncertainty.

The move from applicant to a first professional position as an apprentice/ trainee is a bit like the first days at college. It involves learning the ropes in the new setting, accepting the wisdom and guidance of others about how best to manage responsibilities, building supportive relationships with others, learning to

Table 10-1 Seven Career Stages

	Stage 1	Stage 2	Stage 3	Stage 4	Stage 5	Stage 6	Stage 7
Role	Student	Applicant	Apprentice/Trainee	Colleague	Mentor	Sponsor	Retiree
Central tasks	Developing and discovering one's values, interests, and abilities. Making wise educational decisions. Finding out about occupational possibilities through discussion, observation, and work experience.	Learning how to look for a job, how to apply for a job, how to negotiate a job interview. Learning how to assess information about a job and an organization. Making a realistic and valid job choice.	Learning the ropes of the organization. Helping others. Following directions. Achieving acceptance.	Becoming an independent contributor. Finding a niche in the organization as a specialist.	Training/mentoring others. Interfacing with other units in the organization. Managing team projects.	Analyzing complex problems, shaping the direction of an organization. Handling organizational secrets. Dealing with organizational politics. Developing new ideas. Sponsoring the creative projects of others. Managing power and responsibility.	Adjusting to changes in standard of living and lifestyle. Finding new ways of expressing one's talents and interests.
Major psychological issues	Accepting responsibility for one's choices.	Assertively presenting oneself to others. Tolerating uncertainty.	Depending on others. Dealing with reality, shock of what the organization is like. Overcoming insecurity.	Reassessing original career goals in light of new self-knowledge and growth potential in the organization. Independence. Accepting responsibility for one's successes and failures. Establishing a balanced lifestyle.	Assuming responsibility for others. Deriving satisfaction from the successes of others. If not in management role, accepting role of established professional and finding opportunities from lateral growth.	Disengaging from primary concern about self or ownership to become more concerned with organizational welfare. Managing personal emotional reactions to high levels of stress. Balancing work and family, life planning for retirement.	Finding satisfaction in one's past career accomplishments while being open to new avenues of personal growth.

Sources: Adapted from Dalton, Thompson, and Price, 1977, pp. 19–42; Shein, 1978, pp. 36–48.

Sally Forth, © 1996. Reprinted with special permission of King Features Syndicate.

live with the difference between a fantasy about life in the new place and the reality of the situation, and overcoming the insecurity associated with being less skilled than others in some areas.

Unlike the shift from applicant to apprentice or trainee that occurs shortly after graduation, there may be no clear moment when a person becomes a colleague. For people who have a considerable amount of work experience and a great deal of professional maturity, or who are working in a job that does not involve many complex tasks, the shifts may occur rapidly, sometimes within several months. Others may take considerably longer to reach the new status. Regardless of how long it takes, the benchmarks for successfully moving into the new role are the same: feeling more confidence and a greater sense of belonging in the organization, being able to act as an independent contributor, finding and shaping a personalized professional niche in the organization as a recognized specialist, and developing a mentoring relationship with a senior in experience or in position. As they make the transition, some employees spend time struggling with how best to balance their desire to assert their views of how things ought to be against the realities of past traditions and established policies. Assertively presenting new ideas involves using tact and diplomacy with colleagues and a willingness to take responsibility for one's successes and failures. Successfully moving to the status of colleague often depends on how well a person uses the help or advice of a supervisor or more experienced co-workers and on how well he or she balances non-work-related pursuits against frustrations in the work setting. The period of shaping one's niche may also be accompanied by a time of self-assessment in which one begins to ask, "What does the future look like for me in this organization?"

People who take on the role of mentor usually have a considerable amount of work experience and personal maturity and are viewed as established professionals. Such people derive satisfaction from training and supervising others through informal or formal means and may measure their own success by how they have helped others achieve rather than by what they themselves accomplish. Because they generally have a high level of knowledge and credibility with their peers, they often serve as bridges between staff and the upper levels of management. They may also be involved in making connections with other organizations. Such individuals often have supervisory roles.

The sponsor is usually associated with upper levels of management. People who fill this role are usually responsible for shaping the direction of an organization or a major segment of it. The skills for success in this role are complex: dealing with complicated problems, managing organizational politics, sponsoring the creative ideas of others, originating or promoting new directions for the organization, and managing personal reactions to high levels of stress. Such people must make quick decisions and exercise their authority during crisis periods while having a long-range plan for accomplishing the overall mission of the organization. At times, they may serve as a disciplinarian for an errant staff member, a referee in a staff conflict, a teacher of a new idea or approach that protects company policy, or a team leader. Also crucial to their success are the ability to work for long periods at high levels of involvement and the capacity for taking advantage of social, physical, and other leisure activities for personal restoration and growth.

The retiree role becomes part of the conscious thinking of many workers around the age of 40 as they examine the next steps in their career and realize that their current or next position may be the one from which they will retire. Tasks for the retiree include adjusting to a new standard of living and lifestyle and finding new ways of using interests and talents that may have lain dormant during the working years. People who enjoy their retirement find satisfaction in past career accomplishments but remain open to new pursuits such as hobbies and community involvements.

As you can see, many avenues for career development exist. In the remaining pages of this chapter, we'll examine how you can promote career growth by actively pursuing professional development opportunities and by making wise decisions.

CAREER DEVELOPMENT

When you take a job, you enter into a contract with an employer. In exchange for your labor and talent, you receive wages and certain other benefits. Effective professionals keep in mind that one of their goals throughout their career is their own professional development. Such individuals stay aware of emerging changes in the world marketplace, the changing market, and the professional skills that are currently in demand or will be in the future. Flexible in their orientation toward work, these individuals use their untapped skills and seek training that will maintain their professional value. They also realize that their employer may respond positively to a well-presented statement that explains why they should receive more training or be permitted to add new duties to their current responsibilities. Supervisors spend a good deal of time checking to see that their staff members do their required work. The person who completes essential assignments and asks for more will likely be valued.

As the information revolution now suggests, years from now we'll see a vast number of jobs that don't exist yet. The training you receive today will not necessarily prepare you for jobs 10 years from now. Throughout this book, we have emphasized education, job training, decision making, and adaptability as lifelong processes. Learning and adapting to new situations are skills you'll need to continue throughout your working life.

Professional conferences, workshops, work colleagues, journals, the news media, and the internet help people keep up on significant changes in their professional specialties and related fields. Many employers will pay for some or all of an employee's continuing education. Taking classes and workshops will demonstrate to your employer that you're committed to your professional growth. It will also enhance your value to the employer. In this way, the company benefits by developing talent within its ranks, with an eye toward promotion. Managerial obsolescence, which threatens managers who are more concerned about security rather than growth, presents a major problem to business. By keeping current in your field and exploring related areas, you'll avoid obsolescence and continue to feel fulfilled by your endeavors.

Mentors

The main ingredient in the personal and professional development of many workers is their relationship with a mentor. Often a boss or prestigious older colleague, the mentor functions as a friend, teacher, and surrogate parent. This figure serves as the primary source of the information and confidence that employees need for successful work adjustment. From a mentor, a person can learn how to implement and apply ideas and to develop influence. The mentor relationship is usually personal enough that a new worker can request feedback, ask questions about other people, air misgivings, and get honest advice about how best to use the employment situation for personal development. The mentor also functions as a role model. By watching the way he or she deals with many situations, the young employee can grow personally and professionally.

Female and minority employees may have more difficulty attracting a mentor or keeping such a relationship running smoothly. This may happen because such employees are not totally welcome in a particular work setting or because they seem different and old-timers are afraid of them. Since many potential mentors are men, women may face additional complications: beliefs that many men have about what behaviors are appropriate for women, teasing or gossip about the relationship, and the possibility of sexual attraction. No rules exist for handling these pitfalls effectively, but sensitivity to the mentor and to the work environment will help. Although a mentor must essentially serve as a volunteer, a young professional can invite the support of a potential mentor by asking questions or showing an interest in how that person's job is done. As with any other situations in a new work environment, patience and quiet observation initially provide the best source of learning for a younger staff member.

Promotional Strategies

You should see by now that maintaining a successful career means adapting and growing along with shifts in the environment and changes in yourself. This growth depends on your ability to interact socially, communicate, and continue to learn, as well as make regular use of the first five skills in this book—decision making, self-assessment, information gathering, integration, and job-search strategies.

Keeping abreast of satisfaction and fit in any job requires regular reassessment of your feelings, values, beliefs, goals, interests, skills, and experience—all of which accumulate and change over the years. Also, you need to be sensitive to the job market, the economy, to changing job requirements, and possibilities for other jobs and new learning opportunities.

The attention you give your personal development and growth will inevitably lead to expanded interests and abilities and a desire for new challenges. Depending on your development and the direction your company takes, you can meet your need for change in a variety of ways—for example, a move to another organization or career area, a move up in a company's hierarchy, a lateral move to another area or department, or even just a move toward greater inclusion in the decision-making process of the organization. Moving toward inclusion can be as simple as asking to be included in policy-making or managerial meetings, or as complex as a planned campaign to qualify and be considered for a particular promotion or job.

If you enter a job with the general goal of being promoted or are aiming for advancement to a specific position, you may want to use the following professional and interpersonal tips and strategies to move yourself along your planned path and meet transitions and obstacles more confidently.

1. Begin early to document your successes. When you offer a good idea, institute a new policy, or contribute to the solution of a problem, put it in written reports as a memo to your superior or get it into the minutes of a meeting. Save letters of recommendation. If someone you trust commends or thanks you for a job well done, then ask him or her to put it in writing and/or make sure your superiors hear the news.
2. Be sure that you fully understand the requirements and demands of your target position and are willing and able to meet them.
3. Build a system of formal and informal connections. Make an effort to cooperate with your supervisor and understand his or her problems. Do the same with the others in higher positions who can influence which people will be promoted. Also keep in mind the significant role secretarial and other support staff may play in providing access to resources and individuals who may play an important role in your career. Keep in touch with the friends you make in other areas and departments and in other organizations. Besides enjoying the company of your friends, listen to their shop talk and problems for valuable information about company plans. You can also put in a good word for them if the opportunity arises, as they can for you. You may or may not choose to confide in your immediate supervisor. This decision should be based on the relationship you have and your opinion of the supervisor. If your supervisor is not effective or supportive, a lateral move to another area where the environment is more favorable may be the wisest choice.
4. When you've decided to try for a specific position or to make a move within a given time frame, share this decision with your support group and suggest things your peers might do to help. Whenever it seems

appropriate, share your goals with the people who make the promotions or do the hiring. When appropriate, present your supervisors with documentation of your work successes, your reasons for being interested in the change, and what you believe you can offer in the new position.

Although in our society we're relatively free to aim as high as our potential permits, striving to reach the top may not be that important. It can also be unwise. Being at too high a level creates constant pressure. Too much pressure may cause considerable stress; physical, emotional, and interpersonal damage; and loss of a sense of well-being. Reaching for ever-higher levels of achievement can become a trap if the work does not also provide personal pleasure and satisfaction.

To avoid reaching too high too soon, start by defining the level where you'll be most comfortable and setting a series of moderate goals for continued advancement. These goals will then act as steps you can climb. This method makes an ambitious goal more distant and less overwhelming and provides room for further investigation and redecision.

Regardless of where you start or how high you aim, you'll reach a ceiling at some point in your career. If your upward movement continues at the same time, you may find yourself at a level of responsibility beyond your competence. Laurence Peter (1984) writes that such situations arise frequently and are a prime cause of inefficiency in U.S. society. Here is what he calls his "Peter Principle": "In time, every post tends to be occupied by an employee who is incompetent to carry out his/her duties." The remedy is to halt advancement just below this level: This is the level of working and living well.

It may be difficult to acknowledge that you've reached your ceiling. You may go through a period of anxiety and uncertainty. The rewards of moving up in the hierarchy may seem to outweigh the problems—a trap of rising expectations. During such times, you'll face having to choose between moving up, moving across, or moving out.

Career Expansion: Moving Up, Across, or Out

Harriet Goldhor Lerner, the author of *The Dance of Intimacy,* observes:

> All of us have deeply ambivalent feelings about change. We seek the wisdom of others when we are not making full use of our own and then we resist applying the wisdom that we *do* seek even when we're paying for it. We do this not because we are neurotic or cowardly, but because both the will to change and the desire to maintain sameness coexist for good reason. Both are essential to our emotional well-being and equally deserve our attention and respect. (1989, p. 11)

No work environment is ideal. Each has its peculiarities and problems. Even the job that approaches the ideal will prove unsatisfying some of the time. Though discomfort often precedes growth within a job, how do we know when it's time to look for a different position—to move up, across, or out? How frustrated, bored, or disappointed must we become before saying "enough is enough" and beginning the process of change? These are difficult questions. And with no pat answers or formulas, we must determine for ourselves how to answer them.

Here are some areas to explore and questions we can ask as we sort through our motivations to make a change.

Start with yourself, where the growth cycle begins and ends:

1. Do I want more money? More or less responsibility? A new set of tasks? A more balanced lifestyle and greater attention to my personal well-being?
2. Have my career goals changed since I started at my job? If they have changed, how do they differ?
3. Am I a victim of the Peter Principle?
4. Last, but very important, how much of my dissatisfaction is due to my attitudes and behaviors, which will follow me to any job I choose?

Next, look to the organization:

1. Does it ask too much or give too little, leaving me feeling burned out and unappreciated?
2. Does the job have a negative effect on the other aspects of my lifestyle—my social life, leisure pursuits, spiritual beliefs, physical well-being, and pursuit of my intellectual interests?
3. Has my employer made comments about my work performance falling off, indicating that I'm now seen as less involved in my work than before? Is this an accurate perception?
4. Does my employer support my need for change, or does he or she view such a change as a threat to the status quo?
5. Does any unresolved conflict at work haunt me from day to day?

After you've explored these questions, look at the options you'll have if you stay where you are: Can you redefine your position (sometimes even the slightest alteration can make a big difference) or move to another one within the firm to save the benefits you've accumulated? Finally, look at the benefits of moving out. Where do I want to live? What work would I do there? How would the change affect my personal well-being? Would it allow me to express and expand my growth in all areas of the wellness wheel?

Before we discuss further the process of changing jobs, however, let's look at the whole idea of job change. Years ago, employers tended to view with concern the employee with a vocational history marked by several jobs. People tended to remain with the organization where they began work, moving up or across rather than out. However, in the United States today, workers change jobs more than ever before, with 10 percent of the labor force changing jobs every year. The typical American can expect to change jobs, and sometimes professions, at least three or four times during the course of his or her career.

The increased acceptability of job changes, midlife career changes, and multiple careers stems from the social upheaval of the 1960s. During that period, the motivation for choosing a job ceased to center solely on security. It expanded to include self-growth and personal satisfaction. As an outgrowth of social change, people now leave jobs for many reasons. Whereas people once stayed with a secure job unless extreme problems arose, they can now acceptably change jobs because they realize they chose the wrong job, because they changed, because the job has changed, or because they've done as much as they can in that job and want a new challenge.

The prospective employee who can give a good explanation for seeking a new position can usually locate one. If your record as an employee reflects frequent or directionless moves, however, you could experience difficulty looking for still another job. Informed decisions made in the early stages of a job search can avoid your taking a job that you may want to leave in 6 months.

Consider the advantages and disadvantages of available jobs. Be realistic about your strengths and limitations when you assess the requirements of new jobs. On the basis of adequate information, decide what you'd like to do and how you'll do it. If possible, stay in your present position while conducting your job search—an employer will more likely hire someone who already has a job. Interviewing for information is a useful way of searching out new prospects while maintaining control over your present job situation. So is taking on job responsibilities that involve meeting the public or other people in your field.

An important consideration in changing jobs is when to tell a boss about it. A supportive supervisor will understand an employee's need for advancement or change in position for personal reasons. Just the opposite may be true if the boss is threatened by the employee's need for change. Some supervisors view a staff member's desire to take on a new position as a personal criticism of their management style (which, under some circumstances, may actually be true). Insecure or threatened bosses may judge the employee as disloyal or expect him or her to coast during the remaining days of employment. With these attitudes and beliefs, the supervisor may try to push that person "out the door" as soon as possible.

If you find yourself in such a circumstance, keep in mind that the problem belongs to your boss, not you. Your task is to continue to do a good job during your remaining days of employment.

Ed Stockwell, who works for an executive search firm, suggests that a person who resigns from a position should do so "with grace." He advises that before you resign from a position to be sure you have written confirmation of the new job offer and have prepared a written letter of resignation to give your current employer. Also important, be sure to sit down with your current boss to discuss when you'll leave your job and what needs to be done to make your departure a smooth transition for both of you. It's also wise not to share your new salary level with other employees, especially if it involves a significant pay increase. Finally, be sure to leave on a positive note with your colleagues (Kleman, 1997).

Whatever you do, you need to retain a balanced perspective on where you are, what you want to do, and how you'll go about getting there. This perspective involves being thorough and clear-cut in your approach to building your future. In this way, you can increase the odds of saying to yourself in the future, "I've lived the way I wanted. I've enjoyed my career."

Everyone Has a Turn . . .

A fellow had just been hired as the new CEO of a large high-tech corporation.

The CEO who was stepping down met with him privately and presented him with three numbered envelopes. "Open these if you run up against a problem you don't think you can solve," he said.

Well, things went along pretty smoothly, but 6 months later, sales took a downturn and the new CEO was really catching a lot of heat. About at his wit's end, he remembered the envelopes. He went to his drawer and took out the first envelope. The message read, "Blame your predecessor."

The new CEO called a press conference and tactfully laid the blame at the feet of the previous CEO. Satisfied with his comments, the press and Wall Street responded positively, sales began to pick up, and the problem was soon behind him.

About a year later, the company was again experiencing a slight dip in sales, combined with serious product problems. Having learned from his previous experience, the CEO quickly opened the second envelope. The message read, "Reorganize." This he did, and the company quickly rebounded.

After several consecutive profitable quarters, the company once again fell on difficult times. The CEO went to his office, closed the door, and opened the third envelope.

The message said, "Prepare three envelopes."

Source: Internet

PROMOTING CONSTRUCTIVE CHANGE

Imagine yourself in the following situations:

1. You're a new employee. Your colleagues seem to think you receive preferential treatment because of your gender, race, or social-group membership. You'd like to change their attitudes because you don't think they're judging you fairly.
2. Your supervisor makes heavy demands on your time. You haven't been able to meet those demands without putting in a considerable amount of overtime. The pressure of the job has caused you to cut back on leisure and social pursuits that matter to you. It doesn't look as though the situation will change in the near future.
3. You have a strong but unexpressed difference of opinion with a colleague about the way a project should be done. You've been holding back your opinion for several weeks, and it's beginning to distress you.
4. After a year on the job, you didn't receive the raise you'd hoped for. You believe you deserve a raise and want to take steps to get it.
5. Your recent request for a promotion was denied, but you don't know why.

6. After doing the same job for five years, you've recently been feeling bored and restless. You don't know why your feelings have changed, but you're becoming more and more distressed about your situation.

7. You're a departmental supervisor. Two of your employees have had a considerable amount of conflict recently. You'd like to change this situation as soon as you can, because it's beginning to affect the morale of the entire staff.

8. You're going to retire in 2 years. How will you prepare for the change?

9. Imagine you're the human resources director for a newly formed biotechnology firm. You've been assigned the task of hiring a new staff of technical workers and mid-level managers. How would you go about finding a qualified pool of applicants? What qualities would you look for in the applicants? How would you assess them to make sure they fit your employer's needs?

10. Imagine you're an organizational consultant who's been asked by an employer to work with a group of employees disheartened because they can't resolve a "power struggle" among themselves. What steps would you take to assess the situation and build an action plan to resolve it?

Choose two of the situations just described and apply them to your own future career. For each situation, try to identify its potential causes and outline a strategy for resolving or changing it. Use the following questions to develop your change strategy.

1. What are the causes of this situation?
2. What is the worst possible way I could handle this problem?
3. To change the situation constructively, I would have to alter my behaviors in the following ways. (Identify specific behaviors you would need to change.)
4. To change this situation to make it more positive or constructive, others would have to change their behaviors in the following ways. (Identify specific behaviors they would have to change.)
5. How will you communicate your desire to change the situation to others?
6. How much responsibility will you take for promoting the change? How much responsibility will you share with others?
7. Using the information from your answers to the previous questions, list the specific steps you will take to create this change.

SELF-REVIEW ACTIVITY: HOW MUCH HAVE I CHANGED?

Turn back to the activity entitled "Where Am I in the Career Decision-Making Process?" at the end of Chapter 2. Use the stages presented in the activity to summarize your progress thus far and to plan the next steps in the decision-making cycle.

References and Resources

Boucher, J. (1994). *How to love the job you hate*. Nashville, TN: Thomas Nelson.

Chantilis, P. S. (1997, Oct. 19). Helpful hints for dealing with conflict. *Columbus Dispatch* (OH), Accent section, p. 2.

Cobble, D. (1996, Aug. 18). Certain protocol should be observed at company picnics. *Columbus Dispatch* (OH), p. 33J.

Cosgrave, G. P. (1973). *Career planning: Search for a future*. Toronto: University of Toronto Press.

Dalton, G. W., Thompson, R. H., & Price, R. L. (1997, Summer). The four stages of professional careers: A new look at performance by professionals. *Organizational Dynamics*, pp. 19–42.

Dilenschneider, R. L. (1997). *The critical fourteen years of your professional life*. New York: Birch Lane/Carol Publishing Group.

Dunphy, P. W. (Ed.). (1973). *Career development for the college student*. Cranston, RI: Carroll Press.

Gmelch, W. H. (1983). Stress for success: How to optimize your performance. *Theory into Practice, 22*, 7–14 (Columbus, OH: Ohio State University, College of Education).

Hughes, J. O., & Sandler, B. R. (1986). In case of sexual harassment: A guide for women students. Washington, DC: Association of American Colleges, Project on the Status and Education of Women.

Kleman, C. (1977, Aug. 24). Maintain ties by resigning with grace, consultant says. *Columbus Dispatch* (OH), p. 31F.

Lerner, H. G. (1985). *The dance of anger*. New York: Harper & Row.

Lerner, H. G. (1989). *The dance of intimacy*. New York: Harper & Row.

Levi, L. (1972). *Stress and distress in response to psychological stimuli*. Elmsford, NY: Pergamon Press.

Peter, L. J., & Hull, R. (1984). *The Peter principle*. New York: Bantam.

Project on the Status and Education of Women. (1978, June). *Sexual harassment: A hidden issue*. Washington, DC: Association of American Colleges.

Rowe, M. P. (1981, May–June). Dealing with sexual harassment. *Harvard Business Review*.

Schein, E. H. (1971). The individual, the organization, and the career: A conceptual scheme. *Journal of Applied Science, 7*, 401–426.

Schein, E. H. (1978). *Career dynamics: Matching individual and organizational needs*. Reading, MA: Addison-Wesley.

Tiedeman, D. V., & O'Hara, R. P. (1963). *Career development: Choice and adjustment*. Princeton, NJ: College Entrance Examination Board.

SELF-ASSESSMENT INVENTORY

"Today, our guest lecturer is Dr. Clarence Tibbs, whose 20-year career has culminated in his recent autobiography, *Zoo Vet—I Quit!*"

Preference Inventory   Skill Inventory

Interest Inventory   The Summary Profile

People seeking assistance in planning their careers frequently say, "I'm uncertain about what to major in or what career to pursue. Is there a test that can tell me what I should do with the rest of my life?" The question reflects a common but only partly accurate belief about the career-planning process. Although a number of students have had their tentative educational and occupational goals confirmed by tests, many have found that tests opened up new areas to explore rather than defining a single choice for them. Thus, tests can serve to narrow or to expand one's career options. However helpful they may be for these purposes, you must understand their limitations.

Just as hammers don't make good wrenches, tests don't provide useful aids to career planning when they're misused. Since tests sample around 10 percent of the 20,000 occupations that exist in our society, they provide only a limited view of occupational possibilities. Also, because most are heavily biased toward a person's past experiences, they can reinforce stereotypic notions about which fields men, women, and minorities should enter. For example, the woman thinking about entering a field traditionally dominated by men, such as engineering, will find her expertise as a secretary confirmed by the test but will not learn much about her potential as an engineer. The most beneficial use of a test in this situation would be to help her identify the interests and skills she'll need to develop in order to become an engineer. Pursuing her new goal will require work on her part, but at least the test can provide some suggestions about how to go about it.

Another problem with tests is the way they're scored and interpreted. We remember most those experiences in which we've been actively involved: the poem we spent hours memorizing in grammar school, the recognition we earned for a job well done. In most occupational testing situations we're active only as long as we are taking the test. Computers and technicians score the results, and counselors interpret them for us. Because the expertise for scoring and interpreting the tests rests in someone else's hands, it's easy to feel mystified by the test. We may then passively absorb the results instead of gaining a better understanding of how we've developed our abilities and interests. Small wonder that researchers have found that most people forget the results of testing shortly afterward.

In sharing these points with you, our goal is not to turn you off to tests. Instead, we want you to recognize the limitations inherent in testing and to use the results wisely. It may be helpful to know that other, less complicated ways to assess your personal qualities exist besides taking standardized tests.

One type of exploration involves examining the themes in your fantasies and aspirations and seeing how they match the requirements of different occupations. Similarly, you can make lists of activities that you enjoy and do well and look for commonalities among them that can be translated into work activities. You can also use self-scored inventories that tap into your interests, values, and abilities.

The self-assessment inventories that follow include the preference inventory, the interest inventory, and the skill inventory. They provide you with an opportunity to review your work preferences, interests, and skills in relation to the six general career clusters identified by Prediger and his colleagues at ACT.

PREFERENCE INVENTORY

People tend to gravitate toward job families that match their work orientations. Academic and work preferences tend to cluster around six common work orientations:

1. People in the business contact cluster like to persuade, supervise, or lead others toward common goals or to sell an idea or product.
2. People in the business operations cluster like activities that allow them to organize data, attend to detail, and check results for accuracy.
3. People in the technical cluster like to work with their hands, are often athletic, and tend to enjoy working outdoors with animals, machines, or nature.
4. People in the science cluster enjoy scientific types of activities in which they engage in research to test ideas or to develop new products.
5. People in the arts cluster find that they most enjoy expressing ideas and feelings through writing stories and poems, painting, photography, sculpting, and physical movement.
6. People in the social service cluster find satisfaction in teaching, counseling, assisting, and informing others.

This activity allows you to compare your academic preferences with each of six worker orientations. Your preferences are what you'd ideally do if reality permits.

On the pages that follow, you'll find lists of areas of study that will appeal to you to varying degrees. You can indicate how much you would prefer each area by circling one of the numbers next to it, as in the following examples:

Circle "3" if you have a definite or strong preference for an area.
  For example: engineering   0   1   2   ③
Circle "2" if you have a moderate preference for an area.
  For example: medical technology   0   1   ②   3
Circle "1" if you have little preference for an area.
  For example: anthropology   0   ①   2   3
Circle "0" if you do not prefer this area at all.
  For example: economics   ⓪   1   2   3

Don't be concerned about whether you have the interests and skills to succeed in a particular area. You'll review your interests and skills in the next two sections of this appendix. Because your first reactions will produce the most reliable index of your preferences, work rapidly and respond spontaneously to each area.

Be sure to circle a number beside each area before moving on to the next. Complete the entire inventory before you total your scores. That way, your responses will be fresh and won't be delayed by your stopping to calculate.

My "business contact" preferences are in . . .

1. Hotel management	0	1	2	3
2. Industrial engineering	0	1	2	3
3. Marketing	0	1	2	3
4. Real estate sales and management	0	1	2	3
5. Mortuary science	0	1	2	3
6. Park management	0	1	2	3
7. Radio/TV announcing	0	1	2	3
8. Fashion merchandising	0	1	2	3
9. Business management	0	1	2	3
10. Law	0	1	2	3
11. Financial planning	0	1	2	3
12. Athletic administration	0	1	2	3
13. Health services management	0	1	2	3
14. Urban planning	0	1	2	3

Sum of circled "1s" ☐

+

Sum of circled "2s" ☐

+

Sum of circled "3s" ☐

=

Grand total of "1s," "2s," "3s" ☐

My "business operations" preferences are in . . .

1. Personal clerking	0	1	2	3
2. Computer operations	0	1	2	3

 3. Office machine technology   0   1   2   3
 4. Claims adjusting   0   1   2   3
 5. Business education   0   1   2   3
 6. Budget analysis   0   1   2   3
 7. Office administration   0   1   2   3
 8. Medical records technology   0   1   2   3
 9. Court reporting   0   1   2   3
10. Accounting   0   1   2   3
11. Air traffic controlling   0   1   2   3
12. Finance   0   1   2   3
13. Secretarial science   0   1   2   3
14. Mathematics   0   1   2   3

Sum of circled "1s"   ☐

\+

Sum of circled "2s"   ☐

\+

Sum of circled "3s"   ☐

\=

Grand total of "1s," "2s," "3s"   ☐

My "technical" preferences are in . . .

 1. Agriculture   0   1   2   3
 2. Aviation   0   1   2   3
 3. Geology   0   1   2   3
 4. Industrial arts teaching   0   1   2   3
 5. Emergency medical technology   0   1   2   3
 6. Aerospace engineering   0   1   2   3
 7. Law enforcement   0   1   2   3
 8. Forestry   0   1   2   3
 9. Radiological technology   0   1   2   3
10. Traffic technology   0   1   2   3
11. Photography   0   1   2   3
12. Dental ceramics   0   1   2   3
13. Architectural drafting   0   1   2   3
14. Marine surveying   0   1   2   3

Sum of circled "1s"   ☐

+

Sum of circled "2s"   ☐

+

Sum of circled "3s"   ☐

=

Grand total of "1s," "2s," "3s"   ☐

My "science" preferences are in . . .

1. Economics	0	1	2	3
2. Actuarial science	0	1	2	3
3. Nursing	0	1	2	3
4. Microbiology	0	1	2	3
5. Dentistry	0	1	2	3
6. Medicine	0	1	2	3
7. Natural science teaching	0	1	2	3
8. Veterinary medicine	0	1	2	3
9. Psychology/Sociology	0	1	2	3
10. Mathematics	0	1	2	3
11. Computer networking	0	1	2	3
12. Astronomy	0	1	2	3
13. Aeronautical engineering	0	1	2	3
14. Geography	0	1	2	3

Sum of circled "1s"   ☐

+

Sum of circled "2s"   ☐

+

Sum of circled "3s"   ☐

=

Grand total of "1s," "2s," "3s"   ☐

My "arts" preferences are in . . .

1. Medical illustration	0	1	2	3
2. Fine arts	0	1	2	3
3. Commercial art	0	1	2	3
4. Music	0	1	2	3
5. Library science	0	1	2	3
6. Journalism	0	1	2	3
7. Public relations	0	1	2	3
8. Foreign languages	0	1	2	3
9. Industrial design	0	1	2	3
10. Fashion design	0	1	2	3
11. Dance	0	1	2	3
12. Theater	0	1	2	3
13. Interior design	0	1	2	3
14. Landscape architecture	0	1	2	3

Sum of circled "1s"   ☐

+

Sum of circled "2s"   ☐

+

Sum of circled "3s"   ☐

=

Grand total of "1s," "2s," "3s"   ☐

My "social service" preferences are in . . .

1. Cosmetology	0	1	2	3
2. Occupational therapy	0	1	2	3
3. Physical education	0	1	2	3
4. Dental hygiene	0	1	2	3
5. Social work	0	1	2	3
6. Guidance counseling	0	1	2	3
7. Elementary-school teaching	0	1	2	3
8. Paralegal studies	0	1	2	3
9. Law enforcement	0	1	2	3
10. Psychiatry	0	1	2	3
11. Medicine	0	1	2	3

12. Home economics   0   1   2   3
13. Television production   0   1   2   3
14. Rehabilitation counseling   0   1   2   3

Sum of circled "1s"   ☐

                            +

Sum of circled "2s"   ☐

                            +

Sum of circled "3s"   ☐

                            =

Grand total of "1s," "2s," "3s"   ☐

Check to make sure you've circled a number next to each item. Then add the scores in each preference category and write the totals in the spaces provided. For example, in the "realistic" category you would total all the "1s" (if you had circled three "1s" the sum would be 3), all the "2s" (for three "2s" the sum would be 6), and all the "3s" (for three "3s" the sum would be 9). Next, add the three sums together to get your grand total for that category (from the examples: 3 + 6 + 9 = 18).

After you've determined the grand totals for each of the six preference categories, transfer those totals to the spaces provided below.

Preference grand totals:

_____ Business contact   _____ Science

_____ Business operations   _____ Arts

_____ Technical   _____ Social service

INTEREST INVENTORY

In this activity, you compare your current interests with each of the six worker orientations.

Here you will find a number of study and work activities that will have varying degrees of appeal to you. You can indicate how much you enjoy or are interested in each activity by circling a number next to each item.

Circle "3" if you have a definite or strong interest in the activity.
    For example: making jewelry   0   1   2   ③
Circle "2" if you have a moderate interest in the activity.
    For example: selling insurance   0   1   ②   3
Circle "1" if you have little interest in the activity.
    For example: installing vending machines   0   ①   2   3
Circle "0" if the activity is no appeal to you at all.
    For example: running a photocopier   ⓪   1   2   3

As before, don't be concerned about whether you have the skills to perform a particular activity. You'll review your competencies in the skill inventory. Because your first reactions will produce the most reliable index of your interests, work rapidly and respond spontaneously to each item. Be sure to circle a number beside each item before moving on to another one. Complete the entire inventory before you total your scores. That way, your responses will be fresh and will not be delayed by your stopping to calculate.

My "business contact" interests are in . . .

1. Managing my own firm	0	1	2	3
2. Buying and selling stocks and bonds	0	1	2	3
*3. Buying merchandise for a large store or chain of stores	0	1	2	3
4. Managing the public affairs division of a corporation	0	1	2	3
5. Helping others locate and secure equipment	0	1	2	3
6. Lobbying for the passage of a law	0	1	2	3
7. Settling disputes between labor and management	0	1	2	3
*8. Managing or directing a large enterprise or division of a corporation	0	1	2	3
9. Directing a social service or recreational agency	0	1	2	3
*10. Directing the sales policies for a large firm or managing a group of salespeople	0	1	2	3
11. Helping individuals plan their travels	0	1	2	3
12. Making announcements on radio or television	0	1	2	3
*13. Investigating legal situations and interpreting the law	0	1	2	3
14. Managing and representing performers, speakers, and artists	0	1	2	3

---

*Items marked with an asterisk are from *Occupational Interest Inventory.* Modified and reproduced by permission of the publisher, CTB/McGraw-Hill, 20 Ryan Ranch Road, Monterey, CA 93940. Copyright © 1956 McGraw Hill, Inc. All rights reserved.

Sum of circled "1s"   □

                            +

Sum of circled "2s"   □

                            +

Sum of circled "3s"   □

                            =

Grand total of "1s," "2s," "3s" □

My "business operations" interests are in . . .

		0	1	2	3
1.	Operating office machines	0	1	2	3
2.	Developing an accounting or filing system for a firm	0	1	2	3
3.	Posting bills for a large company	0	1	2	3
4.	Planning or coordinating a conference or convention	0	1	2	3
5.	Assisting others in planning and managing their finances	0	1	2	3
6.	Classifying orders, figuring price quotations, and making out price sheets	0	1	2	3
7.	Keeping financial records	0	1	2	3
8.	Answering the telephone and giving information or routing phone calls	0	1	2	3
9.	Teaching business classes	0	1	2	3
*10.	Preparing payrolls, figuring commissions, and making salary deductions	0	1	2	3
*11.	Meeting clients, making appointments, and doing general office work	0	1	2	3
12.	Taking dictation and typing correspondence	0	1	2	3
*13.	Making bookkeeping entries or keeping inventories	0	1	2	3
14.	Studying how people manage their time and energies to complete work tasks	0	1	2	3

Sum of circled "1s"   □

                            +

Sum of circled "2s"   □

                            +

Sum of circled "3s" ☐

=

Grand total of "1s," "2s," "3s" ☐

My "technical" interests are in . . .

1.	Routing aircraft, ships, trucks, or buses	0	1	2	3
2.	Installing, maintaining, and repairing computers or other office machines	0	1	2	3
*3.	Breeding pedigreed dogs, thoroughbred horses, or other animals	0	1	2	3
4.	Landscaping yards and parks	0	1	2	3
5.	Farming the ocean for fish and other sea products	0	1	2	3
6.	Building or repairing furniture	0	1	2	3
7.	Refining and demonstrating my athletic skills	0	1	2	3
*8.	Enforcing laws to protect life and property	0	1	2	3
9.	Creating blueprints for buildings, machines, or electrical equipment	0	1	2	3
10.	Guarding the safety and feeding of wildlife	0	1	2	3
11.	Building houses or other structures	0	1	2	3
12.	Operating emergency, rescue, or fire-fighting equipment	0	1	2	3
13.	Driving a truck, tractor, or bus	0	1	2	3
14.	Building or operating radio or TV equipment	0	1	2	3

Sum of circled "1s" ☐

+

Sum of circled "2s" ☐

+

Sum of circled "3s" ☐

=

Grand total of "1s," "2s," "3s" ☐

My "science" interests are in . . .

1. Investigating the occupations, style of living, or behavior of others   0 1 2 3
*2. Experimenting with living plants or animals to explore the laws of growth or heredity   0 1 2 3
3. Designing new forms of transportation or communication   0 1 2 3
4. Designing experiments to create or to test new drugs, chemicals, or diets   0 1 2 3
5. Designing buildings, bridges, or other structures   0 1 2 3
*6. Developing methods of long-range weather forecasting and prediction   0 1 2 3
*7. Operating an X-ray machine or other laboratory apparatus   0 1 2 3
*8. Examining the formation of mineral deposits and determining how they may be removed from the earth   0 1 2 3
9. Programming computers to solve complex technical problems   0 1 2 3
10. Studying the causes of or diagnosing and treating diseases and physical impairments in humans or animals   0 1 2 3
11. Navigating a ship or an airplane   0 1 2 3
12. Developing mathematical equations or chemical formulas to solve scientific problems   0 1 2 3
13. Studying the solar system   0 1 2 3
14. Investigating bodies of water, such as lakes, rivers, and oceans   0 1 2 3

Sum of circled "1s"   ☐

+

Sum of circled "2s"   ☐

+

Sum of circled "3s"   ☐

=

Grand total of "1s," "2s," "3s"   ☐

My "arts" interests are in . . .

*1.	Playing musical instruments in a band, orchestra, or other musical organization and/or writing music	0	1	2	3
2.	Designing floor plans and selecting furniture and color combinations for homes or offices	0	1	2	3
3.	Illustrating or designing covers for books or magazines	0	1	2	3
4.	Engaging in creative dance, ballet, or rhythmic gymnastics	0	1	2	3
*5.	Drawing cartoons, comics, or caricatures of people	0	1	2	3
6.	Writing short stories, novels, plays, or poetry	0	1	2	3
7.	Using wood, clay, paint, or other materials to create art objects	0	1	2	3
*8.	Doing creative photography	0	1	2	3
9.	Conducting an orchestra or directing a play	0	1	2	3
10.	Giving presentations or writing descriptions or criticisms of sculpture, plays, books, movies, or music	0	1	2	3
11.	Setting up art, merchandise, or museum displays	0	1	2	3
*12.	Writing dialogue or commercial announcements for radio or TV programs	0	1	2	3
13.	Studying and interpreting foreign languages	0	1	2	3
14.	Designing containers for commercial products	0	1	2	3

Sum of circled "1s" ☐

+

Sum of circled "2s" ☐

+

Sum of circled "3s" ☐

=

Grand total of "1s," "2s," "3s" ☐

My "social service" interests are in . . .

1.	Supervising activities at parks or recreational facilities	0	1	2	3
*2.	Taking care of children and assisting in their education	0	1	2	3

3. Helping people with their personal problems and important decisions in life   0   1   2   3
4. Teaching or helping people to develop their talents and interests   0   1   2   3
5. Teaching others how to care for themselves and improve their health   0   1   2   3
*6. Advising parents about the rearing of children   0   1   2   3
7. Coordinating health and social services for the public   0   1   2   3
8. Working with or helping in the treatment of sick, handicapped, or injured individuals   0   1   2   3
*9. Supervising the selection, placement, and promotion of employees   0   1   2   3
*10. Visiting homes to help people who are in trouble or need assistance   0   1   2   3
11. Teaching arts and crafts to others   0   1   2   3
12. Studying the customs and folkways of different societies and cultures   0   1   2   3
13. Interviewing people for information about their beliefs and habits   0   1   2   3
14. Helping others to develop their physical talents and athletic skills   0   1   2   3

Sum of circled "1s"   [ ]

       +

Sum of circled "2s"   [ ]

       +

Sum of circled "3s"   [ ]

       =

Grand total of "1s," "2s," "3s"   [ ]

Check to make sure you have circled a number next to each item. Then add the scores in each preference category and write the totals in the spaces provided. For example, in the "realistic" category you would total all the "1s" (if you had circled three "1s" the sum would be 3), all the "2s" (if you had circled three of the "2s" the sum would be 6), and all the "3s" (if you had circled three of the "3s" the sum would be 9). Next, add the three sums together to get your grand total for that category (from the above examples: 3 + 6 + 9 = 18).

After you have determined the grand totals for each of the six interest categories, transfer those totals to the spaces provided below.

Interest grand totals:

_____	Business contact	_____	Science
_____	Business operations	_____	Arts
_____	Technical	_____	Social service

SKILL INVENTORY

"Jim and Julia are the math whizzes in our class." "Tina and Bill are the class leaders." Statements such as these are often used to group individuals according to a common skill they possess, many times because they excel at that skill. Although we may not be outstanding at a particular task when compared with our peers, each of us has skills that allow us to function effectively at particular work tasks.

Like the preceding preference and interest inventories, this inventory requires that you look through several sets of skills and evaluate yourself on a scale that runs from 3 to 0.

Circle "3" next to an activity if you have a definite, strong skill in that area.	0 1 2 ③
Circle "2" if you have a moderate degree of skill in that activity.	0 1 ② 3
Circle "1" to indicate that you have enough skill to get by with some help from others.	0 ① 2 3
Circle "0" if you believe you have no skill at all in that particular activity.	⓪ 1 2 3

When evaluating your skills, don't compare yourself with any particular reference group, such as other students or the general population. Rate yourself according to your own judgment of your ability. Be sure that each item has a number circled beside it before moving to the next item.

My "business contact" skills are in . . .

1. Organizing campaigns for candidates in school clubs or other social groups	0	1	2	3
2. Leading others	0	1	2	3
3. Entering new situations with ease and comfort	0	1	2	3
4. Interpreting changes in the economy	0	1	2	3

5. Persuading others to accept a new idea	0	1	2	3
6. Performing effectively in debates	0	1	2	3
7. Managing or supervising others in a work group	0	1	2	3
8. Selling products	0	1	2	3
9. Speaking on behalf of a group	0	1	2	3
10. Helping others resolve their disputes	0	1	2	3
11. Understanding how the legal system operates and how laws are passed	0	1	2	3
12. Finding and capitalizing on bargains and sales	0	1	2	3
13. Soliciting contributions to charities or political organizations	0	1	2	3
14. Giving speeches before large groups	0	1	2	3

Sum of circled "1s" ☐

+

Sum of circled "2s" ☐

+

Sum of circled "3s" ☐

=

Grand total of "1s," "2s," "3s" ☐

My "business operations" skills are in . . .

1. Operating office machines	0	1	2	3
2. Planning a personal budget	0	1	2	3
3. Organizing or filing materials such as records, class notes, stamps, or photographs	0	1	2	3
4. Keeping financial records	0	1	2	3
5. Typing, keypunching, or operating a calculator or office machine	0	1	2	3
6. Keeping an accurate checkbook	0	1	2	3
7. Organizing ideas or numbers so they are clear and understandable	0	1	2	3
8. Proofreading papers or records and finding the mistakes	0	1	2	3
9. Spelling and using punctuation and grammar correctly	0	1	2	3

10. Keeping accurate records   0   1   2   3
11. Examining or keeping budgets for business   0   1   2   3
12. Working in an office setting and doing a good job   0   1   2   3
13. Organizing my time to accomplish tasks   0   1   2   3
14. Acting as a secretary or treasurer in a club or organization   0   1   2   3

Sum of circled "1s"   [ ]

\+

Sum of circled "2s"   [ ]

\+

Sum of circled "3s"   [ ]

\=

Grand total of "1s," "2s," "3s"   [ ]

My "technical" skills are in . . .

*1. Painting, varnishing, or staining wood or metal surfaces   0   1   2   3
2. Working with wood using power tools, hand tools, or other woodworking equipment   0   1   2   3
3. Working outdoors for long periods of time   0   1   2   3
4. Putting together toys, furniture, or machinery that comes unassembled   0   1   2   3
5. Repairing furniture or other objects   0   1   2   3
*6. Cleaning, adjusting, or repairing electric motors, sewing machines, or bicycles   0   1   2   3
7. Completing tasks that require physical endurance or agility   0   1   2   3
8. Making clothes or other wearing apparel from patterns   0   1   2   3
9. Driving a tractor or a truck   0   1   2   3

10. Reading blueprints or schemata   0 1 2 3
*11. Doing odd jobs with a saw, hammer and nails,
     screwdriver, or plane   0 1 2 3
*12. Making drawings with a compass, triangle, ruler,
     or other instrument   0 1 2 3
13. Installing or repairing household electric circuits   0 1 2 3
14. Constructing, planting, or cultivating rock gardens
    or making flower beds   0 1 2 3

Sum of circled "1s"   ☐

    +

Sum of circled "2s"   ☐

    +

Sum of circled "3s"   ☐

    =

Grand total of "1s," "2s," "3s"   ☐

My "science" skills are in . . .

1. Mixing chemicals according to formulas   0 1 2 3
2. Experimenting with and creating recipes   0 1 2 3
3. Naming basic foods and telling why they are nutritious   0 1 2 3
4. Reading data tables, graphs, and charts   0 1 2 3
5. Setting up a scientific demonstration for a class
   or science fair   0 1 2 3
6. Understanding articles in newspapers and magazines
   about recent scientific breakthroughs   0 1 2 3
7. Describing the different classification systems for
   plants or animals   0 1 2 3
8. Reading topographical or navigational maps   0 1 2 3
9. Naming the different cloud formations   0 1 2 3
10. Using a microscope   0 1 2 3
11. Using a hand calculator   0 1 2 3
12. Interviewing others about their attitudes, feelings,
    and beliefs   0 1 2 3
13. Solving puzzles or figuring out how things work   0 1 2 3
14. Identifying the major constellations of the stars   0 1 2 3

Sum of circled "1s"
☐
+

Sum of circled "2s"
☐
+

Sum of circled "3s"
☐
=

Grand total of "1s," "2s," "3s"
☐

My "arts" skills are in . . .

1.	Sketching, drawing, or painting; carving or sculpting objects	0	1	2	3
2.	Creating new ideas and gadgets or expressing myself in original ways	0	1	2	3
3.	Doing interpretive readings of stories, poetry, or plays	0	1	2	3
4.	Impersonating the speech and mannerisms of others	0	1	2	3
5.	Using the color wheel to mix colors or create color complements	0	1	2	3
6.	Writing essays, stories, or poetry	0	1	2	3
7.	Designing and making clothing	0	1	2	3
8.	Singing or acting	0	1	2	3
*9.	Arranging color harmonies and furnishings in a home	0	1	2	3
10.	Speaking a foreign language	0	1	2	3
11.	Playing a musical instrument	0	1	2	3
12.	Following the story line and message in movies, plays, and books	0	1	2	3
13.	Performing ballet, tap dance, or gymnastics	0	1	2	3
14.	Telling stories or jokes	0	1	2	3

Sum of circled "1s"
☐
+

Sum of circled "2s"
☐
+

Sum of circled "3s"   ▢

=

Grand total of "1s," "2s," "3s"   ▢

My "social service" skills are in . . .

1. Performing in athletic competitions	0	1	2	3
2. Planning social events	0	1	2	3
3. Entertaining others	0	1	2	3
4. Getting along with others who are different from myself	0	1	2	3
5. Teaching or tutoring	0	1	2	3
6. Explaining new ideas to others	0	1	2	3
7. Supervising children's activities	0	1	2	3
8. Meeting new people	0	1	2	3
9. Accepting and giving criticism	0	1	2	3
10. Helping others feel comfortable in new situations	0	1	2	3
11. Encouraging and supporting others	0	1	2	3
12. Working with others in a team effort	0	1	2	3
13. Determining the needs of others and helping them find solutions to their problems	0	1	2	3
14. Understanding other people's personalities	0	1	2	3

Sum of circled "1s"   ▢

+

Sum of circled "2s"   ▢

+

Sum of circled "3s"   ▢

=

Grand total of "1s," "2s," "3s"   ▢

As you did with the preference and interest inventories, go back and add the "1s," "2s," and "3s" you have circled for each skill category. Record the results in the spaces provided at the end of each category. After you have determined the grand totals for each of the six categories, transfer these totals to the spaces provided below.

Skills grand totals:

_____ Business contact   _____ Science

_____ Business operations _____ Arts

_____ Technical   _____ Social service

THE SUMMARY PROFILE

The final steps in the self-assessment process will pull together a composite picture of your preferences, interests, and skills. This will allow you to look at them separately and to compare them actively. It will also guide you to occupational clusters that match your general work orientation.

Step 1. Write the grand totals of your preference, interest, and skill scores in the spaces provided. Then, add the grand totals together to develop an overall composite score of your preferences, interests, and skills.

	Job Cluster					
	Business Contact	Business Operations	Technical	Science	Arts	Social Service
Preference grand totals	____	____	____	____	____	____
	+	+	+	+	+	+
Interest grand totals	____	____	____	____	____	____
	+	+	+	+	+	+
Skill grand totals	____	____	____	____	____	____
	=	=	=	=	=	=
Overall composite score	☐	☐	☐	☐	☐	☐

Step 2. Write the name of the job cluster that received the highest overall composite score in your self-evaluation in the box on the following page. (See our example as well.)

Job Cluster: _____

World of Work
Map Regions: _____

Related Job Families:

___ _____

___ _____

___ _____

___ _____

_____ Areas I Would Explore:

_____

_____

_____ Areas I Would Explore:

_____

_____

_____ Areas I Would Explore:

_____

_____

_____

Step 3. From the world of work map (Figure A-1), write in the two numbers found in the inner ring of the family you've chosen. Those numbers correspond to "regions" on the map that can be used to identify job families that best match your preferences, interests, and skills.

Step 4. Write the letters and names of the job families that appear in the two regions. The letters correspond to job families and may be useful to you as you try to locate other occupations on the map.

Step 5. Use the "VIESA Job Family Charts" and the "Index to Description of Occupations" to identify occupations that match your preferences, interests, and skills—in other words, your "Occupational Orientation."

In the case of equally high scores, you have several options to consider. You can look for majors and occupations offering a great deal of diversity or seek op-

---

Example

Job Cluster: _____ Arts _____

World of Work Map Regions: _____ 10, 11 _____

Related Job Families:

P	Social Science
Q	Applied Arts
R	Creative and Performing Arts
S	Applied Arts (Written) and Spoken

Social Science _____ **Areas I Would Explore:**

Anthropology _____

Political Science _____

_____

Applied Arts (visual) _____ **Areas I Would Explore:**

Cartoonist _____

Photography _____

Creative and Performing Arts _ **Areas I Would Explore:**

Actor _____

Writer/Author _____

Teacher _____

---

portunities to work in a variety of settings. You can also identify the specific preferences, interests, and skills you want to capitalize on and look for related majors or occupations. Or you can consider pursuing several fields during the course of your career, which will allow you to capitalize on your preferences, interests, and skills in different ways across time. Finally, you can explore the possibility of pursuing some activities that appeal to you at work and pursuing other activities outside of work through leisure and recreation.

A low profile with equal scores may indicate that you haven't had opportunities to try out the kinds of diverse activities that would allow you to identify your preferences, interests, and skills clearly. In this case you may want to gain more experience through volunteer work, classes, and part-time or summer jobs in areas that appeal to you. This type of profile may also suggest that you may be resistant

Figure A-1 The world of work map (ACT, 1993, p. 1)

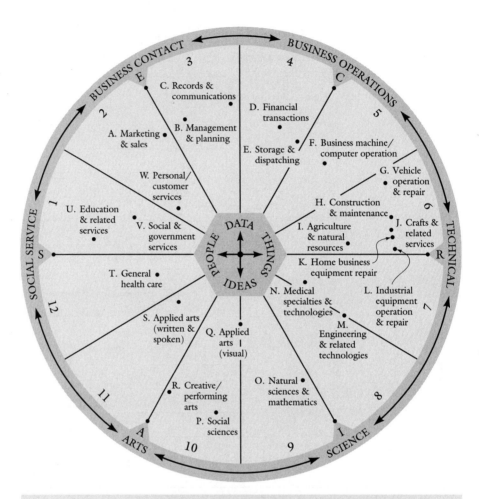

About the Map

- The world of work map arranges job families (groups of similar jobs) into 12 regions. Together, the job families cover all U.S. jobs. Although the locations of the jobs in each family differ, most are located near the point shown.

- A job family's location is based on its primary work tasks — working with DATA, IDEAS, PEOPLE, and THINGS.

- The edge of the map presents six general areas of the work world. The letters RIASEC refer to occupational and personality typologies created by John Holland.

BUSINESS CONTACT JOB CLUSTER

A. MARKETING AND SALES JOB FAMILY

Sales workers in stores; route drivers (milk, etc.); buyers; travel agents; sales workers who visit customers (real estate and insurance agents; stock brokers; farm products; office and medical supplies sales workers)

B. MANAGEMENT AND PLANNING JOB FAMILY

Store, motel, restaurant, and agribusiness managers; office supervisors; purchasing agents; managers in large businesses; recreation/parks managers; medical records administrators; urban planners

BUSINESS OPERATIONS JOB CLUSTER

C. RECORDS AND COMMUNICATIONS JOB FAMILY

Office, library, hotel, and postal clerks; receptionists; computer tape librarians; office, medical, and legal secretaries; court reporters; medical record technicians

D. FINANCIAL TRANSACTIONS JOB FAMILY

Bookkeepers; accountants; grocery check-out clerks; bank tellers; ticket agents; insurance underwriters; financial analysts

E. STORAGE AND DISPATCHING JOB FAMILY

Shipping and receiving clerks; mail carriers; truck, cab, and airline dispatchers; cargo agents; air traffic controllers

F. BUSINESS MACHINE/COMPUTER OPERATION JOB FAMILY

Computer console, printer, etc., operators; office machine operators; typists; word-processing equipment operators; statistical clerks

TECHNICAL JOB CLUSTER

G. VEHICLE OPERATION AND REPAIR JOB FAMILY

Bus, truck, and cab drivers; auto, bus, and airplane mechanics; forklift operators; merchant marine officers; airplane pilots

H. CONSTRUCTION AND MAINTENANCE JOB FAMILY

Carpenters; electricians; painters; custodians (janitors); bricklayers; sheet metal workers; bulldozer and crane operators; building inspectors

I. AGRICULTURE AND NATURAL RESOURCES JOB FAMILY

Farmers; foresters; ranchers; landscape gardeners; tree surgeons; plant nursery workers; pet shop attendants

J. CRAFTS AND RELATED SERVICES JOB FAMILY

Cooks; meatcutters; bakers; shoe repairers; piano/organ tuners; tailors; jewelers

K. HOME/BUSINESS EQUIPMENT REPAIR JOB FAMILY

Repairers of TV sets, appliances, typewriters, telephones, heating systems, photocopiers, etc.

L. INDUSTRIAL EQUIPMENT OPERATION AND REPAIR JOB FAMILY

Machinists; printers; sewing machine operators; welders; industrial machinery repairers; production painters; laborers and machine operators in factories, mines, etc.; firefighters

SCIENCE JOB CLUSTER

M. ENGINEERING AND OTHER APPLIED TECHNOLOGIES JOB FAMILY

Engineers and engineering technicians in various fields; biological and chemical lab technicians; computer programmers; computer service technicians; drafters; surveyors; technical illustrators; food technologists

N. MEDICAL SPECIALTIES AND TECHNOLOGIES JOB FAMILY

Dental hygienists; EEG and EKG technicians; opticians; prosthetics technicians; X-ray technologists; medical technologists; dentists; optometrists; pharmacists; veterinarians

O. NATURAL SCIENCES AND MATHEMATICS JOB FAMILY

Agronomists; biologists; chemists; ecologists; geographers; geologists; horticulturists; mathematicians; physicists

P. SOCIAL SCIENCES JOB FAMILY

Marketing research analysts; anthropologists; economists; political scientists; psychologists; sociologists

ARTS JOB CLUSTER

Q. APPLIED ARTS (VISUAL) JOB FAMILY

Floral designers; merchandise displayers; commercial artists; fashion designers; photographers; interior designers; architects; landscape architects

R. CREATIVE/PERFORMING ARTS JOB FAMILY

Entertainers (comedians, etc.); actors/actresses; dancers; musicians, singers; writers; art, music, etc.; teachers

S. APPLIED ARTS (WRITTEN AND SPOKEN) JOB FAMILY

Advertising copywriters; disk jockeys; legal assistants; advertising account executives; interpreters; reporters; public relations workers; lawyers; librarians; technical writers

SOCIAL SERVICE JOB CLUSTER

T. GENERAL HEALTH CARE JOB FAMILY

Orderlies; dental assistants; licensed practical nurses; physical therapy assistants; registered nurses; dietitians; occupational therapists; physicians; speech pathologists

U. EDUCATION AND RELATED SERVICES JOB FAMILY

Teacher aides; preschool teachers; athletic coaches; college teachers, guidance/career/etc., counselors; elementary and secondary school teachers; special education teachers

V. SOCIAL AND GOVERNMENT SERVICES JOB FAMILY

Security guards; recreation leaders; police officers; health/safety/food/etc., inspectors; child welfare workers; home economists; rehabilitation counselors; social workers

W. PERSONAL/CUSTOMER SERVICES JOB FAMILY

Grocery baggers; bellhops; flight attendants (stewards, stewardesses); waitresses and waiters; cosmetologists (beauticians); barbers; butlers and maids

Figure A-2 Job cluster and job family list (ACT, 1993, pp. 3–4)

to any type of career commitment right now and need to explore what's happening in your life that makes you want to postpone such a commitment. It's not uncommon, for example, for students to feel that if they did what they wanted they'd disappoint someone important to them, or that if they tried and failed they would not know how to cope with it. These and other thoughts, feelings, and conflicts are best worked through with the assistance of a professional counselor.

Interpreting Your Summary Profile

Your summary profile can help you identify college majors and related occupations to explore. In reviewing your profile, consider the following: Do your highest preference, interest, and skill scores match one another? In other words, are your preferred majors in line with the things you like to do daily and the skills you have? If your preferences, interests, and abilities correspond with one another, you'll probably find it relatively easy to come up with a major and an occupation that uses common personal characteristics. If these three personal qualities don't match, however, you should look closely at why they differ and find a way of balancing them that's comfortable and realistic for you.

For example, if the areas you prefer are not matched by your interests and skills, you may have based your choice of study areas on a standard (for example, a family value, stereotypes you have for certain majors or occupations, or the prestige you associate with different fields) that is not consistent with what you really enjoy doing and have the skills to do day in and day out. In this case, if you pursue your preferences, you may go through a period of frustration as you engage in activities that hold little interest for you and as you try to develop skills that coincide with your preferences. Another solution would be to accept the possibility that you may not be able to pursue your preferences and should select a field more consistent with your interests and skills.

If your strongest interests do not match your preferences and skills, you face a similar problem: you'll need to find a way to balance the activities you enjoy most with your academic preferences and current skills. Again, the task is to figure out *what is most important to you*. If you give greatest weight to your interests, you may need to redefine your academic and occupational preferences and acquire new skills to match your interests.

Finally, if your skills lie in an area different from those of your preferences and interests, you may do well at jobs in this area but not seek to invest yourself in them on a continuing basis. For example, you may be good at a variety of office practices or "conventional" activities because you developed these skills to help you with your studies or for summer jobs, but you may not want to make a permanent living with these skills. Suppose your preferences and interests were in the "science" and "arts" areas. You might consider the possibility of combining your interests and skills by using your current skills in settings consistent with your preferences and interests—for example, in a medical or scientific setting or an advertising office—while you work to advance your education. In this way you can use your current skills to support yourself as you develop skills in areas that appeal to you.

Thus, how you balance these three personal qualities when they aren't equally matched will require you to test your ideals and dreams against the realities of your skills and resources and the requirements of different majors and occupations.

For some people, three or more job families in the summary profile might have an equal score. This type of profile can occur in two ways: (1) when all your scores are high, suggesting that you have diverse preferences, interests, and skills and (2) when all your scores are low, indicating that you haven't fully developed your preferences, interests, and skills.

VIESA JOB FAMILY CHARTS

LEVELS 1 & 2 (1997 Revision)

The charts group VIESA Job Families by "regions" of the world of work. Within each Job Family, jobs ("occupations") are arranged by the level of formal preparation (education and training) people in the jobs typically have. More than 500 jobs are listed. As you use the charts, you may come across jobs that seem strange or even amusing. Others will be more appropriate to your background and goals. Each provides a livelihood and way of life for many people.

Note: Consult the most recent edition of the *Occupational Outlook Handbook* for current information on specific occupations.

KEY: Preparation Level: Typical amount of education/training: 1 = High school; 2 = Up to two years beyond high school; 3 = Four or more years beyond high school.

Examples of Courses/Majors: Typical courses and programs/majors are listed by Job Family.

Occupation	Preparation Level	EXAMPLES of Courses, Programs/ Majors Related to Job Family
Region 1: Education & Related Services Job Family		**Basic High School Courses**
EXERCISE/AEROBIC INSTRUCTOR	1	Art; English; Math: General, Algebra,
PRESCHOOL WORKER	1	etc.; Life Sciences; Physical Sciences;
TEACHER AIDE	2	Social Studies; Speech
ATHLETIC COACH	3	**High School + 1 or 2 Years**
ATHLETIC TRAINER	3	Education, General; Elementary Edu-
COLLEGE STUDENT PERSONNEL WORKER	3	cation; Secondary Education; Music
COLLEGE/UNIVERSITY FACULTY	3	Education; Science Education; Psy-
COUNSELOR (career)	3	chology; On-the-job Training
COUNSELOR (school/college)	3	**High School + 4 or More Years**
RESIDENTIAL COUNSELOR	3	Education, General; Elementary Edu-
TEACHER (adult education)	3	cation; Secondary Education; Agricul-
TEACHER (business)	3	ture Education; Business Education;
TEACHER (elementary)	3	Industrial Arts Education; Physical
TEACHER (vocational/technical)	3	Education; Science Education; Social
TEACHER (physical education)	3	Science Education; Special Education;
TEACHER (kindergarten)	3	Student Counseling; Psychology
TEACHER (secondary)	3	
TEACHER (special education)	3	
TEACHER (vocational agriculture)	3	*(continued)*

Occupation	Preparation Level	EXAMPLES of Courses, Programs/ Majors Related to Job Family
Region 1: Social & Government Services Job Family		**Basic High School Courses**
CORRECTION OFFICER	1	Business; Health and Human Care;
SECURITY OFFICER	1	Home Economics; Life Sciences; Phys-
HOMEMAKER/HOME HEALTH AIDE	1	ical Services; Social Studies
HUMAN SERVICES WORKER	1	**High School + 1 or 2 Years**
POLICE OFFICER	1	Investigation and Protection; Law
STORE DETECTIVE	1	Enforcement Training; Food Science
WELFARE ELIGIBILITY WORKER	1	Dietetics; Psychology; Sociology;
DETECTIVE (police)	2	Corrections; Criminal Justice; Law
HAZARDOUS WASTE TECHNICIAN	2	Enforcement; Parks and Recreation;
RECREATION LEADER	2	Social Work; On-the-job Training
COUNSELOR (mental health)	3	**High School + 4 or More Years**
COUNSELOR (rehabilitation)	3	Corrections; Criminology; Law En-
CUSTOMS INSPECTOR	3	forcement Administration; Parks and
DIRECTOR (social services)	3	Recreation; Social Work; Food Sci-
DIRECTOR (social)	3	ence, Dietetics; Home Economics,
ENVIRONMENTAL HEALTH INSPECTOR	3	General; Psychology; Sociology
FARM/HOME MANAGEMENT ADVISOR	3	
FBI AGENT	3	
FOOD AND DRUG INSPECTOR	3	
GERONTOLOGIST	3	
HOME ECONOMIST	3	
PAROLE OFFICER	3	
PROFESSIONAL ATHLETE	3	
PSYCHOLOGIST (counseling, clinical)	3	
SOCIAL WORKER	3	
Region 2: Personal/Customer Services Job Family		**Basic High School Courses**
BARTENDER	1	Home Economics; Math: General,
CHILDCARE WORKER (domestic)	1	Business Math; Trade and Industrial
COUNTER ATTENDANT	1	Education
COUNTER/RENTAL CLERK	1	**High School + 1 or 2 Years**
DINING ROOM ATTENDANT	1	Childcare Aide/Assisting;
FAST-FOOD WORKER	1	Cosmetology/Barbering; On-the-job
FLIGHT ATTENDANT	1	Training; No formal requirement
GAMING OCCUPATIONS WORKER	1	* = Apprenticeship may be required.
HOST/HOSTESS	1	
PARKING LOT ATTENDANT	1	**High School + 4 or More Years**
PORTER	1	Cosmetology/Barbering
PRIVATE HOUSEHOLD WORKER	1	
WAITER/WAITRESS	1	
BARBER	2*	
HAIRSTYLIST/COSMETOLOGIST	2*	
ELECTROLOGIST	2	
MANICURIST	2	
WEIGHT REDUCTION SPECIALIST	2	

Occupation	Preparation Level	EXAMPLES of Courses, Programs/ Majors Related to Job Family
Region 2: Marketing & Sales Job Family		**Basic High School Courses**
AUCTIONEER	1	Business, including Distributive Education; Math: General, Business Math; Speech
BILL COLLECTOR	1	
DRIVER (sales route)	1	
FASHION MODEL	1	**High School + 1 or 2 years**
PRODUCT DEMONSTRATOR	1	Travel Agency Management and Tourism; Travel Agent Reservations; Insurance; Business Management; Contract Management; Insurance/Risk Management; Retailing and Sales; On-the-job Training
SALES WORKER (retail)	1	
SAMPLE DISTRIBUTOR	1	
CLAIMS REPRESENTATIVE	2	
INSURANCE AGENT	2	
MANUFACTURER'S REPRESENTATIVE	2	
REAL ESTATE AGENT	2	**High School + 4 or More Years**
SALES MANAGER	2	Business Administration; Contract Management; Insurance/Risk Management, Retailing and Sales
TRAVEL AGENT	2	
TRAVEL GUIDE	2	
BUYER	3	
FINANCIAL SERVICES SALES REPRESENTATIVE	3	
SECURITIES SALES AGENT	3	
SERVICES SALE REPRESENTATIVE	3	
Region 3: Management & Planning Job Family		**Basic High School Courses**
ADMINISTRATIVE ASSISTANT/ EXECUTIVE SECRETARY	1	Business; English; Home Economics; Math: General, Business Math; Social Studies; Speech; Trade and Industrial Education
AUTO SERVICE STATION MANAGER	1	
ADMINISTRATIVE SERVICES MANAGER	2	
CATERER	2	**High School + 1 or 2 Years**
CLUB/RESORT MANAGER	2	Accounting; Business Management; Business Economics; Contract Management; Institutional Management; Labor/Industrial Relations; Small Business Management; Office Management; On-the-job Training
CONTRACTOR/CONSTRUCTION MANAGER	2	
CREDIT MANAGER	2	
CUSTOMER SERVICE COORDINATOR	2	
EMPLOYMENT INTERVIEWER	2	
EXECUTIVE HOUSEKEEPER	2	
FOOD SERVICE MANAGER	2	
FUNERAL DIRECTOR	2	**High School + 4 or More Years**
HOTEL/MOTEL MANAGER	2	Accounting; Business Administration; Business Economics; Contract Management; Institutional Management; Labor/Industrial Relations; Small Business Management; Public Administration; Home Economics-General
IMPORTER/EXPORTER	2	
INSURANCE MANAGER	2	
MEETING/CONVENTION PLANNER	2	
OFFICE MANAGER	2	
POSTMASTER	2	
PROPERTY MANAGER	2	
RESTAURANT/BAR MANAGER	2	
RETAIL STORE MANAGER	2	
SUPERMARKET MANAGER	2	
ADVERTISING MANAGER	3	
AIRPORT MANAGER	3	

(continued)

Occupation	Preparation Level	EXAMPLES of Courses, Programs/ Majors Related to Job Family
Region 3: Management & Planning Job Family (*continued*)		
BANK OFFICER/MANAGER	3	
BUSINESS AGENT	3	
CITY MANAGER	3	
COMPENSATION MANAGER	3	
CONSULTANT	3	
DIRECTOR (industrial relations)	3	
EDUCATIONAL ADMINISTRATOR	3	
EMPLOYEE BENEFITS MANAGER	3	
FARM MANAGER	3	
FINANCIAL MANAGER	3	
FOREIGN SERVICE OFFICER	3	
GENERAL MANAGER/TOP EXECUTIVE	3	
GOVERNMENT CHIEF EXECUTIVE/ LEGISLATOR	3	
HEALTH SERVICES ADMINISTRATOR	3	
HUMAN RESOURCES MANAGER	3	
HUMAN RESOURCES RECRUITER	3	
JOB ANALYST	3	
LABOR RELATIONS SPECIALIST	3	
MANAGEMENT ANALYST/CONSULTANT	3	
MEDICAL REPORTS ADMINISTRATOR	3	
PRODUCTION MANAGER (industry)	3	
PURCHASER	3	
SPORTS/ATHLETICS MANAGER	3	
TRAINING/EDUCATION MANAGER	3	
URBAN PLANNER	3	

Occupation	Preparation Level	EXAMPLES of Courses, Programs/ Majors Related to Job Family
Region 3: Records & Communications Job Family		**Basic High School Courses** Business; English; Math: General Business Math; Social Studies
ADJUSTMENT CLERK	1	
BILLING CLERK	1	
BROKERAGE CLERK	1	**High School + 1 or 2 Years**
CAREER TECHNICIAN	1	Library Assistant Technology; English, General; English/American Literature; Office Management; Secretarial Science; On-the-job Training
CLERK (GENERAL)	1	
FILE CLERK	1	
FOREIGN TRADE CLERK	1	
HOTEL CLERK	1	
INTERVIEWING/NEW ACCOUNTS CLERK	1	**High School + 4 or More Years** English, General; English/American Literature
MAIL CLERK (except P.O.)	1	
METER READER	1	
POSTAL CLERK	1	
RECEPTIONIST/INFORMATION CLERK	1	
STENOGRAPHER	1	
TRAVEL CLERK	1	
COURT REPORTER	2	
HUMAN RESOURCES ASSISTANT	2	

Occupation	Preparation Level	EXAMPLES of Courses, Programs/ Majors Related to Job Family
HUMAN RESOURCES CLERK	2	
LEGAL SECRETARY	2	
LIBRARY ASSISTANT	2	
LIBRARY TECHNICIAN	2	
MEDICAL RECORDS TECHNICIAN	2	
MEDICAL SECRETARY	2	
ORDER CLERK	2	
SECRETARY	2	
TITLE EXAMINER/SEARCHER	2	

Region 4: Financial Transactions Job Family

Occupation	Preparation Level	EXAMPLES of Courses, Programs/ Majors Related to Job Family
ACCOUNTING CLERK	1	**Basic High School Courses**
BANK TELLER	1	Business; Math: General, Business Math
CASHIER	1	
CHECKOUT CLERK	1	**High School + 1 or 2 Years**
CREDIT CLERK/AUTHORIZER	1	Travel Agent Reservations; Bank Teller and Cashier; Accounting; Banking and Finance; Business Management; Business Economics; Insurance/Risk Management; On-the-job Training
PAYROLL CLERK	1	
RESERVATIONS AGENT	1	
TICKET AGENT	1	
BOOKKEEPER	2	
COST ESTIMATOR	2	**High School + 4 or More Years**
ACCOUNTANT	3	Accounting; Banking and Finance; Business Administration; Business Economics; Insurance/Risk Management
ACTUARY	3	
AUDITOR	3	
BUDGET ANALYST	3	
FINANCIAL ANALYST	3	
INSURANCE UNDERWRITER	3	
LOAN OFFICER/COUNSELOR	3	
REAL ESTATE APPRAISER	3	
TAX ACCOUNTANT	3	

Region 4: Storage & Dispatching Job Family

Occupation	Preparation Level	EXAMPLES of Courses, Programs/ Majors Related to Job Family
DISPATCHER	1	**Basic High School Courses**
MAIL CARRIER	1	Business; Math: General, Business Math; Trade and Industrial Education
MESSENGER/COURIER	1	
RAILROAD CONDUCTOR	1	**High School + 1 or 2 Years**
SHIPPING/RECEIVING CLERK	1	Shipping, Receiving, and Stock Clerk; On-the-job Training
STOCK CLERK	1	
WAREHOUSE WORKER	1	
WAREHOUSE SUPERVISOR	2	
AIR TRAFFIC CONTROLLER	3	
FLIGHT DISPATCHER	3	
TRAFFIC MANAGER	3	

(continued)

Occupation	Preparation Level	EXAMPLES of Courses, Programs/ Majors Related to Job Family
Region 5: Business Machine/Computer Operation Job Family		**Basic High School Courses** Business; Math: General, Business Math
DATA ENTRY KEYER	1	
OFFICE MACHINE OPERATOR	1	**High School + 1 or 2 Years**
STATISTICAL CLERK	1	Business Computer Operation; Data
TELEPHONE OPERATOR	1	Entry Equipment Operator; Business
TYPIST	1	Data Processing; On-the-job Training
COMPUTER/PERIPHERAL EQUIPMENT OPERATOR	2	* = Apprenticeship may be required.
MOTION PICTURE PROJECTIONIST	2*	
WORD PROCESSOR OPERATOR	2*	
Region 6: Vehicle Operation & Repair Job Family		**Basic High School Courses** Math: General, Algebra, etc.; Physical
AUTO SERVICE STATION ATTENDANT	1	Sciences; Trade and INdustrial
AUTOMOTIVE PAINTER	1*	Education
BUS DRIVER	1	**High School + 1 or 2 Years**
CHAUFFEUR	1	Autobody and Fender Repair; Auto-
DELIVERY DRIVER	1	motive Mechanics; Diesel Mechanics;
FORK LIFT OPERATOR	1	Commercial Pilot Training; Truck and
LOCOMOTIVE ENGINEER	1	Bus Driving; Aerospace Engineering
MOTORCYCLE TECHNICIAN	1	TEchnology; Airplane Piloting/
RAILROAD BRAKER	1	Navigation; On-the-job Training
REFUSE COLLECTOR	1	* = Apprenticeship may be required.
TAXICAB DRIVER	1	
TRUCK DRIVER (tractor trailer)	1	**High School + 4 or More Years**
AIRCRAFT TECHNICIAN	2*	Aerospace Engineering
AIRCRAFT PILOT	2	
AUTO BODY REPAIRER	2*	
AUTOMOTIVE TECHNICIAN	2*	
DIESEL TECHNICIAN	2	
FARM EQUIPMENT MECHANIC	2	
GARAGE SUPERVISOR	2*	
MOBILE HEAVY EQUIPMENT MECHANIC	2	
ASTRONAUT	3	
SHIP CAPTAIN	3	
Region 6: Construction & Maintenance Job Family		**Basic High School Courses** Trade and Industrial Education, including Industrial Arts
CONSTRUCTION LABORER	1	
CUSTODIAN	1	**High School + 1 or 2 Years**
DRYWALL INSTALLER	1	Construction/Building Technology;
ELEVATOR MECHANIC	1	Masonry and Bricklaying; Painting and
FLOOR COVERING INSTALLER	1	Wallpapering; Plumbing and Pipefit-
GLAZIER	1	ting; On-the-job Training; No formal
HEAVY EQUIPMENT OPERATOR	1	requirement
MAINTENANCE MECHANIC (general)	1	* = Apprenticeship may be required.
TRACK WORKER (railroad)	1	
BUILDING/CONSTRUCTION INSPECTOR	2*	

Occupation	Preparation Level	EXAMPLES of Courses, Programs/ Majors Related to Job Family
BRICKLAYER/STONEMASON	2	
CARPENTER	2*	
CONCRETE MASON	2*	
ELECTRICAL (construction)	2*	
ELECTRICIAN (maintenance)	2*	
INSULATION WORKER	2*	
PAINTER (construction)	2*	
PAPER HANGER	2*	
PIPEFITTER	2*	
PLASTERER	2*	
PLUMBER	2*	
ROOFER	2*	
SECURITY SYSTEM INSTALLER	2	
SHEET-METAL WORKER	2*	
STRUCTURAL STEEL WORKER	2*	
TILESETTER	2*	

Region 6: Agriculture & Natural Resources Job Family

Occupation	Preparation Level	
ANIMAL CARETAKER	1	**Basic High School Courses**
FISHER	1	Agriculture; Life Sciences; Trade and Industrial Education
GROUNDSKEEPER (gardener)	1	**High School + 1 or 2 Years**
HORTICULTURE (nursery) WORKER	1	Horticulture and Nursery Operations;
LOGGER	1	Forestry, Fishery, and Wildlife;
PEST CONTROLLER	1	Forestry/Related Sciences; Natural
FARMER (owner)	2	Resources Management; Agriculture
FISH AND GAME WARDER	2	Technology, General; Animal Sciences;
FORESTRY TECHNICIAN	2	On-the-job Training
TREE SURGEON (arborist)	2	**High School + 4 or More Years**
FORESTOR	3	Animal Sciences; Forestry/Related Sciences; Agriculture Technology, General

Region 6: Crafts & Related Services Job Family

Occupation	Preparation Level	
BAKER	1*	**Basic High School Courses**
BUTCHER/MEATCUTTER	1*	Home Economics; Trade and Industrial Education
COOK	1*	**High School + 1 or 2 Years**
UPHOLSTERER	1*	Culinary Arts; On-the-job Training;
HOUSEKEEPER (hotel)	1	No formal requirement
KITCHEN HELPER	1	
TAILOR/DRESSMAKER	1*	* = Apprenticeship may be required.
CHEF	2*	
DRYCLEANER	2	
JEWELER	2*	
LOCKSMITH	2*	
MUSICAL INSTRUMENT REPAIRER	2	
SHOE REPAIRER	2	
WATCH REPAIRER	2*	

(continued)

Occupation	Preparation Level	EXAMPLES of Courses, Programs/ Majors Related to Job Family
Region 6: Home/Business Equipment Repair Job Family		**Basic High School Courses**
APPLIANCE SERVICER (home)	1	Math: General, Algebra, etc.; Trade and Industrial Education
CABLE TV SYSTEM INSTALLER	1	
LINE INSTALLER/CABLE SPLICER	1	**High School + 1 or 2 Years**
AIR CONDITIONING/REFRIGERATION/ HEATING TECHNICIAN	2	Electronic Communications; Electrical and Electronic Equipment Repair; On-the-job Training
COMMUNICATIONS EQUIPMENT MECHANIC	2*	
OFFICE MACHINE SERVICER	2	* = Apprenticeship may be required.
"RADIO/TV, ETC. REPAIRER"	2*	
TELEPHONE INSTALLER/REPAIRER	2	
VENDING MACHINE MECHANIC	2	
Region 6: Industrial Equipment Operations & Repair Job Family		**Basic High School Courses**
ASSEMBLER	1	Math: General; Trade and Industrial Education, including Industrial Arts
BLASTER/EXPLOSIVE WORKER	1	
BLUE-COLLAR WORKER SUPERVISOR	1*	**High School + 1 or 2 Years**
BOILERMAKER	1	Machine Tool/Shop Operations: Metallurgy; Painting and Typesetting; Stationary Energy Sources; On-the-job Training; No formal requirement
DOCK WORKER	1	
FORGING PRESS OPERATOR	1*	
FURNACE OPERATOR	1	* = Apprenticeship may be required.
HEAT TREATER	1*	
MACHINE OPERATOR (industrial)	1	
MATERIAL HANDLER	1	
MINER	1	
ROLLER	1	
ROUSTABOUT	1	
SAILOR	1	
SEWING MACHINE OPERATOR	1*	
TEXTILE MACHINE OPERATOR	1	
BOOKBINDER	2*	
COMPOSITOR/TYPESETTER	2*	
ELECTRONIC EQUIPMENT REPAIRER	2*	
FIREFIGHTER	2	
INSTRUMENT REPAIRER	2*	
JOB AND DIE SETTER	2*	
MACHINE REPAIRER (industrial)	2*	
MACHINIST	2*	
MILLWRIGHT	2*	
MOLDER	2*	
NUCLEAR REACTOR OPERATOR	2	
PATTERNMAKER	2*	
PHOTOENGRAVER/LITHOGRAPHER	2*	
POWER HOUSE MECHANIC	2*	
POWER PLANT OPERATOR	2	
PRINTING PRESS OPERATOR	2*	

Occupation	Preparation Level	EXAMPLES of Courses, Programs/ Majors Related to Job Family
STATIONARY ENGINEER	2*	
TOOL AND DIE MAKER	2*	
WATER PLANT OPERATOR	2	
WELDER	2*	
WIRE DRAWER	2*	
WOODWORKER	2	

Region 7: Medical Specialties & Technologies Job Family

Occupation	Preparation Level	EXAMPLES of Courses, Programs/ Majors Related to Job Family
BLOOD BANK TECHNOLOGIST	2	**Basic High School Courses** Health and Human Care; Life Sciences; Physical Sciences; Trade and Industrial Education
CARDIOVASCULAR TECHNICIAN	2	
DENTAL HYGIENIST	2	
DENTAL LABORATORY TECHNICIAN	2	
DIALYSIS TECHNICIAN	2	**High School + 1 or 2 Years** EEG and EKG Technology; Medical/Surgical Assisting; Medical Laboratory Technology; Radiology Technology; Health Science Fields, General; Biochemistry/Biophysics; Biology; Microbiology; Sciences, General
EEG TECHNOLOGIST	2	
EMERGENCY MEDICAL TECHNICIAN	2	
MEDICAL LABORATORY TECHNICIAN	2	
MEDICAL TECHNOLOGIST	2	
NUCLEAR MEDICINE TECHNOLOGIST	2	
OPHTHALMIC LAB TECHNICIAN	2	
OPTICIAN	2*	* = Apprenticeship may be required.
RADIATION THERAPY TECHNOLOGIST	2	**High School + 4 or More Years** Medical Laboratory Technology; Medicine (Pre-Med); Radiology Technology; Health Science Fields, General; Biochemistry/Biophysics; Biology; Chemistry; Microbiology, Sciences, General
RADIOGRAPHER	2	
RESPIRATORY THERAPIST	2	
SONOGRAPHER	2	
SURGICAL TECHNOLOGIST	2	
ANESTHESIOLOGIST	3	
DENTIST	3	
INDUSTRIAL HYGIENIST	3	
INTERNIST	3	
OPTOMETRIST	3	
PHARMACIST	3	
PODIATRIST	3	
PROSTHETIST/ORTHOTIST	3	
RADIOLOGIST	3	
SURGEON	3	
VETERINARIAN	3	

Region 8: Engineering & Related Technologies Job Family

Occupation	Preparation Level	EXAMPLES of Courses, Programs/ Majors Related to Job Family
AEROSPACE ENGINEERING TECHNICIAN	2	**Basic High School Courses** Math: Algebra, Geometry, etc.; Life Sciences; Physical Sciences; Trade and Industrial Education, including Industrial Arts
AVIONICS TECHNICIAN	2	
BIOMEDICAL EQUIPMENT TECHNICIAN	2	
BROADCAST TECHNICIAN	2	
CHEMICAL TECHNICIAN	2	
CIVIL ENGINEERING TECHNICIAN	2	
COMPUTER PROGRAMMER	2	

(continued)

Occupation	Preparation Level	EXAMPLES of Courses, Programs/ Majors Related to Job Family
Region 8: Engineering & Related Technologies Job Family (*continued*)		**High School + 1 or 2 Years** Pre-Engineering and various Engineering Technologies: Aviation, Civil, Electrical, Mechanical, etc.; Applied Mathematics, including Computer Programming
COMPUTER SERVICE TECHNICIAN	2	
COMPUTER-AIDED DESIGN (CAD) TECHNICIAN	2	
DRAFTER	2*	* = Apprenticeship may be required.
ELECTRICAL/ELECTRONICS TECHNICIAN	2*	
ENERGY CONSERVATION TECHNICIAN	2	**High School + 4 or More Years** Engineering, various specialties; Applied Mathematics, including Computer Science
INDUSTRIAL ENGINEERING TECHNICIAN	2	
LABORATORY TESTER	2	
LASER TECHNICIAN	2	
MECHANICAL ENGINEERING TECHNICIAN	2	
METALLURGICAL TECHNICIAN	2	
POLLUTION-CONTROL TECHNICIAN	2	
QUALITY CONTROL TECHNICIAN	2	
ROBOT TECHNICIAN	2	
SCIENCE TECHNICIAN	2	
SURVEYOR TECHNICIAN	2	
SURVEYOR (land)	2	
TECHNICAL ILLUSTRATOR	2	
TEXTILE TECHNICIAN	2	
TOOL DESIGNER	2*	
WEATHER OBSERVER	2	
AEROSPACE ENGINEER	3	
AGRICULTURAL ENGINEER	3	
AUTOMOTIVE ENGINEER	3	
BIOMEDICAL ENGINEER	3	
CARTOGRAPHER	3	
CERAMIC ENGINEER	3	
CHEMICAL ENGINEER	3	
CIVIL ENGINEER	3	
COMPUTER ENGINEER	3	
COMPUTER NETWORK SPECIALIST	3	
COMPUTER SOFTWARE ENGINEER	3	
COMPUTER SYSTEMS ANALYST	3	
CRIMINALIST	3	
DATA PROCESSING MANAGER	3	
ELECTRICAL/ELECTRONICS ENGINEER	3	
FOOD TECHNOLOGIST	3	
INDUSTRIAL DESIGNER	3	
INDUSTRIAL ENGINEER	3	
MATERIALS ENGINEER	3	
MECHANICAL ENGINEER	3	
METALLURGICAL ENGINEER	3	
MINING ENGINEER	3	
NONDESTRUCTIVE TESTER	3	
NUCLEAR ENGINEER	3	

Occupation	Preparation Level	EXAMPLES of Courses, Programs/ Majors Related to Job Family
PETROLEUM ENGINEER	3	
RADIO/TV ENGINEER	3	
SAFETY ENGINEER	3	
SOLAR ENERGY ENGINEER	3	
TIME STUDY ANALYST	3	

Region 9: Natural Sciences & Mathematics Job Family

Occupation	Preparation Level	EXAMPLES
		Basic High School Courses
ANIMAL SCIENTIST	3	Agriculture; Math: Algebra, Geometry,
ASTRONOMER	3	etc.; Life Sciences; Physical Sciences
BIOCHEMIST	3	
BIOLOGIST	3	**High School + 1 or 2 Years**
BOTANIST	3	Biology; Physics; Sciences, General
CHEMIST	3	
ECOLOGIST	3	**High School + 4 or More Years**
GENETICIST	3	Biochemistry/Biophysics; Biology;
GEOGRAPHER	3	Earth Science; Physics; Science,
GEOLOGIST	3	General
GEOPHYSICIST	3	
HORTICULTURIST	3	
HYDROLOGIST	3	
MARINE BIOLOGIST	3	
MATHEMATICIAN	3	
METEOROLOGIST	3	
OCEANOGRAPHER	3	
OPERATIONS RESEARCH ANALYST	3	
PATHOLOGIST	3	
PHARMACOLOGIST	3	
PHYSICIST	3	
PHYSIOLOGIST	3	
PLANT SCIENTIST	3	
RANGE MANAGER	3	
SOIL CONSERVATIONIST	3	
STATISTICIAN	3	
ZOOLOGIST	3	

Region 10: Social Sciences Job Family

Occupation	Preparation Level	EXAMPLES
		Basic High School Courses
ANTHROPOLOGIST	3	English; Math; Social Studies
ARCHAEOLOGIST	3	
ECONOMIST	3	**High School + 1 or 2 Years**
HISTORIAN	3	Economics; International Relations;
MARKET RESEARCH ANALYST	3	Political Science; Sociology; Area/
POLITICAL SCIENTIST	3	Ethnic Studies
PSYCHOLOGIST (developmental, experimental)	3	
SOCIOLOGIST	3	**High School + 4 or More Years**
		Economics; Area/Ethnic Studies; International Relations; Political Science; Sociology

(continued)

Occupation	Preparation Level	EXAMPLES of Courses, Programs/ Majors Related to Job Family
Region 10: Applied Arts (Visual) Job Family		**Basic High School Courses**
FLORAL DESIGNER	1	Art; Home Economics; Trade and In-
MERCHANDISE DISPLAYER	1	dustrial Education, including Drafting
PAINTER (artist)	1	**High School + 1 or 2 Years**
PHOTOGRAPHIC PROCESS WORKER	1	Commercial Art/Photography; Fash-
CAMERA OPERATOR	1	ion Design; Textiles and Clothing;
CARTOONIST	2	Home Economics, General; Applied
FASHION ARTIST	2	Design/Crafts; Art; Photography;
FASHION DESIGNER	2	Photo/Motion Picture Technology;
GRAPHICS ARTIST	2	On-the-job Training
ILLUSTRATOR	2	
INTERIOR DECORATOR	2	**High School + 4 or More Years**
INTERIOR DESIGNER	2	Photo/Motion Picture Technology;
LAYOUT ARTIST	2	Fashion Design; Textiles and
PHOTOGRAPH RETOUCHER	2	Clothing; Applied Design/Crafts;
PHOTOGRAPHER	2	Art; Photography
STAGE TECHNICIAN	2	
ARCHITECT	3	
LANDSCAPE ARCHITECT	3	
MARINE ARCHITECT	3	
Region 10: Creative/Performing Arts Job Family		**Basic High School Courses**
SINGER	1	Art; English; Music, Band, Chorus;
STUNT PERFORMER	1	Speech
ACTOR	2	**High School + 1 or 2 Years**
DANCER/CHOREOGRAPHER	2	Music and Dance, Creative Writing;
MUSICIAN (instrumental)	2	Music (Liberal Arts); Music Perfor-
WRITER/AUTHOR	2	mance; Music Theory/Composition;
COMPOSER	3	No formal requirement
DRAMATIST (playwright)	3	**High School + 4 or More Years**
ORCHESTRA CONDUCTOR	3	Music Education; Creative Writing;
TEACHER (art/drama/music/speech)	3	Speech/Debate/Forensics; Dramatic
		Arts; Music (Liberal Arts); Music
		Performance; Music Theory/
		Composition
Region 11: Applied Arts (Written & Spoken) Job Family		**Basic High School Courses**
PROOFREADER	1	Business; English; Social Studies;
ADVERTISING COPYWRITER	2	Speech
FUND-RAISER	2	**High School + 1 or 2 Years**
LEGAL ASSISTANT/PARALEGAL	2	Creative Writing; English, General;
ACCOUNT EXECUTIVE (advertising)	3	Journalism; Radio/TV Production
ARCHIVIST/CURATOR	3	Technology; Communications Tech-
COLUMNIST	3	nology, Other

Occupation	Preparation Level	EXAMPLES of Courses, Programs/ Majors Related to Job Family
CRITIC (book/theater)	3	**High School + 4 or More Years**
EDITOR	3	Business Administration; Advertising;
FOREIGN LANGUAGE INTERPRETER	3	Journalism; Radio/TV Production
JUDGE	3	Technology; Communications Tech-
LAWYER	3	nology, Other; Library Science; Cre-
LIBRARIAN	3	ative Writing; English, General
LOBBYIST	3	
PUBLIC RELATIONS SPECIALIST	3	
RADIO/TV ANNOUNCER/NEWSCASTER	3	
RADIO/TV PROGRAM WRITER	3	
REPORTER CORRESPONDENT	3	
TECHNICAL WRITER	3	
TV PRODUCTION DIRECTOR	3	

Region 12: General Health Care Job Family		**Basic High School Courses**
DENTAL ASSISTANT	1	Health and Human Care; Life Sci-
GERIATRIC AIDE	1	ences; Social Studies; Speech
MEDICAL ASSISTANT	1	**High School + 1 or 2 Years**
NURSING/PSYCHIATRIC AIDE	1	Nursing; On-the-job Training
DIETETIC TECHNICIAN	2	
NURSE (licensed practical)	2	**High School + 4 or More Years**
OPTOMETRIC ASSISTANT	2	Medicine (Pre-Med); Nursing; Health
PHYSICAL THERAPIST ASSISTANT	2	Science Fields, General; Philosophy;
AUDIOLOGIST	3	Religion; Theology; Biology; Sciences,
CHIROPRACTOR	3	General
DIETITIAN/NUTRITIONIST	3	
MINISTER	3	
NURSE ANESTHETIST	3	
NURSE PRACTITIONER	3	
NURSE (registered)	3	
OCCUPATIONAL THERAPIST	3	
OSTEOPATHIC PHYSICIAN	3	
PEDIATRICIAN	3	
PHYSICAL THERAPIST	3	
PHYSICIAN	3	
PHYSICIAN'S ASSISTANT	3	
PRIEST	3	
PSYCHIATRIST	3	
RABBI	3	
RECREATION THERAPIST	3	
SPEECH-LANGUAGE PATHOLOGIST	3	
SPORTS PHYSICIAN	3	

Index to Descriptions of Occupations: Supplement to the 1996 ACT Job Family Charts

The ACT Job Family Charts refer counselees to descriptions of occupations in the *Occupational Outlook Handbook*. This supplement is designed to help counselees access other useful sources of occupational information, including computer-based files that use U.S. Government ID numbers for retrieving occupational descriptions. This index can be reproduced locally and placed in or near various occupational information resources.

The following sources of occupational descriptions and filing system codes are referenced in this index:

- *World-of-Work Map:* Job Family letter and map region. The World-of-Work Map is used in the following ACT Programs:
  - ACT Assessment Program (the "ACT")
  - PLAN (tenth-grade assessment program)
  - EXPLORE (eighth-grade assessment program)
  - DISCOVER (computer-based career planing and guidance system)
  - CPP (Career Planning Program)
  - VIESA (Vocational Interest, Experience, and Skill Assessment)
  - *Take Hold of Your Future* (career and life planning course text)
  - *Realizing the Dream* (career planning kit for parents and their student)
  - ASSET (print-based course assessment/placement and advising service for community and technical colleges)

  The job family letters and/or the region number can be used to find where a particular occupation is located on the World-of-Work Map and to identify other occupations related to that occupation.

- OOH: *Occupational Outlook Handbook*, 1996–97, 1994–95, and 1992–93 Editions (U.S. Government Printing Office).

- GOE: *Guide for Occupational Exploration* (American Guidance Service, 1993). The *Worker Trait Group Guide* (Meridian Education Corp., 1988) also uses the GOE code

- DOT: *Dictionary of Occupational Titles,* 4th Edition (U.S. Government Printing Office, 1977), the 1986 *Supplement,* and the 1991 Revised 4th edition. Careers, Inc. and Chronicle Guidance Publications publish comprehensive lists of occupational information indexed by the DOT code.

- SOC: *Standard Occupational Classification Manual.* (U.S. Department of Commerce, 1980). The four-digit SOC code is listed.

Occupation	World-of-Work Map[a]		Job Descriptions, OOH[b]			Government ID Numbers[c]		
	JF	Region	96/97	94/95	92/93	GOE	DOT	SOC
Account Executive (advertising)	S	11	247■	246■	229	11.09.01	164.167-010	1250
Accountant	D	4	21	17	15	11.06.01	160.162-018	1412
Accounting Clerk	D	4	282	280	262	07.02.02	216.482-010	4712
Actor	R	10	193	197	180	01.03.02	150.047-010	3240
Actuary	D	4	91	90	79	11.01.02	020.167-010	1732
Adjustment Clerk	C	3	254	253	236	07.01.02	219.362-010	4630
Administrative Assistant (See Administrative Assistant/Executive Secretary)								
Administrative Assistant/ Executive Secretary	B	3	287	286	267	11.05.02	201.362-030	4622
Administrative Services Manager	B	3	24	20	17	11.12.04	162.117-014	1370
Advertising Copywriter	S	11	184	187	171	01.01.02	131.067-014	3313
Advertising Manager	B	3	60	56	48	11.09.01	164.117-010	1250
Aerospace Engineer	M	8	79	77	66	05.01.07	002.061-014	1622
Aerospace Engineering Technician	M	8	226■	228■	210■	05.01.01	007.161-026	3713
Agricultural Engineer	M	8	76■	75■	64■	05.01.08	013.161-010	3719
Air Conditioning/ Refrigeration/ Heating Technician	K	6	360	352	333	05.05.09	637.261-014	6160
Air Traffic Controller	E	4	218■	220	204	05.03.03	193.162-018	3920
Aircraft Pilot	G	6	215	218	202	05.04.01	196.263-014	8250
Aircraft Technician	G	6	342	335	316	05.05.09	621.281-014	6116
Airplane Pilot (See Aircraft Pilot)								
Airport Manager	B	3	44■	40■	34■	11.05.01	184.117-026	1342
Anesthesiologist	N	7	160	161	145	02.03.01	070.101-010	2610
Animal Caretaker	I	6	330	314	295	03.03.02	410.674-010	5624
Animal Scientist	O	9	101	100	88	02.02.01	040.061-014	1853
Anthropologist	P	10	119	119	106	11.03.03	055.067-010	1919
Appliance Servicer (home)	K	6	362	354	335	05.10.03	723.584-010	6156
Archaeologist	P	10	119	119	106	11.03.03	055.067-018	1919
Architect	Q	10	85	84	73	05.01.07	001.061-010	1610
Archivist/Curator	S	11	140	144	129	11.03.03	101.167-010	2520
Artist	Q	10	191■	194■	177■	01.02.02	144.061-010	3250
Assembler	L	6	401	393	372	06.04.22	706.687-010	7720
Astronaut	G	6	—	—	—	05.04.01	196.263-014	8250
Astronomer	O	9	113	111	98	02.01.01	021.067-010	1842
Athletic Coach	U	1	469	458	433■	12.01.01	153.227-010	3400

(continued)

[a]World-of-Work Map Job Family (JF) and Map Region for Job Family.
[b]OOH = *Occupational Outlook Handbook*, 1996–97, 1994–95, and 1992–93 editions. When a specific job is not covered, but related jobs are, a ■ appears.
[c]These ID numbers can be used to find occupational descriptions in various government publications and computer-based information systems. See the previous page or ask your counselor for local specifics.

Occupation	World-of-Work Map[a]		Job Descriptions, OOH[b]			Government ID Numbers[c]		
	JF	Region	96/97	94/95	92/93	GOE	DOT	SOC
Athletic Trainer	U	1	469	—	—	10.02.02	153.224-010	3400
Auctioneer	A	2	234	235	—	08.02.03	294.567-010	4364
Audiologist	T	12	177	179	163	02.03.04	076.101-010	3034
Auditor	D	4	21	17	15	11.06.01	160.167-054	1412
Auto Body Repairer	G	6	344	337	317	05.05.06	807.381-010	6115
Auto Service Station Attendant	G	6	460	450	426	05.10.02	915.467-010	8730
Auto Service Station Manager	B	3	345	338	426	11.11.05	185.167-014	4030
Automotive Engineer	M	8	82	80	69	05.01.08	007.061-010	1635
Automotive Painter	G	6	441	432	411	05.10.07	845.381-014	7669
Automotive Technician	G	6	345	338	319	05.05.09	620.261-010	6111
Avionics Technician	M	8	352	345	326	05.05.10	823.261-026	6151
Baker	J	6	308	304	285	06.02.15	313.381-010	5214
Bank Officer/Manager	B	3	41	36	32	11.05.02	186.117-038	1220
Bank Teller	D	4	258	257	240	07.03.01	211.362-018	4791
Barber	W	2	320	315	296	09.02.02	330.371-010	5252
Bartender	W	2	311	306	287	09.04.01	312.474-010	5212
Beautician/Cosmetologist (See Hairstylist)								
Benefits Manager (See Employee Benefits Manager)								
Bill Collector	A	2	254	253	236	07.03.01	241.367-010	4786
Billing Clerk	C	3	281	279	261	07.06.02	214.482-010	4718
Biochemist	O	9	103	102	89	02.02.03	041.061-026	1854
Biologist	O	9	103	102	89	02.02.03	041.061-030	1854
Biomedical Engineer	M	8	79	75	64	02.02.01	019.061-010	1639
Biomedical Equipment Technician	M	8	473	461	436	05.05.11	719.261-010	6179
Blaster/Explosive Worker	L	6	472	460	435	05.10.06	859.261-010	6530
Blood Bank Technologist	N	7	200	203	185	02.04.02	078.161-010	3620
Blue-Collar Worker Supervisor	L	6	402	394	373	05.12.01	899.131-010	6311
Boilermaker	L	6	407	399	377	05.05.06	805.261-014	6814
Bookbinder	L	6	423	419	398	05.05.15	977.381-010	6844
Bookkeeper	D	4	282	280	262	07.02.01	210.382-014	4712
Botanist	O	9	103	102	89	02.02.02	041.061-038	1854
Bricklayer/Stonemason	H	6	376	368	348	05.05.01	861.381-018	6412
Broadcast Technician	M	8	220	222	206	05.10.05	194.262-010	3930
Brokerage Clerk	C	3	282	280	263	07.02.02	219.362-018	4699
Budget Analyst	D	4	25	22	19	11.06.05	161.267-030	1419
Building Inspector (See Building/ Construction Inspector)								
Building Manager/ Superintendent (See Property Manager)								

Occupation	World-of-Work Map[a]		Job Descriptions, OOH[b]			Government ID Numbers[c]		
	JF	Region	96/97	94/95	92/93	GOE	DOT	SOC
Building/Construction Inspector	H	6	28	24	21	05.03.06	168.167-030	1472
Bus Driver	G	6	446	436	415	09.03.01	913.463-010	8215
Business Agent	B	3	44	40	32	11.12.03	191.117-014	1450
Business Manager/Agent (See Business Agent)								
Butcher/Meatcutter	J	6	404	396	375	05.10.08	316.681-010	6871
Buyer	A	2	69	65	62	08.01.03	162.157-018	1442
Cable TV System Installer	K	6	365	357	338	05.10.03	821.281-010	6151
Camera Operator	Q	10	189	191	175	01.02.03	143.062-022	3260
Cardiovascular Technician	N	7	199	202	191	10.03.01	078.362-018	3690
Career Technician	C	3	282	230	212	11.02.04	249.367-014	4630
Carpenter	H	6	377	369	349	05.05.02	860.381-022	6422
Cartographer	M	8	89	87	76	05.03.02	018.261-026	3739
Cartoonist	Q	10	191	194	177	01.02.03	141.061-010	3250
Cashier	D	4	234	235	219	07.03.01	211.362-010	4364
Caterer	B	3	50	46	40	11.11.04	187.167-106	1351
Cement Mason (See Concrete Mason)								
Ceramic Engineer	M	8	82	81	67	05.01.07	006.061-014	1623
Chauffeur	G	6	453	442	439	09.03.02	913.663-010	8216
Checkout Clerk	D	4	234	235	219	07.03.01	211.462-014	4364
Chef	J	6	308	304	285	05.04.17	313.131-014	5211
Chemical Engineer	M	8	80	78	67	05.01.07	008.061-018	1626
Chemical Laboratory/ Technician (See Chemical Technician)								
Chemical Technician	M	8	231	233	215	02.04.01	022.261-010	3831
Chemist	O	9	107	107	94	02.01.01	022.061-010	1845
Childcare Worker (See Childcare Worker (domestic))								
Childcare worker (domestic)	W	2	328	325	306	10.03.03	301.677-010	5060
Chiropractor	T	12	156	157	141	02.03.04	079.101-010	2890
City Manager	B	3	46	42	36	11.05.03	188.117-114	1120
Civil Engineer	M	8	80	79	67	05.01.07	005.061-014	1628
Civil Engineering Technician	M	8	226	228	210	05.01.01	007.161-026	3713
Claims Adjuster (See Claims Representative)								
Claims Representative	A	2	254	253	236	11.12.01	241.217-010	4782
Clerk (general)	C	3	227	263	246	07.07.03	209.562-010	4630
Club/Resort Manager	B	3	50	46	40	11.11.04	187.167-122	1351
Coal Equipment Operator (See Mining Equipment Operator)								

(continued)

Occupation	World-of-Work Map[a]		Job Descriptions, OOH[b]			Government ID Numbers[c]		
	JF	Region	96/97	94/95	92/93	GOE	DOT	SOC
Coin Machine Mechanic (See Vending Machine Mechanic)								
College Student Personnel Worker	U	1	469■	149■	133■	10.01.02	045.107-038	2400
College/University Faculty	U	1	143	147	131	11.02.01	090.227-010	2200
Columnist	S	11	184	187	171	11.08.03	131.067-010	3313
Commercial Artist (See Illustrator)								
Communications Equipment Mechanic	K	6	352	345	326	05.05.05	822.281-014	6151
Compensation Manager	B	3	63	59	50	11.05.02	116.167-022	1430
Composer (music)	R	10	197	200	183	01.04.02	152.067-014	3230
Compositor/Typesetter	L	6	425	415	394	05.05.13	973.381-010	6841
Computer Engineer	M	8	93■	92■	—	05.01.03	020.062-010	1636
Computer Graphic Artist (See Graphic Artist)								
Computer Network Specialist	M	8	93	92	80	11.01.01	109.067-010	1719
Computer Programmer	M	8	222	224	207	11.01.01	030.162-010	3971
Computer Service Technician	M	8	353	346	326	05.05.10	828.261-022	6153
Computer Software Engineer	M	8	93	92	80	11.01.01	030.062-010	1636
Computer Systems Analyst	M	8	93	92	80	11.01.01	012.167-066	1712
Computer Systems Specialist (See Computer Network Specialist)								
Computer-Aided Design (CAD) Technician	M	8	224■	226■	209■	05.03.02	017.261-042	3720
Computer/Peripheral Equipment Operator	F	5	261	260	243	07.06.01	213.362-010	4612
Concrete Mason	H	6	380	372	352	05.05.01	844.364-010	6463
Construction Laborer	H	6	460	450	426	05.10.01	869.664-014	6479
Consultant	B	3	58	54	46	11.01.02	189.167-010	99
Contractor/Construction Manager	B	3	30	26	23	11.12.04	182.167-010	1330
Cook	J	6	308	304	285	05.05.17	313.361-014	5214
Correction Officer	V	1	297	295	276	04.02.01	372.667-018	5133
Cost Estimator	D	4	32	28	25	05.03.02	169.267-038	1490
Counselor (Career)	U	1	145■	149■	133■	10.01.02	045.107-010	2400
Counselor (employment) (See Counselor (career))								
Counselor (mental health)	V	1	145	149	133	10.01.02	045.107-010	2400
Counselor (rehabilitation)	V	1	145	149	133	10.01.02	045.107-042	2400
Counselor (school/college)	U	1	145	149	133	10.01.02	045.107-010	2400

Occupation	World-of-Work Map[a]		Job Descriptions, OOH[b]			Government ID Numbers[c]		
	JF	Region	96/97	94/95	92/93	GOE	DOT	SOC
Counter Attendant	W	2	311	306	287	09.04.01	311.477-014	5216
Counter/Rental Clerk	W	2	235	236	220	09.04.02	295.467-026	4363
Court Reporter	C	3	289	287	269	07.05.03	202.362-010	4623
Credit Clerk/Authorizer	D	4	263	262	245	07.04.01	205.367-022	4642
Credit Manager	B	3	41	36	32	11.06.03	168.167-054	1419
Criminalist	M	8	231	233	215	02.04.01	029.261-026	3890
Critic (book/theater)	S	11	182	185	169	01.01.03	131.067-018	3313
Custodian	H	6	327	324	303	05.12.18	382.664-010	5244
Customer Service Coordinator	B	3	60	56	48	05.02.03	189.117-018	1250
Customs Inspector	V	1	53	49	43	11.10.04	168.267-022	1473
Dancer/Choreographer	R	10	195	198	181	01.05.02	151.047-010	3270
Data Entry Keyer	F	5	294	292	273	07.06.02	203.582-022	4793
Data Processing Manager	M	8	39	34	31	11.01.01	169.167-030	1260
Delivery Driver	G	6	455	444	421	05.08.03	292.363-010	8218
Dental Assistant	T	12	313	309	290	10.03.02	079.361-018	5232
Dental Hygienist	N	7	202	205	187	10.02.02	078.361-010	3630
Dental Laboratory Technician	N	7	439	429	408	05.05.11	712.381-018	6865
Dentist	N	7	157	158	142	02.03.02	072.101-010	2620
Detective (police)	V	1	303	301	281	04.01.02	375.267-010	5132
Dialysis Technician	N	7	200	203	185	10.02.02	078.362-014	3690
Diesel Technician	G	6	348	341	321	05.05.09	625.281-010	6112
Dietetic Technician	T	12	165	167	151	05.05.17	077.124-010	3020
Dietitian/Nutritionist	T	12	165	167	151	11.05.02	077.124-010	3020
Dining Room Attendant	W	2	311	306	287	09.05.02	311.677-018	5218
Director (industrial relations)	B	3	63	59	50	11.05.02	166.177-010	1230
Director (social services)	V	1	132	136	119	11.07.01	195.117-010	1270
Director (social)	V	1	130	133	121	09.01.01	352.167-010	5269
Dispatcher	E	4	273	272	255	07.05.01	249.167-014	4751
Dock Worker	L	6	458	450	426	06.04.40	922.687-090	8723
Drafter	M	8	224	226	209	05.03.02	007.161-018	3720
Dramatist (playwright)	R	10	184	197	180	01.01.02	131.067-038	3210
Driver (sales route)	A	2	455	444	421	08.02.07	292.353-010	8218
Drycleaner	J	6	475	463	438	06.02.16	362.382-014	7658
Drywall Installer	H	6	382	374	353	05.05.04	842.361-030	6424
Ecologist	O	9	103	102	89	02.01.02	029.081-010	1849
Economist	P	10	121	121	108	11.03.05	050.067-010	1912
Editor	S	11	184	187	171	11.05.01	132.017-010	3312
Educational Administrator	B	3	34	30	27	11.07.03	099.117-018	1282
EEG Technologist	N	7	205	208	190	10.03.01	078.362-022	3690
EKG Technician (See Cardiovascular Technician)								

(continued)

Occupation	World-of-Work Map[a]		Job Descriptions, OOH[b]			Government ID Numbers[c]		
	JF	Region	96/97	94/95	92/93	GOE	DOT	SOC
Electrical/Electronics Engineer	M	8	81	79	68	05.01.08	003.061-010	1633
Electrical/Electronics Technician	M	8	226	228	210	05.01.01	003.161-014	3711
Electrician (construction)	H	6	383	375	355	05.05.05	824.261-010	6432
Electrician (maintenance)	H	6	383	375	355	05.05.05	829.261-018	6153
Electrologist	W	2	320	315	296	09.05.01	339.371-010	5253
Electronic Equipment Repairer	L	6	350	343	325	05.05.10	828.261-022	6153
Elevator Mechanic	H	6	355	348	328	05.05.06	825.361-010	6176
Emergency Medical Technician	N	7	206	209	192	10.03.02	079.374-010	3690
Employee Benefits Manager	B	3	63	59	50	11.03.04	166.267-010	1430
Employment Interviewer	B	3	37	32	29	11.03.04	166.267-010	1430
Energy Conservation Technician	M	8	226	228	—	05.03.07	007.181-010	3713
Environmental Health Inspector	V	1	53	49	43	11.10.03	079.117-018	1473
Executive Housekeeper	B	3	50	46	40	11.11.01	187.167-046	1351
Exercise/Aerobic Instructor	U	1	469	—	—	10.02.02	153.227-014	2390
Farm Equipment Mechanic	G	6	357	349	330	05.05.09	624.281-010	6118
Farm Manager	B	3	331	327	308	03.01.01	180.167-018	5522
Farm/Home Management Advisor	V	1	469	458	433	11.02.03	096.127-010	2390
Farmer (owner)	I	6	331	327	308	03.01.01	421.161-010	5512
Fashion Artist	Q	10	191	194	177	01.02.03	141.061-014	3250
Fashion Designer	Q	10	186	189	173	01.02.03	142.016-018	3220
Fashion Model	A	2	—	—	—	01.08.01	297.667-014	4450
Fast-Food Worker	W	2	311	306	287	09.04.01	311.472-010	5216
FBI Agent	V	1	303	301	281	04.01.02	375.167-042	5132
File Clerk	C	3	264	281	263	07.07.01	206.387-034	4696
Financial Analyst	D	4	25	90	79	11.01.02	020.167-014	1733
Financial Manager	B	3	41	36	32	11.06.02	160.167-058	1220
Financial Services Sales Representative	A	2	247	246	229	08.01.02	250.257-022	4124
Firefighter	L	6	299	297	277	04.02.04	373.364-010	5123
Fish and Game Warden	I	6	334	—	—	04.01.02	379.167-010	5134
Fisher	I	6	334	329	310	03.04.03	441.684-010	5830
Flight Attendant	W	2	324	319	298	09.01.04	352.367-010	5257
Flight Dispatcher	E	4	469	220	204	05.03.03	912.167-010	3920
Floor Covering Installer	H	6	379	371	351	05.10.01	864.381-010	6462
Floral Arranger/Designer (See Floral Designer)								
Floral Designer	Q	10	186	189	173	01.02.03	142.081-010	3220

Occupation	World-of-Work Map[a]		Job Descriptions, OOH[b]			Government ID Numbers[c]		
	JF	Region	96/97	94/95	92/93	GOE	DOT	SOC
Food and Drug Inspector	V	1	53	49	43	11.10.03	168.267-042	1473
Food Service Manager	B	3	72	68	58	09.05.02	319.137-010	5211
Food Service Supervisor (See Food Service Manager)								
Food Technologist	M	8	101	100	88	02.02.04	041.081-010	1853
Foreign Language Interpreter	S	11	—	—	—	11.08.04	137.267-010	3290
Foreign Service Officer	B	3	—	—	—	11.09.03	188.117-106	1139
Foreign Trade Clerk	C	3	—	—	—	07.02.04	214.467-010	4716
Forester	I	6	105	104	91	03.01.04	040.167-010	1852
Forestry Technician	I	6	334	332	313	03.02.02	452.364-010	5720
Forging Press Operator	L	6	475	462	404	06.02.02	611.482-010	7319
Fork Lift Operator	G	6	448	438	417	06.04.40	921.683-050	8318
Fund-Raiser	S	11	179	182	166	11.09.02	293.157-010	4369
Funeral Director	B	3	43	38	433	11.11.04	187.167-030	1359
Furnace Operator	L	6	475	462	438	06.02.10	513.462-010	7675
Furniture Upholsterer (See Upholsterer)								
Gaming Occupations Worker	W	2	—	—	—	09.04.02	343.464-010	5254
Garage Supervisor	G	6	402	394	373	05.05.09	620.131-014	7100
General Manager/Top Executive	B	3	44	40	34	11.05.01	189.117-026	1210
Geneticist	O	9	103	102	89	02.02.01	041.061-050	1854
Geographer	O	9	119	119	106	02.01.01	029.067-010	1849
Geologist	O	9	109	108	95	02.01.01	024.061-018	1847
Geophysicist	O	9	109	108	95	02.01.01	024.061-030	1847
Geriatric Aide	T	12	316	311	292	10.03.02	355.674-014	5236
Gerontologist	V	1	119	126	113	11.03.02	054.067-010	1916
Glazier	H	6	385	377	357	05.10.01	865.381-010	6464
Government Chief Executive/Legislator	B	3	46	42	36	11.05.03	188.117-114	1120
Graphics Artist	Q	10	191	194	177	01.02.03	141.061-018	3220
Groundskeeper (gardener)	I	6	339	321	300	03.04.04	406.684-014	5622
Hairstylist/Cosmetologist	W	2	320	315	296	09.02.01	332.271-010	5253
Hazardous Waste Technician	V	1	53	49	43	11.10.03	168.267-086	0
Health Services Administrator	B	3	48	44	38	11.07.02	187.117-010	1210
Heat Treater	L	6	412	404	381	06.02.10	504.382-014	7544
Heavy Equipment Operator	H	6	448	438	417	05.11.01	859.683-010	8312
Historian	P	10	119	119	106	11.03.03	052.067-022	1913
Home Economist	V	1	—	—	—	11.02.03	096.121-014	2390

(continued)

Occupation	JF	Region	96/97	94/95	92/93	GOE	DOT	SOC
Homemaker/Home Health Aide	V	1	325	322	301	11.02.03	309.354-010	5263
Horticulture (nursery) Worker	I	6	472	460■	435■	03.04.04	405.684-014	5619
Horticulturist	O	9	101	100	88	02.02.02	040.061-038	1853
Host/Hostess	W	2	311	306	287	09.01.01	352.667-010	5269
Hotel Clerk	C	3	267	266	248	07.04.03	238.367-038	4643
Hotel/Motel Manager	B	3	50	46	40	11.11.01	187.117-038	1351
Housekeeper (hotel)	J	6	327	324	435■	05.12.18	323.687-014	5242
Human Resources Assistant	C	3	287■	285■	267■	11.05.02	166.167-030	1230
Human Resources Clerk	C	3	287	285	267	07.05.03	209.362-026	4692
Human Resources Manager	B	3	63	59	50	11.05.02	166.117-018	1230
Human Resources Recruiter	B	3	63	59	50	11.03.04	166.267-010	1430
Human Services Worker	V	1	128	132	118	10.01.02	195.367-010	2032
Hydrologist	O	9	109	108	95	02.01.01	024.061-034	1847
Illustrator	Q	10	191	194	177	01.02.03	141.061-022	3250
Importer/Exporter	B	3	44■	40■	34■	11.05.02	184.117-022	1342
Industrial Designer	M	8	186	189	173	01.02.03	142.061-026	3220
Industrial Engineer	M	8	81	80	69	05.01.06	012.167-030	1634
Industrial Engineering Technician	M	8	226	228	210	05.03.06	012.267-010	3712
Industrial Hygienist	N	7	—	—	—	11.10.03	079.161-010	3690
Instrument Repairer	L	6	352	345	326	05.05.10	710.281-026	6171
Insulation Worker	H	6	387	379	358	05.12.14	863.664-010	6465
Insurance Agent	A	2	236	237	221	08.01.02	250.257-010	4122
Insurance Manager	B	3	44■	40■	34■	11.11.04	186.167-034	4010
Insurance Underwriter	D	4	74	73	60	11.06.03	169.267-046	1414
Interior Decorator	Q	10	186	189	173	01.06.02	142.051-014	3220
Interior Designer	Q	10	186	189	173	01.06.02	142.051-014	3220
Internist	N	7	160	161	145	02.03.01	070.101-042	2610
Interviewing/New Accounts Clerk	C	3	268	266	249	07.04.01	205.362-026	4642
Jeweler	J	6	408	400	378	01.06.02	700.281-010	6822
Job Analyst	B	3	63	59	50	11.03.04	166.267-018	1430
Job and Die Setter	L	6	415	406	385	06.01.03	600.380-018	7329
Judge	S	11	115	114	101	11.04.01	111.107-010	2120
Kitchen Helper	J	6	308	304	285	05.12.18	318.687-010	5219
Labor Relations Specialist	B	3	63	59	50	11.05.02	169.107-010	1430
Laboratory Tester	M	8	406	397	376	02.04.01	029.261-010	3831
Landscape Architect	Q	10	87	85	74	05.01.07	001.061-018	1610
Laser Technician	M	8	226■	228■	210■	05.01.01	019.181-010	3890
Lawyer	S	11	115	114	101	11.04.02	110.107-010	2110
Layout Artist	Q	10	425	415	394	01.02.03	141.061-018	3220

| Occupation | World-of-Work Map[a] | | Job Descriptions, OOH[b] | | | Government ID Numbers[c] | | |
	JF	Region	96/97	94/95	92/93	GOE	DOT	SOC
Legal Assistant (See Legal Assistant/Paralegal)								
Legal Assistant/Paralegal	S	11	229	231	213	11.04.02	119.267-026	3960
Legal Secretary	C	3	287	286	267	07.01.03	201.362-010	4622
Librarian	S	11	148	151	137	11.02.04	100.127-014	2510
Library Assistant	C	3	284	282	264	11.02.04	249.367-046	4694
Library Technician	C	3	227	230	212	11.02.04	100.367-018	2510
Line Installer/Cable Splicer	K	6	365	357	338	05.05.05	822.381-014	6157
Lithographer (See Photoengraver/ Lithographer)								
Loan Officer (See Loan Officer/Counselor)								
Loan Officer/Counselor	D	4	57	53	32	11.06.03	186.267-018	1415
Lobbyist	S	11	179	182	166	11.09.03	165.017-010	3320
Locksmith	J	6	473	461	—	05.05.09	709.281-010	6173
Locomotive Engineer	G	6	450	440	419	05.08.02	910.363-014	8232
Logger	I	6	337	332	313	03.04.02	454.684-018	5730
Machine Operator (industrial)	L	6	412	404	384	05.05.07	601.280-054	7329
Machine Repairer (industrial)	L	6	364	356	336	05.05.09	638.281-014	6130
Machine Tool Operator (See Machine Operator (industrial))								
Machinist	L	6	410	402	380	05.05.07	600.280-022	6813
Mail Carrier	E	4	277	275	258	07.05.04	230.367-010	4743
Mail Clerk/Messenger (See Mail Clerk (except P.O.))								
Mail Clerk (except P.O.)	C	3	270	269	251	07.05.04	209.687-026	4744
Maintenance Mechanic (general)	H	6	358	351	332	05.05.09	899.261-014	6100
Management Analyst/ Consultant	B	3	58	54	46	05.01.06	161.167-010	1420
Manicurist	W	2	320	315	296	09.05.01	331.674-010	5253
Manufacturer's Representative	A	2	238	239	223	08.02.01	279.157-010	4249
Marine Architect	Q	10	85	84	73	05.01.07	001.061-014	1637
Marine Biologist	O	9	103	102	89	02.02.03	041.061-022	1854
Market Research Analyst	P	10	121	121	108	11.06.03	050.067-014	1912
Material Handler	L	6	460	450	426	05.12.03	929.687-030	8726
Materials Engineer	M	8	82	81	70	05.01.06	019.061-014	1623
Mathematician	O	9	96	94	82	02.01.01	020.067-014	1739

(continued)

Occupation	World-of-Work Map[a]		Job Descriptions, OOH[b]			Government ID Numbers[c]		
	JF	Region	96/97	94/95	92/93	GOE	DOT	SOC
Mechanical Engineer	M	8	82	80	69	05.01.08	007.061-014	1635
Mechanical Engineering Technician	M	8	226■	228■	210■	05.01.01	007.161-026	3713
Medical Assistant	T	12	314	310	302■	10.03.02	079.362-010	5233
Medical Laboratory Technician	N	7	200	203	185	02.04.02	078.381-014	3690
Medical Records Administrator	B	3	209	212	195■	11.07.02	079.167-014	1310
Medical Records Technician	C	3	209	212	195	07.05.03	079.362-014	3640
Medical Secretary	C	3	287	286	267	07.01.03	201.362-014	4622
Medical Technologist	N	7	200	203	185	02.04.02	078.261-038	3620
Meeting/Convention Planner	B	3	50■	46■	—	11.11.01	187.167-078	1351
Merchandise Displayer	Q	10	186■	189■	173■	01.02.03	298.081-010	3220
Messenger/Courier	E	4	270	269	251	07.07.02	230.663-010	4745
Metallurgical Engineer	M	8	82	81	70	05.01.06	011.061-018	1623
Metallurgical Technician	M	8	231■	133■	215■	02.04.01	011.261-010	3719
Metallurgist (See Metallurgical Engineer)								
Meteorologist	O	9	111	110	97	02.01.01	025.062-010	1846
Meter Reader	C	3	272	270	253	05.09.03	209.567-010	4755
Millwright	L	6	367	359	339	05.05.06	638.281-018	6178
Miner	L	6	472	460	435■	05.11.02	939.281-010	6560
Mining Engineer	M	8	83	82	70	05.01.06	010.061-014	1624
Minister	T	12	135	138	124	10.01.01	120.107-010	2042
Mobile Heavy Equipment Mechanic	G	6	368	360	341	05.05.09	620.261-022	6117
Molder	L	6	412■	404■	381■	06.01.04	518.361-010	6861
Motion Picture Projectionist	F	5	475	463	438■	05.10.05	960.362-010	7479
Motorcycle Technician	G	6	370	362	343	05.05.09	620.281-054	6114
Musical Instrument Repairer	J	6	372	364	344	05.05.12	730.361-010	6172
Musician (See Musician (Instrumental))								
Musician (Instrumental)	R	10	197	200	183	01.04.04	152.041-010	3230
Nondestructive Tester	M	8	76■	75■	64■	05.01.04	002.261-014	3719
Nuclear Engineer	M	8	84	82	71	05.01.03	015.061-014	1627
Nuclear Medicine Technologist	N	7	210	213	196	10.02.02	078.361-018	3650
Nuclear Reactor Operator	L	6	418	410	389	05.06.01	952.362-022	6932
Nurse (licensed practical)	T	12	208	211	194	10.02.01	079.374-014	3660
Nurse (registered)	T	12	174	175	159	10.02.01	075.364-010	2900
Nurse Anesthetist	T	12	174■	175■	159■	10.02.01	075.371-010	2900
Nurse Practitioner	T	12	174■	175■	159■	10.02.01	075.264-010	2900
Nursery School Attendant (See Preschool Worker)								

Occupation	World-of-Work Map[a]		Job Descriptions, OOH[b]			Government ID Numbers[c]		
	JF	Region	96/97	94/95	92/93	GOE	DOT	SOC
Nursing/Psychiatric Aide	T	12	316	311	292	10.03.02	355.377-014	5236
Occupational Therapist	T	12	166	168	152	10.02.02	076.121-010	3032
Oceanographer	O	9	109	108	95	02.01.01	024.061-018	1847
Office Machine Operator	F	5	294	292	273	07.06.02	214.482-010	4718
Office Machine Servicer	K	6	353	346	326	05.05.09	633.281-018	6174
Office Manager	B	3	260	259	242	07.01.02	169.167-034	1370
Operations Research Analyst	O	9	97	96	84	11.01.01	020.067-018	1721
Ophthalmic Lab Technician	N	7	440	431	410	06.02.08	716.382-018	6864
Optician	N	7	203	206	188	05.05.11	299.361-010	4490
Optometric Assistant	T	12	158	160	144	10.03.02	079.364-014	3690
Optometrist	N	7	158	160	144	02.03.04	079.101-018	2810
Orchestra Conductor	R	10	197	200	183	01.04.01	152.047-014	3230
Orchestra Leader (See Orchestra Conductor)								
Order Clerk	C	3	285	283	265	07.05.03	249.362-026	4664
Osteopathic Physician	T	12	160	161	145	02.03.01	071.101-010	2610
Painter (artist) (See Artist)								
Painter (construction)	H	6	389	380	360	05.10.07	840.381-010	6442
Paper Hanger	H	6	389	380	360	05.05.04	841.381-010	6443
Parking Lot Attendant	W	2	460	450	426	09.04.02	915.473-010	8740
Parole Office	V	1	132	136	119	10.01.02	195.107-046	2032
Pathologist	O	9	160	161	145	02.03.01	070.061-010	2610
Patternmaker	L	6	435	427	406	05.05.07	600.280-050	6817
Payroll Clerk	D	4	287	284	266	07.02.05	215.382-014	4713
Pediatrician	T	12	160	161	145	02.03.01	070.101-066	2610
Personnel Assistant (See Human Resources Assistant)								
Personnel Clerk (See Human Resources Clerk)								
Personnel Manager (See Human Resources Manager)								
Personnel Recruiter (See Human Resources Recruiter)								
Pest Controller	I	6	471	460	435	05.10.09	389.684-010	5246
Petroleum Engineer	M	8	84	83	71	05.01.08	010.061-018	1625
Pharmacist	N	7	168	169	153	02.04.01	074.161-010	3010
Pharmacologist	O	9	103	102	89	02.02.01	041.061-074	1855
Photoengraver (See Photoengraver/ Lithographer)								
Photoengraver/ Lithographer	L	6	425	415	394	01.06.01	971.381-022	6842

(continued)

Occupation	World-of-Work Map[a]		Job Descriptions, OOH[b]			Government ID Numbers[c]		
	JF	Region	96/97	94/95	92/93	GOE	DOT	SOC
Photograph Retoucher	Q	10	444	434	413	01.06.03	970.281-018	6868
Photographer	Q	10	189	191	175	01.02.03	143.062-030	3260
Photographer/Camera Operator (See Photographer)								
Photographic Process Worker	Q	10	444	434	413	06.03.02	976.687-018	4753
Physical Therapist	T	12	169	171	155	10.02.02	076.121-014	3033
Physical Therapist Assistant	T	12	169■	171■	155■	10.02.02	076.224-010	5233
Physician	T	12	160	161	145	02.03.01	070.101-022	2610
Physician Assistant	T	12	171	173	157	10.02.01	079.364-018	3040
Physicist	O	9	133	111	98	02.01.01	023.061-014	1843
Physiologist	O	9	103	102	89	02.02.03	041.061-078	1854
Pipefitter	H	6	392	383	363	05.05.03	862.281-022	6450
Plant Scientist	O	9	101	100	88	02.02.02	041.061-086	1854
Plasterer	H	6	390	382	361	05.05.04	842.361-018	6444
Plumber	H	6	392	383	363	05.05.03	862.381-030	6450
Podiatrist	N	7	162	163	147	02.03.01	079.101-022	2830
Police Officer	V	1	303	301	281	04.01.02	375.263-014	5132
Political Scientist	P	10	119	119	106	11.03.02	051.067-010	1914
Pollution-Control Technician	M	8	231■	233■	215■	05.03.08	029.261-014	3890
Porter	W	2	471	459	434■	09.05.03	357.677-010	5262
Postal Clerk	C	3	277	275	258	07.03.01	243.367-014	4742
Postmaster	B	3	44■	40■	34■	11.05.03	188.167-066	1344
Power House Mechanic	L	6	—	—	—	05.05.09	631.261-014	6130
Power Plant Operator	L	6	418	410	389	05.06.01	952.382-018	6932
Preschool Worker	U	1	321	317	304	10.03.03	359.677-018	5264
Priest	T	12	137	140	126	10.01.01	120.107-010	2042
Printing Press Operator	L	6	428	417	396	05.05.13	651.482-010	7443
Private Household Worker	W	2	328	325	306	05.12.18	301.474-010	5070
Product Demonstrator	A	2	245■	244■	228■	08.02.05	297.354-010	4450
Production Manager (industry)	B	3	52	80■	69■	05.01.06	012.167-050	1634
Production Planner (See Production Manager (industry))								
Professional Athlete	V	1	469	458	433	12.01.03	153.341-010	3400
Proofreader	S	11	470	459	434■	07.05.02	209.387-030	4792
Property Manager	B	3	66	62	53	05.02.02	187.167-190	1353
Prosthetist/Orthotist	N	7	—	—	—	05.05.11	078.261-022	3690
Psychiatrist	T	12	160■	161■	145■	02.03.01	070.107-014	2610
Psychologist	V	1	124	124	110	10.01.02	045.107-026	1915
Public Relations Specialist	S	11	179	182	166	11.09.03	165.167-014	3320
Purchaser	B	3	69	65	56	11.05.04	162.157-038	1449
Purchasing Agent (See Purchaser)								

Occupation	World-of-Work Map[a]		Job Descriptions, OOH[b]			Government ID Numbers[c]		
	JF	Region	96/97	94/95	92/93	GOE	DOT	SOC
Quality Control Technician	M	8	—	—	—	02.04.01	012.261-014	3712
Rabbi	T	12	136	139	125	10.01.01	120.107-010	2042
Radiation Therapy Technologist	N	7	212	214	198	10.02.02	078.361-034	3650
Radio/TV Announcer/ Newscaster	S	11	181	184	167	01.03.03	159.147-010	3330
Radio/TV Engineer	M	8	76■	75■	68	05.01.08	003.061-030	1633
Radio/TV Program Writer	S	11	184	187	171	01.01.02	131.067-050	3210
Radio/TV, Etc. Repairer	K	6	354	347	327	05.10.03	720.281-018	6155
Radiographer	N	7	212	214	198	10.02.02	078.362-026	3650
Radiologist	N	7	160	161	145	02.03.01	070.101-090	2610
Railroad Braker	G	6	450	440	419	09.01.04	910.364-010	8233
Railroad Conductor	E	4	450	440	419	11.11.03	198.167-018	8113
Range Manager	O	9	105	104	91	02.02.02	040.061-046	1852
Real Estate Agent	A	2	240	241	225	11.12.02	186.117-058	1353
Real Estate Appraiser	D	4	540	241	225	11.06.03	191.267-010	4123
Receptionist/Information Clerk	C	3	268	267	250	07.04.04	237.367-038	4645
Recreation Leader	V	1	130	133	121	09.01.01	195.227-014	2033
Recreation Therapist	T	12	172	174	158	10.02.02	076.124-014	3049
Refuse Collector	G	6	460	450	426	05.12.03	955.687-022	8722
Reporter Correspondent	S	11	182	185	169	11.08.02	131.262-018	3313
Reservations Agent	D	4	269	268	250	07.04.03	238.367-018	4644
Residence Hall Director (See Residential Counselor)								
Residential Counselor	U	1	469	149■	133■	10.01.02	045.107-038	2400
Respiratory Therapist	N	7	176	178	162	10.02.02	076.361-014	3031
Restaurant/Bar Manager	B	3	72	68	58	11.11.04	187.167-106	1351
Retail Store Manager	B	3	243	70	34■	11.11.05	185.167-046	4030
Robot Technician	M	8	226	228	210■	05.05.09	638.261-026	6178
Roller	L	6	412	404■	381■	06.02.10	613.362-014	7516
Roofer	H	6	394	385	365	05.10.01	866.381-010	6468
Roustabout	L	6	472	386	366	05.10.01	869.684-046	6560
Safety Engineer	M	8	76■	75■	64■	05.01.02	012.061-014	1634
Sailor	L	6	458	447	424	05.12.18	911.687-030	8243
Sales Manager	A	2	60	56	48	11.05.04	163.167-018	1250
Sales Worker (retail)	A	2	245	244	228	08.02.03	279.357-054	4359
Sample Distributor	A	2	—	—	—	07.07.02	230.687-010	8769
Sanitarian (See Environmental Health Inspector)								
Science Technician	M	8	231	233	215	02.04.02	041.381-010	3820
Secretary	C	3	286	286	267	07.01.03	201.362-030	4622
Securities Sales Agent	A	2	247	246	229	11.06.04	250.257-018	4124

(continued)

Occupation	World-of-Work Map[a]		Job Descriptions, OOH[b]			Government ID Numbers[c]		
	JF	Region	96/97	94/95	92/93	GOE	DOT	SOC
Security Officer	V	1	301	299	279	04.02.02	372.667-034	5144
Security System Installer	H	6	383■	375■	—	05.05.05	822.361-018	6432
Services Sales Representative	A	2	249	248	232	08.02.06	251.357-010	4152
Sewing Machine Operator	L	6	429	421	400	06.02.05	787.682-046	7655
Sheet-Metal Worker	H	6	395	388	367	05.05.06	804.281-010	6824
Ship Captain	G	6	458	447	424	05.04.02	197.167-010	8241
Shipping/Receiving Clerk	E	4	276	274	257	05.09.01	222.387-050	4753
Shoe Repairer	J	6	432	423	402	05.05.15	365.361-014	6854
Singer	R	10	197	200	183	01.04.03	152.047-022	3230
Social Worker	V	1	132	136	119	10.01.02	195.107-010	2032
Sociologist	P	10	132	126	113	11.03.02	054.067-014	1916
Soil Conservationist	O	9	105	104	91	02.02.02	040.061-054	1852
Solar Energy Engineer	M	8	76■	75■	64■	05.03.07	007.161-038	1635
Sonographer	N	7	212	214	198	02.04.01	078.364-010	3690
Speech-Language Pathologist	T	12	177	179	163	02.03.04	076.107-010	3034
Sports Physician	T	12	160■	161■	145■	02.03.01	070.101-022	2610
Sports/Athletics Manager	B	3	44■	40■	34■	11.12.03	153.117-014	34
Stage Technician	Q	10	377■	369■	349■	05.10.04	962.261-014	6179
Stationary Engineer	L	6	420	411	390	05.06.02	950.382-026	6931
Statistical Clerk	F	5	470	459	434■	07.02.03	216.382-062	4794
Statistician	O	9	99	98	85	11.01.02	020.167-026	1733
Stenographer	C	3	289	287	269	07.05.03	202.362-014	4623
Stock Clerk	E	4	275	273	256	05.09.01	222.387-058	4754
Store Detective	V	1	303■	301■	281■	04.02.02	376.367-014	5144
Store Manager (See Retail Store Manager)								
Structural Steel Worker	H	6	397	389	369	05.05.06	801.361-014	6473
Stunt Performer	R	10	193	197	180	12.02.01	159.341-014	3280
Supermarket Manager	B	3	243	70	34■	11.11.05	185.167-046	4030
Surgeon	N	7	160	161	145	02.03.01	070.101-094	2610
Surgical Technologist	N	7	214	216	200	10.03.02	079.374-22	3690
Surveyor Helper (See Surveyor Technician)								
Surveyor (land)	M	8	89	87	76	05.01.06	018.167-018	1643
Surveyor Technician	M	8	89	87	76	05.12.02	869.567-010	8646
Tailor/Dressmaker	J	6	429	421	400	05.05.15	785.261-014	6852
Tax Accountant	D	4	21■	17■	15■	11.06.01	160.162-010	1412
Taxicab Driver	G	6	453	442	439	09.03.02	913.463-018	8216
Teacher (adult/vocational) (See Teacher (adult education))								
Teacher (adult education)	U	1	138	143	128	11.02.01	099.227-030	2390
Teacher (art/drama/ music/speech)	R	10	150■	153■	138■	01.02.01	149.021-010	2390

Occupation	World-of-Work Map[a]		Job Descriptions, OOH[b]			Government ID Numbers[c]		
	JF	Region	96/97	94/95	92/93	GOE	DOT	SOC
Teacher (business)	U	1	150	153	138	11.02.01	091.227-010	2330
Teacher (elementary)	U	1	150	153	135	11.02.01	092.227-010	2320
Teacher (industrial arts) (See Teacher (vocational/technical))								
Teacher (kindergarten)	U	1	150	153	304	10.02.03	092.227-014	2310
Teacher (physical education)	U	1	150	153	138	11.02.01	099.224-010	2390
Teacher (preschool/ kindergarten) (See Teacher (kindergarten))								
Teacher (secondary)	U	1	150	153	138	11.02.01	091.227-010	2330
Teacher (special education)	U	1	153	153	138	10.02.03	094.227-010	2350
Teacher (vocational agriculture)	U	1	138	143	128	11.02.02	097.221-010	2390
Teacher (vocational/ technical)	U	1	150	153	138	11.02.02	097.221-010	2390
Teacher Aide	U	1	291	289	271	07.01.02	099.327-010	3990
Technical Illustrator	M	8	224	226	209	05.03.02	017.281-034	3720
Technical Writer	S	11	184	187	171	11.08.02	131.267-026	3980
Telephone Installer/ Repairer	K	6	354	347	328	05.05.05	822.281-018	6158
Telephone Operator	F	5	293	290	272	07.04.06	235.662-022	4732
Test Engineer (See Nondestructive Tester)								
Textile Machine Operator	L	6	433	424	403	06.02.06	683.000-000	765
Textile Technician	M	8	433	424	403	05.01.08	040.061-026	3820
Ticket Agent	D	4	269	268	250	07.03.01	238.367-026	4644
Tilesetter	H	6	398	391	370	05.05.01	861.381-054	6414
Time Study Analyst	M	8	81	80	69	05.03.06	012.267-010	3712
Title Examiner/Searcher	C	3	470	458	434	07.01.05	119.287-010	396
Tool and Die Maker	L	6	415	406	385	05.05.07	601.260-010	6811
Tool Designer	M	8	82	80	69	05.01.07	007.061-026	1635
Track Worker (railroad)	H	6	450	440	419	05.12.12	910.684-014	6467
Traffic Manager	E	4	469	458	433	11.05.02	184.167-094	1342
Training/Education Manager	B	3	63	59	50	11.07.03	166.167-026	1230
Travel Agent	A	2	251	250	234	08.02.06	252.152-010	4369
Travel Clerk	C	3	269	268	250	07.05.01	238.362-014	4644
Travel Guide	A	2	251	250	234	07.05.01	252.152-010	4369
Tree Surgeon (arborist)	I	6	339	321	300	03.01.03	408.181-010	3820
Truck Driver (tractor trailer)	G	6	455	444	421	05.08.01	904.383-010	8212
TV Production Director	S	11	193	197	180	11.05.02	184.167-030	3240
Typist	F	5	294	292	273	07.06.02	203.582-066	4624

(continued)

Occupation	World-of-Work Map[a]		Job Descriptions, OOH[b]			Government ID Numbers[c]		
	JF	Region	96/97	94/95	92/93	GOE	DOT	SOC
Upholsterer	J	6	435	426	405	05.05.15	780.381-018	6853
Urban Planner	B	3	126	129	115	11.03.02	199.167-014	1920
Vending Machine Mechanic	K	6	373	366	346	05.10.02	639.281-014	6179
Veterinarian	N	7	163	165	149	02.03.03	073.101-010	2700
Waiter/Waitress	W	2	311	306	287	09.04.01	311.477-030	5213
Warehouse Supervisor	E	4	218	394	373	05.09.01	929.137-022	7100
Warehouse Worker	E	4	402	450	256	05.09.01	922.687-058	8769
Watch Repairer	J	6	473	461	436	05.05.11	715.281-010	6171
Water Plant Operator	L	6	421	413	391	05.06.04	955.362-010	6910
Weather Observer	M	8	231	233	215	02.04.01	025.267-014	3890
Weight Reduction Specialist	W	2	—	—	—	09.05.01	359.367-014	5269
Welder	L	6	417	408	387	05.05.06	811.684-014	7714
Welfare Eligibility Worker	V	1	254	253	236	07.01.01	195.267-010	4784
Wire Drawer	L	6	—	—	—	06.02.02	614.382-010	7315
Woodworker	L	6	436	427	406	05.05.08	669.380-014	6832
Word Processor Operator	F	5	294	292	272	07.06.02	203.382-030	4624
Writer/Author	R	10	184	187	171	01.01.02	131.067-046	3210
Zoologist	O	9	103	102	89	02.02.01	041.061-090	1854

APPENDIX *B*

WELLNESS LOG

Overboard, © 1993 Dunham. Dist. by Universal Press Syndicate.
Reprinted with permission. All rights reserved.

The wellness log is meant to stimulate your thinking about your daily wellness activities. At the end of each day, record the activities you engaged in that promoted your personal wellness. For example, if you jogged a mile on Sunday, record that in the "Physical" activity box for that day. Do the same for the other days of the week.

At the end of each week, review your activities to see which areas you're doing well in and which you want to improve. For the latter, try to develop an action plan for making the changes you desire. For example, if you want to cut back on fatty foods, what steps can you take toward your goal? What can you do on your own to make that change? Can other people help you as well? If so, how? How will you know that you've successfully completed your goal (i.e., keeping a log of fatty-food consumption, losing 5 pounds, and so forth)?

Wellness Log   **Week of** _____

Briefly describe the wellness activities you engaged in each day of the week.

	Sunday	Monday	Tuesday	Wednesday	Thursday	Friday	Saturday
Physical							
Social							
Emotional							
Intellectual							
Spiritual							
Occupational							

ADDITIONAL SOURCES OF CAREER INFORMATION

"Oh ya? Well my dad knows more about insider trading than your dad."

STATE AND LOCAL INFORMATION
FROM THE OCCUPATIONAL OUTLOOK HANDBOOK

The *Handbook* provides information for the nation as a whole. For help in locating state or local area information, you may contact the following:

State Occupational Information Coordinating Committee (SOICC)   These committees provide the information directly, or refer you to other sources. The addresses and telephone numbers of the directors of SOICCs are listed below.

State employment security agencies   These agencies develop detailed information about local labor markets, such as current and projected employment by occupation and industry, characteristics of the workforce, and changes in state and local area economic activity. Addresses and telephone numbers of the directors of research and analysis in these agencies are listed below.

Most states have career information delivery systems (CIDS). Look for these systems in secondary schools, postsecondary institutions, libraries, job-training sites, vocational rehabilitation centers, and employment service offices. Job seekers can use the systems' computers, printed material, microfiche, and toll-free hotlines to obtain information on occupations, educational opportunities, student financial aid, apprenticeships, and military careers. Ask counselors and SOICCs for specific locations.

A computerized State Training Inventory (STI) developed by the National Occupational Information Coordinating Committee (NOICC) is also maintained by the SOICCs and available in every state. Education and training data are organized by occupation or training program title, type of institution, and geographic area. The database is compiled at the state level and includes more than 215,000 education and training programs offered by over 17,000 schools, colleges, and hospitals. If you are interested in STI, contact individual SOICCs for state-specific data.

Alabama

Director, Labor Market Information. Alabama Department of Industrial Relations, 649 Monroe St., Room 422, Montgomery, AL 36130. Phone: (205) 242-8855.

Source: U.S. Department of Labor, *Occupational outlook handbook,* pp. 10–13. Lincolnwood, IL: VGM Career Horizons.

Director, Alabama Occupational Information Coordinating Committee, Room 424, 401 Adams Ave., P.O. Box 5690, Montgomery, AL 36103-5690. Phone: (334) 242-2990.

Alaska

Chief, Research and Analysis, Alaska Department of Labor, P.O. Box 25501, Juneau, AK 99802-5501. Phone: (907) 465-6022.

Executive Director, Alaska Department of Labor, Research and Analysis. P.O. Box 25501, Juneau, AK 99802-5501. Phone: (907) 465-4518

American Samoa

Statistical Analyst, Research and Statistics, Office of Manpower Resources, American Samoa Government, Pago Pago, AS 96799. Phone: (684) 633-5172.

Director, Occupational Information Coordinating Council, Department of Human Resources, American Samoa Government, Pago Pago, AS 96799. Phone: (684) 633-4485.

Arizona

Research Administrator, Department of Economic Security, P.O. Box 6123, Site Code 733A, Phoenix, AZ 85005. Phone: (602) 542-3871.

Executive Director. Occupational Information Coordinating Council, P.O. Box 6123, Site Code 733A, 1789 West Jefferson St., First Floor, Phoenix, AZ 85005-6123. Phone: (602) 542-3871.

Arkansas

Chief, Arkansas Employment Security Department, P.O. Box 2981, Little Rock, AR 72203. Phone: (501) 682-3159.

Executive Director. Occupational Information Coordinating Council, Arkansas Employment Security Division, Employment and Training Services, P.O. Box 2981, Little Rock, AR 72203-2981. Phone: (501) 682-3159.

California

Chief, Labor Market Information Division, Employment Development Department, 700 Franklin Blvd., Suite 1100, Sacramento, CA 94280-0001. Phone: (916) 262-2160.

Executive Director. Occupational Information Coordinating Council, 1116 9th St. Lower Level, P.O. Box 944222, Sacramento, CA 94244-2220. Phone: (916) 323-6544.

Colorado

Director, Colorado Department of Labor, Tower 2, Suite 400, 1515 Arapahoe St., Denver, CO 80202-2117. Phone: (303) 620-4977.

Director, Occupational Information Coordinating Council, State Board Community College, 1391 Speer Blvd., Suite 600, Denver, CO 80204-2554. Phone: (303) 866-4488.

Connecticut

Director of Research, State Labor Department, 200 Folly Brook Blvd., Wethersfield, CT 06109. Phone: (203) 566-2120.

Executive Director, Occupational Information Coordinating Council, Connecticut Department of Education, 25 Industrial Park Rd., Middletown, CT 06457-1543. Phone: (203) 638-4042.

Delaware

Chief, Delaware Department of Labor, University Plaza, Building D, P.O. Box 9029, Newark, DE 19714. Phone: (302) 368-6962.

Executive Director, Office of Occupational and Labor Market Information, University Office Plaza, P.O. Box 9029, Newark, DE 19714-9029. Phone: (302) 368-6963.

District of Columbia

Chief, Labor Market Information, District of Columbia Department of Employment Services, 500 C St. NW, Room 201, Washington, DC 90001. Phone: (202) 724-7214.

Executive Director, Occupational Information Coordinating Council, Department of Employment Services, 500 C St. NW, Room 215, Washington, DC 20001-2187. Phone: (202) 724-7237.

Florida

Chief, Florida Department of Labor and Employment Security, 2012 Capitol Circle SE, Room 200 Hartman Bldg., Tallahassee, FL 32399-0674. Phone: (904) 488-1048.

Manager, Bureau of Labor Market Information/Department of Labor and Employment Security, 2012 Capitol Circle SE, Hartman Bldg., Suite 200, Tallahassee, FL 32399-0673. Phone: (904) 488-1048.

Georgia

Director, Labor Information Systems, Georgia Department of Labor, 223 Courtland St. NE, Atlanta, GA 30303-1751. Phone: (404) 656-3177.

Executive Director, Occupational Information Coordinating Council, Department of Labor, 148 International Blvd., Sussex Place, Atlanta, GA 30303-1751. Phone: (404) 656-9639.

Guam

Administrator, Department of Labor, Bureau of Labor Statistics, Government of Guam, P.O. Box 9970, Tamuning, GU 96911-9970.

Executive Director, Human Resources Development Agency, Jay East Blvd., Third Floor, P.O. Box 2817, Agana, GU 96910-2817. Phone: (671) 646-9341.

Hawaii

Chief, Department of Labor and Industrial Relations, 830 Punchbowl St., Rm. 304, Honolulu, HI 96813. Phone: (808) 586-8999.

Executive Director, Occupational Information Coordinating Council, 830 Punchbowl St., Room 315, Honolulu, HI 96813-5080. Phone: (808) 586-8750.

Idaho

Chief, Research and Analysis, Idaho Department of Employment, 317 Main St., Boise, ID 83735. Phone: (208) 334-6169.

Director, Occupational Information Coordinating Council, Len B. Jordan Bldg., Room 301, 650 West State St., P.O. Box 83720, Boise, ID 83720-0095. Phone: (208) 334-3705.

Illinois

Director, Illinois Department of Employment Security, 401 South State St., Suite 215, Chicago, IL 60605. Phone: (312) 793-2316.

Executive Director, Occupational Information Coordinating Council, 217 East Monroe, Suite 203, Springfield, IL 62706-1147. Phone: (217) 785-0789.

Indiana

Director, Labor Market Information, Department of Employment and Training Services, 10 North Senate Ave., Indianapolis, IN 46204. Phone: (317) 232-7460.

Executive Director, Department of Workforce Development, State Occupational Information Coordinating Committee, Indiana Government Center South, 10 North Senate Ave., Room SE 405, Indianapolis, IN 46204-2277. Phone: (317) 232-8528.

Iowa

Chief, Iowa Department of Employment Services, 1000 East Grand Ave., Des Moines, IA 50316. Phone: (515) 281-8181.

Acting Executive Director, Occupational Information Coordinating Council, Iowa Department of Economic Development, 200 East Grand Ave., Des Moines, IA 50309-1747. Phone: (515) 242-4889.

Kansas

Chief, Labor Market Information, Kansas Department of Human Resources, 401 Topeka Blvd., Topeka, KS 66603-3182. Phone: (913) 296-5058.

Director, State Occupational Information Coordinating Committee, 401 Topeka Ave., Topeka, KS 66603-3182. Phone: (913) 296-2387.

Kentucky

Director, Labor Market Research and Analysis, Department of Employment Services, 275 East Main St., Frankfort, KY 40621. Phone: (502) 564-7976.

Information Liaison/Manager, Occupational Information Coordinating Council, 2031 Capital Plaza Tower, Frankfort, KY 40601. Phone: (502) 564-4258.

Louisiana

Director, Research and Statistics Division, Department of Employment and Training, P.O. Box 94094, Baton Rouge, LA 70804-9094. Phone: (504) 342-3141.

Acting Director, Louisiana Occupational Information Coordinating Committee, 1001 North 23rd, Baton Rouge, LA 70802. Phone: (504) 342-5149.

Maine

Director, Economic Analysis and Research, Maine Department of Labor, P.O. Box 309, Augusta, ME 04330-0309. Phone: (207) 287-2271.

Acting Executive Director, Maine Occupational Information Coordinating Committee, State House Station 71, Augusta, ME 04333. Phone: (207) 624-6200.

Maryland

Director, Office of Labor Market Analysis and Information, Department of Labor, Licensing, and Regulations, 1100 North Eutaw St., Room 601, Baltimore, MD 21201. Phone: (410) 767-2250.

Director, Occupational Information Coordinating Council, State Department of Employment and Training, 1100 North Eutaw St., Room 103, Baltimore, MD 21201-2298. Phone: (410) 767-2951.

Massachusetts

Director of Research, Division of Employment Security, 19 Staniford St., 2nd Floor, Boston, MA 02114. Phone: (617) 626-6556.

Director, Occupational Information Coordinating Council, Massachusetts Division of Employment Security, Charles F. Hurley Bldg., 2nd Floor, Government Center, Boston, MA 02114. Phone: (617) 727-5718.

Michigan

Director, Bureau of Research and Statistics, Michigan Employment Security Commission, 7310 Woodward Ave., Room 510, Detroit, MI 48202. Phone: (313) 876-5904.

Executive Coordinator, Michigan Occupational Information Coordinating Committee, Victor Office Center, Third Floor, 201 North Washington Square, Box 30015, Lansing, MI 48909-7515. Phone: (517) 373-0363.

Minnesota

Director, Research and Statistical Services, Minnesota Department of Economic Security, 390 North Robert St., 5th Floor, St. Paul, MN 55101. Phone: (612) 296-6546.

Director, Occupational Information Coordinating Council, Department of Jobs and Training, 390 North Robert Street, St. Paul MN 55101. Phone: (612) 296-2072.

Mississippi

Chief, Labor Market Information Department, Mississippi Employment Security Commission, P.O. Box 1699, Jackson, MS 39215-1699. Phone: (601) 961-7424.

Director, Department of Economic and Community Development, Labor Assistance Division/State Occupational Information Coordinating Committee Office, 301 West Pearl St., Jackson, MS 39203-3089. Phone: (601) 949-2240.

Missouri

Chief, Research and Analysis, Division of Employment Security, 421 East Dunkin St., P.O. Box 59, Jefferson City, MO 65104-0059. Phone: (314) 751-3591.

Director, Missouri Occupational Information Coordinating Committee, 400 Dix Rd., Jefferson City, MO 65109. Phone: (314) 751-3800.

Montana

Chief, Research and Analysis, Department of Labor and Industry, P.O. Box 1728, Helena, MT 59624. Phone: (406) 444-2430.

Program Manager, Montana Occupational Information Coordinating Committee, P.O. Box 1728, 1327 Lockey St., Second Floor, Helena, MT 59624-1728. Phone: (406) 444-2741.

Nebraska

Research Administrator, Labor Market Information, Nebraska Department of Labor, 550 South 16th St., P.O. Box 94600, Lincoln, NE 68509. Phone: (402) 471-2600.

Administrator, Nebraska Occupational Information Coordinating Committee, P.O. Box 94600, 550 South 16th St., Lincoln, NE 68509-4600. Phone: (402) 471-9953.

Nevada

Chief, Research and Analysis/LMI, Nevada Employment Security Division, 500 East 3rd St., Carson City, NV 89713-0001. Phone: (702) 687-4550.

Director, Nevada Occupational Information Coordinating Committee, 500 East 3rd St., Carson City, NV 89713. Phone: (702) 687-4550.

New Hampshire

Director, Labor Market Information, New Hampshire Department of Employment Security, 32 South Main St., Concord, NH 03301. Phone: (603) 228-4123.

Director, New Hampshire State Occupational Information Coordinating Committee, 64B Old Suncook Rd., Concord, NH 03301. Phone: (603) 228-3349.

New Jersey

Director, Labor Market and Demographic Research, New Jersey Department of Labor, CN383, Trenton, NJ 08625. Phone: (609) 292-0089.

Staff Director, New Jersey Occupational Information Coordinating Committee, Room 609, Labor and Industry Bldg., CN056, Trenton, NJ 08625-0056. Phone: (609) 292-2682.

New Mexico

Chief, Economic Research and Analysis Bureau, New Mexico Department of Labor, P.O. Box 1928, Albuquerque, NM 87103. Phone: (505) 841-8645.

Director, New Mexico Occupational Information Coordinating Committee, 401 Broadway NE., Tiwa Bldg., P.O. Box 1928, Albuquerque, NM 87103-1928. Phone: (505) 841-8455.

New York

Director, Division of Research and Statistics, New York State Department of Labor, State Office Building Campus, Bldg. 12, Room 402, Albany, NY 12240. Phone: (518) 457-6369.

Executive Director, New York Occupational Information Committee, Research and Statistics Division, State Campus, Bldg. 12, Room 400, Albany, NY 12240. Phone: (518) 457-6182.

North Carolina

Director, Labor Market Information, Employment Security Commission of North Carolina, P.O. Box 25903, Raleigh, NC 27611. Phone: (919) 733-2936.

Executive Director, North Carolina Occupational Information Coordinating Committee, 700 Wade Avenue, P.O. Box 25903, Raleigh, NC 27611. Phone: (919) 733-6700.

North Dakota

Director, Research and Statistics, Job Service of North Dakota, P.O. Box 5507, Bismarck, ND 58502-5507. Phone: (701) 328-2860.

Coordinator, North Dakota State Occupational Information Coordinating Committee, 1720 Burnt Boat Dr., P.O. Box 1537, Bismarck, ND 58502-1537. Phone: (701) 328-2733.

Northern Mariana Islands

Executive Director, Northern Mariana Islands Occupational Information Coordinating Committee, P.O. Box 149, Saipan, CM 96950-0149. Phone: (670) 234-7394.

Ohio

Administrator, Labor Market Information Division, Ohio Bureau of Employment Services, 78-80 Chestnut, Columbus, OH 43215. Phone: (614) 752-9494.

Director, Ohio Occupational Information Coordinating Committee, Ohio Bureau of Employment Services, P.O. Box 1618, Columbus, OH 43266-0018. Phone: (614) 466-1109.

Oklahoma

Director, Research Division, Oklahoma Employment Security Commission, 305 Will Rogers Memorial Office Bldg., Oklahoma City, OK 73105. Phone: (405) 557-7265.

Executive Director, Occupational Information Coordinating Council, Department of Voc/Tech Education, 1500 W. 7th Ave., Stillwater, OK 74074-4364. Phone: (405) 743-5198.

Oregon

Administrator for Research, Tax and Analysis, Employment Department, 875 Union St. NE, Salem, OR 97311. Phone: (503) 378-5490.

Acting Director, Oregon Occupational Information Coordinating Committee, 875 Union St. NE, Salem, OR 97311-0101. Phone: (503) 378-5490.

Pennsylvania

Director, Bureau of Research and Statistics, Department of Labor and Industry, 300 Capitol Associates Building, 3rd Floor, Harrisburg, PA 17120-9969. Phone: (717) 787-3266.

Director, Pennsylvania Department of Labor and Industry. 1224 Labor and Industry Bldg., 7th and Foster, Harrisburg, PA 17120-0019. Phone: (717) 787-8646.

Puerto Rico

Director, Research and Statistics Division, Department of Labor and Human Resources, 505 Munoz Rivera Ave., 20th Floor, Hato Rey, PR 00918. Phone: (809) 754-5385.

Director, Puerto Rico Occupational Information Coordinating Committee, P.O. Box 366212, San Juan, PR 00936-6212. Phone: (809) 723-7110.

Rhode Island

Administrator, Labor Market Information, Rhode Island Department of Employment and Training, 101 Friendship St., Providence, RI 02903. Phone: (401) 277-2731.

Director, Rhode Island Occupational Information Coordinating Committee, 22 Hayes St., Room 133, Providence, RI 02908-5092. Phone: (401) 272-0830.

South Carolina

Director, Labor Market Information, South Carolina Employment Security Commission, P.O. Box 995, Columbia, SC 29202. Phone: (803) 737-2660.

Director, South Carolina Occupational Information Coordinating Committee, 1550 Gadsden St., P.O. Box 995, Columbia, SC 29202-0995. Phone: (803) 737-2733.

South Dakota

Director, Labor Information Center, South Dakota Department of Labor, 400 S. Roosevelt, P.O. Box 4730, Aberdeen, SD 57402-4730. Phone: (605) 626-2314.

Director, Occupational Information Coordinating Council, South Dakota Department of Labor, 420 South Roosevelt St., P.O. Box 4730, Aberdeen, SD 57402-4730. Phone: (605) 626-2314.

Tennessee

Director, Research and Statistics Division, Tennessee Department of Employment Security, 500 James Robertson Pkwy., 11th Floor-Volunteer Plaza, Nashville, TN 37245-1000. Phone: (615) 741-2284.

Executive Director, Tennessee Occupational Information Coordinating Committee, 500 James Robertson Pkwy., 11th Floor-Volunteer Plaza, Nashville, TN 37219-1215. Phone: (615) 741-6451.

Texas

Director, Economic Research and Analysis, Texas Employment Commission, 15th & Congress Ave., Room 208T, Austin TX 78778. Phone: (512) 463-2616.

Director, Texas Occupational Information Coordinating Committee, Texas Employment Commission Building, 3520 Executive Center Dr., Suite 205, Austin, TX 78731-0000. Phone: (512) 502-3750.

Utah

Director, LMI & Research, Utah Department of Employment Security, P.O. Box 45249, Salt Lake City, UT 84145-0249. Phone: (801) 536-7425.

Executive Director, Utah Occupational Information Coordinating Committee, P.O. Box 45249, 140 East 300 South, Salt Lake City, UT 84145-0249. Phone: (801) 536-7806.

Vermont

Director, Policy and Information, Vermont Department of Employment and Training, P.O. Box 488, Montpelier, VT 05602. Phone: (802) 828-4135.

Director, Vermont Occupational Information Coordinating Committee, 5 Green Mountain Dr., P.O. Box 488, Montpelier, VT 05601-0488. Phone: (802) 229-0311.

Virginia

Director, Economic Information and Services Division, Virginia Employment Commission, P.O. Box 1358, Richmond, VA 23211. Phone: (804) 786-7496.

Executive Director, Virginia Occupational Information Coordinating Committee, Virginia Employment Commission, 703 East Main St., P.O. Box 1358, Richmond, VA 23211-1358. Phone: (804) 786-7496.

Virgin Islands

Chief, Bureau of Labor Statistics, Virgin Islands Department of Labor, 53A and 54B Kronprindsens Gade, Charlotte Amalie, St. Thomas, U.S. Virgin Islands 00820. Phone: (809) 776-3700.

Coordinator, Virgin Islands Occupational Information Coordinating Committee, P.O. Box 3359, St. Thomas, U.S. Virgin Islands 00801. Phone: (809) 776-3700.

Washington

Chief, Labor and Economic Analysis, Washington Employment Security Department, P.O. Box 9046, Olympia, WA 98507-9046. Phone: (360) 438-4804.

Acting Executive Director, Washington Occupational Information Coordinating Committee, c/o Employment Security Department, P.O. Box 9046, Olympia, WA 98507-9046. Phone: (206) 438-4803.

West Virginia

Assistant Director, Labor and Economic Research, Bureau of Employment Programs, 112 California Ave., Charleston, WV 25305-0112. Phone: (304) 558-2660.

Executive Director, West Virginia Occupational Information Coordinating Committee, 5088 Washington St. West, Cross Lanes, WV 25313. Phone: (304) 759-0724.

Wisconsin

Director, Bureau of Labor Market Information, Department of Industry, Labor, and Human Relations, P.O. Box 7944, Madison, WI 53707. Phone: (608) 266-5843.

Administrative Director, Wisconsin Occupational Information Coordinating Council, Division of Jobs, Employment and Training Services, 201 East Washington Ave., P.O. Box 7972, Madison, WI 53707-7972. Phone: (608) 266-8012.

Wyoming

Manager, Research and Planning, Division of Administration, Department of Employment, P.O. Box 2760, Casper, WY 82602-2760. Phone: (307) 473-3801.

Executive Director, Wyoming Occupational Information Coordinating Council, Post Office Box 2760, 100 West Midwest, Casper, WY 82602-2760. Phone: (307) 265-6715.

FACTORS AFFECTING THE UTILIZATION OF OCCUPATIONS WITHIN INDUSTRIES

Occupation	Factor
Accountants and auditors	Small decreases in accounting services result from increasing use of clerk-operated computers to generate routine reports.
Actuaries	Small decreases are expected due to continuing insurance industry downsizing, mergers, and acquisition activity.
Adjustment clerks	Increasing emphasis on customer service to resolve customer billing problems will cause a moderate to significant increase in utilization.
Administrative services managers	Moderate decreases are expected across all industries as the automating of administrative support duties lessens the need for administrative services managers. Moderate increases in engineering and management firms will occur as they increasingly supply administrative services managers to other firms on a contractual basis.
Advertising clerks	Small increases are projected due to the growing popularity of classified advertising. Computer driven productivity enhancements in the newspaper industry is expected to cause a small decrease in utilization.
Agricultural and food scientists	Moderate increases are expected in crops, livestock, and livestock products; drugs; and research and testing services to maintain crop and livestock productivity growth.
Air traffic controllers	Air traffic control technology is improving to allow control of more aircraft in a given area, causing a small reduction in personnel requirements.
Aircraft assemblers, precision	Very significant decreases are expected in guided missiles, space vehicles, and parts industries resulting from declining defense expenditures.
Aircraft pilots and flight engineers	Larger capacity planes and the use of 2-person instead of 3-person crews will lead to small decreases in utilization.
Amusement and recreation attendants	Expanding amusement, recreation, and health facilities will spur moderate to significant increases in utilization.
Animal caretakers, except farm	Growing animal populations will cause a moderate increase in utilization of this occupation.
Artists and commercial artists	Small increases across industries as firms place increasing importance on visual appeal of products.
Automotive body and related repairers	New materials in use for car passenger safety damage easily and are usually replaced, resulting in less non-accident body work, and causing small decreases in utilization.
Automotive mechanics	Gasoline service stations will show small declines in utilization as repair services are slowly phased out of some operations.
Bakers, bread and pastry	Increasing consumer demand for low cost fresh baked goods will cause small increases in bakeries and restaurants and moderate to significant increases elsewhere.
Bakers, manufacturing	The growing popularity of baked goods and heat-and-serve pastry products will spur small increases in utilization.

Occupation	Factor
Bank tellers	Increasing ATM use and bank consolidation will significantly reduce the need for tellers.
Bartenders	Changing societal attitudes and stricter laws dealing with drunk drivers are causing moderate decreases in this occupation.
Bill and account collectors	Expanding use of consumer credit will lead to moderate increases in utilization.
Billing, cost, and rate clerks	Computer software will greatly improve the productivity of these workers, causing significant declines in utilization.
Billing, posting, and calculating machine operators	The outdated machines these workers use likely will continue to be used only by small businesses, resulting in very significant declines in utilization across all industries.
Bindery machine operators and set-up operators	Utilization of these workers in commercial printing businesses and newspapers will moderately decrease as a result of more productive binding machinery.
Biological scientists	Moderate increases in the Federal Government and drug manufacturing reflect steady support of health-related research and increasing use of biotechnological techniques by pharmaceutical firms.
Blue-collar worker supervisors	Restructuring of supervisory positions and using self-managing teams of workers in production settings will cause small declines in utilization.
Boiler operators and tenders, low pressure	Automatic boiler systems are expected to cause significant reductions in the utilization of boiler operators in all industries.
Boilermakers	Automated welding and prefabricated boilers will cause moderate declines overall, but fabricated structural metal products and miscellaneous repair shops are increasingly being contracted for boilermaking services and their utilization will significantly increase.
Bookbinders	New technology that performs finishing operations will moderately decrease demand for this occupation.
Bookkeeping, accounting, and auditing clerks	Automated accounting systems, which perform all functions except the initial entries, will moderately reduce utilization.
Broadcast technicians	Increased productivity of broadcasting technology will cause moderate declines in radio and TV broadcasting and in film production.
Brokerage clerks	The computerization of brokerage house clerical duties will cause moderate declines, with significant declines expected in security and commodity exchanges. As they increasingly offer brokerage services, utilization in banking and closely related functions will increase slightly.
Bus and truck mechanics and diesel engine specialists	Trucking companies will show small increases in utilization as increasing competition increases the importance of keeping trucks operational and generating revenue.
Bus drivers, except school	As more people commute using public transportation, there will be small increases in local and suburban transportation.

(continued)

Occupation	Factor
Bus drivers, school	Slow increases in the school-age population and contracting out of student transportation will cause small decreases in the utilization of school bus drivers.
Butchers and meatcutters	These workers are being replaced by lower earning hand cutters, causing small to moderate decreases in utilization.
Camera operators, television, motion picture, and video	Improved camera technology allows lower skilled workers to operate cameras; the effect of this will be a small decrease in utilization.
Camera operators	Direct conversion from electronic data to plate will moderately decrease demand for camera operators in all industries.
Captains and other officers, fishing vessels	Technological innovations will increase productivity of fishing vessels causing small declines in utilization.
Carpenters	More efficient tools are increasing productivity, causing moderate declines in utilization.
Carpet installers	Installation work is shifting to self-employed contractors, resulting in significantly decreased utilization.
Ceiling tile installers and acoustical carpenters	This work will increasingly be done by other construction workers as well as "do-it-yourselfers," causing moderate declines in utilization.
Cement and gluing machine operators and tenders	Increasing automation of gluing machines will result in significantly reduced utilization of these workers.
Central office and PBX installers and repairers	Digital electronic switching systems will replace PBXs, very significantly reducing utilization of this occupation.
Central office operators	Voice recognition, call waiting, call switching, and ISDN centrex services are leading to very significant declines in utilization.
Chemical engineers	Small to moderate increases are expected as chemical firms develop more productive processes amid growing foreign competition.
Chemical equipment controllers, operators and tenders	Increasing use of computers to control chemical reactions will cause small decreases in the utilization of these workers.
Chemical plant and system operators	The expanding uses of specialty chemicals will spur significant increases in utilization in miscellaneous chemical products industry.
Child-care workers	The declining population of children under age 5 through 2005 will lead to small declines in utilization, except in child daycare services.
Civil engineers, including traffic engineers	Increasing investment in the infrastructure is expected to cause moderate increases in utilization by construction firms.
Claims examiners, property and casualty insurance	Small increases are expected in fire, marine, and casualty insurance firms and a moderate increase in insurance agents, brokers, and in service firms as increasing competition focuses on the speed of claims processing.
Clinical laboratory technologists and technicians	Contracting out of lab services to medical and dental laboratories will moderately decrease utilization in hospitals and physicians' offices.
Coil winders, tapers, and finishers	As coils are replaced by electronic components, the utilization of this occupation will moderately decrease.

Occupation	Factor
Coin and vending machine servicers	Improved technology will reduce breakdowns, decrease service needs, and cause a moderate decrease in utilization.
College and university faculty	Shrinking university budgets will lead to cost cutting, increasing reliance on part-time faculty, increasing class sizes, and small decreases in utilization for this occupation.
Combination machine tool setters, set-up operators, and tenders	The utilization of workers with skills on a number of machines will increase slightly as cellular manufacturing advances.
Communication, transportation, and utilities operations managers	Rapidly advancing communications technology, increasing competition in communications and utilities, and consolidation of management responsibilities in transportation firms will cause moderate to significant decreases in utilization.
Compositors and typesetters, precision	Technological improvements are causing significant declines in the utilization of workers that arrange type by hand, replacing them with those that use electronic and word processing methods.
Computer engineers	The continuing demand for new applications and rapid advancements in technology will result in significant to very significant increases in utilization of computer engineers across all industries.
Computer operators, except peripheral equipment	Client-server environments and the automation of operator tasks are expected to cause significant decreases in utilization.
Computer programmers	Computer aided software engineering, wider programming skills of systems analysts, and the outsourcing of low-level programming will improve productivity and cause moderate declines in utilization.
Construction and building inspectors	Moderate decreases are expected in the utilization of inspectors in Federal and State government agencies, as they contract out their inspection responsibilities to engineering and architectural firms, which in turn are expected to have significant increases.
Construction managers	Increasing complexity of construction projects and regulations related to the industry will lead to moderate to significant increases in this occupation's utilization by construction-related firms.
Cooks, institution or cafeteria	Contracting out cooking services will cause significant increases in utilization in eating and drinking places, and moderate declines elsewhere.
Cooks, restaurant	Growth of mid-priced, casual dining establishments will cause a small increase in utilization.
Cooks, short order and fast food	Significant increases in food stores are expected as consumers increasingly demand ready to eat foods.
Cooks, private household	Lower cost services and more easily prepared foods will significantly reduce utilization of these workers.
Corrections officers	Tougher sentencing provisions and an increasing prison population will cause increased construction of correctional facilities, which, in turn, will spur significant increases in State and local governments.

(continued)

Occupation	Factor
Correspondence clerks	Increasing office technology will cause moderate to significant reductions in utilization.
Cost estimators	Small to moderate increases across most construction industries as firms increasingly use these specialists to aid in bidding for projects.
Counselors	Small increases in education and job training services will arise from increasing concern with preparing individuals with the skills necessary to pursue higher education or enter the workforce.
Counter and rental clerks	Increasing demand for rented items such as cars or movies will cause small to moderate increases in utilization.
Court clerks	Increased volume of court cases at the local level is fueling small increases in utilization.
Crane and tower operators	Increased use of robotic cranes will moderately reduce the need for operators in all industries.
Credit analysts	Moderate decreases expected across all industries as credit reporting services become increasingly concentrated in commercial banks, mortgage bankers and brokers, and credit reporting and collection.
Credit authorizers	Automated credit card authorization data centers will cause significant reductions in utilization as businesses increase their use of credit card scanners.
Credit checkers	Specialized firms with access to huge databases will be increasingly contracted to check credit histories, causing very significant decreases in utilization.
Crossing guards	Police will increasingly assume the role of crossing guards, moderately reducing utilization in local government.
Curators, archivists, museum technicians, and restorers	Tightening budgets and reliance on increasingly scarce funding should cause small decreases in government-run and funded institutions.
Custom tailors and sewers	Decreasing demand for tailoring services will significantly decrease utilization in key industries.
Customer service representatives, utilities	The growing number of services offered by telephone utilities will cause a moderate increase in utilization.
Dancers and choreographers	Small to moderate increases in related industries are expected as dance grows in popularity as a form of artistic expression.
Data entry keyers, except composing	Scanners and bar code readers are automating the data entry process, resulting in significant declines in utilization.
Data entry keyers, composing	Desktop publishing will significantly reduce utilization.
Data processing equipment repairers	Falling prices will rapidly expand equipment sales, spurring significant increases in repairers employed by retail stores.
Dental assistants	Dentists will use small increases in utilization of assistants to help meet increased demand.
Dental hygienists	Utilization of this occupation will increase slightly to meet the demand for dental services.

Occupation	Factor
Dental laboratory technicians, precision	Healthier consumers and improved dental lab technology will significantly reduce demand for these workers.
Dentists	There will be a moderate decrease in dental offices as increasing demand is met through the employment of more hygienists and dental assistants.
Designers, except interior designers	Increased emphasis on product quality, safety, design of new high technology products, and growing demand for floral and fashion designers will result in small increases in utilization across industries.
Detectives, except public	Department stores and miscellaneous business services are projected to show small increases in their employment of these workers to deter crime, cut losses, and protect customers. Hotels are projected to show very significant increases.
Dietitians and nutritionists	There will be small decreases in the utilization of these workers in hospitals and personal care facilities as providers are increasingly contracting out dietetic and nutritional services or employing more nonregistered personnel to perform these services.
Dining room and cafeteria attendants and bar helpers	Hotels are minimizing eating facilities, and mid-priced casual dining is replacing cafeterias, causing moderate decreases.
Directory assistance operators	Voice recognition, call waiting, call switching, and ISDN centrex services are leading to very significant declines in utilization.
Drafters	Increasing use of computer assisted design (CAD) by architects and engineers will cause small decreases in the utilization of drafters.
Drilling and boring machine tool setters and set-up operators, metal and plastic	Computer controlled machine tools reduce the need for set-up operators and will spur moderate decreases in utilization.
Driver/sales workers	Increasing demand for a wider variety of fresher foods will cause small increases in utilization in grocery stores and eating and drinking places. Centralized ordering will cause small decreases in utilization in other industries.
Drywall installers and finishers	Very significant declines in the utilization of these workers are expected in most industries as work is increasingly contracted to masonry, stonework, and plastering businesses.
Duplicating, mail, and other office machine operators	Computer technology will reduce demand significantly.
Economists	There will be very significant increases in the utilization of economists and marketing research analysts in research firms due to increased needs for statistical quality control.
Education administrators	Cost management by school districts will cause small decreases in utilization, with other school occupations growing faster in response to increases in the school age population.
EEG technologists	There will be small increases in this occupation's utilization in hospitals as technology improves and medical procedures involving the brain become more common.

(continued)

Occupation	*Factor*
EKG technicians	Significant decreases in utilization are expected as other health technicians are increasingly performing this skill.
Electric meter installers and repairers	Increased reliability of electric meters will moderately reduce demand for installers and repairers.
Electrical and electronic assemblers	Jobs for this assembly occupation are being shipped overseas or automated, resulting in small declines in utilization.
Electrical and electronic technicians and technologists	Computers can simulate components and systems more easily and less expensively than technicians can build the components and systems for testing purposes. This will cause small declines in the utilization of this occupation.
Electrical and electronics engineers	Because electronics-intensive manufacturing firms are reinvesting large portions of their revenues on research and development and latest technology production equipment, these workers will have moderate increases in utilization.
Electromedical and biomedical equipment repairers	Increasing complexity, cost of equipment, and necessity of proper repairs will spur a moderate increase in demand for repairers.
Electronic home entertainment equipment repairers	Microelectronic circuitry has reduced maintenance and repair requirements, and will significantly reduce utilization.
Electronic pagination systems workers	Technological improvements are replacing paste-up artists with electronic pagination workers, leading to very significant increases in utilization.
Electronic semiconductor processors	As chips get more complicated, manufacturing techniques become more automated, resulting in small reductions in utilization.
Emergency medical technicians	A growing urban and elderly population will increasingly demand the services of these workers, causing small to moderate increases of utilization in key industries.
Employment interviewers, private or public employment service	Decreasing Federal support of State employment services and increasing use of computer systems in job service offices will cause moderate decreases in State governments.
Engineering, mathematical, and natural science managers	Moderate increases across all industries are linked to growth of engineering, science, mathematical, and especially computer-related occupations.
Excavation and loading machine operators	Increasing construction of water and sewer services and the growth of surface mining will moderately increase the need for these workers.
Extruding and forming machine operators and tenders, synthetic or glass fibers	Increasing demand for synthetic fibers will cause very significant increases in utilization for this occupation.
Fallers and buckers	Increasing use of heavy equipment to fell and delimb trees will cause small decreases for these workers.
Farm equipment mechanics	As farming equipment becomes more advanced, repairs become critical but less frequent, and are increasingly performed at the dealership, causing a small increase.
Farm workers	Improving productivity of agricultural machinery will cause small declines in the utilization of farm workers.
File clerks	Very significant declines are expected as computer file storage systems grow in use.

Occupation	Factor
Fire fighters	Increasing concern for public safety will spur small increases in local governments.
Fishers, hunters, and trappers	Technological innovations will increase productivity and cause small decreases in utilization.
Fitters, structural metal, precision	More structural metal products are being produced that are easier to assemble and will require significantly lower utilization of fitters.
Flight attendants	Growth in airline seating capacity, with ratio of 1 attendant per 50 seats mandated by Federal regulations, will cause small increases in utilization.
Food counter, fountain, and related workers	Mid-priced, casual dining is replacing cafeterias and diners, causing a moderate decline in eating and drinking places.
Food preparation workers	Increasing consumer demand for ready-to-eat foods is driving moderate increases in food stores and eating and drinking places.
Food service and lodging managers	A significant decrease in utilization is expected in hotels and other lodging places, which are increasingly contracting out or eliminating food services.
Foresters and conservation scientists	Small to moderate increases in utilization across all levels of government reflect more emphasis on wildlife and land management of national forests.
Freight, stock, and material movers, hand	Material moving equipment is moderately reducing the need for hand movers.
Funeral directors and morticians	Small decreases in utilization are expected as the percentage of cremations increases.
Gardeners and grounds-keepers, except farm	Landscaping services companies will have significant increases in utilization as other industries reduce utilization by contracting out for these services.
General office clerks	Some industries are increasing the utilization of clerks with general skills, but most are moderately reducing it as clerical duties become computerized.
Geologists, geophysicists, and oceanographers	Environment-related concerns will moderately increase utilization, while firms engaged in oil and gas extraction are expected to moderately decrease utilization in response to reductions in domestic oil and gas extraction.
Glaziers	Glazing work will be done increasingly by contractors, moderately reducing utilization in paint, glass, and wallpaper stores.
Grader, dozer, and scraper operators	Emphasis on road repair and widening rather than new road construction will moderately reduce utilization in highway and street construction.
Grinding machine setters and set-up operators, metal and plastic	Computer controlled machine tools reduce the need for set-up operators and will spur moderate decreases in utilization.
Guards	Guard services will increasingly be contracted out to security service firms, resulting in small declines across industries.
Hairdressers, hair stylists, and cosmetologists	Department stores are expected to significantly increase hairdressing and cosmetology services.
Hand packers and packagers	Although sometimes difficult to automate, improved packaging methods will cause small reductions in the utilization of these workers.
Hard tile setters	Greater use of tile substitutes, plastic or fiberglass bathtub and shower enclosures, and the "do-it-yourself" trend will cause small declines for these workers.

(continued)

Occupation	*Factor*
Head sawyers and sawing machine operators and tenders, setters and set-up operators	Sawing machine operators will continue to be replaced by automated machinery, resulting in moderate to very significant decreases in utilization.
Heat, air conditioning, and refrigeration mechanics and installers	New construction and increasing retrofit work driven by energy consciousness will lead to a moderate increase in plumbing, heating, and air-conditioning businesses.
Highway maintenance workers	Increased maintenance as a percentage of road work will cause a moderate increase in highway and street construction.
Home appliance and power tool repairers	Longer lasting parts, micro electronics, and the trend to replace rather than repair items will cause moderate declines in utilization.
Home health aides	Hospitals and residential care establishments will continue to rapidly open and expand home health care departments, spurring very significant increases in utilization.
Hosts and hostesses, restaurant, lounge, or coffee shop	Newer hotels increasingly do not have dining establishments as part of operations, leading to moderate declines.
Housekeepers and butlers	Increasing use of firms to supply household services will moderately reduce demand for this occupation.
Human services workers	Small to moderate increases across government and private social services as cost-conscious organizations replace professionals with these workers.
Industrial engineers, except safety engineers	Small to moderate increases across all industries as firms use industrial engineers to streamline production, increase productivity, and minimize costs. Significant increases will occur in manufacturing firms producing expensive per-unit items, such as planes and automobiles.
Industrial machinery mechanics	As American factories become more capital intensive, the utilization of these workers will increase in varying degrees to perform needed repairs and maintenance.
Inspectors, testers, and graders, precision	Automated inspection machines and increased production worker attention to quality and inspection will moderately reduce utilization in manufacturing firms producing highly complicated products such as cars and electrical components.
Inspectors and compliance officers, except construction	Increased activity in law enforcement and regulatory actions at each level of government will cause small increases in utilization.
Instructors, adult (nonvocational) education	Expanding adult education programs and community college course offerings should cause small increases in utilization.
Instructors and coaches, sports and physical training	Moderate increases in recreation services and small increases in education reflect increased public interest in physical fitness for adults and children.
Insulation workers	Moderate increases in the utilization of specialty trade contractors will arise from increasing industrial pipe and boiler insulation to reduce costs.
Insurance adjusters, examiners, and investigators	Insurance company efforts to reduce claim fraud and control costs will cause small increases in utilization.
Insurance policy processing clerks	Insurance applications are being directly input into computer systems during the interview process, causing small to moderate decreases in utilization.

Occupation	Factor
Insurance sales workers	Computer network-based software will allow agents to handle more clients and serve more insurance companies; this will result in a small increase in utilization in insurance agents, brokers, and service firms while utilization in insurance carriers decreases.
Janitors and cleaners, including maids and housekeeping cleaners	Janitorial services are being increasingly contracted out to temporary help and cleaning services firms, causing moderate declines in utilization in nonservice industries.
Jewelers and silversmiths	There will be small decreases in utilization as workers in this occupation are being replaced by sales clerks in stores.
Job printers	Technological improvements in word processing are causing significant decreases by increasing productivity of typesetters and those who make corrections in proofs.
Lathe and turning machine tool setters and set-up operators, metal and plastic	Computer controller machine tools reduce the need for set-up operators and will spur moderate decreases in utilization.
Legal secretaries	Legal secretaries will experience moderate declines in utilization due to growing office automation.
Letterpress operators	Demand for letterpress operators will decline very significantly as many shops switch to newer, faster printers.
Librarians, professional	Small decreases in employment in education and local government are projected as library services are automated and as libraries hire library technicians to contain costs.
Library assistants and bookmobile drivers	Library technicians will pick up many of the key duties of these personnel as automation progresses, resulting in small decreases in utilization.
Licensed practical nurses	As the length of the average hospital stay decreases, quality of care becomes critical, resulting in small decreases in the utilization of these workers as hospitals and residential care facilities switch to registered nurses (RN's) and other higher level health professionals to provide primary patient care.
Loan and credit clerks	Despite automation, this occupation will experience only moderate declines in utilization because of the need for personal contact in the loan process.
Loan officers and counselors	Moderate increases are expected in banking institutions as the industry consolidates. Small increases are expected as the growth of nonbank lenders continues.
Logging tractor operators	These versatile workers can perform more tasks than less skilled logging industry employees, and will experience small increases in utilization.
Machine assemblers	In large electronics and automobile parts manufacturing firms, automating assembly lines will moderately reduce demand for these workers.
Machine feeders and offbearers	Computer controlled loading and unloading machinery will cause small reductions in utilization.
Machine forming operators and tenders, metal and plastic	Computer controlled machine tools reduce the need for set-up operators and will spur moderate decreases in utilization.

(continued)

Occupation	Factor
Machine tool cutting operators and tenders, metal and plastic	Computer controlled machine tools reduce the need for set-up operators and will spur moderate decreases in utilization.
Mail clerks, except mail machine operators and postal service	Facsimile transmissions, electronic mail, and automated mail processing will moderately reduce utilization across industries.
Management analysts	Expected significant increases in the use of management analysts and consultants, across all but management consulting businesses, will help firms downsize, expand, merge, compete, form alliances, and/or cope with technological change, and will create increased demand for these workers.
Manicurists	Increased demand for manicuring services will very significantly increase utilization in beauty shops.
Marketing, advertising, and public relations managers	Small increases in utilization by firms in all industries will result from increasing importance of well-organized customer relations.
Mathematicians and all other mathematical scientists	Cutbacks in basic research expenditures will cause small decreases in utilization.
Meat, poultry, and fish cutters and trimmers, hand	Relatively low wages, compared to skilled meat cutters, will cause small utilization increases in the meat products industry.
Mechanical engineers	Small to moderate increases in utilization are expected across all industries, with significant increases in motor vehicles, as firms concentrate on the quality of product design.
Medical assistants	The growth of group practices requires moderate increases of personnel who can perform both clinical and clerical duties.
Medical records technicians	Efforts to control health care costs will cause third-party payers to increasingly scrutinize medical records, causing significant increases in utilization for this occupation.
Medical scientists	Moderate increases are expected in most related industries except hospitals, where there is a movement from teaching and research to for-profit hospitals, and a resulting decrease in utilization.
Medical secretaries	Each medical secretary will support an increasing number of professionals as automation ensues, leading to small utilization decreases.
Messengers	Private delivery companies will moderately increase utilization in response to demand as other industries moderately decrease it due to expanded use of facsimile transmissions and electronic mail.
Metallurgists and metallurgical, ceramic, and materials engineers	There will be small increases in primary metal industries, and moderate increases in stone, clay, and glass products, due to increased applications and demand for specialty materials. However, there will be moderate decreases in aircraft and parts as the percent of defense related aircraft manufactured falls.
Meter readers, utilities	Remote reading of meters will spread throughout utilities companies, improving productivity and significantly reducing utilization.
Millwrights	Machinery designed to last longer and be more dependable will cause moderate decreases in utilization of millwrights.

Occupation	Factor
Mining, quarrying, and tunneling occupations	Larger, more productive equipment will cause a moderate decline in metal mining.
Motion picture projectionists	The growth of multi-screen theaters will cause very significant decreases in utilization of projectionists.
Municipal clerks	Computers will increase productivity and reduce utilization in local government offices.
Nuclear engineers	Small decreases in utilization will arise from the virtual halt in nuclear plant construction. Moderate increases in research and testing services reflect the contracting of these service firms to develop applications for nuclear technology outside power production.
Nuclear medicine technologists	Technological improvements in nuclear diagnostic procedures and expanding use will cause a small increase in hospital utilization.
Numerical control machine tool operators and tenders, metal and plastic	The demand for more flexibility and precision in the manufacturing sector will lead to an increasing number of numerically controlled machine tools in American factories, causing moderate to very significant increases in utilization.
Occupational therapists	Significant increases in utilization are expected as outpatient services expand in response to cost consciousness, an aging population, and advances in medical treatment that allow people to survive severe trauma.
Occupational therapy assistants and aides	The health care industry's continued increase in the level of outpatient rehabilitative services will cause very significant increases in the utilization of these workers.
Operations research analysts	Availability of low-cost, high-powered computing ability will allow organizations to significantly increase utilization of these workers to solve operations management problems and optimize efficiency.
Optical goods workers, precision	Jobs will continue to shift to retail establishments with on-site lens crafting, causing a small increase in retail stores.
Opticians, dispensing and measuring	Moderate decreases in utilization by health services are offset by small increases in retail trade as employment shifts from offices of health practitioners to retail stores.
Order clerks, materials, merchandise, and service	Growing home catalog shopping will cause a significant increase in nonstore retailers.
Order fillers, wholesale and retail sales	Warehouse and billing automation should cause small declines in utilization.
Other law enforcement occupations	Public concern about crime will cause moderate increases in the utilization of these workers in State and local government.
Painters, transportation equipment	Increased use of plastics and automated painting machines will cause significant decreases in motor vehicle manufacturing and moderate declines in aircraft manufacturing.
Paper goods machine setters and set-up operators	New automated equipment is expected to moderately reduce the demand for these operators.
Paralegals	Paralegals will experience moderate increases at law firms as the cost of hiring them is significantly below lawyers.

(continued)

Occupation	*Factor*
Paste-up workers	Electronic pagination is causing significant declines in the utilization of these workers.
Paving, surfacing, and tamping equipment operators	Increasing road maintenance will spur moderate increases in the highway and street construction and concrete work industries.
Payroll and timekeeping clerks	Computer software developed for payroll processing will cause moderate to significant declines in utilization.
Peripheral EDP equipment operators	Automated peripheral equipment will very significantly decrease the utilization of these workers. ·
Personal and home care aides	Shift to less costly and more accessible care in the home, whenever possible, for the elderly, convalescent, and disabled will drive significant increases in social services.
Personnel, training, and labor relations specialists	Increased training needs to keep pace with technology will cause small to moderate increases in utilization across most industries despite decreasing labor relations needs.
Personnel clerks, except payroll and timekeeping	Computer software will allow personnel specialists to store information during interviews and subsequent personnel actions, leading to significant decreases in utilization.
Pharmacists	There will be a small increase in utilization in hospitals as large health care networks will be more likely to own and operate their own pharmacies.
Pharmacy assistants	Large health care networks will be more likely to own and operate their own pharmacies, causing small increases in utilization.
Photoengravers	Increased use of direct digital printing does not require hand preparation of printers and should moderately decrease the need for photoengravers.
Photoengraving and lithographic machine operators and tenders	Increasing use of electronic and computer technology should very significantly reduce the demand for these workers.
Photographers	Increased use of photography and visual images will cause a moderate increase in use of these workers by miscellaneous business services, which includes photofinishing and photography brokers.
Photographic process workers, precision	Increased use of computers to edit and manipulate photos will increase productivity and moderately reduce utilization.
Photographic processing machine operators and tenders	Improved processing technology and the growth of digital cameras will cause significant declines in this occupation in photo processing labs.
Physical and corrective therapy assistants and aides	Increasing use of physical therapists in group practices and for outpatient therapy will moderately to significantly increase demand.
Physical therapists	Expanded use of physical therapy services in hospitals and group medical practices will cause a significant increase in utilization.
Physician assistants	There will be a small increase in utilization in hospitals as health care organizations will increasingly rely on physician assistants because they provide care at a lower cost.

Occupation	Factor
Physicists and astronomers	Shrinking defense expenditures and movement from basic research to product development will cause a moderate decline overall and small declines in the Federal Government.
Platemakers	Technology in which data and images are moved directly from computers to the press will moderately reduce demand for these workers.
Plumbers, pipefitters, and steamfitters	The growing use of plastic pipe makes plumbers more efficient, causing small decreases in utilization. Contracting out plumbing work will cause very significant decreases in heavy construction and the Federal Government.
Police and detective supervisors	Public concern about crime will cause small increases in the utilization of this occupation.
Police detectives and investigators	Public concern about crime will cause small increases in employment in local governments and moderate to significant increases at the State and Federal (?) government level.
Police patrol officers	Public concern about crime will cause moderate increases in State and local government.
Postal mail carriers	A growing population and an expanding volume of mail will require a small increase in utilization despite improved route-sequence sorting technology.
Postal service clerks	Expanding mail volume will require a small increase in utilization of clerks to process mail.
Power distributors and dispatchers	Legislation to increase competition in utilities will cause firms to automate the functions and moderately reduce utilization of distributors and dispatchers to reduce costs.
Power generating and reactor plant operators	Legislation to increase competition in utilities will cause a small reduction in utilization by electric services firms to reduce costs.
Printing press machine setters, operators and tenders	New printing presses with more highly automated controls will cause small reductions in utilization for these workers.
Procurement clerks	Inventory control, EDI, and automated ordering should cause small decreases in all industries except hospitals and the Federal Government, where significant decreases are projected.
Producers, directors, actors, and entertainers	Rising domestic and foreign demand for film and television productions, as well as a growing movie rental market, will spur significant increases in the utilization of these workers by radio and television broadcasting and advertising industries.
Proofreaders and copy markers	Software that checks spelling and grammar will significantly reduce utilization in all industries.
Psychiatric technicians	A small decrease is expected in this occupation in hospitals due to decreasing State hospital employment.
Punching machine setters and set-up operators, metal and plastic	Punch-press machines are being replaced by automated equipment which requires less set-up time, handles a greater variety of materials, and operate significantly faster, resulting in moderate reductions in utilization.

(continued)

Occupation	Factor
Purchasing managers	Moderate decreases in utilization are expected in wholesale and retail trade as computer inventory and ordering systems grow in use. Significant increases are expected in manufacturing as firms operating JIT inventory systems rely on purchasing managers to keep proper amounts of raw materials available.
Radio mechanics	Increased reliability of radios will cause moderate to significant reductions in the utilization of radio mechanics.
Radiologic technologists and technicians	Technological advancements in diagnostic imaging will continue to make radiological procedures a viable way of diagnosing ailments and will cause a small increase in utilization by hospitals and a very significant increase in medical and dental laboratories.
Rail yard engineers, dinkey operators, and hostlers	Switching, locomotive, and dinkey engine automation will cause moderate declines in this occupation.
Railroad brake, signal, and switch operators	Computer controlled switches will cause small decreases in this occupation.
Receptionists and information clerks	Firms using advanced phone systems will show small to moderate utilization decreases; firms perceiving personal contact as important will not.
Recreational therapists	Expanding hospital outpatient rehabilitation services cause a moderate increase in utilization; a significant decrease due to contracting out for services is expected in nursing and personal care facilities.
Registered nurses	Moderate utilization increases are expected in home health care and nursing facilities as levels of patient care increase, but small decreases in doctor's offices as medical assistants increasingly take over clerical and light clinical duties.
Reservation and transportation ticket agents and travel clerks	Improved ticket reservation systems will increase productivity of ticket agents and significantly reduce utilization by air carriers.
Respiratory therapists	Growing numbers of cardiopulmonary cases will cause a moderate increase in utilization by hospitals.
Roofers	More efficient tools and materials will increase productivity of roofers, leading to small decreases in utilization.
Roustabouts	Computerized equipment, more powerful tools and machinery, electronic testers, and handheld computers are increasing productivity. This combined with diminished domestic drilling and closing of existing wells is causing significant to very significant declines in utilization.
Sales agents, real estate	The growing practice of using sales agents to show rental properties will cause a moderate increase in real estate operators and lessors, whereas the projected small decrease in utilization by real estate agents and managers is due to the increasing use of self-employed agents.
Science and mathematics technicians	Biotech firms moving into production phases and government-required air and water sampling should cause small increases in utilization in the pharmaceuticals and research and testing services industries.
Screen printing machine setters and set-up operators	The increasing popularity of apparel decorated with screen prints will spur moderate increases in utilization of this occupation.
Secretaries, except legal and medical	Traditional secretarial duties are being automated, leading to various levels of decline in all industries.

Occupation	Factor
Securities and financial services sales workers	Global expansion of financial markets and growing involvement in these markets by banks will lead to small to moderate increases in utilization.
Service station attendants	Self-service and the decrease in auto repairs being done at gas stations will very significantly reduce utilization in this occupation at gasoline service stations.
Sewing machine operators, garment	Productivity increases and increasing overseas production will cause a small reduction in demand for these workers in the apparel industry.
Sheet metal workers and duct installers	Increasing use of robotics and substitute materials will significantly reduce demand for these workers in fabricated structural metal products, motor vehicles and equipment, and in the Federal Government.
Sheriffs and deputy sheriffs	Public concern about rising crime rates will cause moderate increases in utilization in local government.
Shipfitters	Defense cutbacks will moderately reduce utilization in the Federal Government.
Shoe and leather workers and repairers, precision	Inexpensive imports and the rising sales of athletic footwear have made consumers more likely to purchase new shoes than to repair old ones, resulting in small decreases in utilization.
Shoe sewing machine operators and tenders	Overseas production of shoes is significantly reducing demand for these workers.
Small engine specialists	Longer lasting, more efficient small engines will reduce demand for repair services and cause small decreases in utilization.
Social workers	Efforts to coordinate hospital care and outpatient health services, and projected fast growth of public welfare and health services at the State and local government level should cause small increases in this occupation's utilization in these industries.
Soldering and brazing machine operators and tenders	Continuing increases in the use of computer controlled soldering and brazing equipment will cause small decreases in demand for these workers.
Speech-language pathologists and audiologists	Growing hospital outpatient services will lead to a very significant increase in utilization; expanded group practice services will cause a small increase.
Statement clerks	Computers will increasingly perform statement processing in financial institutions, causing very significant decreases in utilization.
Station installers and repairers, telephone	Very significant declines will occur as replacement heavily outweighs repair, and modular plugs allow consumers to install their own phones.
Stationary engineers	Computer monitored and controlled building systems are expected to continue to cause small reductions in the need for these workers.
Statistical clerks	Increased computer power and advanced statistical software will significantly reduce demand for these workers.
Stenographers	Increasing court case volume and demand for transcriptions of medical records will cause small to moderate increases in employment.
Stock clerks	Automation such as pre-labeling, hand held scanners, inventory control systems, guided vehicles, and mechanized stackers will cause moderate declines in utilization across industries and small declines in retail trade.

(continued)

Occupation	*Factor*
Subway and streetcar operators	Growing mass transit systems will moderately increase the need for these workers.
Surgical technologists	Increasing numbers of outpatient surgical procedures and substitution for RN's and surgeons' assistants to control costs should cause a small increase in the utilization of these workers in hospitals and a very significant increase in physicians offices.
Surveyors	Small decreases in this occupation will occur due to increasing use and falling cost of the Global Positioning System and the Geographic Information System.
Switchboard operators	Voice recognition, call waiting, call switching, and ISDN centrex services are leading to significant declines in utilization.
Systems analysts	Very significant increases in utilization across all industries will result as more emphasis is placed on network applications, and rapidly advancing technology continues to merge computers, telecommunications, and video.
Teacher aides and educational assistants	Increasing attention to the quality of education is leading schools to moderately increase utilization of support staff for teachers.
Teachers, preschool and kindergarten	Cost-cutting measures by social service organizations will cause small decreases in utilization.
Teachers, elementary	There will be a small decrease in utilization as the proportion of elementary school students decreases.
Teachers, secondary school	A small increase in utilization will result as proportion of high school students increases.
Teachers, special education	Legislative mandates stipulating that special needs students are entitled to public education will moderately increase utilization.
Technical assistants, library	Schools will contain costs by automating library tasks, enabling them to increase the utilization of library technical assistants in place of more highly paid librarians.
Telephone and cable TV line installers and repairers	Television cable lines are almost completely installed and fiber-optic cables have significantly lower maintenance requirements, causing moderate declines in utilization. Electrical contractors will benefit from the increasing contracting out of this work, and will significantly increase utilization of these workers.
Tire building machine operators	The highly automated tire industry will show moderate increases in this occupation in response to increased demand for tires.
Tire repairers and changers	Moderate declines in utilization are expected in gas service stations and auto repair shops due to a shift in business to discount tire retailers.
Title examiners and searchers	This work is being taken over by paralegals and legal assistants, resulting in moderately decreasing utilization.
Tool and die makers	CNC equipment and quick-die changing extrusion presses will cause moderate declines in utilization of this occupation.
Traffic, shipping, and receiving clerks	Automation and self-guided vehicles in distribution centers and warehouses will cause small decreases in utilization.
Truck drivers, light and heavy	The growth of chain stores and centralized ordering will cause moderate declines in utilization in wholesale and retail firms.

Occupation	Factor
Typesetting and composing machine operators and tenders	The increasing use of electronic and computer technology should very significantly reduce the demand for these workers.
Typists and word processors	The increasing use of computers by professional and managerial staff for their own word processing is very significantly reducing utilization of this occupation.
Underwriters	Moderate increases are expected in life insurance businesses as the population grows older and demands more life insurance. However, there will be moderate decreases in the utilization of insurance agents, brokers, and in service firms stemming from growing competition and entrance into insurance markets by various financial institutions.
Upholsterers	More durable fabrics will cause small reductions in utilization of this occupation, because less reupholstery will be required.
Urban and regional planners	A moderate increase in utilization by local government reflects increased zoning, ecological, and land use questions faced by local government.
Ushers, lobby attendants, and ticket takers	The increasing quality of service in response to competition from video rental businesses will cause theaters to moderately increase utilization of this occupation.
Vehicle washers and equipment cleaners	Self-service car washes will cause moderately declining utilization of these workers.
Waiters and waitresses	Rapid growth of mid-priced eating and drinking places will cause small increases in utilization.
Watchmakers	More reliable watches and popular "throw-away" watches will cause moderate to significant decreases in utilization for watchmakers.
Welders and cutters	The increasing use of automated welding machines will cause small utilization declines.
Welding machine setters, operators, and tenders	Numerically controlled welding equipment will make its way into the medium-sized firms that now must adopt the technology to remain competitive on cost and quality, causing small reductions in demand for these workers.
Welfare eligibility workers and interviewers	A moderate decrease in local government utilization will be offset by a moderate increase in State government as responsibility shifts from local to State authorities.
Wholesale and retail buyers, except farm products	Centralization and consolidation of purchasing operations to improve efficiency should cause small decreases in utilization.
Woodworking machine operators and tenders, setters and set-up operators	Woodworking machine operators will continue to be replaced by automated machinery and experience moderate to very significant declines in utilization.
Writers and editors, including technical writers	Increasing use of technical writers in high-tech companies will lead to small increases in utilization.

Source: U.S. Department of Labor (1996). *Employment outlook: 1994–2005. Job quality and other aspects of projected employment growth.* Bulletin 2472, pp. 64–70. Washington, DC: U.S. Government Printing Office.

INDEX

CREDITS

Chapter 3: 49: From *The World's Best Proverbs and Maxims,* by Gilchrist Lawson, Grosset & Dunlap, 1926. **50:** "With the blink of an eye, time flies and they're no longer little" by Barbara Brotman, as appeared in *Columbus Dispatch,* June 29, 1997. Reprinted by permission. **52:** From *All I Really Need to Know I Learned in Kindergarten,* by Robert L. Fulghum, pp. 4–6. Copyright © 1986, 1988 Robert L. Fulghum, Random House Publishers. Reprinted by permission of Villard Books, a division of Random House, Inc. **61:** Table 3-3; **62:** Figure 3-2; **63:** Figure 3-3: Copyright 1997 by American College Testing (ACT), Iowa City, IA 52243. All rights reserved. Reprinted by permission of ACT.

Chapter 4: 84: "Coming and Going" from *Ric Masten Speaking,* by Ric Masten. Copyright © 1979 SunInk Publications. Reprinted with permission.

Chapter 5: 100: Figure 5-5; Figure 5-6: From *199–97 Occupational Outlook Handbook.* U.S. Department of Labor, Lincolnwood, IL: VGM Career Horizons. Reprinted by permission.

Chapter 6: 111: Table 6-1: From *1996–97 Occupational Outlook Handbook.* U.S. Department of Labor, Lincolnwood, IL: VGM Career Horizons. Reprinted by permission. **127:** Table 6-3: Reprinted with the permission of Simon & Schuster from *The Day America Told the Truth* by James Patterson and Peter Kim. Copyright © 1991 by James Patterson and Peter Kim.

Chapter 7: 130: Excerpt from "Getting Lost: The Case for Creative Ineptitude," by Tim Cahill, 1986, *Outside,* 11, 25–28. Copyright © 1986 Mariah Publications Corporation. Reprinted with permission of Outside magazine.

Chapter 8: 170: From "Give Yourself Permission to Pursue the Career You Really Want," by Howard Figler, from *Planning Job Choices: 1995,* with permission of the National Association of Colleges and Employers, copyright holder. **177:** Adapted from "Give Yourself Permission to Pursue the Career You Really Want," by Howard Figler, from *Planning Job Choices: 1995,* with permission of the National Association of Colleges and Employers, copyright holder.

Chapter 9: 185: "Translations tell story between the lines of help-wanted ads" by Al Sicherman as appeared in *Columbus Dispatch,* October 11, 1992. **191:** Items 1–11 are from *Career Development for the College Student* (pp. 89–90), ed. by P. Dunphy, 2nd ed., 1973, as adapted from *The Resume Workbook: A Personal Career File for Job Applications* by C. Nutter, 3rd ed.,

1970. Copyright © 1973 by The Carroll Press. Reprinted with permission. **202:** Reprinted from *The Campus Interview—Are You Ready?* (audiotape) with the permission of the National Association of Colleges and Employers, copyright holder. **204:** From Edgar H. Schein, *Career Dynamics* (pp. 103–104), © 1978 by Addison Wesley Longman. Reprinted by permission of Addison Wesley Longman. **205:** From *The Northwestern Lindquist-Endicott Report* by Victor R. Lindquist, Northwestern University Placement Center, Evanston, Illinois. Reprinted with permission. **214:** Table 9-2: From *Questioning Applicants for Employment and Membership in Labor Organizations: A Guide for Application Forms and Interviews,* by the Ohio Civil Rights Commission. Copyright © 1990 Ohio Civil Rights Commission. Reprinted with permission. **221:** From *About Getting Hired: The Job Search,* by Marvin Walberg. Copyright © 1992 Marvin Walberg. Reprinted with permission.

Chapter 10: 245: Figure 10-1: Reprinted with permission from NTL Institute, "The Individual, the Organization, and the Career," by Edgar H. Schein, p. 404, *Journal of Applied Behavioral Science,* 7, No. 4, copyright © 1971. **252:** From *The Dance of Intimacy,* by H. G. Lerner, p. 11. Copyright © 1989 Harriet Goldhor Lerner, Harper & Row Publishing. Reprinted with permission.

Appendix A: 260: Portions of this material were adapted reproduced by permission of the Publisher, Psychological Assessment Resources, Inc., Odessa, Florida 33556, from the *Self-Directed Search Assessment Booklet and Occupations Finder* by John L. Holland, Ph.D. Copyright 1985 by PAR. Further reproduction is prohibited without permission from PAR, Inc. The *Self-Directed Search Assessment Booklet and Occupations Finder* can be purchased from Psychological Assessment Resources, Inc., by calling 1-800-331-TEST. **267:** Items marked with an asterisk are from *Occupational Interest Inventory.* Modified and reproduced by permission of the publisher, CTB/McGraw-Hill, 20 Ryan Ranch Road, Monterey, California 93940. Copyright © 1956 McGraw-Hill, Inc. All rights reserved. **274:** Items marked with an asterisk are from *Occupational Interest Inventory.* Modified and reproduced by permission of the publisher, CTB/McGraw-Hill, 20 Ryan Ranch Road, Monterey, California 93940. Copyright © 1956 McGraw-Hill, Inc. All rights reserved. **282:** Figure 283; Figure: Copyright 1997 by American College Testing (ACT), Iowa City, IA 52243. All rights reserved. Reprinted by permission of ACT. **285:** "VIESA Job Family Charts"; **298:** "Index to Descriptions of Occupations: Supplement to the 1996 ACT Job Family Charts": Copyright 1997 by American College Testing (ACT), Iowa City, IA 52243. All rights reserved. Reprinted by permission of ACT.

Appendix C: 318: From *1996–97 Occupational Outlook Handbook.* U.S. Department of Labor, Lincolnwood, IL: VGM Career Horizons. Reprinted by permission.

TO THE OWNER OF THIS BOOK:

We hope that you have found *Working Well, Living Well: Discover the Career within You*, Fifth Edition, useful. So that this book can be improved in a future edition, would you take the time to complete this sheet and return it? Thank you.

School and address: _____

Department: _____

Instructor's name: _____

1. What I like most about this book is: _____

_____

_____

2. What I like least about this book is: _____

_____

_____

3. My general reaction to this book is: _____

_____

4. The name of the course in which I used this book is: _____

_____

5. Were all of the chapters of the book assigned for you to read? _____

   If not, which ones weren't? _____

6. In the space below, or on a separate sheet of paper, please write specific suggestions for improving this book and anything else you'd care to share about your experience in using the book.

_____

_____

_____

_____

_____

Optional:

Your name: _____ Date: _____

May Brooks/Cole quote you, either in promotion for *Working Well, Living Well: Discover the Career within You,* Fifth Edition, or in future publishing ventures?

Yes: _____ No: _____

Sincerely,

Clarke G. Carney
Cinda Wells

IN-BOOK SURVEY

At Brooks/Cole, we are excited about creating new types of learning materials that are interactive, three-dimensional, and fun to use. To guide us in our publishing/development process, we hope that you'll take just a few moments to fill out the survey below. Your answers can help us make decisions that will allow us to produce a wide variety of videos, CD-ROMs, and Internet-based learning systems to complement standard textbooks. If you're interested in working with us as a student Beta-tester, be sure to fill in your name, telephone number, and address. We look forward to hearing from you!

In addition to books, which of the following learning tools do you currently use in your counseling/human services/social work courses?

_____ **Video** _____ in class _____ school library _____ own VCR

_____ **CD-ROM** _____ in class _____ in lab _____ own computer

_____ **Macintosh disks** _____ in class _____ in lab _____ own computer

_____ **Windows disks** _____ in class _____ in lab _____ own computer

_____ **Internet** _____ in class _____ in lab _____ own computer

How often do you access the Internet? _____

My own home computer is:

_____Macintosh _____DOS _____Windows _____Windows 95 _____Windows 98

The computer I use in class for counseling/human services/social work courses is:

_____Macintosh _____DOS _____Windows _____Windows 95 _____Windows 98

If you are NOT currently using multimedia materials in your counseling/human services/social work courses, but can see ways that video, CD-ROM, Internet, or other technologies could enhance your learning, please comment below:

_____

_____

_____

Other comments (optional): _____

_____

Name _____Telephone _____

Address _____

School _____

Professor/Course_____

You can fax this form to us at (408) 375-6414; e-mail to: info@brookscole.com; or detach, fold, secure, and mail.

NO POSTAGE
NECESSARY
IF MAILED
IN THE
UNITED STATES

BUSINESS REPLY MAIL

FIRST CLASS   PERMIT NO. 358   PACIFIC GROVE, CA

POSTAGE WILL BE PAID BY ADDRESSEE

ATT: MARKETING

Brooks/Cole Publishing Company
511 Forest Lodge Road
Pacific Grove, California 93950-5098